T0214750

Lecture Notes in Computer Science   11227

Commenced Publication in 1973
Founding and Former Series Editors:
Gerhard Goos, Juris Hartmanis, and Jan van Leeuwen

More information about this series at http://www.springer.com/series/7411

Subir Biswas · Animesh Mukherjee
Mun Choon Chan · Sandip Chakraborty
Abhinav Kumar · Giridhar Mandyam
Rajeev Shorey (Eds.)

Communication Systems and Networks

10th International Conference, COMSNETS 2018
Bangalore, India, January 3–7, 2018
Extended Selected Papers

 Springer

Editors
Subir Biswas
Michigan State University
East Lansing, MI, USA

Abhinav Kumar
Indian Institute of Technology Hyderabad
Kandi, India

Animesh Mukherjee
Indian Institute of Technology
Kharagpur, India

Giridhar Mandyam
Qualcomm Inc.
San Diego, CA, USA

Mun Choon Chan
National University of Singapore
Singapore, Singapore

Rajeev Shorey
Tata Consultancy Services
Bangalore, India

Sandip Chakraborty
Indian Institute of Technology
Kharagpur, India

ISSN 0302-9743   ISSN 1611-3349   (electronic)
Lecture Notes in Computer Science
ISBN 978-3-030-10658-4   ISBN 978-3-030-10659-1   (eBook)
https://doi.org/10.1007/978-3-030-10659-1

Library of Congress Control Number: 2018965736

LNCS Sublibrary: SL5 – Computer Communication Networks and Telecommunications

This Springer imprint is published by the registered company Springer Nature Switzerland AG
The registered company address is: Gewerbestrasse 11, 6330 Cham, Switzerland

Preface

Following a successful tenth edition of the International Conference on Communication Systems and Networks (COMSNETS) in January 2018, this book of proceedings records the highlights of the conference. COMSNETS 2018 had 134 submissions. Of these, 30 high-quality papers were chosen, after a rigorous review by a 90-strong Program Committee, leading to 15 sessions over two parallel tracks in the program.

This book contains the 12 best papers originally presented during the main technical program. These papers were significantly extended and reviewed again for this highlights edition.

October 2018

Subir Biswas
Animesh Mukherjee
Mun Choon Chan
Sandip Chakraborty
Abhinav Kumar
Giridhar Mandyam
Rajeev Shorey

Contents

Improved Physical Downlink Control Channel for 3GPP Massive Machine Type Communications

M. Pavan Reddy$^{(\boxtimes)}$, G. Santosh, Abhinav Kumar, and Kiran Kuchi

Indian Institute of Technology Hyderabad, Hyderabad 502285, India
{ee14resch11005,ee12m1018,abhinavkumar,kkuchi}@iith.ac.in

Abstract. To provide cellular connectivity to massive machine type communications, 3rd Generation Partnership Project (3GPP) has come up with an enhanced machine type communications (eMTC) standard. The eMTC is a low power wide area network technology. It can cater to the needs of massive MTC devices providing voice support, required data rates, low latency, wide area coverage, and mobility. The eMTC is built on LTE framework and necessary modifications are made as per the requirements of MTC. A chunk of 1.4 MHz from the LTE bandwidth is required to deploy eMTC. Similar to LTE, delivering Downlink Control Information (DCI) to end devices is crucial in eMTC. The DCI carries information about modulation and coding scheme, uplink grant, and scheduling of downlink resources. The DCI of multiple eMTC devices are multiplexed over a region of time and frequency resources. Hence, the eMTC devices have to blindly decode this control channel region. Significant computational power is required from an eMTC device to decode this region. This paper explains the processes involved in the delivery of DCI for eMTC. We propose a novel mapping of repetition and aggregation level to each eMTC device based on the available channel state information. We identify the under utilization of the time and frequency resources in the existing eMTC scheme used for rate matching the DCI information bits. We present system level simulations considering the proposed novel mapping. Further, through extensive simulations and hardware emulations, we show that the proposed rate matching scheme results in significant improvement in performance as compared to the existing scheme.

Keywords: Blind decoding · Control channel
Machine type communications · Physical downlink control channel
Rate matching

1 Introduction

Enhanced machine type communications (eMTC) has recently been introduced by the 3rd Generation Partnership Project (3GPP) to provide cellular connectivity to massive MTC devices [2,3,5]. The major challenge in eMTC is to provide

© Springer Nature Switzerland AG 2019
S. Biswas et al. (Eds.): COMSNETS 2018, LNCS 11227, pp. 1–25, 2019.
https://doi.org/10.1007/978-3-030-10659-1_1

coverage to massive number of eMTC devices operating at much lower signal-to-noise ratios (SNRs) as compared to the existing long term evolution (LTE) based cellular networks. The eMTC technology can be deployed on a much smaller bandwidth of the existing LTE network infrastructure to cater the growing needs of Internet-of-things (IoT) based devices. The technical specifications of eMTC are under development. The eMTC devices (also termed as LTE-M devices) are expected to have a coverage gain of 21 dB as compared to the legacy LTE device. This wider coverage has to be supported without increasing the base station's transmit power and the end device's maximum transmit power must be limited to 20 dBm as compared to 23 dBm for a legacy LTE device [4]. Thus, the eMTC has to provide larger coverage along with lower power consumption at the end device making it a suitable technology for the low power IoT applications [1,13].

The cell search and synchronization procedures for eMTC devices are similar to LTE. However, eMTC has fewer physical downlink channels than LTE as follows. The eMTC has a physical broadcast channel (PBCH) to carry the broadcast information for the devices trying to access the network, an M-physical downlink control channel (MPDCCH) to carry the downlink control information (DCI), and a physical downlink shared channel (PDSCH) to carry the downlink data for the eMTC devices. Repetitions have been introduced in the eMTC for the data carried in these physical channels to enhance the coverage area. Hence, these control and shared channel procedures in eMTC are modified as compared to the LTE. In this work, we focus on the MPDCCH.

In MPDCCH, the DCI is a set of bits transmitted to convey the information required by the eMTC devices for decoding their data and finding resources for uplink transmissions [2]. The DCIs of different devices are multiplexed and transmitted in MPDCCH. A DCI is repeated to achieve a pre-determined length called the aggregation level (AL). The size of DCI bits vary depending on the information being carried. In LTE, as size of DCI information bits is not known a-priori to the LTE device, it tries to decode the DCI blocks/aggregation levels received by blindly searching for all possible combinations (termed as blind decoding in the literature). In the eMTC specifications [2], to simplify this complex decoding procedure, different DCI sizes have been unified to the maximum possible DCI size by padding zeros. Then, these maximum sized DCIs are repeated to form ALs. This ensures that an eMTC device need not search for all possible DCI lengths. However, during this process, the time and frequency resources are under utilized. For e.g., with a DCI repeated over 256 subframes and aggregation level of 24, a maximum of 62 subframes can potentially be left unused (a detailed example is available in Sect. 3.9). For a technology that targets to serve massive number of devices per cell, this is a highly inefficient way of utilizing resources. To overcome this problem without violating the device decoding complexity as per the specifications [12], we propose a novel and efficient rate matching scheme that unifies DCI sizes and results in better performance.

The contributions of this work are as follows. We explain the MPDCCH in detail as per the 3GPP standard [2,3,5]. We identify the limitations of the existing rate matching scheme for eMTC. Motivated by the underutilized resources in the existing scheme, we propose a novel rate matching scheme for MPDCCH in eMTC. We propose a novel mapping between the eMTC device's channel state information and its allocated repetition and aggregation levels. We compare the performance of the proposed scheme with the existing scheme in terms of the block error rate (BLER) and show the improvement in performance for the proposed scheme. We extend the simulation results presented in [20] for various repetition and aggregation level configurations. Further, we present the system level and hardware level performance analysis for the proposed and the existing schemes as compared to [20].

The rest of the paper is organized as follows. The Sect. 2 presents related eMTC work in the literature. In Sect. 3, MPDCCH transmission and reception is explained in detail and its limitations are discussed. The novel rate matching scheme is discussed in Sect. 4. In Sect. 5, a novel scheme for mapping the repetition and aggregation levels is proposed. The analysis of the proposed scheme is presented in Sect. 6. In Sect. 7, simulation model is explained and the numerical results are discussed. Some concluding remarks and possible future works are presented in Sect. 8.

2 Related Work

The key features of the 3GPP MTC have been discussed in [23]. Note that MTC is the predecessor technology for eMTC which doesn't have the IoT related enhancements. In [11], the development of physical layer design for MTC across different releases of LTE has been presented. In [22,23], the effect of repetitions on the coverage enhancement of MTC has been discussed. In [8,10,21], resource allocation schemes for the control channel in LTE and LTE-Advanced systems have been presented. In [19], the design rationale and scheduling of control channel for Narrowband-IoT have been discussed. In [7,18], control channel performance has been analysed for LTE. However, the control channel design for MTC is different from LTE and Narrowband-IoT, and hence the same cannot be extended in the context of MTC. In [14], an enhanced control channel design has been presented for MTC. The simulation results in [23] indicate that for low signal-to-interference-plus noise ratios (SINRs), a cross-subframe based channel estimation can improve the coverage by 2 dB. However, the effects of various configurations of aggregation levels and repetitions have not been considered in [23]. In [17], it has been shown that the receiver gain is restricted in MTC due to the long lengths of cyclic redundancy check (CRC). Thus, a novel CRC processing on top of the compact PDCCH for MTC devices has been proposed in [17]. The proposed smart technique reduces the subframe repetition and accordingly the required resources, transmission delays and power consumption. Further, the proposed smart CRC processing results in coverage gain of 13.8%. However, the zero padding in eMTC has not been considered in [17]. In [9], for a given R and AL configuration, the scheduling of the control channel has been discussed for eMTC. To the best of our knowledge, this is the first paper which presents a detailed explanation and performance analysis of downlink control channel for eMTC.

In [24], the motivation for blind decoding attempts of a UE to receive its DCI information has been discussed. A novel DCI scheme has been proposed in [24] that reduces the blind decoding attempts at the expense of link level performance loss of around 1 dB. However, the proposed scheme in [24] cannot be adapted directly for eMTC as its structure is very different from the proposed DCI for the 3GPP standards [2,3,5]. A method to reduce blind decoding attempts for LTE carrier aggregation has been proposed in [16]. The proposed method in [16], unifies the aggregation levels in a search space to the maximum possible level on the secondary carriers. This results in reduced blind decodings on the secondary carrier. However, the primary carrier blind decoding attempts remains the same. Further, the proposed method in [16] is not applicable for eMTC as eMTC has no carrier aggregation. Thus, even though attempts have been made to design better blind decoding schemes for MTC, the problem of resource under utilization in eMTC due to zero padding of unified DCI sizes has not been addressed in the literature. Hence, this work is the first attempt to improve the coverage performance for eMTC by more efficiently padding the DCI for the blind decodings. Next, we explain in detail the MPDCCH as per the 3GPP standard [2]. The reader's familiar with the MPDCCH can skip to the Sect. 3.9, where we explain the limitations of the current MPDCCH design.

3   Physical Downlink Control Channel for eMTC

In this section, we first present the DCI information defined in the 3GPP specifications for the eMTC [2]. This is followed by a detailed description of the transmitter and receiver structure for MPDCCH. Lastly, we explain the limitations of the existing rate matching scheme for eMTC.

3.1   Downlink Control Information (DCI)

The DCI carries information regarding modulation and coding scheme, resources to be monitored for decoding the transmitted information, and the resources for uplink transmission for the eMTC device. The DCI is transmitted in multiple scenarios like random access procedure, paging, and user intended data transmission in the shared channel. This DCI for multiple eMTC devices is multiplexed over a set of time frequency resources called search spaces. The DCI is transmitted in the search spaces in a specific format called DCI format. These DCI formats are defined as follows [2]:

1. The *DCI Format 6-0* is intended for uplink resource grants.
2. The *DCI Format 6-1* is intended for downlink resource information.
3. The *DCI Format 6-2* is intended for paging.

The DCI information is transmitted over MPDCCH as shown in Fig. 1. The DCIs of multiple eMTC devices after encoding and rate matching are multiplexed to form a search space. This search space is the region over which all the DCIs intended for devices are present. The eMTC devices have to blindly

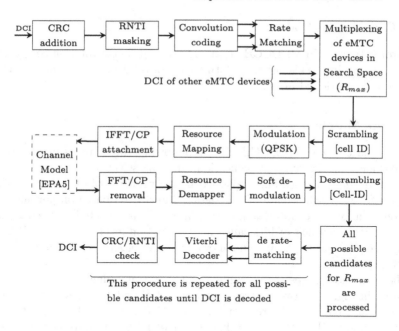

Fig. 1. The MPDCCH transmitter and receiver structure

search this region to receive respective DCIs. Let the length of search space be denoted by R_{max}. This R_{max} is conveyed to all the devices through system information blocks. Further, in this search space, the encoded DCI is repeated over R subframes for coverage enhancement. In MPDCCH, $R_{max} \in \{1, 2, \ldots, 256\}$, with repetitions $R \in \{R_{max}/8, R_{max}/4, R_{max}/2, R_{max}\}$. The Fig. 1 also presents the typical decoding scheme for MPDCCH. Next, we explain each block in the MPDCCH transmitter and receiver structure as shown in Fig. 1.

3.2 Cyclic Redundancy Check (CRC)

The DCI format to be transmitted is attached with a 16 bit CRC. This CRC helps in verifying that the received DCI by the eMTC device is error free.

3.3 Radio Network Temporary Identifier (RNTI) Masking

The RNTI is used to identify the type of DCI format being decoded. The CRC padded to the DCI is masked with the RNTI. Hence, whenever a device receives a block of DCI data, it first unmasks the CRC bits using its RNTI before going for a CRC. The RNTI is the key identifier for the type of the information being conveyed in the DCI. An eMTC device will have unique RNTIs for different procedures. For example, RA-RNTI is used for random access, P-RNTI is used for paging, SI-RNTI is used for receiving system information, and C-RNTI is used for receiving device specific data.

3.4 Convolution Coding

For error correction in MPDCCH, a rate-1/3 tail biting convolution code is used for channel coding. This block performs the convolution coding based on the polynomials mentioned in [3].

3.5 Rate Matching

The rate matching in MPDCCH has the following three stages of processing. (1) sub-block interleaving, (2) collection, and (3) selection and pruning. The rate 1/3 convolution encoding explained in the previous block results in three streams of data. Each stream of this data is interleaved based on permutations mentioned in [3]. After interleaving, the data is then collected and repeated to attain a certain number of bits called an aggregation level (AL). In MPDCCH, one AL is equivalent to 72 bits, and allowed number of ALs is such that $AL \in \{1, 2, 4, 8, 16, 24\}$.

The complete process of encoding a DCI and mapping to search space is presented in Fig. 2 for two different lengths. Let S and L represent the lengths of smaller and larger DCIs, respectively. Let M denote the difference between their lengths such that $M = L - S$. For the smaller DCI, M zero bits are padded to make its length equal to L, as per the 3GPP specifications [2]. Further, a 16 bit CRC is attached to the DCI and masked with the RNTI of the eMTC device. The resultant K number of bits, where $K = L + 16$, are passed through the rate-1/3 convolution coding block. This block generates three streams of bits, each of length K. Let E denote the number of bits after rate matching such that $E = AL \times 72$. Then, $3K$ bits of output from the convolution coding block is interleaved, concatenated side by side and repeated to achieve output E bits post rate matching. Note that when E is not a multiple of $3K$ this process results in an incomplete repetition of data with $3r$ bits, where $3r = E \bmod 3K$.

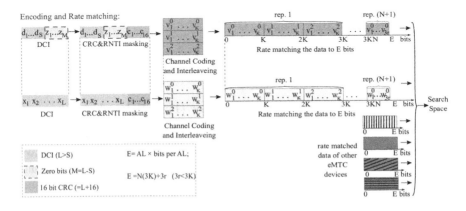

Fig. 2. Existing rate matching scheme for eMTC

In case there exists no zero padding in MPDCCH, the receiver would have to de-rate match the data for two different lengths. Hence, the receiver would have to perform two complete decodings. However, with zero padding, the de-rate matching and the convolution decoding has to be performed only for the maximum length (L). Thus, zero padding has been included in MPDCCH to reduce the number of de-rate matching and convolution decoding operations at the eMTC receiver.

In the end, the eMTC device validates DCI by unmasking with two RNTIs and performing CRC check twice. One for each possible length of the DCI. Next, we explain the process of multiplexing the rate matched DCI data of various eMTC devices into a search space.

3.6   Search Space

The search space is a set of subframes where the rate matched data of various eMTC devices is transmitted. The Fig. 3 presents this multiplexing of rate matched device data into a search space of 4 subframes. MPDCCH supports two types of search spaces, UE specific search space (USS) and common search space (CSS). DCI transmitted in USS conveys information regarding downlink and uplink grants, whereas DCI transmitted in CSS communicates information related to paging and random access procedures. Hence, the DCIs in USS are specific to each device. Whereas, the DCIs in CSS are common to all devices. Whenever a device starts decoding the search space, it has no prior knowledge of the position and length of its DCI, AL, and repetition level. Hence, it tries to decode for all possible combinations of DCI, AL, and repetition level. This results in MPDCCH decoding being a power consuming operation. To remove the dependency of decodings on the size of DCI, all the DCIs are made equal in size by padding extra zeroes as explained previously. This way a device can perform the decoding process for only one DCI size and validate it using multiple CRC checks. Note that the zero padded bits also get repeated during rate matching and repetition over subframes. These zero padded bits convey no extra information and hence, they result in poor resource utilization. Next, we explain scrambling and modulation.

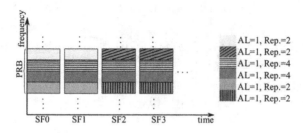

Fig. 3. Devices multiplexed in a search space of 4 subframes

3.7 Scrambling and Modulation

A pseudo-noise (PN) sequence is initialized with the physical cell identifier. This PN sequence is used for scrambling the bit sequence generated after search space allocation [3]. The scrambling of data offers protection from inter cell interference. This is followed by quadrature phase shift keying (QPSK) modulation in MPDCCH. Next, we explain the resource mapping in MPDCCH.

3.8 Resource Mapping

The smallest unit of frequency and time that can be allocated to a device in eMTC is called a Resource Element (RE). The RE is also the basic unit of resource assignment in legacy LTE. In MPDCCH, resources are allocated in units of Enhanced Control Channel Elements (ECCEs). A group of nine REs is termed as an Resource Element Group (REG) and four such REGs form the ECCE. Thus, each ECCE is made up of 36 REs, with QPSK as the modulation scheme, it can accommodate 72 bits. In MPDCCH, the bits in one AL are mapped to one ECCE. The mapping of these ECCEs to REs is performed as follows. In a PRB pair, the resource elements are numbered from 0 to 15, in the increasing order of first frequency and then time [3]. The REs with reference signal are excluded from this numbering. All the REs with same number form an EREG as shown in Fig. 4. eMTC has two types of mapping, localised and distributed. In localised mapping, four EREGs from same PRB pair are grouped together to form an ECCE. In a distributed mapping, EREGs are picked from different PRB pairs to form an ECCE. Localised mapping of MPDCCH is depicted in Fig. 4. Each small block in the figure represents an RE and every fourth EREG in the PRB pair are grouped to form an ECCE. This is followed by the inverse fast Fourier transform (IFFT), addition of cyclic prefix (CP) and transmission as shown in Fig. 1. Next, we discuss the limitations of the existing rate matching scheme in MPDCCH.

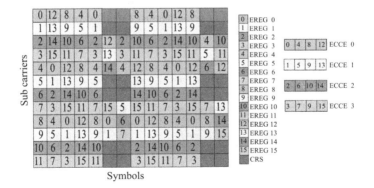

Fig. 4. Resource mapping in MPDCCH

3.9   Limitations of the Existing Rate Matching Scheme

The limitations of the rate matching in MPDCCH are explained as follows.

- **Resource Utilization:** Example 1 presents the under utilisation of resources for a worst case scenario.

Example 1.   From [2], we consider the largest and the smallest DCI lengths as $L = 25$ and $S = 15$, respectively.
The difference in DCI lengths is $M = L - S = 10$ bits.
With a 16 bit CRC, the length of data block is $K = 25 + 16 = 41$ bits for each of the DCIs.
The fraction of DCI block unused for the device with $S = 15$ is $10/41 = 0.2431 = 24.31\%$.
For an $AL = 24$, $AL = \lfloor 0.2431 \times 24 \rfloor = 5$ is not used by the eMTC device with $S = 15$.
Similarly, for a repetition of 256 subframes, $62 = \lfloor 0.2431 \times 256 \rfloor$ subframes are under utilized for the same eMTC device with $S = 15$.

From the Example 1, we can observe that upto 24% resources might be wasted for devices with the smaller DCI lengths. Given the various formats of DCI and various procedures corresponding to each RNTI, the DCI sizes used in a search space can significantly vary between the eMTC devices. The eMTC has limitations on the available bandwidth and has to address scheduling of a massive number of devices. Hence, this poor utilization of resources has significant impact on the system performance. Thus, there exists a need to design more efficient schemes than simply zero padding for rate matching in MPDCCH. This is the key motivation of this work.

- **Power Consumption:** The search space in eMTC spans over large number of subframes. An eMTC device tries to decode the various combinations of subframes in the search space, as explained earlier. The power consumed in the process of decoding the whole search space is large. Further, every time the search space region is conveyed to the devices, at most eight devices get allocated in the search space. However, the search space has to be decoded by all the eMTC devices that are expecting a DCI. Thus, if a device fails to decode the DCI in its allocated search space, it ends up decoding a lot more search spaces before its next allocation. Hence, every DCI decode failure results in significant increase in power consumption.
- **Unnoticed Downlink Grants:** In case an eMTC device fails to decode a DCI, its corresponding downlink grant is left unnoticed. Even if there is no acknowledgement for DCI reception from the eMTC device, its corresponding shared channel resources (in PDSCH) are used irrespective of the device decoding the DCI. Since repetition is allowed in PDSCH, any unnoticed downlink grants result in further poor resource utilization. Hence, we next propose the novel rate matching scheme which adheres to the receiver capabilities mentioned in the 3GPP specifications [12] and at the same time addresses the above mentioned limitations of the existing MPDCCH rate matching.

4   Proposed Rate Matching Scheme

The proposed rate matching scheme has two stages:

1. Pre-collection stage and
2. Block-wise rate matching stage.

The Fig. 5 illustrates the complete process of proposed rate matching scheme.

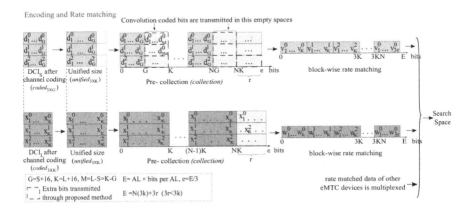

Fig. 5. The proposed rate matching scheme

Pre-collection

- Let S and L denote the size of smaller and larger DCI lengths, respectively, such that $S < L$.
- A 16 bit CRC is attached to each DCI and an RNTI is masked with each of these CRCs. Since zero padding is not performed, it results in $G = S + 16$ and $K = L + 16$ bits, respectively.
- Then, convolution encoding results in three streams of data. This stream of $3K$ bits of data is termed as *coded*. For the DCI of original length S, we assume for now that an empty space of length $(K - G)$ bits are appended at the end of each stream of *coded* to achieve a unified size of $3K$ bits. This new block is termed as *unified*. Please note that this is not equivalent to zero padding as we will be inserting bits in these appended empty spaces as explained next.
- The number of bits in any AL is given by $E = AL \times 72$.
- Since the data is now in three streams, the new block to be configured is of size $3 \times e$, where, $e = E/3$. This new block is termed as *collection*.
- The *unified* is repeated N times in pre-collection stage as shown in Fig. 5. Note that $3r$ bits at the end of this pre-collection stage might remain as empty spaces. We fill all the empty spaces as explained next.

– A small block of size $3(K - G)$ will remain as empty spaces in a *collection* for DCIs of size S. For these DCIs of length S, the convolution coded bits from *coded* are filled sequentially in these empty spaces as shown in Fig. 5. Thus, these bits are in the same order as they appear in *unified*. Further, the empty space at the end of the N repetitions, represented by r are also used to fill these convolution coded bits as shown in Fig. 5.

Algorithm 1: Modified rate matching scheme

Input : Lengths G and K, aggregation level AL,
convolution coded data $coded_{3 \times G}$.
Output: Rate matched data of length E
/* stage I: Pre collection   */

1 Let $unified = [coded_{3 \times G}\ NULL_{3 \times (K-G)}], \quad N = \left\lfloor \dfrac{E}{3K} \right\rfloor, E = 72 \times AL;$

2 **for** $var = 1$ *to* N **do**

3 $\quad |$ Append *unified* to *collection*;

4 **end**

5 Let $rem = \dfrac{E\ mod\ 3K}{3}$, $temp_{3 \times rem} = 0$, $var3 = 0$

6 **for** $var = 1$ *to* rem **do**

7 $\quad |$ $temp(var) = unified(var)$;

8 **end**

9 Append *temp* to *collection*;

10 **for** $var2 = 1$ *to* E **do**

11 $\quad |$ **if** $collection(var2) == NULL$ **then**

12 $\quad\quad$ **repeat**

13 $\quad\quad\quad |$ $var3 = var3 + 1$

14 $\quad\quad$ **until** $unified((var + var3)\ mod\ 3K) \neq NULL$;

15

16 $\quad\quad$ $collection(var2) = unified((var + var3)\ mod\ 3K)$;

17 $\quad |$ **end**

18 **end**

/* stage II:Block wise rate matching   */

19 **for** $var = 1$ *to* N **do**

20 $\quad |$ Do rate-matching of $collection(1 : 3, (var - 1)K + 1 : var \times K)$

21 $\quad |$ Append it to *aggregate*;

22 **end**

23 Let $temp = collection_{3 \times rem}$

24 **for** $var = 1$ *to* rem **do**

25 $\quad |$ Do rate-matching of $temp((var - 1)K + 1 : var \times K)$;

26 $\quad |$ Append it to *aggregate*;

27 **end**

28 **return** *aggregate*

4.1 Block Wise Rate Matching

- For each block of size $3 \times K$ from *collection*, perform a rate matching of size $3k$ bits.
- A $3 \times r$ block of data which is less than $3 \times K$ will remain unattended for block wise rate matching. For the bits in this block of $3 \times r$ data, perform rate match for every K bits as per the specifications given in [3].

The proposed rate matching scheme including both the pre-collection and block wise rate matching is presented as a generalized algorithm in Algorithm 1.

4.2 Decoding for the Proposed Scheme

The decoding procedure for the proposed rate matching scheme is presented in Fig. 6. In Stage I, the device can perform the decoding simultaneously for both the DCI sizes by soft combining the received bits. The device has to de-rate match the received data assuming the length of DCI as L $(> S)$ bits. In case the DCI transmitted was of length L, then the procedure followed results in correct CRC post the de-rate matching. However, if the DCI transmitted was of length S, then the de-rate matching of length L results in a correct combination of first $G = S + 16$ bits (with CRC) while discarding the last $M = K - G$ bits. This way the proposed scheme simultaneously performs the decoding for both the lengths. Note that at this stage the proposed scheme does not alter the receiver performance, as the receiver has not yet utilized the extra bits transmitted in place of the zero padded bits in the existing eMTC scheme.

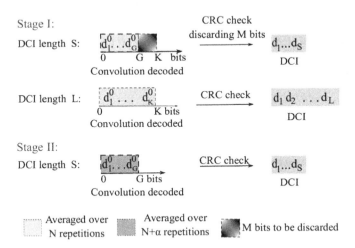

Fig. 6. Decoding procedure for the proposed rate matching scheme

In case a device fails to decode a DCI, with the proposed scheme there is a chance of performing a second decode. In Stage II, the device can de-rate match the data considering the bits of the convolutional code added in the empty space as shown in the Fig. 5. Thus, as shown in Fig. 6, existing scheme results in combination of N times repeated data in Stage I, whereas, the proposed scheme results in combination of additional α times of repetitions. Note that, second decoding is possible only for DCI of length S. This decoding has a better combination of resource elements and hence results in improved performance at the receiver. The Fig. 7 compares the decoding process of proposed scheme with that of the current eMTC rate matching scheme. In case a device decodes the DCI in Stage II, second decode with the proposed scheme as shown in Fig. 7, it helps the device to skip the whole process of waiting for a new allocation and the base station can use these resources for some other eMTC device. This results in efficient resource utilization, reduced power consumption and in turn efficient downlink grant allocation through the usage of the proposed rate matching scheme.

Next, we propose a novel mapping between eMTC device's CQI and its allocated repetition and aggregation levels.

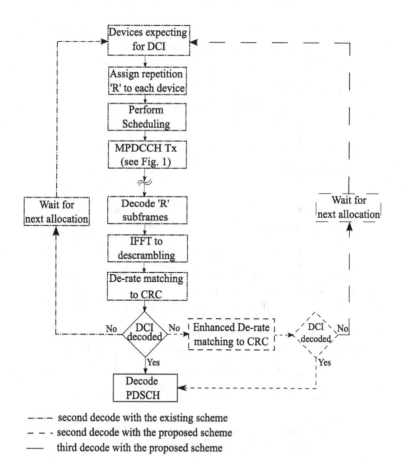

Fig. 7. Comparison of the decoding process of the proposed scheme with the existing rate matching scheme for eMTC

5   Proposed Adaptive Repetition and Aggregation Level Selection (ARALS)

In physical uplink control channel (PUCCH), the channel quality index (CQI) conveys the channel conditions of the device to the base station. The PUCCH in eMTC is the same as that of LTE. Given the CQI, a base station has flexibility in selecting from the various configuration of repetitions and ALs. Motivated by the Modulation and Coding Scheme (MCS) procedure in LTE, we propose a novel method for choosing R and AL using the CQI.

The allocation is based on the link level simulation results generated for each possible R and AL configuration over a wide range of signal to interference-plus-noise ratio (SINR) values. A base station can map CQI to the possible SINR value for each device [15]. Given a BLER threshold β, we select the R and AL configuration for the devices as shown in Fig. 8. Initially, the CQI of each device is mapped to a possible SINR value. A reference SINR value is chosen as follows.

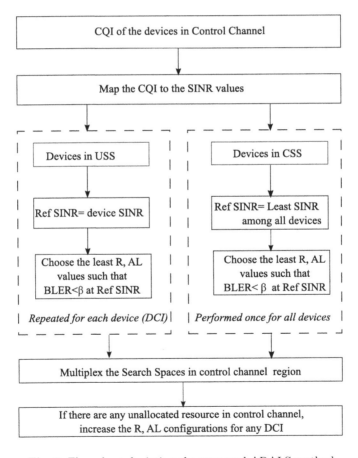

Fig. 8. Flow chart depicting the proposed ARALS method

In USS, reference SINR is the SINR of the respective device, whereas in CSS, the reference SINR is the least SINR among all the active devices. From the link level simulation results, the least possible R and AL configuration is selected such that it has a BLER less than or equal to β for the SINR greater than or equal to the reference value. All the DCIs are then multiplexed in their respective search spaces. The search spaces are then multiplexed in the control channel region. Further, if there are any unallocated REs in the control channel region, the allocated R and AL values can be increased to optimise the resource utilization, accordingly. Next, we analyse the performance of the proposed scheme.

6   Analysis of the Proposed Scheme

In this section, we present the feasibility of the proposed scheme given the eMTC device decoding capabilities as per the 3GPP specifications. We then discuss the enhancements brought in by the scheme both at the eMTC device and the base station (BS) level.

6.1   Feasibility of the Proposed Scheme

In LTE, the smallest time-frequency resource that can be allocated to a device is defined as a resource element (RE). A set of REs over 12 sub-carriers and 14 symbols is termed as one physical resource block (PRB). The eMTC works in coherence with LTE over a bandwidth of 1.4 MHz, i.e., using six PRBs. It can also operate across larger bandwidths (for e.g., 10 or 20 MHz) of LTE over a pre-defined set of six PRBs called Narrowbands. This group of six PRBs are frequency hopped over LTE bandwidth to improve the receiver performance in eMTC. There are two enhanced coverage modes (CE Modes) defined in eMTC, CE Mode A and CE Mode B. In CE Mode A, repetition of data is performed over fewer subframes, whereas, the CE Mode B provides the best possible coverage using frequency hopping and repetition over larger number of subframes.

The most important aspect of proposed scheme is the opportunity to utilize the padded bits, evidently devices in poor channel conditions can gain the maximum benefit from this scheme. The proposed scheme gives device an opportunity to go for second decoding trial on the same search space by utilizing the padded data. An eMTC device has the capability to perform 16 decodes per subframe (1 msec) [12]. However, the number of blind decodings to be performed varies for each configuration. Hence, the maximum number of decodings an eMTC device is expected to perform are calculated for each configuration as mentioned in [5]. A summary of it is presented in Table 1. The search space (N_{PRB}) configurations with Narrowband spanning over 2, 4, and 6 PRBs are considered.

From Table 1, it can be observed that, in CE Mode B device capability is never altered with proposed scheme as maximum decodes are always less than 16. Hence, with the proposed scheme, a device can always perform a second decoding attempt. Therefore, performance enhancement is guaranteed as compared to

Table 1. No. of decodes/subframe with existing and proposed schemes for $R_{max} = 8$

Mode	N_{PRB}	Decodes/subframe with the existing scheme	Decodes/subframe with the proposed scheme (second decode)
CE Mode A	2	8	16
	4	8	16
	6	10	20
CE Mode B	2	2	**4** (<16)
	4	4	**8** (<16)
	6	6	**12** (<16)

the existing scheme in CE Mode B. Further, even in CE Mode A, second decoding attempt is still possible for most of the configurations. Only in case of the CE Mode A with 6 PRBs as the decodes per subframe, i.e., 20 decodes/subframe for the proposed scheme exceeds the maximum permitted decode of 16. Hence, the second decode cannot be performed in this scenario. Everywhere else, the proposed scheme will result in gain in performance within the 3GPP eMTC device specifications.

6.2 Enhancements at Device Level

Enhanced Coverage. Theoretically, the DCI size of information bits can range from 15 to 25 bits. The number of bits in the empty spaces can be anywhere between 0 to 10 bits. An illustration of improved resource utilization is explained in Example (1). The same can generalized using the following equation.

$$AL_{Enhanced} = AL_{Alloted} \left(1 + \frac{L - S}{L + 16}\right) \qquad (1)$$

For typical values of $L = 25$ and $S = 15$ the additional combining gain obtained can be observed from Fig. 9. The gain is measured per subframe in units of ALs. From Fig. 9, for AL $= 24$, upon using 10 padded bits, a device can receive 5 ALs of additional data which can be used for combining. It is this additional data that brings the decoding gain for the proposed rate matching scheme.

Reduced Power Consumption. A successful DCI decoding in second attempt implies that the whole process of waiting for next allocation from BS, re-receiving data at the base band level, and new decoding attempt on the entire search space region for the DCI are all not required. This brings in significant power saving at the eMTC device and also avoids the delay associated with all the above processes.

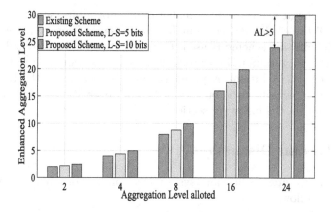

Fig. 9. Aggregation level gain with the proposed rate matching scheme as compared to the existing eMTC scheme

6.3   Enhancements at Base Station

The coverage of BS is increased significantly as the cell edge eMTC devices that require heavy repetitions are effectively served by the proposed scheme. The cell edge devices and devices with poor channel conditions receive DCI with maximum possible repetitions configured by the BS. Hence, the proposed scheme can also be viewed as a BS configuration with further repetitions. Every successful decoding of DCI with proposed scheme at BS saves large time and frequency resources and reduces the overall scheduling delay in the network. Since, the eMTC BS supports massive number of devices, at any point of time there would be large number of devices utilizing the proposed scheme. Thus, the combined power and resource savings brought in by the scheme are significant and make the proposed scheme most desirable to eMTC technology. Further, the overall DCI decoding failure rate in the network goes down with the proposed rate matching scheme as shown next through simulations.

6.4   Subframes Required (η) as a Performance Metric

All the active eMTC devices decode the whole control channel region to obtain the DCI. The increase in the number of errors occurring in a control channel results in a larger number of DCI re-transmissions. Further, if the base station allocates larger R and AL configurations, then all the active devices decode the control channel for a longer period of time. In such cases, the eMTC devices observe a larger power consumption. The power consumed by the eMTC devices is a function of the number of subframes that the base station takes to communicate the DCI to all the devices. Hence, we define the subframes required (η) by the base station for successfully communicating the DCI as a performance metric for power consumption.

Given any SINR value, with the proposed rate matching scheme, the R and AL configuration value should be smaller than that of the existing scheme. Then, the proposed scheme will result in a smaller number of subframes to communicate the DCI to all the eMTC devices. Further, if the same R and AL configuration as that of the existing scheme is used, then it will result in a lower block error rate. This, in turn, results in fewer re-transmissions as compared to the existing scheme. Hence, the subframe required (η) will be smaller with the proposed scheme. The comparison of the same is carried out over Monte Carlo simulations and is presented in the following section.

7   Results and Discussion

In this section, we present link and system level simulations, and hardware level emulations as follows.

7.1   Link Level Simulations

The link level simulations of control channel with both the existing and the proposed schemes are preformed as per the 3GPP specifications [2,3,5]. The block error rate (BLER) is generated for both the schemes for varying ALs and repetition levels using Monte Carlo simulations in MATLAB. The simulation parameters considered are presented in the Table 2 as per [6].

Table 2. Link level simulation parameters

Parameter	Value
LTE bandwidth	10 MHz
eMTC bandwidth	1.4 MHz
DCI size S (without CRC)	15
DCI size L (without CRC)	25
Mapping	Localised
(N_{PRB}) PRBs per Narrowband	6 (2+4)
Aggregation levels	1, 2, 4, 8, 16, 24
Repetition levels	32, 64, 128
Channel model	EPA 5
Sampling rate	15.36 MHz
Antenna configuration	2×1 (SFBC)

In Figs. 10, 11 and 12 the variation of the BLER with respect to the SNR is presented for 32, 64, and 128 repetition levels, respectively. All the possible ALs are considered for each scenario. It is observed that the proposed rate matching scheme always performs better than the existing 3GPP mechanism. The performance of both the schemes increases with the increase in aggregation and repetition levels. Further, increasing ALs result in more empty spaces in the

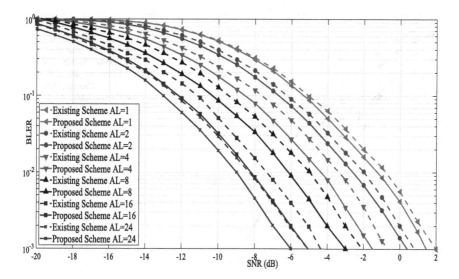

Fig. 10. Variation of BLER with SNR for various ALs in existing and proposed schemes with repetition level R = 32.

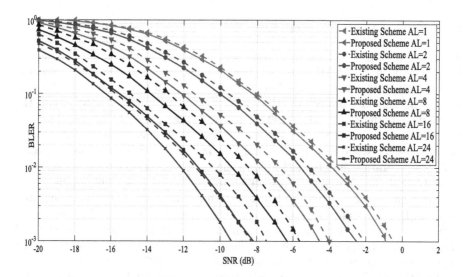

Fig. 11. Variation of BLER with SNR for various ALs in existing and proposed schemes with repetition level R = 64.

pre-collection stage as discussed in Sect. 4. The proposed scheme utilises these empty spaces more efficiently. Hence, with increasing AL, performance of the proposed scheme improves as observed in the Figs. 10, 11 and 12. This gain in performance can significantly improve the coverage of the eMTC network. Next, we present results for system level simulations.

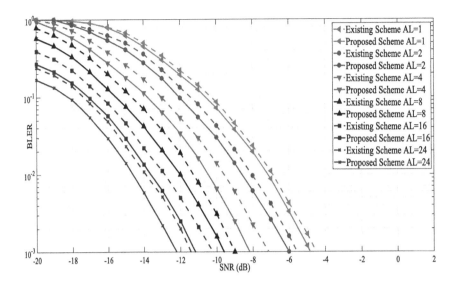

Fig. 12. Variation of BLER with SNR for various ALs in existing and proposed schemes with repetition level R = 128.

7.2   System Level Simulations

The simulation parameters considered are mentioned in Table 3. The simulation is carried out in MATLAB as follows. Initially, the devices are dropped randomly in the hexagonal cell site. Based on the assumed path loss model and the simulation parameters, the SINR values are calculated for each device. Given the SINR values, the R-AL configuration is selected as per ARALS mentioned in Sect. 5. Considering the order of the arrival of devices as the scheduling order, the devices are scheduled in a round-robin fashion. Each device has a specific R-AL configuration, and is checked for a successful reception based on the BLER at that SINR. This checking is performed by generating a random number ranging between 0 and 1. If the BLER is less than the generated random number then the DCI transmitted is assumed to be successfully received by the device. If the reception of DCI is not successful then the device is stacked at the end of the existing order of the devices. The simulation is carried out until all the eMTC devices in the network successfully decode a DCI.

The CDF of subframes required (η) for successful DCI communication for all devices is presented in Fig. 13 for both the proposed and existing schemes. The simulation considers the varying number of devices as 200, 400, 1000 and is carried out for 1000 iterations. In every iteration, the subframes required (η) is calculated for both the schemes. For any R-AL configuration, the proposed scheme always has a better BLER and hence has a better success rate. Thus, the

Table 3. System level simulation parameters

Parameter	Value
Cellular layout	Hexagonal Grid, Single Cell Site
Cell radius	500 m
Pathloss model	Urban Macro (UMa)
Number of devices	200, 400, 1000
Transmission power, antenna	40 dBm, omni-directional
Antenna height	25 m (BS), 1.5 m (UE)
Carrier frequency	2.0 GHz
eMTC bandwidth	1.4 MHz (6 PRBs)
R	1, 2, 4, ..., 256
AL	1, 2, 4, 8, 16, 24
R, AL allocation	ARALS with $\beta = 0.01$
Scheduling	Round Robin

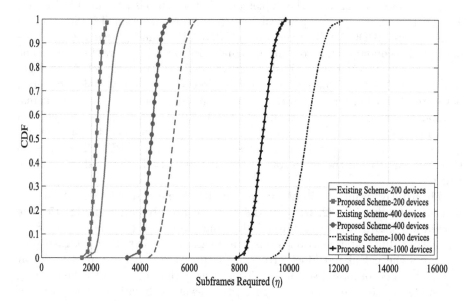

Fig. 13. CDF of subframes required (η) by existing and proposed scheme for varying number of devices

proposed scheme always has less η when compared with the existing scheme. It is observed that with the increase in the number of devices the subframes required (η) to schedule the devices increases. Further, the difference in the subframes required (η) by both the schemes also increases with the increase in the number of the devices. Next, we present results for hardware level emulations.

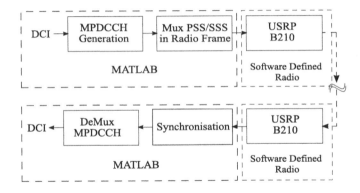

Fig. 14. Block diagram of hardware level emulation

7.3   Hardware Level Emulation

The hardware level emulation is carried out as per the parameters mentioned in Table 4. A block diagram of the implementation scenario is presented in Fig. 14. The DCI undergoes all the physical layer procedures mentioned in Sect. 3 and results in an MPDCCH. The generated MPDCCH is multiplexed with the primary and secondary synchronisation signals (PSS/SSS) in a radio frame. The radio frame is then transmitted using software defined radio connected to a desktop. We use MATLAB based LTE System Tool box to achieve this. Universal Software Radio Peripheral (USRP) - B210 are used for the purpose of transmission and reception over the air. At the receiver, the samples are received for a long period of time. The received samples are then used to find the frequency offset and are synchronised at symbol level. The MPDCCH channel is then separated from the radio frame, decoded for a DCI, and analysed for the BLER.

The BLER results for both the proposed scheme and existing scheme for repetition levels of 8, 32, 64 and ALs of 8, 16 are presented in Fig. 15. The calculation of BLER is carried over 1000 frames. For a better comparison of the schemes at different repetition levels, the y-axis is presented on a logarithmic scale and the calculated block error rate is presented on the top of each bar in Fig. 15. The proposed scheme performs better than or equal to the existing scheme for all the repetition and aggregation level combinations. The proposed and existing schemes result in an equal BLER with a configuration of R = 64 and AL = 16. Note that, this is because the performance improvement of the proposed scheme is limited by the number of frames over which emulation is carried out.

The emulation results presented in Fig. 15 are without any added interference, and the BLER is averaged over various SNR values. Hence, the link level simulation results in Sect. 7.1 cannot be directly compared with the emulation results in Fig. 15. However, the improvement in BLER with the proposed scheme is similar to the simulation results in Sect. 7.1. The BLER decreases with the increase in the repetition levels and aggregation levels. Further, for all the

Table 4. Hardware level emulation parameters

Parameter	Value
eMTC bandwidth	1.4 MHz (6 PRBs)
USRP radios	B210
Carrier frequency	2.6 GHz
Interface	MATLAB LTE System Toolbox
Sampling rate	1.92 MHz
FFT Size	128
Tx gain control	60 dB (Tx power $= -12$ dBm)
Rx gain control	50 dB
Distance between two USRPs	1.5 m
Antenna configuration	1×1
DCI size S (without CRC)	15
DCI size L (without CRC)	25
Mapping	Localised
(N_{PRB}) PRBs per Narrowband	6 (2+4)
PRB set used	2+4
Aggregation level	1, 2, 4, 8, 16, 24
Repetition level	1, 2, 4, ..., 256

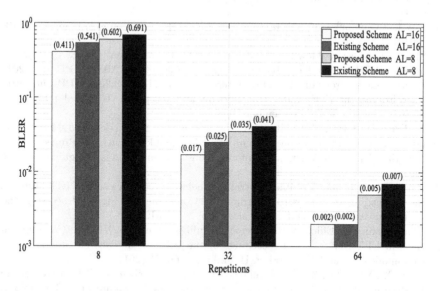

Fig. 15. Variation of BLER with various repetition and aggregation levels for proposed and existing schemes.

repetition levels, the BLER of the proposed scheme with AL = 8 is lower than the existing scheme with AL = 8 and greater than the existing scheme with AL = 16. Next, we present conclusion and directions for future work.

8   Conclusion and Future Work

In this paper, we explained in detail the MPDCCH for eMTC. We demarcated the limitations in existing rate matching for eMTC. Motivated by these limitations, we proposed a novel rate matching for MPDCCH. We propose a novel mapping of the repetition and aggregation level to each eMTC device. The performance of the proposed rate matching scheme is compared with the existing rate matching scheme for MPDCCH using aggregation levels and BLER as performance measure. Further, we show that the proposed scheme significantly outperforms the existing scheme through extensive link and system level simulations, along with hardware level emulations. In future, we plan to do the quantitative analysis for resource utilization and energy efficient eMTC.

References

1. Coverage Analysis of LTE-M (White paper). https://altair-semi.com/wp-content/uploads/2017/02/Coverage-Analysis-of-LTE-CAT-M1-White-Paper.pdf
2. Multiplexing and Channel Coding. Technical report, TS 36.212, v 13.2.0, 3GPP (2016)
3. Physical Channels and Modulation. Technical report, TS 36.211, v 13.2.0, 3GPP (2016)
4. Study on provision of low-cost Machine-Type Communications (MTC) User Equipments (UEs) based on LTE. Technical report, TS 36.888, v 12.0.0, 3GPP, June 2013
5. Physical Layer Procedures. Technical report, TS 36.213, v 13.2.0, 3GPP, June 2016
6. User Equipment (UE) radio transmission and reception. Technical report, TS 36.101, v 14.1.0, 3GPP, September 2008
7. de Andrade, T.P.C., Astudillo, C.A., daFonseca, N.L.S.: Impact of M2M traffic on human-type communication users on the LTE uplink channel. In: Proceedings of the 7th IEEE Latin-American Conference on Communications, Arequipa, pp. 1–6 (2015)
8. Balamurali: Optimal downlink control channel resource allocation for LTE systems. In: Proceedings of the 2010 International Conference on Signal Processing and Communications (SPCOM), Bangalore, pp. 1–5 (2010)
9. Chakrapani, A.: Efficient Resource Scheduling for eMTC/NB-IoT Communications in LTE Rel. 13. In: Proceedings of the IEEE conference on Standards for Communication and Networking, Helsinki, pp. 66–71 (2017)
10. Chen, X., Yang, W., Xu, C.: Novel resource allocation schemes in LTE PDCCH. In: Proceedings of the IEEE International Conference on Communication Technology, pp. 128–132 (2012)
11. Elsaadany, M., Ali, A., Hamouda, W.: Cellular LTE-A technologies for the future internet-of-things: physical layer features and challenges. IEEE Commun. Surv. Tutor. **19**(4), 2544–2572 (2017)

12. Ericsson: RAN1 agreements for Rel-13 eMTC. Technical report, TSG-RAN1, R1–161546, 3GPP, February 2016
13. Ericsson: RAN1 agreements for Rel-13 NB-IoT. Technical report, TSG-RAN1, R1–161548, 3GPP, February 2016
14. Hu, J., Wang, M., Zou, K.J., Yang, K.W., Hua, M., Zhang, J.: Enhanced LTE physical downlink control channel design for machine-type communications. In: Proceedings of the 7th International Conference on New Technologies, Mobility and Security (NTMS), Paris, pp. 1–5 (2015)
15. Kawser, M.T., Hamid, N.I.B., Hasan, M.N., Alam, M.S., Rahman, M.: Downlink SNR to CQI mapping for different multiple antenna techniques in LTE. Int. J. Inf. Electron. Eng. 2(5), 757 (2012)
16. Mu, Q., Ji, X., Zhu, J., Liu, L., Chen, L., She, X.: A novel blind decoding method in carrier aggregation. In: Proceedings of the ICCTA, Beijing, pp. 291–295 (2011)
17. Mu, Q., Liu, L., Jiang, H., Yasuakawa, S.: A new physical downlink control channel design for MTC in LTE-Advanced. In: Proceedings of the WPMC, pp. 204–209 (2014)
18. Osti, P., Lassila, P., Aalto, S., Larmo, A., Tirronen, T.: Analysis of PDCCH performance for M2M traffic in LTE. IEEE Trans. Veh. Technol. 63(9), 4357–4371 (2014)
19. Reddy, M.P., Santosh, G., Kumar, A., Kuchi, K.: Downlink control channel scheduling for 3GPP narrowband-IoT. In: IEEE 29th Annual International Symposium on Personal, Indoor and Mobile Radio Communications (2018) (Accepted)
20. Reddy, M.P., Santosh, G., Kumar, A., Kuchi, K.: Novel rate matching scheme for downlink control channel in 3GPP massive machine type communications. In: Proceedings of the 10th International Conference on Communication Systems and Networks (COMSNETS), pp. 183–190 (2018)
21. Salihu, B.A., Yang, D., Zubair, S.: New remapping strategy for PDCCH scheduling for LTE-Advanced systems. J. Commun. 9(7), 563–571 (2014)
22. Saxena, V., Wallen, A., Tirronen, T., Razaghi, H.S., Blankenship, J.B.Y.: On the achievable coverage and uplink capacity of machine-type communications in LTE Release 13. In: Proceedings of the IEEE 84th Vehicular Technology Conference-Fall, Montreal, pp. 1–6 (2016)
23. Saxena, V., Bergman, J., Blankenship, Y., Wallen, A., Razaghi, H.S.: Reducing the modem complexity and achieving deep coverage in LTE for machine-type communications. In: Proceedings of the IEEE Global Communication Conference, Washington, D.C., pp. 1–7 (2016)
24. Wu, Y.C., Zhang, Y.P., Feng, S., Zhang, P.: A new downlink control channel scheme for LTE. In: Proceedings of the IEEE VTC Spring, pp. 1–6 (2013)

Implementation of Energy Efficient WBAN Using IEEE 802.15.6 Scheduled Access MAC with Fast DWT Based Backhaul Data Compression for e-Healthcare

Tanumay Manna$^{(\boxtimes)}$ and Iti Saha Misra

Department of ETCE, Jadavpur University, Kolkata 700032, India
tmanna@research.jdvu.ac.in

Abstract. This work describes the implementation of a complete Wireless Body Area Network (WBAN) that is capable of monitoring multiple physiological signals of a patient by means of IEEE 802.15.6 scheduled access MAC protocol. In the WBAN setup, data from multiple sensors are sent to a Body Network Controller (BNC) using low power transceivers. To this end, the BNC is designed to multiplex the data from multiple sensors, and send them to a remote server over the Internet using a backhaul cellular network, thereby enabling ubiquitous remote health monitoring. Furthermore, to facilitate an energy efficient backhaul transmission that incurs low data transfer costs to the users, we introduce the concept of data compression at the BNC. In this regard, we propose a fast Discrete Wavelet Transform (DWT) based data compression algorithm at the BNC, termed herein as B-DWT, that is implementable in real-time using the limited on-board resources. The remote server is configured to accept data from multiple patients, de-multiplex different data of a single patient and store them in a database for pervasive access. Issues related to the hardware implementation of sensor nodes and BNC, and the design of the scheduled access mechanism and B-DWT are addressed. Detailed performance analysis of the WBAN is performed in OPNET simulator to determine the optimum allocation intervals for the sensor nodes that maximizes network capacity while maintaining a frame delay constraint. Further, in order to prolong the battery life of sensor nodes, we obtain the optimal payload sizes that maximizes their energy efficiency. Additionally, through implementation of B-DWT at the BNC we determine the optimal wavelet filer and compression levels, that allow maximum data compression within acceptable limits of information loss. The resulting B-DWT algorithm is shown to

The first author deeply acknowledges the financial assistance by CSIR, Govt. of India.

The original version of this chapter was revised: Reference no. 23 ("References" section) has now been corrected. The correction to this chapter is available at https://doi.org/10.1007/978-3-030-10659-1_13

© Springer Nature Switzerland AG 2019
S. Biswas et al. (Eds.): COMSNETS 2018, LNCS 11227, pp. 26–51, 2019.
https://doi.org/10.1007/978-3-030-10659-1_2

outperform traditional DWT with significant gains in execution speed and low memory footprint at the BNC.

Keywords: WBAN · IEEE 802.15.6 · MAC · Scheduled access Energy efficiency · DWT · OPNET · e-Healthcare

1 Introduction

Future healthcare systems should provide proactive management of wellness rather than illness, and focus on prevention and early detection of disease. The present healthcare systems which are structured and optimized for illness management are also facing two major challenges- increase in life expectancy [1] and rising healthcare costs [2]. This necessitate the need to shift toward more scalable and affordable solutions. Wireless Body Area Networks (WBANs) [3] are considered as a key solution to all these problems enabling proactive, affordable and ubiquitous healthcare monitoring. It comprises of a network of intelligent, low-power, micro and nano-technology sensors and actuators, which can be placed on the body, or implanted in the human body (or even in the blood stream), providing timely data. They allow citizens/patients to have more responsibility in managing their own health and interacting, whenever is necessary, with care providers. In addition to proactive healthcare, long-term use of WBANs also reduces healthcare costs by removing the need for costly in-clinic visits or in-hospital monitoring of patients.

Further, due to the remarkable progress in Internet and Communication Technologies (ICT), WBANs can be integrated with Internet by transmitting the data using long distance backhaul technologies comprising Wide-Area Access Networks (WANs) like cellular communications, e.g. GSM, GPRS, 3G, 4G. The backhaul layer provides mobility to the patients allowing them to carry on their daily activities in both outdoor as well as indoor environments while still facilitating ubiquitous remote monitoring of the patient's health over the Internet. Importantly, as WBANs provide large time intervals of medical data, doctors will have a clearer view of the patient's status [4].

WBAN consists of multiple sensors and a hub or Body Network Controller (BNC). The sensors are placed on, or implanted in the human body measuring physiological attributes of a human body (e.g. electrocardiogram (ECG), electroencephalogram, temperature, etc). The data is then sent over the wireless medium to the hub. Thus, WBAN allows real-time tracking of patient's conditions. Earlier works related to design of WBANs considered low power Wireless Personal Area Network (WPAN) technologies such as Zigbee (IEEE 802.15.4) [5–7] and and Bluetooth (IEEE 802.15.1) [8–10]. However, WPAN technologies do not comply with the medical standards in terms of QoS, reliability and increased data rate. To address this, IEEE has recently come up with a new standard IEEE 802.15.6 [11]. The standard provides a new set of PHY and MAC layer specifications. The MAC layer supports both contention based access using CSMA/CA, slotted Aloha and contention free scheduled access. Scheduled access mechanism allows the sensor nodes to transmit their data during specific Allocation Intervals (AIs). Since it is based on the concept of TDMA, it provides advantages like energy efficient transmission, bounded delay, reduced collision, thereby prolonging sensor battery life time.

Literature survey revealed that implementation of a WBAN MAC protocol as envisioned in IEEE 802.15.6 standard is scarce. Moreover, to the best of authors' knowledge no work has implemented the scheduled access mechanism of IEEE 802.15.6 in a WBAN for real-time health monitoring. To this end, the aim of this work is to implement a WBAN that is based on the IEEE 802.15.6 scheduled access MAC protocol, capable of tracking multiple attributes of a patient in real-time. WBAN when viewed as a standalone network allows patients to have a real-time view of their vitals, giving them more control over their own health. However, in this work, to stay true to the IoT vision, we devise a remote heath monitoring e-Healthcare system that supports database storage of samples of near real-time, also termed as non-real time (NRT), data transmitted at regular intervals by WBANs of multiple patients located anywhere in the world. For this, we design our WBAN BNC to multiplex multiple sensor data and transfer them over the Internet using backhaul technology to a Remote Server (RS). The RS de-multiplexes the data and stores them in a database to provide complete patient health history to healthcare personnel and patients via web and mobile apps. Hardware and software designs have been developed to reach our goals.

Moreover, with the need to reduce data transfer costs and energy consumption over backhaul, we were motivated to look into compression of non-stationary signals (such as ECG) collected by WBAN prior to backhaul transmission without significant loss of information. Additionally, the transmitted compressed data can also be leveraged for efficient storage of the huge volume of healthcare information at the remote database of an e-healthcare system. For signal compression, the transformed compression techniques are one of the most widely employed approaches [12]. These are based on transformation of the time domain signal to another domain, and properly encoding the transformed output. Signal reconstruction is achieved by an inverse transformation process. The transform techniques [12] include Short time Fourier transform (STFT), Wigner-Ville transform (WVT), Choi-Williams distribution (CWD) and the Discrete Wavelet Transforms (DWT). Among these DWT has been the popular choice for non-stationary signal compression because of its localized and non-stationary property and the well-proven ability of wavelets to see through signals at different resolutions [13]. So in order to make our system more energy efficient, we implement a modified version of the DWT compression and conduct extensive analysis to determine the best combination of wavelet filter and compression, and provide benchmarks in performance for future works. Our focus is to implement DWT in real-time on WBAN BNC exploiting the limited on-board resources and with low memory foot-print. To this aim, our proposed *BNC DWT (B-DWT)* implementation based on the concept of Finite Impulse Response (FIR) filters [14] showed significant performance improvements in terms of execution speed and memory utilization over the traditional DWT.

Furthermore, motivated by the need to prolong battery life of the sensor nodes, we made our WBAN energy efficient. For this, we performed performance analysis of our setup in OPNET simulator [15] using a custom-made WBAN model based on IEEE 802.15.6 scheduled access MAC. Through performance analysis we derived the optimal AIs that maximize network capacity while satisfying the frame delay constraints and also obtained the payload sizes needed to maximize the energy efficiency of sensor nodes.

Some of the applications of our system include- (i) remote monitoring as a cost-effective, comfortable alternative to in-clinic cardiac treatment follow up, e.g. periodic transmission of short intervals ECGs, (ii) regular monitoring of patients with hypertension, and (iii) keeping track of conditions of chemo patients.

The paper is organized as follows. Section 2 gives an overview of the e-healthcare system model, IEEE 802.15.6 scheduled access MAC and DWT based data compression. Sections 3 and 4 present the design of sensor nodes and BNC respectively. The implementation of scheduled access MAC is provided in Sect. 5. Section 6 describes the implementation of the proposed B-DWT algorithm at BNC. In Sect. 7, we discuss the performance analysis and characterization of our WBAN setup and B-DWT algorithm. Section 8 deals with the RS and database design. Finally, we conclude the paper in Sect. 9.

2   System Model

This section provides an overview of our e-healthcare architecture and briefly introduces the scheduled access mode of IEEE 802.15.6 and basics of DWT.

2.1   WBAN Based e-Healthcare System

Our developed WBAN based e-Healthcare system uses a three-tier architecture as shown in Fig. 1. The first tier known as the *access layer* is comprised of the WBAN operating over 433 MHz ISM band. At the WBAN, multiple sensors connected to a patient/human body sense and collect physiological data and transmits them over the 433 MHz band to a BNC. The communication in this layer is short-range communication. The sensor nodes communicate in a star topology, with the BNC acting as the hub that coordinates the sensors in transmitting their data. We use the terms BNC and hub interchangeably with respect to WBAN. In this paper, we implement, characterize and optimize, first of its kind, the scheduled access MAC protocol as envisioned in IEEE 802.15.6 to control and coordinate the different sensors nodes in the WBAN. The 433 MHz band is selected as - (i) it is un-licensed and thus no licensing issues, (ii) it encounters less penetration loss, and (iii) it allows high-level integration with radio frequency IC technology leading to smaller size and lower power consumption.

In this work, we mainly focus on designing WBAN for an e-healthcare application that uses a database to store small portions of real-time WBAN data. To demonstrate the feasibility of just couple of the several use-case scenarios, we

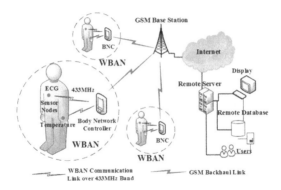

Fig. 1. WBAN based e-healthcare architecture

consider monitoring ECG and temperature of a patient with individual sensors. For ECG tracking, we allow the ECG sensor to transmit a 2 s ECG data to the BNC at regular intervals of 2 h. While for temperature monitoring, only one sample is transmitted every 2 h. After sending the data, the sensors go to sleep. It is worth mentioning that the designed WBAN based on scheduled access MAC can be easily altered to monitor data continuously at the BNC (see Fig. 13b). A possible scenario can be bed-side monitoring (connecting a PC to BNC) or tracking of ones' vitals in real-time on smartphone (considering BNC as part of a smartphone). This is achieved by disabling the sleep periods and allowing the sensors to transmit continuously.

The BNC after multiplexing data from the sensor nodes, compresses the signals that comprise of several samples of information. In our example scenario, we compress the 2 s ECG signal into considerably smaller number of samples using our proposed memory/computationally efficient B-DWT algorithm. This reduces the energy consumed and the data transfer cost involved in backhaul transmission. The compressed data stream is also appended with additional header information that facilitates future reconstruction of the original signal. After multiplexing and compression, the BNC sends the data to a RS over a TCP/IP Internet connection via a WAN Base Station (BS). In this work, for transferring the data collected from WBAN to the BS, the BNC uses General Packet Radio Service (GPRS) over a Global System for Mobile Communications (GSM) network operating in 850/900 MHz band. This comprises the second tier known as the *convergence layer or backhaul*. The backhaul supports wide area communication, thereby enabling patient mobility.

Lastly, after being forwarded by the BS, the data enters the *service layer*. The BS is connected to the service layer through an Internet gateway. The service layer is application specific. In our design, we intend to capture small amounts of medical data at the RS and store them in a database. The physiological signals which are compressed at the BNC are stored in the database in their compressed form along with their associated header information, thereby saving database storage resources. When the compressed signal needs to be read from the database for further diagnosis, the RS or a user application uses the additional header information to implement inverse DWT for signal reconstruction.

2.2 Overview of IEEE 802.15.6 Scheduled Access Mechanism

In IEEE 802.15.6, the time axis is divided into superframes or beacon periods bounded by periodic beacon transmissions (B) by the hub as shown in Fig. 2. The hub places different access phases- Exclusive Access Phases (EAP1, EAP2), Random Access Phases (RAP1, RAP2), Managed Access Phase (MAP), and Contention Access Phase (CAP). EAP, RAP and CAP are meant for contention based access, whereas MAP is for contention free scheduled access. All the access phases except RAP1 may be set to zero. Since we are interested in the scheduled access, we arrange the access phases as shown in Fig. 2. Here, every sensor node is assigned a specific AI within the MAP. A sensor node is permitted to transmit only in its own AI in every superframe. This is termed as scheduled 1-periodic allocation. Figure 2 shows the assignment of specific allocation intervals for ECG and temperature nodes.

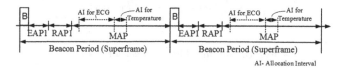

Fig. 2. WBAN superframe structure with scheduled access

2.3 Overview of DWT Based Data Compression

DWT provides an effective data reduction scheme for non-stationary signals like ECG wave [16]. This is because DWT provides time localization of frequency content of the signal. Since the main information in most of the common non-stationary signals lies at low frequencies, the time localization of these lower frequencies will be more precise. Moreover, the high frequency DWT coefficients are less prominent and can be discarded without any major loss of information.

The major challenge in incorporating DWT at BNC is to make the microcontroller of the BNC perform real-time signal processing in addition to digitization, data storage and communication. It is not a trivial task considering that the microcontroller's ability is limited in terms of memory resources, arithmetic power and its ability to handle complex algorithms. We propose a B-DWT algorithm to optimize the DWT through advanced wavelet filters for its calculation by the low-power and low-memory microcontrollers in the BNC. Traditional DWT-based compression algorithm [17] performs several unnecessary arithmetic operations, which implies significant performance penalty. Through our proposed B-DWT algorithm we performed several implementation optimizations for improved execution time and optimal memory utilization, as subsequently explained.

The success of decomposition of a signal into DWT coefficients, followed by compression and then reconstruction to retrieve the original signal depends not only on the level of compression but also on the high-pass and low-pass filters used in sub-band coding [17]. In Sect. 7.2, a comprehensive performance testing of all the major wavelet filters is provided, and depending on the level of compression and the associated permissible information loss, a suitable wavelet filter is selected for the system.

In the following sections, we discuss the design and implementation details of the different components needed to realize the system model of Fig. 1.

3   Wireless Sensor Node Design and Data Generation

We design our own sensor nodes that have the capability of capturing the physiological signals with high fidelity and transmit the captured data wirelessly over 433 MHz ISM band. The basic block diagram of this design is given in Fig. 3.

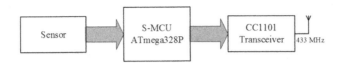

Fig. 3. Building blocks of sensor node

As shown in Fig. 3, the sensor node comprises of an 8-bit 16 MHz ATmega328P Microcontroller Unit (S-MCU) that is interfaced with a sensor and a wireless CC1101 transceiver [18]. The S-MCU is part of an Arduino Uno microcontroller board and has 2 KB of SRAM and 1 KB of EEPROM [19]. The sensors are application specific. For ECG monitoring we use AD8232 sensor [20], which is an integrated signal conditioning block. It is designed to collect, amplify and filter small bio-potential signals from a human body in the presence of noisy conditions, such as those created by motion or remote electrode placement. While for temperature monitoring we employ LM35 sensor. Figure 4 shows the hardware realizations of the ECG setup, and Fig. 5 represents the major components of the sensor node through a functional layered diagram with inter-layer coupling. The S-MCU samples the analog data of the signals, digitizes them with the help of the ADC and stores them. After obtaining the data, the S-MCU will pack the data into MAC frames called MAC Protocol Data Units (MPDUs) by appending headers. Based on the scheduled access mechanism, the S-MCU will transmit the data to the hub over the 433 MHz ISM band using the CC1101 transceivers. The CC1101 wireless chip is selected because of low-power consumption, overall cost saving, small size, fast data transfer and less penetration loss at 433 MHz bands. Furthermore, the CC1101 along with its open-source Panstamp library [21] for Arduino gives the flexibility of designing our own MAC protocols. In the following, we elaborate on the sensing and transmission mechanisms in more detail.

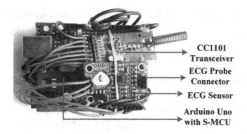

Fig. 4. Developed sensor node with ECG sensor

3.1   Sensing Mechanism

For sensing the physiological signals, the S-MCU takes help of timer interrupts. Atmega328P has 3 timers. Each of the timers has a counter that is incremented on each tick of the timer's clock. In Clear Timer on Compare match (CTC) mode, timer interrupts are triggered when the counter reaches a specified value stored in the compare match register. Once a timer counter reaches this value, it will clear on the next tick of the timer's clock and continue to count up to the compare match value again. We can also set the speed at which the timer increments the counter using a prescaler. Upon setting the compare match value and prescaler, we generate timer interrupts at the required sampling intervals for the signals. When interrupted, S-MCU executes its Interrupt Service Routine (ISR), which triggers the ADC to read the analog value of the signal and enqueue its corresponding digital value in a First-In-First-Out (FIFO) queue (see Fig. 5).

3.2   Interfacing CC1101 with S-MCU

CC1101 provides extensive hardware support for data buffering, packet handling, burst transmissions, link quality indication and clear channel assessment. The main operating parameters and 64-byte transceiver FIFOs of CC1101 can be controlled via a Serial Peripheral Interface (SPI), where the S-MCU is the "master", while the CC1101 serves as its "slave".

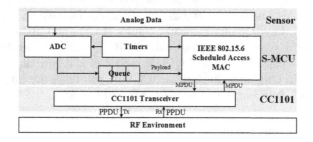

Fig. 5. Layered diagram of sensor node with inter-layer coupling

We use Panstamp library [21] for Arduino to communicate between S-MCU and the CC1101. More specifically, we implement the CC1101 class contained in the Panstamp library. It provides simple mechanisms to configure the CC1101 registers to operate in 433 MHz band and use GFSK modulation scheme. The CC1101 class also allows us to send and receive wireless frames termed as Physical Layer Protocol Data Units (PPDUs). The most interesting methods are the receiveData and sendData. In order to detect an incoming packet, we configure CC1101 to interrupt the S-MCU Interrupt Pin (INT0). Whenever the INT0 pin of S-MCU goes low, the interrupt is triggered and the S-MCU reads the incoming PPDU stored in the RX FIFO register of CC1101 using the receiveData command. While, the sendData is a method which enables S-MCU to send a data packet via the CC1101 RF transmitter. It takes the PPDU to be sent as an argument. Next, we discuss the CC1101 PPDU frame format.

3.3   CC1101 PPDU Frame Format

A CC1101 PPDU frame is configurable and consists of fixed length preamble, a synchronization (SYNC) word, optional length byte, optional address byte (not used as similar field is in the MPDU), variable length MPDU and an optional 2-byte Cyclic Redundancy Check (CRC) field as shown in Fig. 6 [18]. The *preamble*, *SYNC word* and *CRC* fields are defined at the CC1101 registers and are inserted automatically during transmission (Tx) and removed during reception (Rx).

Fig. 6. CC1101 PPDU frame format

We employ a variable packet length mode, where the MPDU length is configured by the first byte after the *SYNC word*. The maximum length of MPDU is 60 bytes. This is governed by the CRC capabilities of CC1101. We set the *Length* field to 'MPDU size' bytes. The actual length of CC1101 data buffer is 63 bytes. However, 3 status bytes are inserted within a received PPDU adjacent to its MPDU. These three status bytes contain Received Signal Strength Indicator (RSSI), Link Quality Indicator Values (LQI) and CRC_OK values. In Rx mode, when a sync word is detected, the RSSI value at the RSSI register is inserted in the RSSI byte. The LQI is a metric of the current quality of the received signal. In CRC auto flush mode, CC1101 will flush the entire Rx FIFO if the CRC check fails and it will set CRC_OK field to '0'.

3.4   MPDU Frame Format

The MPDU frame prepared by S-MCU (Fig. 5) consists of a fixed length MAC header and a variable-length MAC frame body/payload containing the sensor

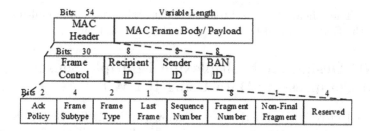

Fig. 7. CC1101 MPDU frame format

data as shown in Fig. 7 [11]. The *Recipient ID* denotes the ID of the recipient of the current frame. The *Sender ID* is set to the ID of the sender of the current frame. The *BAN ID* field is set to the ID of the BAN in which the current frame is transferred. The *Ack Policy field* is set to I-Ack to indicate the immediate acknowledgment requirement of data, connection request and connection assignment frames. The *Frame Type* and *Frame Subtype* fields respectively indicate the type and sub-type of the current frame according to Table 1. It must be pointed out that the *Frame Subtype* field for allocation mapped data is user configurable that we use for representing 15 different physiological signals. If more number of sensors are needed in a WBAN, then we can use the reserved fields in the MPDU. The *Last Frame* field indicates the last frame in an AI.

The *Sequence Number* field prevents reception of duplicate MAC Service Data Unit (MSDU) at the receiver. For frames containing fragments of the same MSDU, the *Sequence Number* remains unchanged. In such scenario, the *Fragment Number* field is used to indicate the data frames containing the fragments of the same MSDU. In this regard, the *Non-Final Fragment* field is set to one if the frame contains a non-final fragment of a fragmented MSDU.

For example, in case of transfer of a 2 s ECG data sampled at 200 Hz, a total of 400 integer samples are generated. If we fragment the data stream into 20 data samples (each of 2 bytes), then there will be 20 such 40-byte data payloads. Each of these data payloads constitute an MSDU fragment. Then, there will be 20 data fragments having same *Sequence Number* but incrementing *Fragment Number*. Whereas, the *Sequence Number* will be incremented for the next 2 s

Table 1. Frame type and frame subtype field encoding [11]

Frame type value	Frame type name	Frame subtype value	Frame subtype name
00	Management	0000	Beacon
00	Management	1000	Connection request
00	Management	1001	Connection assignment
01	Control	0000	I-Ack
10	Data	1000–1111	Allocation mapped data

ECG data. These fields play vital roles in multiplexing data from multiple sensor nodes at the BNC and will be discussed in the next section.

4   BNC Design for Multiplexing Multiple Sensors and Compressing Data Using B-DWT

We designed a BNC to realize the scenario shown in Fig. 1. The BNC is developed based on the internal structure as shown in Fig. 8. The ATmega328P MCU of the BNC (H-MCU) controls the WBAN communication as a hub using CC1101 transceiver. The WBAN communications needs to satisfy QoS constraints as mentioned in IEEE 802.15.6 standard [11]. Therefore, it comes as a straight forward deduction that it is not possible to engage H-MCU in backhaul communication Therefore, we add another MCU comprising of an 8-bit 16 MHz ATmega2560 MCU termed as the Client MCU (C-MCU) as shown in Fig. 8. We will justify the terminology shortly. The C-MCU is part of an Arduino Mega microcontroller board and has 8KB of SRAM and 4KB of EEPROM [22]. The higher specifications of ATmega2560 is needed for (1) queuing data from multiple sensors, (2) handle TCP-IP communications, (3) B-DWT based compression of data such as the ECG samples, and (4) to allow scope for future optimizations with respect to the backhaul communication. For supporting backhaul communication, we have a GSM shield connected to the C-MCU. With the GSM shield, it is possible to leverage the GPRS data communication to access the Internet.

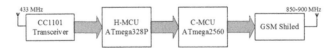

Fig. 8. Building blocks of body network controller

Figure 9 shows the hardware realization of the BNC. The interfacing of CC1101 with H-MCU is similar to that of the sensor nodes. However, the interfacing between H-MCU and C-MCU needs an elaborate explanation.

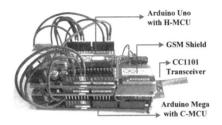

Fig. 9. Developed body network controller

4.1   Interfacing H-MCU with C-MCU for Data Multiplexing with B-DWT Based Compression

The H-MCU communicates with C-MCU via Universal Asynchronous Receiver/ Transmitter (UART) interface. Here, the H-MCU takes bytes of data and transmits the individual bits in a sequential fashion to the C-MCU. Figure 10 illustrates the process of transferring and multiplexing the data collected by H-MCU from multiple sensors to the C-MCU. When the H-MCU receives a data MPDU from a sensor within an AI, it extracts the payload, the *Frame Subtype* (FS) field, the *Non-Final Fragment* (NFF) field and prepares H-MCU packet. It then transfers the H-MCU packet, as shown in Fig. 10, to the C-MCU over the UART interface. The FS field helps C-MCU decode the signal, while the NFF helps C-MCU identify the final payload of a fragmented MSDU.

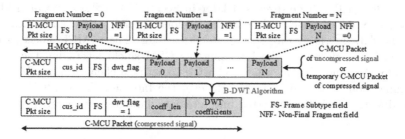

Fig. 10. Multiplexing different data fragments from sensors that require either no compression or B-DWT based compression for preparation of C-MCU packets

Upon detecting a packet over the UART interface, C-MCU parses the incoming integer numbers. The first number of an incoming H-MCU packet corresponds to its size, which helps C-MCU identify the boundaries of the packet. The next field is the *Frame Subtype* field. For our proposed BNC, we employ this field to multiplex data from multiple sensors within a particular WBAN of a patient. To enforce minimal memory utilization, we employ a multiple queue memory management system for the C-MCU. Where one queue corresponds to one particular physiological signal (having distinct *Frame Subtype*) as shown in Fig. 10. The advantage of the queue management system is that the individual queues are flexible enough to adjust their lengths as per the number of samples within an MSDU (fragmented or non-fragmented) that it stores. This leads to less wastage of memory space, unlike fixed length array. The intelligent nature of the BNC allows the C-MCU to take action when a complete MSDU is received from H-MCU. This is identified from the *Non-Final Fragment* field (see Fig. 10). It must be noted, that prior to queuing the data bytes from H-MCU into C-MCU packets, the integer data are re-converted to actual analog floating-point values that were digitized at the ADC of the sensor nodes. Upon reception of a complete MSDU, the BNC is pre-programmed to perform B-DWT data compression on certain signals with particular *Frame Subtype*. The compression status of a signal is indicated by the *dwt_flag* field of C-MCU packet which is set to '1' if a signal is to be compressed, else it is set to '0'. The *dwt_flag* will intimate the RS about the compression status of a received C-MCU packet, which needs to be stored accordingly. In case a signal is to be transmitted in uncompressed form (eg. Temperature values), the resulting C-MCU packet is prepared directly from the H-MCU packets as shown in Fig. 10. However, for signals that require compression (eg. ECG samples), prior to preparing the final C-MCU packet with DWT coefficients, the C-MCU prepares a 'temporary C-MCU packet' comprising of all the payloads of the concerned H-MCU packets as illustrated in Fig. 10. Thereafter, the C-MCU compresses the original signal using B-DWT to prepare the final C-MCU packet. In addition to the already existing fields, the C-MCU appends an extra field denoted by *coeff_len* ahead of the DWT coefficients. The *coeff_len* denotes the length of different levels of DWT coefficients which are instrumental in facilitating future reconstruction of the signal. Preparation of the *coeff_len* field will be discussed later in Sect. 6.1. Finally, a *cus_id* field is inserted by C-MCU which will help the RS identify the patient and efficiently store the data in the database, more on this later. The C-MCU packet thus prepared is transferred to the RS using the GSM shield leveraging the GSM library for Arduino, that allows the C-MCU to act as a client and use TCP/IP communication to send data to the RS over the Internet. The C-MCU packet received at the RS is then inserted into a remote database (see Sect. 8).

5   Implementation of Scheduled Access MAC

In order to achieve a seamless and reliable communication between different sensor nodes and the BNC, we use the scheduled access mechanism of IEEE 802.15.6. For this, the S-MCU of sensor nodes and H-MCU of BNC needs to handle the following three kinds of operations: (i) superframe generation, (ii) connection establishment, and (iii) data transmission/reception.

5.1   Superframe Generation

In our designed WBAN, the sensors and hub operate within the superframe structure as depicted in Fig. 2. To achieve this, the H-MCU and S-MCU takes help of Timer interrupts, whose ISR pseudo-code is given in Algorithm 1.

We maintain a variable *mac_state* that defines the current access phase of the sensor node/hub. A timer interrupt executes the ISR, checks the current *mac_state*, and based on it changes *mac_state* to the value corresponding to next access phase. The ISR also updates the compare match register of the timer to trigger the next interrupt at the end of the current access phase. Additionally, at the beginning of EAP1, the hub broadcasts a Beacon MPDU allowing the sensor nodes to tune their individual timer clocks to the hub's clock and also update the access phase lengths in case of a change.

Algorithm 1. Timer interrupt subroutine for superframe generation

---

```
 1: ISR(TIMER1_COMPA_vect){
 2:     switch (mac_state){ // MAC states
 3:         case EAP1: //End of EAP1
 4:             mac_state = RAP1; //Start of RAP1
 5:             set compare match register for interrupt at end of RAP1
 6:         break;
 7:         case RAP1: //End of RAP1
 8:             mac_state = MAP1; //Start of MAP1
 9:             set compare match register for interrupt at end of MAP1
10:         break;
11:         case MAP1: //End of MAP1
12:             mac_state = EAP1; //Start of EAP1
13:             set compare match register for interrupt at end of EAP1
14:         break; } }
```

5.2 Connection Establishment

Prior to beginning its transmission, a sensor node must obtain a scheduled allocation from the hub by sending a Connection Request frame within EAP1 or RAP1. The MSDU of Connection Request frame contains the requested AI. If the hub can fit the requested AI within the available MAP barring the already granted allocations, then the hub sends a Connection Assignment frame, informing the acceptance. Note that IEEE 802.15.6 [11] has the provision for both secured and un-secured WBAN session. An implementation of the secured communication is beyond the scope of this paper, however it will be incorporated in our setup in the future.

For transferring the Connection Request or Connection Assignment frames, the S-MCU and H-MCU uses Tx-if-Clear Channel Assessment (CCA) mechanism of CC1101. The CCA functionality makes use of the Carrier Sense (CS) feature of CC1101. The CS is asserted when the RSSI is above a programmable absolute threshold, and de-asserted when RSSI is below the same threshold. The RSSI threshold value (in dBm) in our setup is set at -91.5 dBm based on the CC1101 specification sheet [18]. In Tx-if-CCA mode, before transmission, the CC1101 strobes the Rx, waits 500 µs for a valid RSSI, and compares it with the threshold for CS. If CS is asserted, then the channel is busy or else the PPDU loaded in Tx FIFO buffer of CC1101 is transmitted.

5.3 Data Transmission and Reception

Upon obtaining a scheduled uplink allocation, if the queue of the sensor node is not-empty, then the sensor node can initiate a frame transaction with the hub within its AIs. However, the sensor node will only initiate transmission if the frame transaction and an appropriate guard time fit within the current timer instant and the end of the AI, as shown in Fig. 11. If the frame cannot be transmitted, it will be deferred till the next AI. A frame transaction comprises of the sensor node transmitting a CC1101 PPDU and waiting for a corresponding Immediate Acknowledgment frame (I-Ack) from the hub, separated by a Short Inter-Frame Spacing (SIFS). If an I-Ack is not received within the expected time, the node resends the data frame. The maximum number of such resends is denoted by R. The I-Ack timeout is detected by enabling another timer, termed I-Ack timer, within the sensor node. The timeout is set to the time required to transmit an I-Ack frame plus the SIFS period. In this regard, the superframe parameters, frame lengths and other system parameters are given in Table 2.

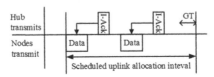

Fig. 11. Frame transactions in scheduled uplink allocations

Upon reception of a PPDU at the hub, the H-MCU examines its CRC_OK status bit. If the CRC check fails, then the hub discards the received frame. Upon timeout, the sensor node will retransmit the frame. However, if the PPDU passes the CRC check, then the MPDU will be extracted. Next, we check if the MPDU is actually meant for the sensor node by comparing the *BAN ID, Sender ID* and *Recipient ID* present in the MPDU header (Fig. 7) respectively with the *BAN ID, Recipient ID* of the expected sensor node and hub ID. H-MCU also checks for a duplicate frame using the *Sequence Number* and *Fragment Number* fields of the MPDU. Upon successfully filtering the incoming PPDU, the sensor data is handled by H-MCU and sent to C-MCU, as described in Sect. 4.1. In response to the successful filtering of the received MPDU, H-MCU prepares the corresponding I-Ack frame by setting its *Recipient ID* field to the sensor node ID, *Sender ID* field to the hub ID and *Sequence Number* and *Fragment Number* to that of the received MPDU frame. Upon successfully receiving the I-Ack frame, the sensor node loads the TX FIFO with the next PPDU.

6   Implementation of B-DWT for Data Compression

DWT, in practice, employs wavelet filters comprising of a pair of finite half-band low and high pass filters [17]. Let us assume that the impulse response of these FIR filters be represented by $H_d[n]$ and $L_d[n]$ respectively, and the length of these filters be denoted by K. The procedure starts with passing the input sequence $x[n]$ comprising of N samples through $H_d[n]$ and $L_d[n]$ simultaneously, which doubles the frequency resolution. As per Nyquist theorem, half the samples now become redundant and hence are removed through down sampling by 2. The down sampling process reduces the time-resolution by half. The output of $H_d[n]$ followed by the down sampling, known as *Detail Coefficients*, comprises the first level of DWT coefficients. Whereas, the output of $L_d[n]$ after down sampling, called *Approximation Coefficients*, is again subjected to filtering through $H_d[n]$ and $L_d[n]$ with subsequent sub-sampling, and the process continues until L levels of decomposition are performed. We now introduce our proposed B-DWT.

6.1   Proposed B-DWT Algorithm

For the proposed B-DWT algorithm, we employ the analysis of moving average filters [14], that allows us to mathematically express the DWT process as,

$$y_{high}[n] = \sum_{t=0}^{K-1} (H_d[t]x[2n - t]) \tag{1}$$

$$y_{low}[n] = \sum_{t=0}^{K-1} (L_d[t]x[2n - t]) \tag{2}$$

Where, $y_{high}[n]$ and $y_{low}[n]$ are the outputs of the high-pass and low-pass filters after sub-sampling by 2. By intelligently exploiting (1) and (2), our proposed B-DWT can provide improvement in execution speed by effectively reducing the number of arithmetic operations. Additionally, B-DWT intelligently utilizes the C-MCU memory allocated for storing input signal to hold the output data that will be utilized in the calculation of DWT coefficients of subsequent levels. This saves memory space in the resource constrained C-MCU which can now be more efficiently utilized. The pseudo-code of B-DWT is provided in Algorithm 2.

At the beginning of the B-DWT algorithm, initialization of all the variables is performed. *tot_dwt_len* denotes the length of the L level DWT of the input signal $x[n]$ without any compression, and it can be obtained mathematically. $y[n]$ is the set of yet to be attained DWT coefficients. M keeps track of the length of the input signal at each filtering stage. *start_ind* and *end_ind* marks the beginning and end of the location in $y[n]$ where the DWT coefficients at each stage are to be inserted. As discussed previously, in DWT based compression, the first level of high frequency DWT coefficients of length $\lfloor (N + K - 1)/2 \rfloor$ are generally discarded. Therefore, in order to save memory space and reduce execution time, the length of $y[n]$ is reduced as in (line: 4 of Algorithm 2). Thereafter, in the *for* loop of (line 8 of Algorithm 2) the detail and approximation coefficients are obtained from sub-loops in (lines: 10 and 21 of Algorithm 2) respectively. Note that, an advantage in terms of less number of computations can be gained from (lines: 12 and 22 of Algorithm 2) which essentially performs the down sampling but prior to the filtering process. More specifically, at each filtering stage the proposed B-DWT technique uses $(L-1)(L+M-2)/2$ number of additions and $L(L + M - 1)/2$ multiplications. Whereas, normal DWT implementation takes $(L-1)(L+2M-1)/2$ number of additions and $L(L+2M-1)/2$ multiplications to get the same result. Hence, at each filtering stage B-DWT requires almost half the number of computations as compared to normal DWT, thereby drastically reducing the execution time. After evaluating the DWT coefficients at a particular level, the final stage of the B-DWT pertains to the utilization of the

---

Algorithm 2. Computation of DWT Coefficients by B-DWT Algorithm

---

Initialization

1: tot_dwt_len=length of dwt output;

2: N= length of input signal, K=length of filter, C=length of compressed signal;

3: $x[0 : N - 1]$=input signal, $x[N : N + K - 2] = 0$;

4: $y[0 : tot\_dwt\_len - \lfloor (N + K - 1)/2 \rfloor - 1] = \{0\}$;

5: $H_d[0 : K - 1]$=High pass filter coefficients;

6: $L_d[0 : K - 1]$=Low pass filter coefficients;

7: $M = N$, $end\_ind = tot\_dwt\_len$, $start\_ind = 0$, $k = 0$, $i = 0$, $j = 0$;

8: **for** $j = 1 : L$ **do**

9:     $start\_ind = end\_ind - \lfloor (M + K - 1)/2 \rfloor$;

Calculation of Detail Coefficients

10:     **for** $k = 0 : \lfloor (M + K - 1)/2 \rfloor - 1$ **do**

11:         **if** $j > 2$ **then**

12:             $i = 2k + 1$;

13:             **if** $i < (K - 1)$ **then**

14:                 $y[start\_ind + k] = \sum_{t=0}^{i} H_d[t] \times x[i - t]$;

15:             **else**

16:                 $y[start\_ind + k] = \sum_{t=0}^{K-1} H_d[t] \times x[K - 1 - i]$;

17:             **end if**

18:         **end if**

19:     **end for**

20:     $end\_ind = start\_ind$;

Calculation of Approximation Coefficients

21:     **for** $k = 0 : \lfloor (M + K - 1)/2 \rfloor - 1$ **do**

22:         $i = 2k + 1$;

23:         **if** $i < K - 1$ **then**

24:             $y[k] = \sum_{t=0}^{i} L_d[t] \times x[i - t]$;

25:         **else**

26:             $y[k] = \sum_{t=0}^{K-1} L_d[t] \times x[K - 1 - t]$;

27:         **end if**

28:     **end for**

29:     **if** $j < L$ **then**

30:         **for** $k = 0 : \lfloor (M + K - 1)/2 \rfloor - 1$ **do**

31:             $x[k] = y[k]$;

32:         **end for**

33:     **end if**

34:     $M = \lfloor (M + K - 1)/2 \rfloor$;

35: **end for**

36: $output\_signal = y[0 : C - 1]$, where $C \leq \lfloor (N + K - 1)/2 \rfloor$;

---

approximation coefficients for the next level. Since, we opt to enforce minimal memory utilization, the *for* loop of (line 30 of Algorithm 2) aptly overwrites the input signal at $x[n]$ with the approximation coefficients. Thereafter, M, *start_ind* and *end_ind* are updated before proceeding to the next level. Finally, after the computation of L levels of DWT, depending on the required degree of compression, the output signal of length C is generated from $y[n]$ in (line 36 of Algorithm 2). Lastly, the length of each of the L levels of DWT coefficients and the actual input signal length N are updated in *coeff_len* field of C-MCU packet (Fig. 10).

7   Performance Evaluation and Optimization

In this section, we analyze the performance of our designed WBAN access layer. For this, we have developed a simulation model for WBAN in OPNET simulator [15] based on the scheduled access mechanism of IEEE 802.15.6 MAC protocol. Using the custom-made OPNET simulation model we analyze the system performance metrics namely, average frame delay, average throughput and energy consumption of the sensor nodes. Through performance analysis, we choose the appropriate system parameters. We determine the AIs to maximize network capacity while maintaining a frame delay constraint, and also select a payload size to achieve maximum energy efficiency of sensor nodes.

This section also deals with the analysis of the proposed B-DWT based compression of ECG signal samples generated by AD8232 sensor. The two metrics that are commonly used to measure the performance of DWT analysis are [13]: (i) *Percentage Root Mean Difference (PRD)* to measure distortion between the original signal and the reconstructed signal, and (ii) *Compression Ratio or Compressed Data Ratio (CDR)*, defined as the ratio of the number of bits representing the original signal to the number of bits required to store the compressed signal. Using these metrics, we report the most suitable wavelet filter to achieve optimal compression within acceptable information loss. Finally, we provide some real test-bed results pertaining to implementation of B-DWT in C-MCU to establish its superior real-time performance with respect to normal DWT process.

7.1   Performance Analysis of WBAN Communication

We evaluate the performance of our setup in terms of the afore-mentioned metrics through simulations in our OPNET model. For simulation, the parameters followed are same as the hardware setup. The complete list of system parameters is given in Table 2. The transceiver specific parameters of CC1101 are obtained from its data-sheet [18]. The OPNET model is designed based on a slotted time-reference, with each slot equivalent to 2 ms. Accordingly, we refer to superframe parameters in terms of time-slots. However, for building our hardware setup, we implement the equivalent times in floating point variables. The requirements stated in [11] mention an operating range of 3 m for WBANs. At this distance, we were not able to record any CRC error for the received frames. We, therefore, consider an ideal channel for our OPNET model.

As highlighted in Sect. 2, we tested our hardware model for ECG and temperature monitoring. The monitoring of ECG signal is more complicated as

Table 2. System parameters

Parameters	Values	Parameters	Values
Data rate	38.4 kbps	MAP length	0.4 s
SIFS	75 μs	Voltage supply, V_s	3 V
Guard Time, GT	120 μs	Transmit current	16 mA
Beacon period	0.5 s	Receive current	15 mA
EAP1 length	0.05 s	Idle current	1.7 mA
RAP1 length	0.05 s	Sleep current, I_{sleep}	0.2 μA

compared to temperature. Unlike temperature (0.1 sample/s), sending an ECG signal requires continual and undisturbed sampling period of 200 samples/s or 400 bytes/s. Therefore, performance analysis for ECG sensor node needs special attention. We run the simulations in OPNET for 5 mins in case of ECG and 2 h in case of temperature, where the nodes generate data continuously without any sleep interval during the simulation run. This helps us get accurate average values for the performance metrics.

The nodes generate traffic with constant traffic distribution. In case of ECG sensing, for a selected payload size (of a single fragment) of P_{size} bytes/packet, the arrival rate is obtained as $\lambda = \dfrac{400}{P_{size}}$ packets/s.

Figure 12a shows the variation of average frame delay for ECG monitoring with respect to the size of the payloads for different AIs. It must be noted, that the CC1101 PPDU frame format limits the maximum payload size to 52 bytes. In this figure, it can be observed that as the AI increases, delay decreases. For larger AIs, the event of deferral of frame transmissions decreases. Less deferral corresponds to less waiting delay for the frames in the queue. This leads to the perception that higher AIs are better for the system. However, as we increase the AI, the network capacity also decreases. Hence, we select an AI that just satisfies the maximum frame delay constraint. For our setup, we consider a delay constraint of 150 ms [11]. From Fig. 12a, we can observe that an AI of 90 slots (0.18 s) satisfies this delay constraint. It is also observed that for a fixed AI, variation in moderate payload sizes does not affect frame delay significantly. Larger payloads lead to more deferrals, but reduced packet arrival rates tend to balance that effect. Thus, the queue length and waiting delay does not vary much with changes in payload size. However, very small payload sizes (<20 slots) lead to high frame delay due to high packet arrival rate. A high packet arrival rate will cause buffer overflow and thus packet loss and high delay.

We illustrate the variation of average throughput and total energy consumption of the ECG node transceiver with respect to the payload sizes in Figs. 12b and c respectively. It is observed that as payload size increases, both the throughput and energy consumption decreases. Due to increase in the size of the payloads, the deferral in frame transmission within an AI increases. This leads to decrease in the number of frame transmissions within a particular time, thereby

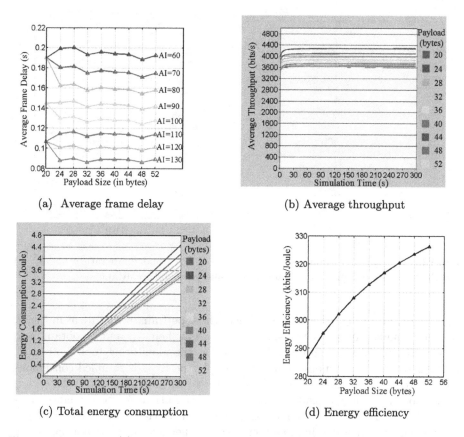

(a) Average frame delay

(b) Average throughput

(c) Total energy consumption

(d) Energy efficiency

Fig. 12. Variation of (a) average frame delay against different AIs, (b) average throughput, (c) total energy consumption for continuous transmission, (d) energy efficiency of ECG node for varied payload sizes

reducing both the throughput and energy consumption. So, to address this inherent tradeoff we consider the energy efficiency metric as shown in Fig. 12d. It can be observed that higher payload size leads to more energy efficient transmissions. Thus, we conclude that decrease in energy consumption overpowers the decrease in throughput, resulting in better energy efficiency. Hence, we consider a payload size of 52 bytes for ECG node (limited by CC1101 CRC ability).

Compared to ECG, modeling temperature monitoring is much simpler. Only one 2-byte sample needs to be transmitted every sleep interval. So, determining a payload size is not required. As for AI, we performed a delay analysis in OPNET and determined 5 slots (0.01 s) as the AI length for temperature monitoring.

Likewise, the WBAN sensor nodes in our setup have been tuned to the optimal AIs and payload sizes. To validate the functionality and capability of the scheduled access mode in providing real-time tracking of physiological parameters, the H-MCU was directly monitored via a serial monitoring tool. As shown in

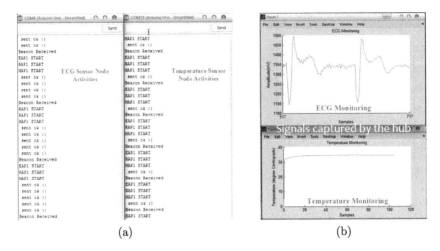

Fig. 13. Snapshot: (a) Simultaneous activities of ECG and temperature nodes, (b) Simultaneous monitoring of continuous ECG and temperature at hub

the screenshots of Fig. 13, the hub arranges the superframe structure as in Fig. 2, the sensor nodes efficiently transmit the frames in their AIs and we obtain both ECG and temperature data simultaneously at the monitoring tool. Note that, in order to get a continuous monitoring graph, the ECG is sampled continuous and the temperature is sent in every superframe without sleep intervals.

Although, we have considered ideal channel conditions for performance analysis. It is worth noting that the necessary mechanisms (I-Ack and CRC check) to address bit errors arising due to a non-ideal channel, such as a log-normal fading channel, have been incorporated, as described in Sect. 5.3. An effective way to handle a changing channel condition is to allow a sensor node to to adapt its AI and PS based on the channel SNR using pre-loaded Look-up Tables stored in its memory. The overall objective can be maximization of the energy efficiency under frame delay and reliability constraints. Analytical modeling of Scheduled Access MAC under non-ideal channel conditions is conducted by us in [23].

7.2   Peformance Analysis of Proposed B-DWT

Table 3 compares the output PRD and CDR averaged over the 400 sample ECG signal for B-DWT performed using different DWT filters over 5 levels (i.e. $L = 5$). With increasing compression, the CDR improves, however the PRD also increases. This is expected because more compression means discarding more number of DWT coefficients, which results in eliminating increased number of coefficients at lower frequency levels containing significant meaningful information. Therefore, a tradeoff is required between the desired level of compression (CDR) and the acceptable PRD.

The relationship between the measured PRD and the diagnostic distortion is established based on the work of Zigel et al. on the weighted diagnostic

Table 3. CDR and PRD at different levels of DWT for varied wavelet filters

Wavelet family	Wavelets	Level-1		Level-2		Level-3		Level-4		Level-5	
		CDR	PRD	CDR	PRD	CDR	PRD	CDR	PRD	CDR	PRD
Biorthogonal	bior1.1	15.38	4.56	7.84	3.79	3.96	3.07	1.99	1.97	1	0
	bior1.3	11.76	4.66	6.35	3.97	3.42	2.40	1.82	2.00	0.95	0
	bior2.2	11.76	5.06	6.35	2.92	3.42	2.03	1.82	1.12	0.95	0
	bior2.4	9.52	4.24	5.33	3.41	3.03	1.76	1.68	1.11	0.90	0
	bior3.1	13.33	6.20	7.02	3.97	3.67	2.27	1.90	0.69	0.97	0
	bior4.4	9.52	4.25	5.33	3.40	3.03	1.68	1.68	0.94	0.90	0
Reverse biorthogonal	rbio1.1	15.38	4.56	7.84	3.79	3.96	3.07	1.99	1.96	1.0	0
	rbio1.3	11.76	4.36	6.35	3.49	3.42	1.79	1.82	1.51	0.95	0
	rbio1.5	9.52	4.41	5.33	3.46	3.03	2.58	1.68	1.39	0.90	0
	rbio2.2	11.76	4.59	6.35	3.31	3.42	2.68	1.82	1.47	0.95	0
	rbio2.6	8.00	4.35	4.60	3.60	2.70	2.52	1.56	0.94	0.86	0
	rbio3.1	13.33	14.75	7.02	9.79	3.67	6.95	1.90	2.27	0.97	0
	rbio3.5	8.70	4.55	4.94	3.60	2.86	2.61	1.61	0.54	0.88	0
Daubechies	db1	15.38	4.56	7.84	3.79	3.96	3.07	1.99	1.96	1.0	0
	db4	10.53	4.20	5.80	3.53	3.20	2.36	1.74	0.61	0.92	0
Coiflets	coif1	11.76	4.47	6.35	2.89	3.42	2.26	1.82	1.31	0.95	0
	coif2	8.70	4.29	4.94	3.51	2.86	2.64	1.61	1.04	0.88	0
	coif3	7.14	4.37	4.17	3.51	2.50	2.41	1.47	0.95	0.83	0
	coif4	5.88	4.39	3.51	3.71	2.17	2.45	1.33	0.90	0.78	0
Symlets	sym2	13.33	5.14	7.02	3.78	3.67	1.86	1.90	1.31	0.97	0
	sym4	10.53	4.24	5.80	3.18	3.20	2.46	1.74	1.22	0.92	0

measure for ECG signal compression [24], which classifies the different values of PRD based on the signal quality perceived by a specialist. A filter is selected which provides an acceptable PRD with the maximum amount of compression. *Biorthogonal 4.4 filter* produces the best results for B-DWT. A "very good" signal reconstruction quality (corresponding to PRD below 2% [24]) can be reached for CDRs up to 3.03. Finally, it is worthwhile mentioning that the used metric, PRD may not always reflect the reconstruction quality. Hence, Fig. 14 is plotted to illustrate that the proposed B-DWT algorithm produces acceptable signal after signal reconstruction. As evident from Fig. 14b the last 310 DWT coefficients are insignificant and hence omitted. From Fig. 14c it can be easily seen that transmitting only the first 132 DWT coefficients (3.03 CDR or 67% compression) followed by signal reconstruction preserves the original signal information. Interestingly, the reconstructed signal does not contain the high frequency noise and is smoother than the original signal in Fig. 14a. Consequently, while incurring no significant information loss, B-DWT could efficiently provide three-fold energy and cost saving in transmission over long distance backhaul.

Finally, we study the B-DWT performance in compressing 400 sample ECG signal in real-time using Biorthogonal 4.4 filter at C-MCU (ATmega2560). The results of the study are summarized in Table 4. As evident, our proposed B-DWT outperforms traditional DWT [17] based implementation in terms of 64%

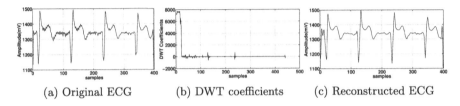

(a) Original ECG   (b) DWT coefficients   (c) Reconstructed ECG

Fig. 14. (a) 2 s ECG signal captured by AD8232 sensor, (b) DWT signal compressed using Bior.4.4 filter, (c) Reconstructed signal from 1st 132 DWT coeff.

Table 4. Performance of B-DWT and traditional DWT based compression

Algorithm	Time taken (ms)	Program storage (bytes)
Proposed B-DWT	97.06	17262 (6% of total memory)
Traditional DWT	267.3	20654 (8% of total memory)

faster execution speed and 2% less memory utilization of the resource constrained ATmega2560. These improvements are a result of down sampling before filtering and intelligent utilization of memory space for intermediate filtering stages.

8   Remote Server and Database

In this section, the implementation of the Remote Server (RS) and the development of a database to store the captured data is described. For the RS, we have used MATLAB TCP server framework. As highlighted previously, the RS receives the C-MCU packets from the BNC. The RS is further configured to insert the data into a database called Remote DB in a formatted manner as illustrated in Fig. 15. As seen in Fig. 15, the database maintains separate Microsoft Excel files (*.xlsx*) for each patient and names them according to their Customer IDs. Each *.xlsx* file has separate worksheets for storing records of different physiological signals in chronological order of the time the data were collected. The time of the data collection is registered by the RS. To achieve this structured and sorted Remote DB, the RS exploits the header information contained with C-MCU packets. More specifically, the *cus_id* helps in selecting the *.xlsx* file, the *Frame Subtype* field allows to identify the worksheet, and the *dwt_flag* field facilitates in identifying whether the data contained in the C-MCU packet is compressed. If *dwt_flaq* = 1 (as in in case of ECG), the corresponding DWT coefficients are stored along with the contents of the *coeff_len* field of C-MCU packet. As shown in Fig. 15, for a single record of ECG monitoring we store the all the 132 DWT coefficients preceded by the *coeff_len*, values, while for temperature only a single value (uncompressed) is stored. In must be highlighted that, instead of storing all the 400 samples of a 2 s ECG signal, B-DWT allows Remote DB to store the same signal in terms of 132 DWT coefficients and seven *coeff_len* values leading to a significant 65.25% reduction in database utilization.

Fig. 15. Snapshot of remote database

The database when coupled with different analytics tools such as Microsoft Power BI will allow visualizing the received data providing deeper insights into a patient's conditions and also enable integration with cloud and web services.

9   Conclusion

In this paper, we present a WBAN that can be used to remotely monitor and store multiple physiological signals of patients. For this, we implement, first of its kind, schedule access mechanism of IEEE 802.15.6 to monitor ECG and temperature simultaneously. In this regard, detailed hardware implementation involving interfacing of MCU of sensor nodes with CC1101 low power transceiver is discussed. Furthermore, multiplexing of data from multiple sensor nodes at the BNC is elaborated. In addition, we introduce the concept of data compression at BNC and propose a fast B-DWT algorithm to compress long data streams into DWT coefficients in real-time that would allow the BNC to transfer the data over a backhaul network in an energy efficient and cost effective manner. Further, the BNC is used to connect to a GSM cellular network to send the collected data over the Internet to a Remote Server (RS). Moreover, the RS is configured to accept data from multiple patients and store them in a database. This would allow users to access patient data anywhere, anytime through web service and mobile applications.

To characterize and optimize the designed WBAN, we perform its performance analysis in OPNET. To this aim, we obtain the optimal Allocation Intervals (AIs) for ECG and temperature monitoring, that maximizes the network capacity within a frame delay constraint. Furthermore, the optimal payload sizes are obtained to maximize the energy efficiency of the sensor nodes. Additionally, through a comprehensive performance analysis of the proposed B-DWT algorithm we found Bi-orthogonal 4.4 Wavelet filter as the most suitable filter providing 67% signal compression with less than 2% information loss. Moreover, B-DWT is found to be 64% faster in terms of execution speed and 2% more memory efficient as compared to traditional DWT. To add to this, the storage of the physiological signals in their compressed form at the remote database also allows a significant 65.25% reduction in database storage utilization. Currently we are working to make the WBAN communication secured, and interface the database with analytics tool and cloud services to provide a user interface for secured pervasive access of the data.

References

1. World Health Organization: Life expectancy at birth (years) (2017). http://www.gamapserver.who.int/gho/interactive_charts/mbd/life_expectancy/atlas.html
2. The World Bank: World health organization global health expenditure database (2018). https://data.worldbank.org/indicator/SH.XPD.TOTL.ZS?end=2014&start=1995
3. Movassaghi, S., Abolhasan, M., Lipman, J., Smith, D., Jamalipour, A.: Wireless body area networks: a survey. IEEE Commun. Surv. Tutorials **16**(3), 1658–1686 (2014)
4. Latré, B., Braem, B., Moerman, I., Blondia, C., Demeester, P.: A survey on wireless body area networks. Wirel. Netw. **17**(1), 1–18 (2011)
5. IEEE: IEEE standard for local and metropolitan area networks - Part 15.4: Low-rate wireless personal area networks (LR-WPANs). IEEE Std (2011)
6. Gao, T., Greenspan, D., Welsh, M., Juang, R.R., Alm, A.: Vital signs monitoring and patient tracking over a wireless network. In: 27th Annual International Conference of the IEEE Engineering in Medicine and Biology Society, EMBS, China, pp. 102–105. IEEE (2006)
7. Chan, C.H., Poon, C.C.Y., Wong, R.C.S., Zhang, Y.T.: A hybrid body sensor network for continuous and long-term measurement of arterial blood pressure. In: 4th IEEE/EMBS International Summer School and Symposium on Medical Devices and Biosensors, ISSS-MDBS, United Kingdom, pp. 121–123. IEEE (2007)
8. IEEE: IEEE standard for local and metropolitan area networks - Part 15.1: Wireless personal area networks (WPANs), IEEE Std (2005)
9. Choi, J.M., Istepanian, R.S.H., Alesanco, A., Wang, H.: Hardware design and compression issues in compact bluetooth enabled wireless telecardiology system. In: 2nd International Conference on Broadband Networks, BroadNets, MA, USA, pp. 1014–1015. IEEE (2005)
10. Rasid, M.F.A., Woodward, B.: Bluetooth telemedicine processor for multichannel biomedical signal transmission via mobile cellular networks. IEEE Trans. Inf. Technol. Biomed. **9**(1), 35–43 (2005)
11. IEEE: IEEE standard for local and metropolitan area networks - part 15.6: Wireless body area networks. IEEE Std. (2012)
12. Manikandan, M.S., Dandapat, S.: Wavelet-based electrocardiogram signal compression methods and their performances: a prospective review. Biomed. Sig. Process. Control **14**, 73–107 (2014)
13. Lu, Z., Kim, D.Y., Pearlman, W.A.: Wavelet compression of ECG signals by the set partitioning in hierarchical trees algorithm. IEEE Trans. Biomed. Eng. **47**(7), 849–856 (2000)
14. Proakis, J.G., Manolakis, D.G.: Digital Signal Processing: Principles, Algorithms, and Applications. Pearson Prentice Hall, Upper Saddle River (2007)
15. Riverbed Technolgies: OPNET (2012). www.opnet.com
16. Jalaleddine, S.M.S., Hutchens, C.G., Strattan, R.D., Coberly, W.A.: ECG data compression techniques: a unified approach. IEEE Trans. Biomed. Eng. **37**(4), 329–343 (1990)

17. Mallat, S.G.: A theory for multiresolution signal decomposition: the wavelet representation. IEEE Trans. Patt. Anal. Mach. Intell. **11**(7), 674–693 (1989)
18. Texas Instruments: CC1101 low-power sub-1 GHz RF transceiver datasheet (2018). www.ti.com/lit/ds/symlink/cc1101.pdf
19. Interaction Design Institute: Arduino Uno (2018). www.arduino.org/products/boards/arduino-uno
20. Analog Devices Inc.: AD8232 datasheet (2018). www.analog.com/media/en/technical-documentation/data-sheets/AD8232.pdf
21. panStamp: Panstamp library (2018). http://www.github.com/panStamp/panstamp/wiki
22. Interaction Design Institute: Arduino mega (2018). www.arduino.cc/en/Main/ArduinoBoardMega
23. Manna, T., Misra, I.S.: Performance analysis of scheduled access mode of the IEEE 802.15.6 MAC protocol under non-ideal channel conditions. IEEE Trans. Mobile Comput. **PP**(99) (2019). https://doi.org/10.1109/TMC.2019.2901852
24. Zigel, Y., Cohen, A., Katz, A.: The Weighted Diagnostic Distortion (WDD) measure for ECG signal compression. IEEE Trans. Biomed. Eng. **47**(11), 1422–1430 (2000)

Leveraging SDN for Early Detection and Mitigation of DDoS Attacks

Neelam Dayal[✉] and Shashank Srivastava

Motilal Nehru National Institute of Technology Allahabad, Allahabad, India
{rcs1408,shashank12}@mnnit.ac.in

Abstract. Distributed Denial of Service (DDoS) attacks being one of the most challenging security issues in the current network requires a lot of attention from the research community. Detection and mitigation of DDoS attacks at early stages could reduce the impact of the attack on legitimate users. Software Defined Networking (SDN) has emerged as a technique to aid the resolution of DDoS attacks effectively. This paper proposes one such detection scheme that utilizes Radial Basis Function networks optimized with Particle Swarm Optimization for early detection of DDoS attacks in SDN networks. A feature set for training and testing of detection module is also proposed that allows the identification of DDoS attacks. The proposed detection scheme is efficient enough to classify the heavy load of network traffic from that of DDoS attacks. Not only detection is important in such scenario, but the mitigation technique also needs to be selected very carefully in order to meet the desired network requirements as well as to secure the legitimate users. For the purpose of identification of suitable mitigation scheme an analytical comparison of possible controller based mitigation techniques is presented. These techniques are further compared based on several parameters governing the effect of mitigation on network users and processing.

Keywords: Software Defined Networking (SDN)
Distributed Denial of Service (DDoS) · Radial Basis Function (RBF)
Particle Swarm Optimization (PSO) · Dynamic blocking
Rate limiting · Controller migration

1 Introduction

Distributed Denial of Service (DDoS) attack aims at hindering the availability of network resources. Controlling the impact of these attacks in the traditional network is certainly a challenging task. In the state of Internet of Things, it has become more challenging to curtail the impact of evolving DDoS attacks. Software Defined Networking (SDN) with the help of its global monitoring and dynamic maintenance feature, facilitates handling these attacks effectively. Security reports and web articles, such as [1], also suggest that SDN has the potential to mitigate DDoS attacks. The SDN having global information of the network

© Springer Nature Switzerland AG 2019
S. Biswas et al. (Eds.): COMSNETS 2018, LNCS 11227, pp. 52–75, 2019.
https://doi.org/10.1007/978-3-030-10659-1_3

can help in easy detection of DDoS attacks in the network; and to mitigate these attacks, desired rules could be generated dynamically to be followed by the entire network with immediate effect. Many researchers have proposed several DDoS attack detection and mitigation schemes leveraging SDN.

The main challenge for any DDoS detection technique is to differentiate the DDoS attack traffic from the genuine traffic. It becomes more difficult when there is a heavy load of genuine traffic in the network. In such scenarios, attack detection with the help of statistics threshold or policy exploitation could be misleading. That motivates the use of machine learning based techniques to classify the network traffic as normal or attack traffic. Machine learning techniques have self-learning capabilities that make the detection scheme more efficient. These techniques being reactive adapts themselves according to the network characteristics. We propose one such system model to detect and mitigate DDoS attacks in the network, which has Radial Basis Function (RBF) network with Particle Swarm Optimization (PSO) optimized training for the classification of traffic patterns. RBF network increases the dimensionality of the features making the detection more robust than other techniques. When any optimization technique for training is incorporated, it can provide more optimized classification. It is the first attempt to introduce such optimized detection module in SDN environment.

Detection is important to identify the DDoS attack but to immediate removal of the attack flows from the network is also important. Instant mitigation of these attacks could reduce the impact of the attack on legitimate users. But mitigation techniques need to be selected very carefully in order to meet the desired network requirements. Different type of networks have distinct requirements, hence the mitigation technique appropriate for one of the network could not be relevant for another type of network. Therefore different techniques need to be evaluated for correlating them with distinct network requirements. An analysis of possible ways of mitigating DDoS attacks from the network is presented in this paper, to identify the best possible mitigation technique in SDN environment. Based on the literature of DDoS attack mitigation in SDN network and in traditional network, we identified four possible categories of mitigation schemes used by the researchers for mitigating DDoS attacks. We implemented three of these mitigation techniques in SDN. These techniques are analyzed based on several parameters of interest in selecting appropriate mitigation technique. The selected parameters are based on the effect of mitigation technique on attack packets, legitimate packets and overall processing in the network. The overall contributions of this paper are as follows:

- proposes a set of features useful for optimal classification of traffic patterns as DDoS attack traffic and normal traffic.
- proposes a DDoS detection module with optimized machine learning that provides better classification than existing research works for DDoS detection in SDN.
- the proposed system model is capable of distinguishing between heavy load of genuine traffic in the network from that of DDoS attacks.

- proposes a mitigation module that drops the attack packets destined to victim using specific IP protocol.
- presents the real-time implementation of the proposed system model, verifying the use of detection model with SDN controller for handling the attacks at initial phase itself, to lower the risk for legitimate users.
- mitigation techniques are implemented in SDN environment for comparison.
- it simplifies the selection of the best possible scheme for mitigation of DDoS attack, according to network requirement.

This paper is organized into several sections. Section 2 proposes the system model for DDoS detection and mitigation including the background of detection scheme. Section 3 presents three different approaches for mitigation of DDoS attacks. In Sect. 4, implementation details, such as the creation of topology, dataset generation and finalizing feature set has been discussed. Section 5 presents the results of testing the model in off-line mode and with real-time traffic. Section 6 discusses the implementation results of all the three mitigation schemes. In Sect. 7, conclusion followed by future work has been provided.

2   DDoS Detection

Machine learning techniques having self learning capability, analyze the traffic based on their patterns. With accurate features and dataset, the classification of normal traffic from that of attack traffic becomes much easier, making the DDoS attack detection more reliable. We have proposed a DDoS detection scheme based on Radial Basis Function Network (RBF network) with optimized training of Particle Swarm Optimization (PSO). With each iterations these particles get optimized and becomes accurate in predicting the behavior of network traffic. Further a comparison for the proposed model with recent neural network based DDoS detection proposals in SDN environment in [2–4], has been done.

2.1   Background

Most of the DDoS attack detection module in SDN are based on statistical analysis or static policy. This can only be helpful in detection of volumetric attacks. For detection of all type of DDoS attacks, including volumetric attacks as well as protocol exploitation attacks with low traffic, analysis of appropriate traffic patterns is required. It can be achieved with the help of machine learning techniques. Only a few machine learning based research works for DDoS detection in SDN are available till date.

One such detection scheme is suggested by Braga *et al.* in [2], it utilizes Self-Organizing Maps (SOM) to classify network flows. Self-Organizing Maps (SOM) are based on neural network that uses neighborhood properties in the network to create topological properties. Their proposed model has several modules such as flow collector module, feature extractor module, and classifier module. Flow collector module collects the network flows periodically, whose features are extracted with feature extractor module. With the help of these features, the classifier module implemented using SOM, classifies the network flow as an attack or non-attack flow. Authors in this paper proposed one of the most popular feature set for DDoS detection in SDN environment. We have proposed our features and compared them with these features.

Another machine learning based DDoS detection scheme in SDN was proposed by Kokila et al. [5] that utilized support vector machine for detection purpose. Authors suggested that use of support vector machine for detection of DDoS with a previously trained dataset will give the least number of false positive results compared to other machine learning techniques such as Naive Bayes, RBF, Bagging, J48 and Random Forest. The authors even mentioned that SVM has similar results compared to RBF due to better training time, SVM was used by them. This proposal was also tested in offline mode only. Also, support vector machines provide linear classification only.

Li et al. in [6] also suggested using support vector machines for detection of DDoS attacks in SDN network. They further optimized the learning of SVM with Genetic Algorithms (GA). The approach was to optimize the DDoS detection module. But the learning of GA is quite slow, making training of the detection module slower.

Mihai-Gabriel et al. in [3] proposed DDoS detection scheme using Feed-Forward Backward-Propagating Neural Network based on two input layers, ten hidden layers and one output layer for analyzing the incoming traffic for anomalies. Traffic in the overall network was monitored with the help of sFlow, and at each layer, the computation of risk at certain node was computed with the help of biological danger theory of risk. But it is just a proposal, it does not provide simulated proof of applicability.

In the latest attempt in [4], Cui et al. suggested using Back-propagation Neural Network for DDoS detection in SDN. The author suggested that using the neural network with back-propagation could facilitate better DDoS detection results in Software Defined network.

The proposed detection model in this paper is based on Radial Basis Function (RBF) Network that is better than other neural networks, in terms of learning and classification. For making the detection module even more efficient, the training of the network has been optimized with Particle Swarm Optimization (PSO). It has not yet been done by any researcher in SDN environment. Optimization of detection module helps in reducing the error rates in classification, hence making the module more accurate. The results of comparison between proposed model and techniques used by other researchers are compared in Sect. 5.1.

The machine learning techniques used to design the proposed DDoS detection module is Radial basis function (RBF) network, which is a feed forward artificial neural network with a single hidden layer. This network was proposed by Broomhead et al. in 1988 [7]. It is a non-linear classifier that makes the problem domain linear by increasing the dimensionality of feature set. The output of the network is linear combination of radial basis functions of the inputs and parameters of neuron. These networks could be beneficial in many domains, such as classification, series prediction, and function approximation. The training of RBF network is further optimized with Particle Swarm Optimization (PSO) that is an iterative computational method proposed by Kennedy *et al.* in 1995 [8]. This algorithm is inspired by the social behavior of birds. The swarm of bird moves dynamically in search space based on their personal experience and the experience of every other bird in the swarm. Similar to the behavior of the swarm of birds, PSO has a swarm of several particles that optimize the swarm based on the computations with each particle's position and velocity. This algorithm is helpful in optimizing the search domain.

2.2 Proposed System Model

For detecting the DDoS attacks, we propose a system model integrated with floodlight controller. The system model has three modules. First module is Statistics Collection & Monitoring module that keeps track of the network traffic and is responsible for initial detection of DDoS attack, second module is DDoS Detection module that verifies whether the traffic being initially detected as attack is attack traffic or not, and the third module is Mitigation module that generates and imposes the rules to remove attack flows from the network. Overall Detection Model is presented in Fig. 1.

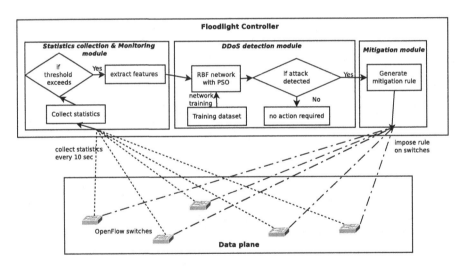

Fig. 1. Detection model

Statistics Collection & Monitoring Module. Statistics Collection & Monitoring module is responsible for continuous monitoring of the network with the help of statistics collected from the network switches. The Statistics collector module of Floodlight [9] is modified to fetch the flow statistics from the switches after every 10 s. These statistics are further parsed to extract the desired features. Based on the initial DDoS detection criteria, a threshold (DDoS_{tr}) is set for the monitoring module. As discussed in our previous work [10], during a DDoS attack, the randomness of IP address of the destination is quite low, as all the attack packets are destined to a single host or small group of hosts. Hence, we selected the entropy of destination IP addresses as our initial DDoS detection criteria. Since, the randomness of destination is low during DDoS attack that makes entropy of destination low. So, the base threshold i.e. entropy of destination IP addresses ($DestIP_{entropy}$) should be greater than or equal to 0.5 (i.e.$DDoS_{tr} = 0.5$) for normal traffic.

The network is further monitored as per the Algorithm 1. As the Statistics Collection module collects the statistics from network switches, in Line 4, the $DestIP_{entropy}$ for a switch is computed and in Line 5, this $DestIP_{entropy}$ is compared with $DDoS_{tr}$. If the $DestIP_{entropy}$ is less than 0.5, then in Line 6 DDoS_Alarm is flagged and

---

Algorithm 1. Statistics Collection & Monitoring

Input: $DDoS_{tr}$
Output: DDoS_Alarm
1: **procedure** STATISTICS COLLECTION & MONITORING
2:     **for** each Switch in Network **do**
3:         Collect the network statistics
4:         Calculate $DestIP_{entropy}$
5:         **if** $DestIP_{entropy} \leq DDoS_{tr}$ **then**
6:             DDoS_Alarm
7:                 **call** Detection Module
8:         **else** continue
9:         **end if**
10:     **end for**
11: **end procedure**

DDoS Detection module is triggered in Line 7. This process is repeated for all the switches in network.

DDoS Detection Module. DDoS Detection module is designed with RBF network having PSO optimized training, where the RBF-PSO network is pre-trained with the training dataset providing a Trained_RBF_PSO_network that is used for attack classification. After the initial DDoS_Alarm from Algorithm 1, the DDoS Detection module is triggered for analyzing the flows and identifying whether the alarm is true or false. As per the Algorithm 2, for the initial DDoS_Alarm, Line 3 extracts the desired features of the flow statistics as Feature-

---

Algorithm 2. Detection Module

Input: Trained_RBF_PSO_network, Flow statistics, DDoS_Alarm
Output: ATTACK, NON-ATTACK
1: **procedure** DETECTION MODULE
2:     **for** DDoS_Alarm **do**
3:         extract FeatureSet
4:         **for** FeatureSet **do**
5:             test   FeatureSet   with Trained_RBF_PSO_network
6:                 set FLAG = ATTACK or NON-ATTACK
7:             **end for**
8:             **if** FLAG = ATTACK **then**
9:                 **call** Mitigation
10:             **else** exit
11:             **end if**
12:     **end for**
13: **end procedure**

Set. The FeatureSet, in Line 5 is tested with Trained_RBF_PSO_network. After the testing is completed, based on the decision by the detection module, a FLAG is set as ATTACK or NON-ATTACK in Line 6. Line 8 checks the value in FLAG, if the FLAG is ATTACK, that means the incoming flow is classified as an attack flow by detection module, then Mitigation module will be called in Line 9, else no action is required and the DDoS_Alarm will be ignored.

DDoS Mitigation Module. To mitigate the attack, a Mitigation module is written in Floodlight controller that generates the rule to drop the specific type of flow destined to specific destination. As soon as the attack is confirmed, statistics is analyzed to identify the protocol used to perform attack and the victim of the attack, which is nothing but the most frequent IP protocol and destination

---
Algorithm 3. Mitigation

Input: Switch, VictimIP, ProtocolType
Output: insert block flow rule on switches
1: **procedure** MITIGATION
2:     **for** Switch **do**
3:         generate a block flow rule with destination IP of victim and specific protocol type
4:         write the flow rule onto switch
5:     **end for**
6: **end procedure**

IP address. As discussed in Algorithm 3, for the switch under attack, a flow rule is generated to drop the flows destined to the victim utilizing the specific type of IP protocol in Line 3. In Line 4, this flow rule is imposed onto the switch for blocking any such future flows. This rule will only block the flows to specific destination IP address with specific IP protocol, all other flows will be normally communicated in the network.

3   DDoS Mitigation Techniques in SDN

This paper focuses on the mitigation techniques discussed with respect to the SDN controller, as we are interested in imposing mitigation rules dynamically on entire network with the help of SDN controller. The four broad categories of DDoS attack mitigation are filtering, rate limiting, access control, and resource migration.

3.1   Background

Filtering at a network device refers to removing of suspicious flows and only allowing the non-suspicious flows through that device. Blocking, aggressive aging, dynamic filtering are few of the examples. Filtering of network traffic and dropping the attack is one of the approach acquired by most of the researchers to mitigate DDoS attacks in SDN. Dillon *et al.* [11], Lim *et al.* [12] and Luo *et al.* [13] in their respective research work proposed to drop the detected potential DDoS attack traffic. But all the suspicious flows are not necessarily attack flows, such a mitigation technique affects the legitimate flows as well. Giotis *et al.* [14], Liu *et al.* [15] and Wang *et al.* [16] proposed to drop the flows from a suspicious source, the suspicious sources in these techniques are identified either based on IP addresses or by their past behavior. But in the case of source spoofing, such IP based source identification is not appropriate. Another source based blocking technique for mitigation was used by Cui *et al.* [4], which identified the attack source dynamically using SDN backtracking and dropped the flows from the backtracked attack source. Wei *et al.* in [17] proposed rate limiting of flows based on the past behavior of the users. The users are prioritized based on their past behavior and are allowed to transmit with their provided bandwidth only.

Access control refers to restricting the communication and resources to the network users. Such a scheme may be useful for a small network but for a large network with an Internet connection this method is not useful as it is not feasible to authenticate each and every device connected to the Internet. Another method for mitigation of DDoS attack adopted in SDN is authentication or access control. DaMask [18] by Wang *et al.* provide one such technique that virtualizes the network into separate slices. Slice for enterprise network communication is always kept separate from outside communication. Any outside communication is firstly verified, then only allowed to enter the enterprise network. Another authentication based mitigation technique OPERETTA was proposed by Fichera *et al.* [19] to secure any web server. It suggested that any device, trying to have communication with a web server have to establish TCP connection with OPERETTA enabled controller and if authenticated as a genuine user, then only is allowed to connect to the web server. SDSNM [20] by Wang *et al.* was another authentication based technique that suggested to create a secure perimeter to provide access control, communication was provided only after authentication.

Rate limiting refers to limiting the rate for communication. Rate limiting techniques include source rate limiting, granular rate limiting, and flow rate limiting. Kalliola *et al.* [21] proposed to limit the rate of suspicious flows after controller migration.

Migration refers to sending the suspicious traffic to a secure state where they can be analyzed further, it includes, flow migration, controller migration and server migration. Migration of server or resources to mitigate DDoS attack was also adopted by researchers in SDN to mitigate DDoS attacks. Different research works by Sahay *et al.* [22], Shtern *et al.* [23] and Xu *et al.* [24] suggested redirecting the suspicious flows to middle-boxes or secure applications after initial attack detection, where further filtering is applied to these flows to identify the malicious and legitimate ones. Kalliola *et al.* [21] proposed to migrate the controller during attack phase and limit the rate of services provided to suspicious flows, in order to lower the chances of dropping any legitimate flow falling into the suspicious category.

For analyzing the mitigation techniques, they are implemented and tested on SDN network. The techniques are implemented on SDN controller and once the attack is detected, SDN controller generates the mitigation rule to implement on switches, hence all the three techniques are controller based mitigation techniques. The implementation details are given in Sect. 4.1. Access control is not considered for comparison as it is not possible to restrict the communication among devices in the era of Internet.

3.2 Dynamic Blocking

For analyzing the filtering technique, dynamic blocking is implemented in SDN environment. In spoofing or bot based DDoS attack, it is not possible to identify the source of the attack at initial stages, therefore for analysis purpose, the filtering is done based on IP address of victim and type of packets being exploited to perform the attack. Tracebacking to identify the attack source and implementing mitigation scheme near attack source is our future scope. Based on the filtering criteria, the suspicious packets will be blocked. This paper refers this technique as dynamic blocking. Diagrammatic representation of the technique is provided in Fig. 2, and the procedure is explained in Algorithm 4. As per the Algorithm 4, after detecting a DDoS attack using any of the conventional methods in Line 2, the Controller will generate a Block_Rule in Line 3 to block all the packets with Victim's IP address as destination IP and IP protocol type similar to attack protocol. In Line 4–5 the block rules are implemented onto the switches under attack. At the switches, each time a new flow arrives, it will be compared to block rule in Line 11. If the flow matches the block rule, it will be dropped immediately in Line 12, else a packet_In will be send to the controller. With this technique, all the attack flows are barred in the network but few of the legitimate packets which are using similar IP protocol and destination IP address are also restricted to enter the network.

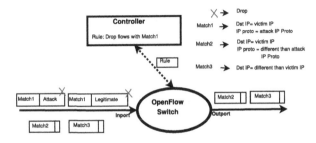

Fig. 2. Blocking specific type of flows

Algorithm 4. Algorithm to Dynamically Blocking Potential Attack Flows

---

Input: Attack_Detection, Victim_IP, Attack_Protocol
Output: Attack Flow Block
1: **procedure** GENERATE BLOCK_RULE AT CONTROLLER
2:     **for** Attack_Detection **do**
3:         Block_Rule = block packets with {DestinationIP==Victim_IP && Protocol==Attack_Protocol}
4:             **for** each switch under attack **do**
5:                 Insert Block_Rule
6:             **end for**
7:     **end for**
8: **end procedure**
9: **procedure** BLOCK SUSPICIOUS FLOWS AT SWITCH
10:     **for** Each new Flow **do**
11:         **if** incoming Flow matches Block_Rule **then**
12:             Drop Flow
13:         **else**
14:             send Packet_In to controller
15:         **end if**
16:     **end for**
17: **end procedure**

3.3   Rate Limiting

For analyzing the efficiency of rate limiting to mitigate DDoS attacks, flow rate limiting based on victim IP address and attack IP protocol. To implement the rate limiting technique, two queues are created at each switch, one with normal transmission rate and another with slower transmission rate. All the suspicious flows are sent to queue with slower transmission rate and others are allowed to carry on the communication with normal speed in the queue with normal transmission rate. Figure 3 represents the process and Algorithm 5 describes the procedure of rate limiting. In Line 3 of algorithm, the controller generates a RateLimit_Rule on attack detection. the RateLimit_Rule is to send all the flows matching Victim_IP address in destination IP field and attack protocol in IP protocol field to the queue with slower transmission rate. This rule is inserted into each switch under attack in Line 4–5. At switches under attack, each incoming flow is matched to rate limiting rule in Line 10–11, if the flow

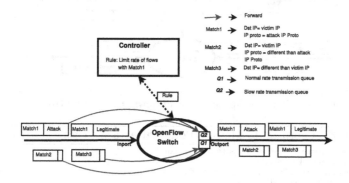

Fig. 3. Limiting the rate of specific type of flows

Algorithm 5. Algorithm to Limit the Rate of Potential Attack Flows

---

Input: Attack_Detection, Victim_IP, Attack_Protocol, Queue2: Slow Rate Queue, Queue1: Normal Rate Queue
Output: Attack Flow Rate Limit
1: **procedure** GENERATE RATELIMIT_RULE AT CONTROLLER
2:     **for** Attack_Detection **do**
3:         RateLimit_Rule = send Flows with {DestinationIP==Victim_IP && Protocol==Attack_Protocol} to Queue2 of outport to Vicitm
4:             **for** each switch under attack **do**
5:                 Insert RateLimit_Rule
6:             **end for**
7:     **end for**
8: **end procedure**
9: **procedure** LIMIT RATE FOR SUSPICIOUS FLOWS AT SWITCH
10:     **for** Each new Flow **do**
11:         **if** incoming Flow matches RateLimit_Rule **then**
12:             send Flow to Queue2
13:         **else**
14:             send Packet_In to controller
15:         **end if**
16:     **end for**
17: **end procedure**

---

matches the rule it is inserted to slow rate queue in Line 12, else corresponding packet_In is sent to the controller. Rate limiting of suspicious traffic is useful for providing services to legitimate traffic that is under suspicion but at the same time, it provides slow services to the malicious traffic as well.

3.4 Controller Migration

The resource migration technique selected in this paper is Controller migration. A proxy controller is placed in the network to handle the suspicious packets in order to reduce the load and potential damage to the actual controller. Once

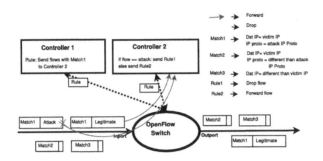

Fig. 4. Migrating specific type of flows to proxy controller

Algorithm 6. Algorithm to Migrate Potential Attack Flows

Input: Attack_Detection, Victim_IP, Attack_Protocol
Output: Attack Flow Removed
1: **procedure** GENERATE DROP FLOW RULE AT CONTROLLER
2:     **for** Attack_Detection **do**
3:         Generate Migrate_Rule = migrate packets with {DestinationIP==Victim_IP && Protocol==Attack_Protocol} to proxy controller
4:             **for** each switch under attack **do**
5:                 Insert Migrate_Rule
6:             **end for**
7:     **end for**
8: **end procedure**
9: **procedure** MIGRATE SUSPICIOUS FLOWS AT SWITCH
10:     **for** Each new Flow **do**
11:         **if** incoming Flow matches Migrate_Rule **then**
12:             send flow to Proxy Controller
13:         **else**
14:             send Packet_In to controller
15:         **end if**
16:     **end for**
17: **end procedure**
18: **procedure** FLOW ANALYSIS AT PROXY CONTROLLER
19:     **for** Each new Flow **do**
20:         Analyze the flow for potential attack threat
21:         **if** incoming Flow matches attack criteria **then**
22:             Drop Flow
23:         **else**
24:             send a Packet_Out to forward legitimate flow
25:         **end if**
26:     **end for**
27: **end procedure**

---

attack traffic is detected all the suspicious traffic is redirected to the proxy controller. The actual controller handles only the normal network traffic. The proxy controller analyzes each and every suspicious flow to determine whether the flow is attack flow or not. If the flow is attack flow, it is immediately discarded and if the flow is legitimate, it is forwarded to the destination. The controller migration based mitigation technique is diagrammatically represented in Fig. 4 and the procedure for the same is given in Algorithm 6. As per the Algorithm 6, as soon as the attack is detected, in Line 3, Migrate_Rule is generated at the controller to migrate all flows to the proxy controller, whose Destination_IP is same as of Victim IP address and protocol in use is also similar to attack protocol. This Migration_Rule is inserted onto switches under attack in Line 4–5. When a switch receives a new flow matching the Migrate_Rule in line 10–11, it forwards the flow to proxy controller in line 12, else the corresponding packet_In message is sent to the controller in Line 14. At proxy controller, each incoming flow is analyzed for potential attack threat in Line 20. If the flow is identified as an attack, it is dropped in Line 22 else the corresponding packet_Out message is sent to the switch in Line 24. Hence, removing the attack flows from the network without dropping legitimate flows by analysis of suspicious flows.

4   Implementation Details

4.1   Topology and Dataset Generation

The topology used to implement the system model is Claranet topology taken from Zoo topologies [25]. The topology is implemented on Mininet [26] network emulation tool that provides realistic virtual network on a single system. Mininet executable python file for Claranet topology is generated with help of a mininet parser [27]. The system on which mininet is running has 16 GB RAM and core i7 processor. The remote controller Floodlight [9] is running on a different system having 8 GB RAM and core i5 processor.

Due to unavailability of standard dataset for DDoS in SDN, lab generated DDoS attack dataset in SDN environment is used in this paper. The dataset generated is based on the study by Borgnat et al. [28] that analyzes the distribution of Internet traffic between USA and Japan over the period of seven years. The analysis suggests that Internet traffic consists of 85% TCP, 15% UDP & 5% ICMP traffic. Such a lab generated dataset is also used by researchers in [2,4]. Distributed Internet Traffic Generator (D-ITG) [29] tool that facilitates the replication of Internet traffic is used for normal traffic generation in mininet network. Attack tools, such as scapy [30], hyenae [31], hping3 [32] are utilized to generate DDoS attack traffic of ICMP flood, UDP flood, Smurf, TCP_SYN flood and HTTP flood. To create the training and testing dataset, network statistics is collected at Floodlight controller. Floodlight's statistics collector module is modified to collect the flow statistics from the switches at an interval of 10 s. Featureset extracted for every sample is added to the dataset.

4.2 Features

For implementing machine learning algorithms, one needs to determine the features to be used for training the algorithm. These features are basically the traffic patterns that help the algorithm for learning the network behavior. Single feature alone is not sufficient to analyze the network characteristics, but an appropriate set of features together could be very helpful in classifying the attack patterns efficiently. One of the popular research work by Braga *et al.* in [2] considers six features for training their neural network. These features are Average of Packets per flow (APf), Average of Bytes per flow (ABf), Average of Duration per flow (ADf), Percentage of Pair-flows (PPf), Growth of Different Ports (GDP), Growth of Single-flows (GSf).

Further, in our previous work [10], we analyzed several patterns of DDoS attacks that are noteworthy for identification of attacks. These patterns, as well as, feature set proposed by Braga *et al.* in [2], helped to deduce the final set of features for training the proposed system model, which are as follows:

- **Average packets per flow (APf):** in a volumetric DDoS approach, the packets in each flow will be increased drastically to consume the network bandwidth. On the other hand, in protocol exploitation based DDoS approach, huge amount of flows will be sent with less number of packets. In both the cases, average number of packets per flow is either too small or too large making it a key feature to identify the attack pattern.
- **Average bytes per flow (ABf):** similar to the APf average bytes per flow will be either too high or too low during an attack phase, making it an important feature in the identification of DDoS attack.
- **Number of flows per second (NFs):** in attacks, such as TCP_SYN flood attack, attacker aims at holding all the connections at victim for long duration using large number of flows. These are actually idle flows, resulting in less communication of bytes or packets, but the number of flows keeps on increasing. So, it is needed to consider NFs as one of the features for DDoS identification.
- **Average duration per flow (ADf):** during DDoS attack, time duration of attack flow is either very small or very long, making it another important feature of DDoS attack detection.
- **Entropy of destination IP addresses per second (EDIPs):** as discussed in our previous work [10], during a DDoS attack all the attack packets are destined either to a single host or a small pool of host, making the randomness of destination IP address quite small. Hence, entropy of destination IP address during an attack is low.
- **Entropy of source IP address per second (ESIPs):** as DDoS attack is distributed in nature, i.e. the attack sources are either distributed in the network via a bot or attacker is using spoofed IP addresses to attack the victim. Hence, the randomness of source IP addresses in the attack flows will be quite high, making the entropy of source IP address large.
- **Entropy of IP protocol per second (EPs):** the protocol utilized to perform a DDoS attack would be same in most of the cases, more the number

of attack flows, less will be the randomness of the IP protocol being used to perform the attack. Hence, the entropy of the IP protocol per second will be lower during attack phase than during regular traffic.

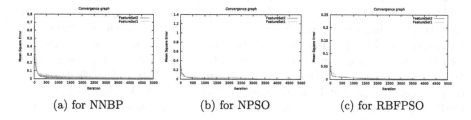

(a) for NNBP	(b) for NPSO	(c) for RBFPSO

Fig. 5. Training convergence for different algorithms

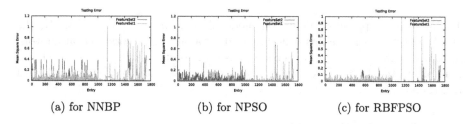

(a) for NNBP	(b) for NPSO	(c) for RBFPSO

Fig. 6. Testing errors per iteration for different algorithms

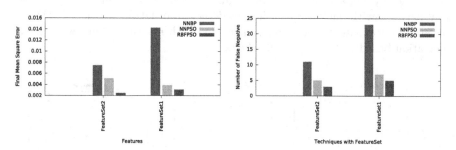

(a) Final Network Score after training   (b) False Negative Results during Testing

Fig. 7. Comparison of FeatureSet1 and FeatureSet2

The proposed feature set in this paper (referred by FeatureSet2) is compared with the feature set proposed by Braga *et al.* [2] (referred as FeatureSet1). For comparing the feature sets different neural network techniques have been used. The results are shown in Figs. 5, 6, and 7. For Neural Networks with back-propagation (Fig. 5a), FeatureSet2 has better convergence rate during training than FeatureSet1. As well as, during testing phase also (Fig. 6a), FeatureSet2 seems less error prone for each entry compared to that of FeatureSet1. When the PSO optimization is added to Neural Network and RBF network, the training convergence becomes better and is almost similar for both feature sets, as seen in Fig. 5b and c. But during testing phase of networks with PSO optimization (Fig. 6b and c), the error for each entry in testing dataset for FeatureSet2 is slightly less than that of error in FeatureSet1. Figure 7a shows that final score after the training of network for FeatureSet2 is better for all the three self-learning networks. Also, Fig. 7b shows that number of False Negative detection for FeatureSet2 is less than that of FeatureSet1. From these results, it seems that for overall detection of DDoS attacks FeatureSet2 is better than FeatureSet1. Hence, FeatureSet2 that includes seven features (APf, ABf, NFs, ADf, EDIPs, ESIPs, EPs) is used to train the RBF network in the detection module of the proposal.

5   Analysis of Detection Module

The analysis of proposed detection model is done in two phases. Firstly, the DDoS detection scheme has been finalized by analyzing several neural network methods in off-line testing. In second phase, the best possible detection scheme is implemented to SDN controller and proposed system model is tested with real-time traffic.

5.1   Off-Line Testing of Model

Two of the most recent works proposing the machine learning based DDoS detection scheme, by Mihai-Gabriel et al. [3] and Cui et al. [4], suggests the use of neural network with back-propagation for detection of DDoS attacks in SDN. It motivated us to compare our proposed scheme with neural network with back-propagation based DDoS detection scheme.

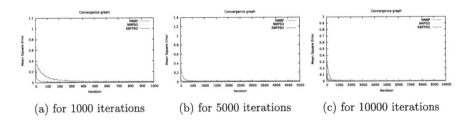

(a) for 1000 iterations   (b) for 5000 iterations   (c) for 10000 iterations

Fig. 8. Training convergence for algorithms

Hence, the three neural networks compared in this section and in Figs. 8, 9, and 10 are, Neural Network with back-propagation denoted as NNBP, Neural Network with PSO optimization denoted as NNPSO, and RBF with PSO optimization denoted as RBFPSO. The parameters selected for comparison of

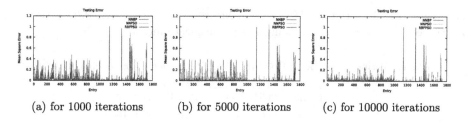

(a) for 1000 iterations   (b) for 5000 iterations   (c) for 10000 iterations

Fig. 9. Testing results per dataset entries

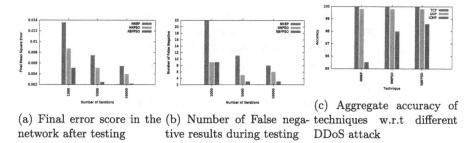

(a) Final error score in the network after testing   (b) Number of False negative results during testing   (c) Aggregate accuracy of techniques w.r.t different DDoS attack

Fig. 10. Comparison results

these techniques are the rate of convergence during training, testing errors for each entry during testing, false positive and false negative results while testing, accuracy of techniques and accuracy of detecting particular type of DDoS attack (i.e. TCP_SYN flood, UDP flood and ICMP flood). The accuracy of a technique is calculated as per the Eq. 1.

$$\text{Accuracy} = \frac{TP+TN}{TP+TN+FP+FN} * 100\% \tag{1}$$

Where, TP is True Positive values, TN is True Negative values, FP is False Positive values, and FN is False Negative values.

For testing these techniques a labeled dataset with 1730 entries of traffic is taken, out of which 1003 entries are patterns for normal traffic and 727 entries are DDoS attack patterns. The comparison of these techniques is done three times with different iterations (1000, 5000 and 10000). Figure 8a, b and c represents the rate of convergence of all the three techniques with three different iterations 1000, 5000 and 10000 respectively. In all the cases, RBF network with PSO has better convergence rate than that of Neural Networks and Neural Network with PSO optimization. In Fig. 9a, b and c, testing errors for each technique with respect to each entry is plotted, where networks have been trained in 1000, 5000 & 10000 iterations respectively. RBF network with PSO optimization is plotted on topmost, it is clear that the testing error for RBFPSO is least as compared to other techniques. In Fig. 10a, as we can observe that more the number of iterations less is the error in any type of network. Still, the final score that is nothing but the final mean square error in network, is least for RBFPSO network.

Also, as in Fig. 10b, the number of False Negative results for RBFPSO network is least compared to others, making it most accurate method.

Table 1. Testing results for DDoS detection (iterations: 1,000, 5000 & 10000)

It.	Technique	TCP Acc.	UDP Acc.	ICMP Acc.	Overall Accuracy
1000	NNBP	100%	99.80%	92.55%	98.73%
	NNPSO	100%	99.80%	97.16%	99.47%
	RBFPSO	100%	99.80%	97.16%	99.47%
5000	NNBP	100%	99.80%	96.45%	99.36%
	NNPSO	100%	99.80%	98.58%	99.71%
	RBFPSO	100%	99.80%	99.29%	99.83%
10000	NNBP	100%	99.80%	97.52%	99.54%
	NNPSO	100%	99.80%	98.22%	99.65%
	RBFPSO	100%	99.80%	99.29%	99.83%

The comparison results for accuracy of all the three techniques w.r.t. different iterations are tabulated in Table 1. For 1000 iterations, as seen in Table 1, all the methods are able to detect 100% of TCP attacks and 99.80% of UDP attacks. While ICMP attacks are detected with a success rate of 92.55%, 97.16% and 97.16% respectively for NNBP, NNPSO, and RBFPSO. The overall accuracy of RBFPSO and NNPSO is similar for 1000 iterations that is 99.47%.

For 5000 iterations, for all the techniques, TCP attacks are detected with 100% accuracy and UDP attacks with 99.80% accuracy. For ICMP attacks, the accuracy of NNBP is 96.45%, accuracy of NNPSO 98.58%, while the accuracy of RBFPSO is 99.29%. Here, the overall accuracy of the RBFPSO is 99.83%, which is better than NNBP and NNPSO having 99.36% and 99.71% respectively.

For 10000 iterations, all the techniques are detecting TCP attacks accurately with 100% efficiency, but UDP attacks are detected with 99.80% accuracy. For ICMP attacks, the detection accuracy is 97.52%, 98.22% and 99.29% respectively for NNBP, NNPSO and RBFPSO. Here also, RBFPSO is more efficient compared to others, for detecting DDoS attacks with an accuracy of 99.83%. The efficiency of all the techniques for detecting different type of DDoS attacks is compared in Fig. 10c.

These comparison results shows that RBF network with PSO optimized training takes less time for training, it is less error prone while testing and is more accurate. Hence, The detection module of the proposed model is designed with the same.

5.2   Real-Time Implementation of System Model

For the real-time emulation of the proposed system model, the topology is created as discussed in Sect. 4.1. The results are analyzed using sFlow-rt real-time analytics tool [33]. The DDoS detection model is implemented on floodlight controller having RBF network with PSO optimized training. With the help of statistics collector module, baseline threshold of incoming traffic is monitored. As soon as the baseline threshold is crossed, desired features are extracted and detection module is triggered. The pre-trained RBF-PSO network tests the traffic patterns and decides whether the traffic is attack traffic or non-attack traffic. If the tested traffic is detected as attack traffic, the mitigation module is triggered. Mitigation module written in floodlight controller takes the DPID of switch on which attack is detected and sends a rule to block all such flows for 100 s destined to victims destination IP address having the IP protocol same as that of attack packets. After 100 s the flow rule is removed from the flow table. In case, the attack is still ongoing, the flow will be again marked as attack flow, and the rule to drop such flows will be inserted to flow table once again.

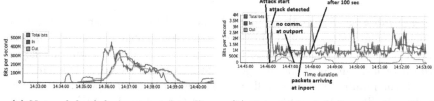

(a) Network load during normal traffic   (b) Network load during attack traffic

Fig. 11. Network statistics from sFlow-rt

One of the biggest challenge of DDoS attack detection is to distinguish heavy load of benign traffic from that of DDoS attack traffic. As seen in the network statistics from sFlow-rt (Fig. 11), in the network during normal communication, the traffic load (Fig. 11a) has even reached to 500 Mbps, while in case of attack statistics (Fig. 11b), the attack traffic load is even not able to exceed 3.5 Mbps and is detected on time. Hence, the proposed system model is capable of classifying the normal traffic from that of attack traffic successfully.

For the legitimate traffic load, Fig. 11a, the incoming and outgoing traffic is almost equivalent, that implies, the communication is taking place normally. But in case of attack traffic, Fig. 11b, as the attack starts, within 10 s the controller gets the information through monitoring module and generates the flow rule to drop all such attack packets. The rule is imposed on the switches and attack packets are being dropped. Although, the attack packets are still incoming at the in-port of the switch, but they are no more being forwarded; this could be verified by out-port statistic which has dropped down. After 100 s, as the packet drop rule has been timed-out, hence the flow has been allowed for few seconds only and again identified and dropped immediately. The peaks in the diagram represent the timeout of the flow rule but as the attack is instantaneously detected hence the peak is immediately dropped.

The proposed system model is capable of detecting the DDoS attacks successfully and distinguishes the attack traffic from that of the heavy load of legitimate traffic as well. With SDN's capability to instantly impose the rules to switches, the DDoS attacks are instantly stopped before they could harm the network. The flows with attack protocol and victim destination IP address are only dropped. Hence, other hosts and even the victim (with different IP protocol) is capable of carrying out normal communication in the network. Only few of the legitimate flows are affected, which are actually using the same protocol as of attack protocol and have destination IP address as victims IP address.

6   Analysis of Mitigation Techniques

The mitigation techniques discussed in Sect. 3 are analyzed with the help of statistics obtained by sFlow-RT, while these techniques are implemented to mitigate UDP based DDoS attack from the network using the proposed DDoS detection scheme.

Dynamic Blocking. Figure 12 presents the network statistics while attack flows are being dynamically blocked after detection. As we can see in Fig. 12a, with start of attack at T1, the number of datapath flows have grown enormously in the network, but since the attack is immediately detected and dynamically blocked, the number of datapath flows have significantly dropped down withing few seconds. The dynamic blocking drops all the potential attack flows in the network, hence the number of datapath flows are kept on normal level afterwards. The mitigation is simply removing the attack flows in the network, hence not affecting the normal flows. It can be inferred from Fig. 12b, where the TCP, UDP and ICMP traffic is being transmitted at regular rate without much deviation.

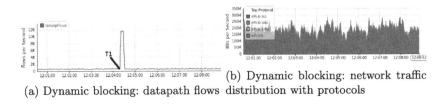

(a) Dynamic blocking: datapath flows

(b) Dynamic blocking: network traffic distribution with protocols

Fig. 12. Dynamic blocking statistics

Rate Limiting. The implementation results of rate limiting are presented in Fig. 13. As the attack starts at time T1 in Fig. 13a, it is detected and rate limiting is applied for the suspicious flows. Since the attack flows are also allowed in the network, the datapath flows are reaching to a high peak but gradually decreasing when the queue with slow rate is being overflown and no more flows are allowed in the network. Once the queue has space, it again allows the attack flows in the network. Hence the datapath flows are continuously varying in the network. It shows that rate limiting incurs additional traffic overhead in the network. Figure 13b presents the network traffic variation based on protocols being used.

Although, UDP flows are being used to perform DDoS attacks in the network, but since they are being forwarded through slow rate queue, hence a normal level of communicated UDP flow is throughout maintained in the network. But there are certain sharp valleys in the network statistics, which indicates that certain times, network communication is dropped for a while due to network overload.

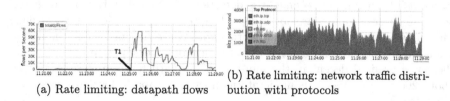

(a) Rate limiting: datapath flows   (b) Rate limiting: network traffic distribution with protocols

Fig. 13. Rate limiting statistics

Controller Migration. Figure 14 presents the network statistics from sFlow-RT, when controller migration is applied. Figure 14a presents the datapath flows in the network while controller migration is used to mitigate DDoS attacks. Controller migration is a method to reduce the load of traffic on actual controller, by redirecting the suspicious traffic to a proxy controller that analyzes each suspicious flow and decides whether to drop the flow or to forward the flow. Hence we can observe in Fig. 14 that after the attack is started, controller is migrated but it took some time to mitigate the attack flows from the network as additional policies and verification of all suspicious flows is required. But gradually all the attack flows are removed; and from Fig. 14b, it can be observed that during mitigation phase, the normal flow is not much affected, as there are no sharp valleys in network statistics indicating drop of communication.

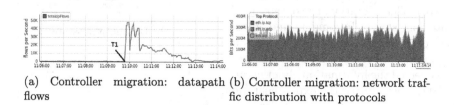

(a) Controller migration: datapath flows   (b) Controller migration: network traffic distribution with protocols

Fig. 14. Controller migration statistics

6.1 Result Analysis

Comparison results for the mitigation techniques, i.e., dynamic blocking, rate limiting, and controller migration w.r.t. attacks without any mitigation technique, are presented in Fig. 15. Figure 15a shows the datapath flows in the network under different scenarios. When attack is started at time T1 (247th s), for network with no mitigation scheme, the datapath flows are hiked and shows an abrupt peaks and valleys, even some times the communication in the network is also dropped. As rate limiting is also allowing the attack flows to be forwarded in the network. Hence datapath flows for this techniques also show almost similar behavior as of without mitigation technique, but the intensity of attack flows is less, and abrupt drop of communication in the network is also not observed for rate limiting. In case of dynamic blocking mitigation, as soon as the attack is starts at T1, within few seconds it is detected and immediately blocked. Afterwards no peaks or valleys are observed and legitimate communication is normally carried out in the network. For mitigation with controller migration, the datapath flows are moderately removed from the network over a period of time, hence there is a gradual decent in the number of datapath flows in the network for about 200 s, and afterwards moderate number of datapath flows are present in the network.

The Fig. 15a shows that rate limiting incurs the highest amount of additional traffic load on the network, which is constantly varying, while dynamic blocking induces least amount of additional traffic load and removes the attack flows immediately. Controller migration although removes the attack flows gradually over a period, but puts least impact on the legitimate traffic, as compared to other two mitigation techniques.

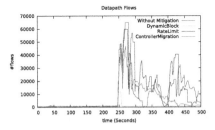

(a) Datapath flows

Figure 15b represents the same results where the datapath missrate, i.e., the percentage of flows not matching any of the entry in flows table is high for rate limiting and least for dynamic blocking, while for controller migration, the datapath missrate has slowly become normal over a period of time. Since the UDP flows are exploited to perform DDoS attack, hence we collected the information about number of UDP flows during the experimentation, Fig. 15c presents the results under different scenarios. As we can observe that when no mitigation technique is used, the UDP flows keeps growing. While for dynamic blocking the UDP flows are continuous and at normal level. For rate limiting and controller migration, the number of UDP flows are changing after the start of attack, but has never reached to a high level than it was during a non-attack phase before 247th second.

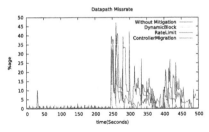

(b) Datapath missrate

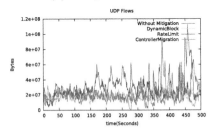

(c) UDP Flows in network

Fig. 15. Implementation results for mitigation techniques

From the results in Fig. 15, it is clear that dynamic blocking is beneficial when immediate removal of attack is needed, but it may also block certain legitimate flows that falls under suspicious category. Controller migration although takes some time to remove all the malicious flows from the network, but less number of legitimate flows are suffered. While rate limiting forwards malicious flows as well, incurring additional traffic load at a slow rate, as the attack traffic is slow enough, the impact of attack on normal flow is very low.

Each of the mitigation technique has its advantages and disadvantages over the other. The probability of drop a legitimate flow during dynamic blocking technique is highest and least for rate limiting; but rate limiting induces high load on the network and also high waiting times for the services. Rate limiting and controller migration reduces the probability of loss of legitimate packets, but rate limiting also serves the attack packets, although at slow rates. In overall results, it can be observed that Controller migration is the best mitigation technique, which induces less additional load on the network, effects least number of legitimate traffic and removes all the attack packets from the network. But it has its limitations too, as it requires additional resources to setup and maintain proxy server and its processing.

7   Conclusion and Future Work

This paper proposed a system model for DDoS detection with RBF and PSO optimization. This was the first attempt to propose such an optimized scheme for DDoS detection in SDN environment. For the training of RBF network, DDoS detection feature set has been proposed and compared with one of the most popular feature set in SDN. Further, the proposed scheme has been compared with several existing DDoS mitigation schemes in SDN, deducing the conclusion that RBF network with PSO optimization is best of its type to effectively detect DDoS attacks. The final system model is implemented on mininet and floodlight controller for analyzing real-time efficiency of the model. The detection module is capable of identifying and distinguishing DDoS attacks from the normal traffic and removes the attack flows from the network in initial stage itself.

The paper further analyzed various possible DDoS mitigation techniques. The analysis of all the mitigation techniques shows that each technique has its pros and cons. Based on the network requirement specific type of mitigation technique must be implemented. In the network that does not have to guarantee delivery of each and every packet, dynamic filtering techniques such as blocking could be useful, where certain amount of legitimate packets are lost but no additional network load or additional resources are required to implement the mitigation. But dynamic blocking is not appropriate for the networks with high reliability requirements, in such networks rate limiting or migration based mitigation techniques could be useful. In scarcity of additional resources for additional processing rate limiting based mitigation techniques could be utilized. But if the network requires high reliability of packet delivery and network administrator could afford additional resources and processing, then migration based techniques such as controller migration is the best possible technique to mitigate DDoS attacks from the network. Combination of these techniques could also be designed for prominent attack mitigation. The mitigation will be more effective if it is implemented to the switch nearest to attack source. Hence, our future plan is to design an effective traceback technique that is capable of tracing exact source of attack.

Acknowledgments. The authors would like to acknowledge financial support of Ministry of Human Resource Development, ISEA Phase II project and TEQIP Phase II for the related doctoral research work.

References

1. InfoWorld: 2017: The year of widespread SDN adoption and DDoS attack mitigation (2017). http://www.infoworld.com/article/3156344/internet/2017-widespread-sdn-adoption-and-ddos-attack-mitigation.html
2. Braga, R., Mota, E., Passito, A.: Lightweight DDoS flooding attack detection using NOX/OpenFlow. In: IEEE 35th Conference on Local Computer Networks (LCN), pp. 408–415. IEEE (2010)
3. Mihai-Gabriel, I., Victor-Valeriu, P.: Achieving DDoS resiliency in a software defined network by intelligent risk assessment based on neural networks and danger theory. In: IEEE 15th International Symposium on Computational Intelligence and Informatics (CINTI), pp. 319–324. IEEE, November 2014
4. Cui, Y., et al.: SD-Anti-DDoS: fast and efficient DDoS defense in software-defined networks. J. Netw. Comput. Appl. **68**, 65–79 (2016)
5. Kokila, R.T., Selvi, S.T., Govindarajan, K.: DDoS detection and analysis in SDN-based environment using support vector machine classifier. In: Sixth International Conference on Advanced Computing (ICoAC), pp. 205–210. IEEE, December 2014
6. Li, X., Yuan, D., Hu, H., Ran, J., Li, S.: DDoS detection in SDN switches using support vector machine classifier. In: Joint International Mechanical, Electronic and Information Technology Conference (JIMET-15). Atlantis Press (2015)
7. Broomhead, D.S., Lowe, D.: Radial basis functions, multi-variable functional interpolation and adaptive networks. Technical report (1988)
8. Kennedy, J., Eberhart, R.: Particle swarm optimization. In: IEEE International Conference on Neural Networks, pp. 1942–1948. IEEE (1995)
9. Floodlight documentation (2016). https://floodlight.atlassian.net/wiki/display/floodlightcontroller/For+Developers
10. Dayal, N., Srivastava, S.: Analyzing behavior of DDoS attacks to identify DDoS detection features in SDN. In: 9th International Conference on Communication Systems and Networks (COMSNETS-2017), pp. 274–281. IEEE (2017)
11. Dillon, C., Berkelaar, M.: Openflow DDoS mitigation, February 2014
12. Lim, S., Ha, J., Kim, H., Kim, Y., Yang, S.: A SDN-oriented DDoS blocking scheme for botnet-based attacks. In: Sixth International Conference on Ubiquitous and Future Networks (ICUFN), pp. 63–68 (2014)
13. Luo, S., Wu, J., Li, J., Pei, B.: A defense mechanism for distributed denial of service attack in software-defined networks. In: Ninth International Conference on Frontier of Computer Science and Technology (FCST), pp. 325–329. IEEE (2015)

14. Giotis, K., Argyropoulos, C., Androulidakis, G., Kalogeras, D., Maglaris, V.: Combining OpenFlow and sFlow for an effective and scalable anomaly detection and mitigation mechanism on SDN environments. Comput. Netw. **62**, 122–136 (2014)
15. Liu, J., Lai, Y., Zhang, S.: Fl-guard: a detection and defense system for DDoS attack in SDN. In: Proceedings of the 2017 International Conference on Cryptography, Security and Privacy, pp. 107–111. ACM (2017)
16. Wang, R., Jia, Z., Ju, L.: An entropy-based distributed DDoS detection mechanism in software-defined networking. In: Trustcom/BigDataSE/ISPA, vol. 1, pp. 310–317. IEEE (2015)
17. Wei, L., Fung, C.: FlowRanger: a request prioritizing algorithm for controller DoS attacks in software defined networks. In: IEEE International Conference on Communications (ICC), pp. 5254–5259 (2015)
18. Wang, B., Zheng, Y., Lou, W., Hou, Y.T.: DDoS attack protection in the era of cloud computing and software-defined networking. Comput. Netw. **81**, 308–319 (2015)
19. Fichera, S., Galluccio, L., Grancagnolo, S.C., Morabito, G., Palazzo, S.: OPERETTA: an OPEnflow-based REmedy to mitigate TCP synflood attacks against web servers. Comput. Netw. **92**, 89–100 (2015)
20. Wang, X., Chen, M., Xing, C.: SDSNM: a software-defined security networking mechanism to defend against DDoS attacks. In: Ninth International Conference on Frontier of Computer Science and Technology (FCST), pp. 115–121. IEEE (2015)
21. Kalliola, A., Lee, K., Lee, H., Aura, T.: Flooding DDoS mitigation and traffic management with software defined networking. In: IEEE 4th International Conference on Cloud Networking (CloudNet), pp. 248–254. IEEE (2015)
22. Sahay, R., Blanc, G., Zhang, Z., Debar, H.: Towards autonomic DDoS mitigation using software defined networking. In: NDSS Workshop on Security of Emerging Networking Technologies (2015)
23. Shtern, M., Sandel, R., Litoiu, M., Bachalo, C., Theodorou, V.: Towards mitigation of low and slow application DDoS attacks. In: IEEE International Conference on Cloud Engineering (IC2E), pp. 604–609. IEEE (2014)
24. Xu, T., Gao, D., Dong, P., Zhang, H., Foh, C.H., Chao, H.C.: Defending against new-flow attack in SDN-based Internet of Things. IEEE Access **5**, 3431–3443 (2017)
25. The internet topology zoo (2012). http://www.topology-zoo.org/dataset.html
26. Mininet: An instant virtual network on your laptop (or other pc) (2016). http://mininet.org/
27. Grobmann, M., Schuberth, S.J.: Auto-mininet: assessing the internet topology zoo in a software-defined network emulator. Technical report, Otto-Friedrich University (2013)
28. Borgnat, P., et al.: Seven years and one day: sketching the evolution of internet traffic. In: INFOCOM 2009. IEEE (2009)
29. Botta, A., Dainotti, A., Pescape, A.: A tool for the generation of realistic network workload for emerging networking scenarios. Comput. Netw. **56**(15), 3531–3547 (2012)
30. Scapy v2.1.1-dev documentation (2010). http://www.secdev.org/projects/scapy/doc/usage.html
31. Hyenae (2010). https://sourceforge.net/projects/hyenae
32. hping3(8)-Linux man page (2010). https://linux.die.net/man/8/hping3
33. sFlow-RT (2015). http://sflow-rt.com/index.php

Use of Facial Landmarks for Adaptive Compression of Videos on Mobile Devices

Garima Chhikara[1], Ruchika Banerjee[1], Vinayak Naik[2(✉)],
A. V. Subramanyam[1], and Kuntal Dey[3]

[1] IIIT Delhi, New Delhi, India
{garima15014,ruchika1453,subramanyam}@iiitd.ac.in
[2] BITS Pilani, Sancoale, Goa, India
vinayak@goa.bits-pilani.ac.in
[3] IBM Research, New Delhi, India
kuntadey@in.ibm.com

Abstract. Challenges, such as requirements of resources, limited availability of storage space on devices, and mobile bandwidth spectrum, inhibit unconstrained and ubiquitous video consumption. We propose a first-of-its-kind methodology to compress videos that stream human faces. We detect facial landmarks on-the-fly and compress the video by storing a sequence of distinct frames extracted from the video, such that the facial landmarks of a pair of successively stored frames are significantly different. We use a dynamic thresholding technique to detect the significance of difference and store meta-information for reconstructing the missing frames. To reduce glitches in the decompressed video, we use morphing technique that smoothens the transition between successive frames. We measure the objective goodness of our technique by evaluating the time taken to compress, the entropy per frame, peak signal-to-noise ratio (PSNR), structural similarity index (SSIM), and compression ratio. For subjective analysis, we perform a user study observing user satisfaction at different compression ratios. We provide an extension of our technique to handle videos with multiple faces. Our approach is complementary to the existing compression techniques, e.g. JPEG. By using the complementary approach, we further improve the compression ratio without compromising on the quality.

Keywords: Multimedia · Compression · Mobile

1 Introduction

Smart mobile phones have been widely adopted. Mobile applications have firmly established their presence on smart phones [12,13]. Many applications today use end-to-end streaming video transmission [20,28] such as Skype, Youtube and Facebook. These often generate live user video streams and video playback applications having large video repositories, including human faces, and transmit the faces over the network on a regular basis [24].

Although new-generation mobile networks with enhanced data transmission capacity have emerged, such as 3G and 4G, the transmission bandwidth and commercially imposed usage limits (such as monthly usage quota) remain concerns.

© Springer Nature Switzerland AG 2019
S. Biswas et al. (Eds.): COMSNETS 2018, LNCS 11227, pp. 76–101, 2019.
https://doi.org/10.1007/978-3-030-10659-1_4

Video data requires much more network data transmission volume, compared to text and image. It is important to compress videos, for better storage and network resource utilization.

We adopt a frame-by-frame compression approach to compress the human face videos, wherein we examine each frame from the video, and adaptively choose to retain or discard the frame. Towards this, we first find the facial landmarks, such as eye corners, eye center, lip corners, and cheek muscles. We note that verbal communication leads to a variation of facial expressions [18], and thus, in positions of facial landmarks. In a given video, after retaining a frame f_i, we choose to retain the first among the following frames f_j, where the difference between f_j and f_i is significant, measured using a dynamic thresholding technique, and otherwise discard the frame. To enable decompression (reconstruction), we maintain a count of discarded frames following each retained frame. The value of the dynamic threshold adapts to different variation rates of the facial videos, using changes in facial landmark positions. We observe that the dynamic threshold significantly enhance the user experience.

While videos are stored and transmitted in compressed forms and formats, our system selects a subset of these frames for storage and transmission and discards the remaining frames. We experiment with real-life Youtube videos, and observe significant additional compression with facial videos, over and beyond what traditional video storage and transmission systems use.

The key contributions of our paper are following:

- We propose a facial landmark based framework for compression of videos which involve human face.
- We follow a frame-by-frame facial landmark comparison based decision of frame transmission, using a dynamic threshold that adapts to different variation rates of the facial videos. We retain only a few frames, and meta-information about discarded frames, for the compression.
- Our proposed method works for videos with multiple faces.
- We provide a lightweight implementation of the framework and demonstrate the system to perform well on a mobile platform (Android) with inherent resource limitations.
- We study the goodness of our system against multiple static baselines and validate with an elaborate user study. We further provide an entropy-based objective measurement, as well as, analyze the signal-to-noise ratio and structural similarity index, and observe favorable outcomes.
- Our method can be applied using other compression technologies, e.g. JPEG, to further improve the results.

2   Related Work

Video compression, for example, MPEG-4, H.264, and HEVC exploit the spatial and temporal redundancies to facilitate storage and transmission [19,22]. However, our work differs from these, as it uses facial landmarks in video sequences for compression.

Ekman and Friesen [5] develop the Facial Action Coding System (FACS) to describe facial expressions, using 44 Action Units (AU). [15] implemented three convergent modules for feature extraction, dense flow extraction, facial-feature tracking, and high gradient component detection, all of which could capture subtle motions in facial displays. The paper focused on recognizing 15 AUs in a face and yielded an average recognition accuracy of 81–91%. The objective was to identify facial expressions using AUs. Our work, however, uses AUs to identify a change in a person's facial expressions, without tagging it to any emotion. Otsuka and Ohya [17] worked on spotting segments, that display facial expressions, from image sequences. The motion of the face is modeled using HMM. Each state in HMM represents the condition of the facial muscles and is associated with a forward probability. When the probability reaches a certain threshold value, they tag that state to a facial expression. Our work is not identifying facial expressions; instead we are identifying a difference between the facial expression for consecutive frames.

The amount of work done using action units and facial expression recognition using mobile phones is less, as these models are quite heavy for mobile phones to execute using their limited CPU and memory. Emotion detection from mobile phones is done in [21], using a template matching technique, which yields a 72% accuracy rate for 6 basic emotions and a neutral expression. Jo et al. [9] work on mobile platform using Neural Network and CK Database. Unlike the above-mentioned work which detect emotions, our work uses the mobile platform and facial landmarks recognition to eliminate redundant frames from a video.

Facial animation systems have been developed to animate cartoon characters using facial features [6]. Facial landmark detection in video sequences have proved to be an important step towards facial recognition and tracking in videos [10, 14], recognizing human facial expressions to understand the level of interests in a video [26], and facial gesture recognition [7].

3   Methodology

We present our algorithm in this section. The algorithm takes a video as an input and performs the following steps.

3.1   Detecting Facial Landmarks

Facial landmarks are the facial feature points, such as corners of eyes, a tip of nose, and corners of lips. When a person communicates, these landmarks change, from frame to frame, in a video. Our algorithm first divides input video into frames. Within each frame, it identifies the face of the person and then identifies eight major landmarks as shown in Fig. 1. The landmarks are two eye centers, nose tip, two cheek muscle tip points, two lip corners, and one point in the lower lip jaw. It then records the coordinates of these landmarks within the frame.

Fig. 1. The eight selected facial landmarks for a frame.

3.2 Detecting Distinct Frames

A frame, which differs in a position of these landmarks from its previous one by more than a certain threshold, is called a *distinct frame* in our setting. In principle, the set of distinct frames carry more information than the others. Once the facial landmarks are detected in a frame, the next step is to store those landmarks and check the difference of the landmarks' positions on the next frame in the queue.

Introducing Static and Dynamic Thresholds: The difference in the facial landmarks is compared using two methods, *using dynamic threshold* and *using static threshold*. The threshold to detect distinct frames can be constant for the entire video, or it can be adaptive. Static threshold speeds up the processing. However, it would hamper the visual quality of the compressed video if the frames have a variable rate of change in a video. We propose dynamic thresholding, where the threshold value automatically adjusts itself concerning change of rate of frames. The threshold is decided by looking at the maximum and minimum changes in the difference for any of the eight landmarks' coordinates, in the two successive frames. A frame is considered to be distinct if the minimum change is greater than half of the maximum change. With dynamic thresholding, segments where entropy per frame is higher have a lower degree of compression and vice-versa. This safeguards quality of the compressed video.

3.3 Formulation of the Compression Algorithm

We calculate the Euclidean distance of each landmark in the current frame from the stored landmark information of the previously transmitted frame. For any landmark j in the $(i+1)^{th}$ frame, the Euclidean distance $d_{i+1,j}$ is given as:

$$d_{i+1,j} = \sqrt{\left(cx_{i+1,j} - cx_{i,j}\right)^2 + \left(cy_{i+1,j} - cy_{i,j}\right)^2} \tag{1}$$

where $(cx_{i,j}, cy_{i,j})$ is the coordinate of the landmark in last transmitted frame. A frame i is categorized as "distinct" if it satisfies:

$$(\forall j \in \{1..M\})\ min(d_{i,j}) >= max(d_{i,j})/2 \tag{2}$$

All the facial landmarks chosen in this paper are the ones, which change when a person changes any expression. According to the proposed Eq. (2), when the minimum change in a landmark in any i^{th} frame is greater than at least half of the maximum change of any other landmark in that same frame, it can be inferred that the ith frame has a significant information and hence can be considered as a distinct frame.

Our algorithm needs only a pair of frames to calculate threshold and thus making it computationally efficient. For illustration, consider a video comprising of 100 frames, namely $f_1, f_2, ..., f_{100}$. Of these, say frames f_1, f_{12}, f_{23}, f_{24}, f_{25}, f_{47}, f_{55}, and f_{90} are distinct, and the rest are not. Our algorithm transmits only these distinct frames and discards the rest. The sequence numbers of the discarded frames are transmitted as $2, 3, \cdots, 11, 13, \cdots$. Note, audio is transmitted separately, using standard transmission techniques. The detailed algorithm is mentioned in Sect. 3.4 [2].

3.4   Compression Algorithm

Algorithm 1. VIDEO COMPRESSION USING DYNAMIC THRESHOLD

$N \leftarrow$ No. of frames
$SequenceNo \leftarrow 1$
Transmit and store <the first frame, SequenceNo>
$lx \leftarrow$ x coordinates of the landmarks in the first transmitted frame
$ly \leftarrow$ y coordinates of the landmarks in the first transmitted frame
for $k = 2 \rightarrow N$ **do**
    $\{face_k\} \leftarrow$ An array of points detected as a face for the kth frame using Face API
    for $landmark : face_k.getlandmarks()$ **do**
        $cx_{k,j} \leftarrow$ landmark.getposition().x
        $cy_{k,j} \leftarrow$ landmark.getposition().y
        $j = j + 1$
    end for
    $M \leftarrow$ No. of landmarks
    for $j = 1 \rightarrow M$ **do**
        $d_{k,j} = \sqrt{\left(cx_{k,j} - lx_j\right)^2 + \left(cy_{k,j} - ly_j\right)^2}$
    end for
    for $j = 1 \rightarrow M$ **do**
        $min\_diff \leftarrow MIN(d_{k,j})$
    end for
    for $j = 1 \rightarrow M$ **do**
        $max\_diff \leftarrow MAX(d_{k,j})$
    end for
    if $min\_diff >= max\_diff/2$ **then**
        Mark the kth frame as a distinct frame
        Transmit and store ¡the kth frame, SequenceNo¿
        $lx \leftarrow cx_k$
        $ly \leftarrow cy_k$
    else
        Discard the kth frame
        SequenceNo = SequenceNo + 1
        Transmit SequenceNo
    end if
end for

3.5 Decompression

We reconstruct the original video from the compressed content, by repeating the most recently transmitted distinct frame for each missing frame. This reconstruction makes the compressed video equivalent to the original video in time length. In our example, the compressed video is received as f_1, f_{12}, $\cdots$, f_{23}, f_{24}, f_{25}, $\cdots$, f_{47}, $\cdots$, f_{55}, $\cdots$, f_{90}, and only the sequence numbers of the other non-distinct frames. The missing frames are inserted by replicating the most recently received distinct frame. Thus the final output at the receiver's end becomes f_1(11 times), f_{12}(11 times), f_{23}(1 time), f_{24}(1 time), f_{25}(22 times), f_{47}(8 times), f_{55}(35 times), and f_{90}(10 times). Any associated audio is received separately and superimposed with the video as-is.

3.6 Block Diagram of Our Algorithm

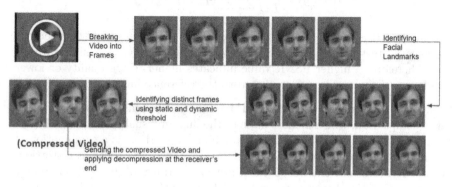

(Decompressed Video)

3.7 Evaluation of Our Algorithm

We measure the performance of our algorithm, in terms of accuracy and efficiency, as follows.

Time Taken by the Algorithm: We measure the efficiency of the algorithm, in terms of time taken to compress the video, using a separate clock.

Compression Ratio: It is a ratio of uncompressed size to compressed size. We compute the ratio for each of the threshold used.

Peak Signal to Noise Ratio (PSNR): PSNR is a well known image quality assessment metric [8]. Given a reference image or frame f and a test image or frame g, both of dimensions $P \times Q$ and represented using 8 bits, the PSNR between f and g is defined as

$$PSNR(f,g) = 10log_{10}\frac{255^2}{MSE(f,g)} \tag{3}$$

Fig. 2. A set of images that show how facial landmarks change with different expressions of a given individual.

where,

$$MSE(f,g) = \frac{1}{PQ}\sum_{i=1}^{P}\sum_{j=1}^{Q}(f(i,j) - g(i,j))^2 \qquad (4)$$

Since the PSNR is inversely proportional to the mean square error between the reference and test image pixel values, a lower error value gives a higher PSNR value. Therefore, a higher PSNR value indicates higher image quality or lower degradation of the test image compared to the reference image.

Structural Similarity (SSIM): SSIM is another popular metric for image quality comparison, which is more close to the human visual system than PSNR [8]. The SSIM is designed by modeling any image distortion as a combination of three factors, loss of correlation, luminance distortion, and contrast distortion. The positive values of the SSIM index are in the range of $[0, 1]$. A value of 0 means no correlation between images, and 1 means the images are identical.

Entropy Per Frame: A successful video compression is to reduce its size without affecting quality or information content much. To determine the average information stored in the video, the following evaluation metric is used.

- Calculate the pixel-wise difference between each consecutive frames for all the frames of the entire video.

$$I_z = I_x - I_y \qquad (5)$$

where I_x and I_y are 2 consecutive frames of a video
- Calculate the average by taking the sum of the entropy of the difference calculated for each consecutive pair of frames and dividing it to the number of entropies.

$$Entropy\ per\ frame = \frac{\sum_{i=1}^{N-1} E(I_{z_i})}{N - 1} \qquad (6)$$

Here, N is the total number of frames in the video, I_{z_i} is the difference of ith and $i + 1^{th}$ frames, and $E(I_{z_i})$ gives the entropy of the difference. A higher entropy per frame will result in a better compression ratio. However, it may result in a poor subjective quality of the video.

For comparison, we use a static value of threshold as the baseline. Between two successive frames, every time any landmark changes its position by a margin above that of the threshold, the frame is categorized as a distinct frame. As evident from Fig. 2, the landmarks positions changes with changing the expression on face. If the change is above a certain threshold, the frame is considered to be distinct. We consider four static threshold values of 3, 5, 8, and 10. We chose these values empirically.

3.8 Smoothing Decompressed Video Using Morphing Technique

A naive decompression technique that uses replication of frames, between the selected frames, result into sudden transitions between each pair of the replicated frame and the selected frame. The result is visually unpleasant. To overcome this problem, we add morphed frames instead of replicating the frames. Such addition gives a gradual transition between frames and the video is visually better. Following are the steps for obtaining morphed frames.

Fig. 3. Landmarks obtained using DLib.

- **Find Point Correspondences Using Facial Feature Detection:** For each facial image, we calculate 68 facial landmarks using DLib as shown in Fig. 3 [11].
- **Delaunay Triangulation:** In the previous step, we obtained 68 landmark locations. 8 more points are added to the boundary of the output image (shown in green) to calculate Delaunay Triangulation (shown in red) in Fig. 4. Delaunay Triangulation breaks the image into triangles. The result of Delaunay Triangulation is a list of triangles, represented by the indices of points in the 76 points (68 face points + 8 boundary points) array [27].
- **Warping Images and Alpha Blending:** The amount of blending is controlled by a parameter α.

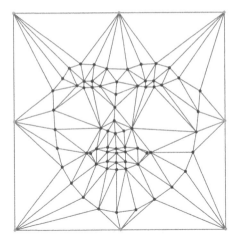

Fig. 4. Triangles obtained after Delaunay Triangulation. (Color figure online)

- Find location of feature points in morphed image: In the morphed image M, we find the location of all 76 points (x_m, y_m) using Eqs. 7 and 8.

$$x_m = (1 - \alpha)x_i + \alpha x_j \tag{7}$$

$$y_m = (1 - \alpha)y_i + \alpha y_j \tag{8}$$

$$M(x_m, y_m) = (1 - \alpha)I(x_i, y_i) + \alpha J(x_j, y_j) \tag{9}$$

- Calculate affine transforms: Affine transformation preserves collinearity and ratios of distances. We have a set of 76 points in image I, another set of 76 points in image J, and the third set of 76 points in the morphed image. We also know the triangulation defined over these points. Pick a triangle in the image I and the corresponding triangle in the morphed image. We calculate the affine transform that maps the three corners of the triangle in image I to the three corners of the corresponding triangle in the morphed image. Then calculate the affine transform for every pair of a triangle and repeat the process on image J and the morphed image.
- Warp triangles: For each triangle in the image I, we use the affine transform, which is calculated in the previous step to transform all pixels inside the triangle to the morphed image. This process is repeated for all triangles in image I to obtain a warped version of image I. Similarly, a warped version of image J was obtained.
- Alpha blend warped images: In the previous step, we obtained warped version of the image I and image J. These two images can be alpha blended using Eq. 9 and this is the final morphed image [3]. α parameter is selected empirically. Let us consider that we want to reconstruct f_k frame. Let f_i be the first distinct frame just before the kth frame and f_j be the first distinct frame just after the kth frame. α for reconstructing

f_k will be equal to $(k-i)/(j-i)$. We illustrate using an example. Let us assume the original image frames are f_1, f_2, f_3, f_4, and f_5. We further assume that the frames f_1 and f_5 are selected as distinct frames and f_2, f_3, f_4 are discarded. For reconstructing f_2, f_3, and f_4 we need to decide the α parameter. For f_2, $k = 2$, $i = 1$, $j = 5$ and hence $\alpha = (2-1)/(5-1)$ = 0.25. For f_3, $k = 3$, $i = 1$, $j = 5$ and hence $\alpha = (3-1)/(5-1) = 0.5$. Similarly, for f_4, $k = 4$, $i = 1$, $j = 5$ and hence $\alpha = (4-1)/(5-1) = 0.75$.

3.9   Complementing with the Existing Compression Techniques

Figure 5 shows the flow of our proposed algorithm. We are sending all the distinct frames over the network i.e. raw frames are being sent.

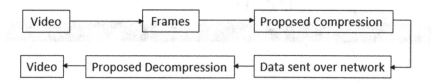

Fig. 5. A block diagram to represent the basic proposed approach

We complement our proposed compression with the existing standard compression techniques, such as JPEG. Benefit of using existing compression techniques, on top of our proposed compression algorithm, is that we are able to get the best of both the worlds. We proceed as follows. We first obtain all the distinct frames using our proposed algorithm and we then apply JPEG compression on these distinct frames. This results in the compressed data. At the receiver end, we first do JPEG decompression and obtain the distinct frames, possibly with some loss of information. Then, we apply our decompression algorithm, i.e., reconstructing the original frames using morphing. Figure 6 represents these steps in a block diagram.

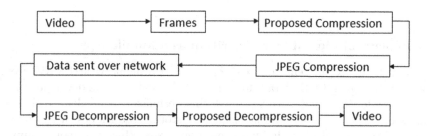

Fig. 6. A modified block diagram to represent the complemented approach

Fig. 7. Screenshots of our mobile app.

Table 1. The various characteristics of all the videos rated on a scale of *High, Medium, and Low.*

Video names	Gender	Talking	Smiling /laughing	Staring quietly	Hand gestures	Multiple expressions	Background lighting conditions	Head movements	Entropy per frame
$Video_1$	Male	Low	High	High	Medium	High	High	Low	High
$Video_2$	Female	High	Low	Medium	Low	Low	High	Medium	Medium
$Video_3$	Male	High	Low	Low	High	Low	High	Low	High
$Video_4$	Male	Medium	Medium	Low	High	Medium	Low	Medium	Medium
$Video_5$	Female	High	Low	Low	Low	Low	Low	High	Low

4   Experimental Setup

In this section, we describe our experimental setup for evaluating the proposed solution.

4.1   Implementation of Our Algorithm as a Mobile App

We conduct our experiments using Google Nexus 5 phone with 1.3 MP front camera Quad-core 2.3 GHz Krait 400 CPU. The mobile app we developed, uses front camera for ingesting video input, which is technically equivalent to clicking pictures in the burst mode and subsequently storing the frames in the phone memory. The app takes in this video as input. Note that, the mobile app is stand alone. It does not use any cloud-based APIs. Figure 7 shows screenshots of our app compressing $Video_1$. We use a well-established Google API [1] to detect the facial landmarks. Note that, in principle, our algorithm works with any other API providing facial landmarks.

4.2 Data for Evaluation

We evaluate our methodology on two standard benchmark databases, the Talking Face Video [4] and the Youtube Faces DB [25]. The Talking Face video [4] consists of 1000 frames, is about 26 MB in size, recorded from a video of a person engaged in a conversation with another person. This database is suitable for evaluation as the subject displayed different facial expressions while talking, such as smiling, laughing, staring silently, *etc.*, as seen in Fig. 8 $Video_1$. The Youtube Faces DB [25] is captured while people are either interviewing or participating in a press conference. Thus, the main focus of each video is the single individual, shown in the frame. We use five videos of 5 different subjects from this database. Figure 8 shows the chosen videos, $Video_1$, $Video_2$, $Video_3$, $Video_4$, and $Video_5$. Table 1 contains a description of the characteristics of these videos, as found in most of the conversations. The five selected video cover the spectrum of characteristics' scale, from Low to High.

4.3 User Study for Subjective Evaluation

We perform a subjective evaluation of our technique by conducting a user study. The original videos from the two benchmark databases and the five compressed videos corresponding to each database were presented to user. Each video was shown at five different threshold levels, four static and one dynamic threshold. Thus, each user was shown a total of 30 videos, 5 original and 25 compressed. The user study was conducted by first showing the original video to the users and then at a random order showing the different compressed videos, without conveying the threshold for any of the randomly-ordered videos. They were then asked to rate them on a Likert scale [16] of 1 to 5 along each of the three dimensions, with 5 being the highest and 1 being the least rating. We ask each user to rate the compressed videos over three key dimensions.

1. Perceived video quality: This was defined to the user as the perception of resolution (pixel quality) of the video, in the perception of the viewers.
2. Smoothness of frame transition: This captures the perception of smoothness (continuity) as a video moves from one frame to the next.
3. Perception of loss of information: This captures whether the user feels any information has been lost.

4.4 Subjective Evaluation of Decompression Using Morphing

A second user study was conducted to evaluate our decompression technique based on replication and morphing. Three versions of the video, original, decompressed using replication, and decompressed using morphing, were shown to 10

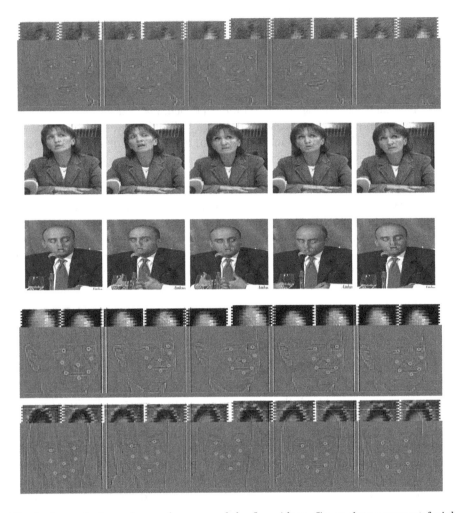

Fig. 8. A row features frames from one of the five videos. Green dots represent facial landmarks on the frames of the individual video. (Color figure online)

different users. We did not inform subjects which of the video uses which technique for decompressing. Since there was a data set of 5 videos and each video had three versions, so in all a user was shown 15 videos. Each user was asked to rate the videos on three parameters: Quality, Transition, and Information Loss.

4.5 Objective Evaluation of the Complemented Approach

For complementing the proposed algorithm with JPEG compression, we experimented with $Video_6$ from YouTube. It consists of 1660 frames in PNG format and is about 1.42 GB in size. In this video, a Psychologist is being interviewed and involves different facial expressions.

We provide frames of $Video_6$ as input to the proposed algorithm and obtain distinct frames for five different thresholds. Then, these distinct frames at five different thresholds are compressed using JPEG. We evaluate the complemented approach in term of compression ratio, PSNR, and SSIM. We compare the compression ratio after the proposed compression, and compression ratio after JPEG compression on the top. We calculate PSNR, and SSIM between the original frames and the frames obtained using proposed decompression.

5   Results

Before proceeding with the evaluation, we take a sample video and show what output we get. Figures 9 and 10 show five successive frames of $Video_1$ before and after compression respectively. The compressed video skips last two frames from the video.

Fig. 9. Images from $Video_1$ before compression.

Fig. 10. Images from $Video_1$ after compression with static threshold.

5.1   Impact of Static Thresholds

Our algorithm for dynamic thresholding is based on the premise that, it is impractical to attempt to design a unique and ubiquitous static threshold, which would yield a satisfactory performance for all video segments, with varying degrees of movements of facial landmarks.

In our user study, outlined in Table 2, we observe the above hypothesis to hold true for all the axes of our user study, namely the perceived video quality, the smoothness of transition, and the perceived information loss.

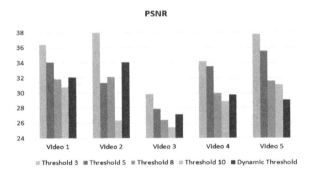

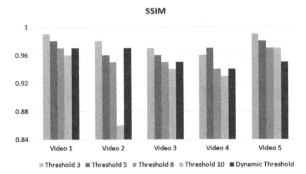

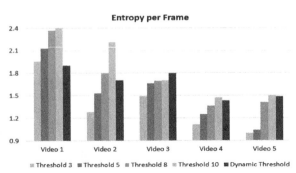

Fig. 11. The plot shows comparison of PSNR, SSIM and Entropy per frame for static and dynamic thresholds.

Further, as the static threshold increases, although the compression ratio (shown in Table 3) and entropy per frame (shown in Fig. 11) of the compressed video increase, the PSNR (shown in Fig. 11) and user experience quality consistently (shown in Table 2) deteriorate. The SSIM values (shown in Fig. 11) have a relatively marginal dip. Thus, our experimenting with static threshold values reveals the need of a dynamically determined threshold.

5.2 Impact of Dynamic Threshold

As seen in Table 2, the ratings indicate that the dynamic threshold based compression delivers quality, which is almost the same as that for the videos with a low static threshold. As shown in Table 3, for all the videos, the compression ratio achieved by the dynamic thresholding method is higher than the lowest static threshold that we experimented. For $Video_3$, $Video_4$, and $Video_5$, the compression ratio is close to that for the static threshold of 10. Although, the dynamic threshold is not absolutely the best in terms of user rating and compression ratio for all the videos, it comes close to the optimal.

Table 2. Overall user ratings for all the videos. Dynamic threshold performs satisfactory.

Threshold	Overall user rating					Mean of user ratings	Standard deviation of user ratings
	$Video_1$ (/15)	$Video_2$ (/15)	$Video_3$ (/15)	$Video_4$ (/15)	$Video_5$ (/15)		
3	13.4	12.8	12.5	13.2	11.8	12.74	0.6309
5	12.8	12.5	12.5	13.1	11.2	12.42	0.7259
8	11.9	11.2	12.4	11.8	11	11.66	0.5639
10	11.4	11.1	12	11.8	10	11.26	0.7861
Dynamic	13.1	12.9	13	12	12.8	12.76	0.4394

Table 3. Compression ratios for all the videos.

Threshold	Overall compression ratio (CR)					Mean of compression ratio	Standard deviation of compression ratio
	$Video_1$ 25.89 MB	$Video_2$ 25.25 MB	$Video_3$ 20.14 MB	$Video_4$ 2.85 MB	$Video_5$ 21.20 MB		
3	2.2909	2.0546	1.4819	1.2127	1.2397	1.6559	0.4904
5	3.9169	6.9013	3.0469	2.1588	1.500	3.5047	2.1063
8	7.8926	8.7336	4.4267	3.4965	4.2229	5.7544	2.3798
10	10.3199	22.3214	5.0479	4.7732	5.2219	9.5368	7.5086
Dynamic	3.0211	5.3163	4.3878	4.2105	5.9206	4.5712	1.1115

5.3 Comparison Based on Time Taken to Compress

The time taken by our algorithm is in the order of a few hundred milli-seconds per compression frame, both for static thresholds (demonstrated with a threshold value of 5, for illustrative purposes) and dynamic compression thresholds, as shown on Table 4. Multiple interesting observations emerge.

– The compression time per frame varies significantly across videos. This is attributed to the fact that the compression time taken per frame varies with

Table 4. Time taken to compress for static and dynamic thresholds.

Video names	Dynamic threshold			Static threshold = 5		
	Time taken by facial landmark API per frame (ms/frame)	Time taken by our algorithm per frame (ms/frame)	Time taken by our algorithm per MB (s/MB)	Time taken by facial landmark API per frame (ms/frame)	Time taken by our algorithm per frame (ms/frame)	Time taken by our algorithm per MB (s/MB)
$Video_1$	26	288	**11.124**	25	225	**8.691**
$Video_2$	23.6	334.2	**10.059**	25	280.3	**8.436**
$Video_3$	25.6	410.3	**9.533**	29.9	322.6	**7.498**
$Video_4$	18.5	137.1	**12.982**	18.5	96.29	**9.123**
$Video_5$	24.1	181.95	**11.415**	22.5	153.4	**9.623**

the rate of movement of facial landmarks, which in turn, translates to higher entropy per frame in our settings. Thus, videos with higher entropy per frame take longer to compress.

- The dynamic compression consistently takes around 20%–30% more than its static counterpart, as apparent from Table 4. The overhead of computing the dynamic thresholds requires the additional time.
- A significant fraction of the time is invested in the actual compression process while computing the landmarks do not provide too heavy overhead.

5.4 Impact of Morphing While Decompressing

Compression using replication, results into jerks in the video, i.e., the transition between frames is not smooth. In Figs. 12 and 13, $Frame_1$ and $Frame_3$ are distinct frames. In Fig. 12, $Frame_2$ is re-constructed by replicating the $Frame_1$. Such creation creates a visual jerk when $Frame_3$ comes on the screen. To have a smooth transition, morphed frames are added instead of replicating the frames. $Frame_2$ in Fig. 13 is re-constructed by obtaining a morphed frame with $Frame_1$ and $Frame_3$ as input to the morphing algorithm.

For reconstructing the video, generated morphed frames are combined with the distinct frames. Table 5 shows the time taken by the algorithm while decompression using morphing and replication. Decompression time for the replication technique is considerably less as compared to the morphing. This is due to the fact that last distinct frame is simply replicated in the former. Whereas in the case of morphing, new morphed frames are created which needs computation for facial feature detection, warping, and blending. In the future, we will use a faster algorithm [23] for blending, though we use the current one for its simplicity. The former has an additional benefit of preserving color in blended images as well as computational efficiency.

Fig. 12. Frame sequences from $Video_2$ obtained while decompression using replication.

Fig. 13. Frame sequences from $Video_2$ obtained while decompression using morphing.

Table 5. Time taken during decompression using morphing and replication technique.

Video name	Facial feature detection using DLib (ms/frame)	Triangulation (ms/frame)	Warping images and alpha blending (ms/frame)	Total time for generating morphed frames (ms/frame)	Time for generating replicated frames (ms/frame)
Video 1	355	10	157	**521**	**4.15**
Video 2	222	6	81	**309**	**5.38**
Video 3	324	9	122	**454**	**5.83**
Video 4	96	4	52	**152**	**4.74**
Video 5	160	5	61	**226**	**4.75**

Table 6. User ratings for decompression using replication and decompression using morphing.

Technique	Overall user rating					Mean of user ratings	Standard deviation of user ratings
	$Video_1$ (/15)	$Video_2$ (/15)	$Video_3$ (/15)	$Video_4$ (/15)	$Video_5$ (/15)		
Replication	9.6	8.7	9.9	10.6	7.7	9.3	1.124
Morphing	11.9	11.1	11.3	11.9	11	11.44	0.4335

Table 6 shows the result of a subjective comparison. Compression technique, which uses morphing, has greater rating than the one which uses replication. In case of morphing, the transition is smooth because inter-mediate frames are added, and there is less loss of information.

5.5   Impact of Using Complementing Compression

Table 7 shows the compression ratio when proposed and JPEG compression are used together. All the distinct frames are passed through the JPEG compression. For a threshold of 8, original size of the video is 1.42 GB, the output of our algorithm is 631 MB, giving compression ratio of 2.25. This dataset of 631 MB is given as an input to the JPEG compression, which gives the output as 143 MB, hence we are able to achieve compression ratio of 9.93. We send this 143 MB to the receiver, receiver first does the JPEG decompression, which is lossy, and the file size on JPEG decompression is 561 MB. We then use morphing to reconstruct the original frames. Here, we have used JPEG compression which is a lossy compression but still algorithm works because the facial landmarks can still be detected. We calculate PSNR and SSIM between the original frames and the result that is obtained using morphing. For most of the thresholds, SSIM value is greater than 0.9, which indicates that the video is similar to the original one and gives a pleasant experience.

Table 7. Compression ratio, PSNR and SSIM when proposed algorithm is used with JPEG compression.

Threshold	CR after proposed algorithm	CR after JPEG compression	CR after JPEG decompression	Time for JPEG compression + decompression (in sec)	PSNR	SSIM
3	1.2	5.13	1.35	300	30	0.989
5	1.53	6.73	1.72	212	30	0.977
8	2.25	9.93	2.53	127	29	0.961
10	2.75	12.14	3.09	104	28	0.950
Dynamic	15.78	67.62	17.42	28	23	0.851

Benefit of Using JPEG Compression: Table 8 shows the size of the frames when proposed compression algorithm is used alone. All original frames are given as input to the proposed compression algorithm, which gives distinct frames as output. Then, these district frames are sent to the receiver. For a threshold of 8, total 631 MB is sent to the receiver and then the receiver applies proposed decompression algorithm, which gives output as morphed frames.

Table 8. Compression ratio, PSNR, and SSIM when we use only the proposed algorithm.

Threshold	CR after proposed algorithm	PSNR	SSIM
3	1.2	31	0.992
5	1.53	30	0.980
8	2.25	29	0.964
10	2.75	28	0.953
Dynamic	15.78	23	0.852

The benefit of using JPEG on top of our algorithm is that we are sending lesser no. of frames, i.e., the bandwidth requirement is low. When we are complementing both the approach then we just need to send 143 MB, whereas when we are using only the proposed algorithm then 631 MB is sent. So we are sending about 4 times less data when both the approaches are used together. The PSNR and SSIM values are approximately the same as shown in Tables 7 and 8. PSNR and SSIM are not much affected when we use existing compression methods on top of our algorithm. But we do gain on the amount of data sent, in case of proposed with JPEG we sent about 4 times less data.

Benefit of Using Our Compression: Now we consider the case when we are doing only JPEG Compression and no other algorithm is used.

Frame 1   Frame 2   Frame 3

Fig. 14. Original frames from $Video_6$

Original size is 1.42 GB, when we apply JPEG Compression on 1.42 GB then the output is 335 MB. In case of complemented approach the amount of data sent for threshold 8 was 143 MB, whereas when we are going to use JPEG then we have to send 335 MB to the receiver. We have to send less data in the complemented approach because the proposed algorithm will select the frames on the basis of facial landmarks and hence less frames are given as input to the JPEG Compression.

Figure 14 shows the original frames 1, 2, and 3. On using our algorithm, Frame 1 and Frame 3 are categorized as the distinct frames as shown in Fig. 15. Frame 1 and 3 undergoes JPEG compression. Encoded data is sent to the receiver

Frame 1   Frame 2   Frame 3

Fig. 15. Frame 1 and Frame 3 are the distinct frames

Frame 1   Frame 2   Frame 3

Fig. 16. Frames obtained using JPEG decompression

Frame 1   Frame 2   Frame 3

Fig. 17. Frame 2 is reconstructed by using morphing

and JPEG decompression is applied on encoded Frame 1 and Frame 3 (Fig. 16). Then, our proposed decompression method is used to reconstruct the Frame 2 via morphing (Fig. 17).

The video frames used for the comparison had changes primarily in the facial expression. The background and the other body parts were relatively still. This ensures we fairly compare our technique with the JPEG.

6   Compressing Videos Containing Multiple Faces

We extend the compression algorithm to handle videos containing multiple faces. This allows us to handle videos of press conferences, tutorials, video conferencing etc. which involve more than one person. The algorithm for a single face differs from this algorithm in terms of choosing the distinct frames. The former first breaks the video into frames, then it identifies facial landmarks on each of the frames. The latter also does the same, but it identifies a frame as distinct if any of the faces in the video shows a substantial change in the expression from its previous frame. We modify the equation to a new Eq. 10. After identifying the distinct frames using this condition, the algorithm works similar to the single face compression algorithm.

For multiple face videos, the Eq. 2 changes as following:

$$(\forall j \in \{1..M\})\ min(d_{i,j,f_1}) >= max(d_{i,j,f_1})/2)$$

$$\cup (\forall j \in \{1..M\})\ min(d_{i,j,f_2}) >= max(d_{i,j,f_2})/2)$$

$$\cup \cdots (\forall j \in \{1..M\})\ min(d_{i,j,f_n}) >= max(d_{i,j,f_n})/2) \tag{10}$$

where f_1, f_2, $\cdots$ f_n are all the faces.

In Fig. 18, the first set of frames is taken from $MultifaceVideo_1$ which is a video of two people in a press conference where the $Person_1$ has quite a few change in expressions along with hand gestures whereas $Person_2$ has almost a constant expression throughout the video. In $MultifaceVideo_2$, the two people are engaged in an online tutorial and both of them have almost similar change in expressions throughout the video. But since it is a tutorial, the moment $Person_1$ stops talking, the $Person_2$ starts. There are relatively lesser frames where both of them are quiet. The size of $MultifaceVideo_1$ is 37.57 MB while that of $MultifaceVideo_2$ is 328 MB.

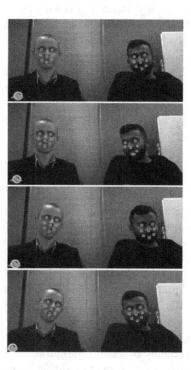

Fig. 18. A set of consecutive frames from $MultifaceVideo_1$ and $MultifaceVideo_2$ when our proposed algorithm was executed on them.

Table 9. Compression ratios of $MultifaceVideo_1$ and $MultifaceVideo_2$. We achieve better compression ratio for $MultifaceVideo_1$ as one face changes its expressions relatively lesser.

Overall compression ratio (CR)		
Threshold	$MultifaceVideo_1$	$MultifaceVideo_2$
3	2.0092	1.3292
5	3.0349	1.6614
8	4.3956	2.0100
10	5.2110	2.1450
Dynamic	2.3900	2.2667

Evaluation of the Algorithm: As mentioned above, the $Person_1$ in $MultifaceVideo_1$ has changes of expression but the $Person_2$ has a relatively constant expression throughout. According to Eq. 10, the frames, in which there is a change in expression, will be selected as distinct. Since the change in expression of $Person_2$ is far less, this video has in effect became a single person video. Hence, the compression ratio given in Table 9 is only dependent on the $Person_1$ of the video. Although $Person_1$ has a few hand gestures in the video, the algorithm is only focused in the change of expressions of his face. On the other hand, in $MultifaceVideo_2$ both of them has almost similar expressions but there is a relatively less overlap of expressions in time. When one person is quiet, another one is active and vice versa. This in effect is equivalent to two single-face videos. With the increase in the number of people, that have different expressions in each frame, the number of distinct frame decreases drastically and hence the compression ratio decreases. We achieve better compression ratio for $MultifaceVideo_1$ as one face changes expressions relatively less.

7   Discussion

Our experimental results establish the validity of our primary hypotheses, both in terms of achieving video compression as well as retaining the perception of users about the given videos. In that, (a) facial video compression technique using the change of facial landmarks over successive video frames, is an effective solution and (b) dynamic threshold based compression is often more effective compared to static threshold based videos. While it is not feasible to provide any quantitative metric to jointly capture the user satisfaction and video compression ratio for facial videos, we observe that, with dynamic thresholding, as a whole the user satisfaction is significantly retained. In addition, the compression ratio is optimal or near-optimal, across several videos having different rates of movements of facial landmarks.

The average overall rating, a measure of our subjective rating, is the best with dynamically thresholded video, shown in Table 2. The compression size with dynamic thresholding is not the maximum for a few of the videos; however, in those cases, the user perception factor significantly indicate in favor of the dynamic thresholding technique, over static. Table 3 shows that, while dynamically adapting to the difference in the rate of change of facial landmark movements prohibits the dynamically thresholded algorithm from having the highest compression ratio, it caters the most consistent compression ratio over all the videos. This benefit is reflected by the fact that the standard deviation is the smallest in case of the dynamically thresholded video, compared to all the statically thresholded videos. The above observations demonstrate the consistent user satisfaction that our dynamic thresholding based methodology produces, over statically thresholded methods.

Decompression using morphing proves better as compared to using replicated frames because the sudden transition is removed and new intermediate frames are added which provides a smooth transition from one frame to another. Our algorithm can be used with other existing compression algorithms. Benefit of complementing proposed algorithm with existing compression method is that we are sending lesser data to the receiver as compared to what was sent when we were using only the proposed algorithm.

8   Future Work

In this paper, we have proposed an algorithm to compress videos containing multiple faces. Considering a frame with multiple faces, currently our algorithm identifies a frame as a distinct frame if any one of the faces in that frame shows substantial changes in its expressions. But there is a concern with this kind of approach.

Consider video in which one of the faces has a lot of changes in facial expressions. Our algorithm will anyway select the entire frames. There is a way to further optimize this. We can identify the different faces in a single frame and break them into distinct subframes. Say, the frame f with two faces becomes subframe f_1 with one face and subframe f_2 with the second one. This will result in two series of subframes, one consisting of only $f_1 s$ and another consisting of $f_2 s$. Now, we will apply our compression-decompression algorithm in isolation on each series of two subframes, i.e., we identify the facial movements in isolation on the two series and select the subframes in isolation. While decompressing, we stitch back the two corresponding two subframes to form a frame. This will result in more compression as we will only send a subframe, instead of a frame, if only one subframe is changing. The work in this paper targets facial landmarks.

There are APIs that track landmarks on an entire body, e.g., OpenNI API for the Kinect motion sensor. Our work can be extended to read these landmarks, determine body movements in successive frames of a video, and eliminate the redundant frames that have less movements.

9   Conclusion

We presented a technique to compress videos, constituting human faces, based on detected movements of facial landmarks across video frames. We explored two compression scenarios, one with a static compression policy based upon a static threshold and another with a dynamic decision process to compress videos with the compression process automatically adjusting to the change rate of frames. We benchmarked against two databases, Talking Face Video DB and YouTube Face DB, and obtained significant compression for both. We evaluated our algorithm via a user study on real videos. The dynamic threshold based implementation was seen to deliver a more consistent performance compared to the static one and often delivered the highest user satisfaction as well as high compression ratios. We tested our methodology on smart mobile phones having inherent resource limitations, showing its practicality. The quality of the decompressed video was improved using the morphing technique. Morphed frames provide better visual feel as compared to replicated frames. Our system can be used to compress real-life human face based videos, supplementing traditional video compression systems.

References

1. Google API for detecting facial landmarks. https://developers.google.com/android/reference/com/google/android/gms/vision/face/Landmark
2. Banerjee, R.: Video compression technique using facial landmarks on mobile devices. Master's thesis, IIIT Delhi (2016). https://repository.iiitd.edu.in/jspui/handle/123456789/435
3. Bichsel, M.: Automatic interpolation and recognition of face images by morphing. In: Proceedings of the Second International Conference on Automatic Face and Gesture Recognition, pp. 128–135 (1996)
4. Cootes, T.: Talking face video database. Images. https://www-prima.inrialpes.fr/FGnet/data/01-TalkingFace/talking_face.html
5. Ekman, P., Friesen, W.V.: Measuring facial movement. Environ. Psychol. Nonverbal Behav. **1**(1), 56–75 (1976)
6. Facerig, F.: Facial animation system. https://facerig.com/
7. Heizmann, J., Zelinsky, A.: Robust real-time face tracking and gesture recognition. In: IJCAI, pp. 1525–1530 (1997)
8. Hore, A., Ziou, D.: Image quality metrics: PSNR vs. SSIM. In: ICPR, pp. 2366–2369. IEEE (2010)
9. Jo, G.S., Choi, I.H., Kim, Y.G.: Robust facial expression recognition against illumination variation appeared in mobile environment. In: CNS, pp. 10–13. IEEE (2011)
10. Kim, M., Kumar, S., Pavlovic, V., Rowley, H.: Face tracking and recognition with visual constraints in real-world videos. In: CVPR, pp. 1–8. IEEE (2008)
11. King, D.E.: Dlib-ml: A machine learning toolkit. J. Mach. Learn. Res. **10**, 1755–1758 (2009). http://dl.acm.org/citation.cfm?id=1577069.1755843
12. Lane, N.D., Miluzzo, E., Lu, H., Peebles, D., Choudhury, T., Campbell, A.T.: A survey of mobile phone sensing. IEEE Commun. Mag. **48**(9), 140–150 (2010)

13. Lane, N.D., et al.: Bewell: a smartphone application to monitor, model and promote wellbeing. In: ICST Conference on Pervasive Computing Technologies for Healthcare, pp. 23–26 (2011)
14. Lee, K.C., Ho, J., Yang, M.H., Kriegman, D.: Video-based face recognition using probabilistic appearance manifolds. In: CVPR, vol. 1, pp. 313–320. IEEE (2003)
15. Lien, J.J.J., Kanade, T., Cohn, J.F., Li, C.C.: Detection, tracking, and classification of action units in facial expression. Robot. Auton. Syst. **31**(3), 131–146 (2000)
16. Likert, R.: A technique for the measurement of attitudes. Archives of psychology (1932)
17. Otsuka, T., Ohya, J.: Spotting segments displaying facial expression from image sequences using HMM. In: Conference on Automatic Face and Gesture Recognition, pp. 442–447. IEEE (1998)
18. Paleari, M., Lisetti, C.L.: Toward multimodal fusion of affective cues. In: Workshop on Human-centered Multimedia, pp. 99–108. ACM (2006)
19. Richardson, I.E.: H. 264 and MPEG-4 Video Compression: Video Coding for Next-generation Multimedia. Wiley, Chichester (2004)
20. Setton, E., Yoo, T., Zhu, X., Goldsmith, A., Girod, B.: Cross-layer design of ad hoc networks for real-time video streaming. IEEE Wirel. Commun. **12**(4), 59–65 (2005)
21. Suk, M., Prabhakaran, B.: Real-time mobile facial expression recognition system-a case study. In: CVPR Workshops, pp. 132–137. IEEE (2014)
22. Sullivan, G.J., Ohm, J.R., Han, W.J., Wiegand, T.: Overview of the high efficiency video coding (HEVC) standard. IEEE Trans. Circ. Syst. Video Technol. **22**(12), 1649–1668 (2012)
23. Tanaka, M., Kamio, R., Okutomi, M.: Seamless image cloning by a closed form solution of a modified poisson problem. In: SIGGRAPH Asia 2012 Posters, SA 2012, p. 15:1. ACM, New York (2012). https://doi.org/10.1145/2407156.2407173
24. Wang, J., Cohen, M.F.: Very low frame-rate video streaming for face-to-face teleconference. In: Data Compression Conference, pp. 309–318. IEEE (2005)
25. Wolf, L., Hassner, T., Maoz, I.: Face recognition in unconstrained videos with matched background similarity. In: CVPR, pp. 529–534. IEEE (2011)
26. Yeasin, M., Bullot, B., Sharma, R.: Recognition of facial expressions and measurement of levels of interest from video. Trans. Multimedia **8**(3), 500–508 (2006)
27. Yi Tao, W.I.G.: Delaunay triangulation for image object indexing: a novel method for shape representation. In: Proceedings of the Seventh SPIE Symposium on Storage and Retrieval for Image and Video Databases, pp. 23–29 (1998)
28. Zhang, Z.L., Wang, Y., Du, D.H., Shu, D.: Video staging: a proxy-server-based approach to end-to-end video delivery over wide-area networks. IEEE/ACM Trans. Netw. (TON) **8**(4), 429–442 (2000)

PKHSN: A Bilinear Pairing Based Key Management Scheme for Heterogeneous Sensor Networks

Madhurima Buragohain[1(✉)] and Nityananda Sarma[2]

[1] Indian Institute of Technology Guwahati, Guwahati, India
madhurima.2015@iitg.ernet.in
[2] Tezpur University, Tezpur, India
nitya@tezu.ernet.in

Abstract. Some applications of Wireless sensor network such as military and health-care applications require high level of security. Such a level of security cannot be provided through traditional key management schemes due to resource-constrained sensor nodes. Keeping this in mind, we propose a novel key management scheme with the following design objectives: (i) reduction of computation overhead (ii) reduction of communication overhead (iii) mitigation of node capture attack and (iv) protection from clone attack and replay attack. Here, we apply Identity-based cryptography which uses bilinear pairing on elliptic curves. The security of the proposed scheme is proved through Strand Space model. The analysis and experimental results infer that the proposed scheme provides better performance as compared to other similar protocols in the literature.

Keywords: Wireless sensor network · Key management
Strand space model · Identity-based cryptography

1 Introduction

Wireless sensor network comprises one or more Base Stations (BS) and a collection of battery powered nodes having the sensing, computation and wireless communication capability [16]. It provides easy deployment, low cost, and dynamic configuration as compared to traditional wired networks. Today, we can see a vast range of applications such as home automation, military, and health-care application. Sometimes, nodes are deployed in an unattended environment where they may be subjected to different types of attacks. The naive way to safeguard the network is to share a key among all the network nodes. But, this does not provide the source message authentication. Moreover, a single node compromise will simply breach the whole security of the network. To solve this problem, we can go for symmetric key cryptography. Here, one single node capture will not affect other nodes. But, each node needs to store 'n(n − 1)/2' number of keys if there are 'n' nodes in the network which is not scalable. We can solve these

© Springer Nature Switzerland AG 2019
S. Biswas et al. (Eds.): COMSNETS 2018, LNCS 11227, pp. 102–125, 2019.
https://doi.org/10.1007/978-3-030-10659-1_5

problems with the help of public key cryptography, where each node needs to store only two keys: private and public key. The public key is used for encryption and private is for decryption of the message. But the major issue is the verification of public keys. In the traditional network, the public key certificate issued by the Certifying Authority (CA) is used for verification of public keys. But management of CA is a complex job and for resource-constrained nodes, management of CA is quite difficult. Moreover, in public key cryptography, huge computation is required which slows down the processing.

Advancement of Identity-based cryptography (IBC) [4] opens the door for secure implementation of Wireless sensor network (WSN). The name Identity-based itself reflects the meaning. Here, only the IDs are sufficient to determine the shared key. So using the IBC, two nodes can derive the shared key just knowing the IDs of each other. There is no need for communication between them. For that, each node must have a unique ID and a private key. But the question comes: where do they get the secret key from? Each of them gets it from a Trusted Authority. This authority generates the secret key from the node ID and its own master key. This trusted authority has another name called Private Key Generator (PKG). The reason of applicability of IBC in WSN is that here BS can play the role of PKG. IBC utilizes bilinear pairing for the pairwise key generation. These keys are very secure as they don't need to share any information except the unique ID. Though they are highly secure, one can not solely depend on them. The generation of pairwise keys requires high computation cost which will reduce the lifespan of the sensor nodes. So, our aim is to design a new scheme where less number of pair-wise keys are required. For that, we consider the model of cluster-based Heterogeneous Sensor network (HSN) which consists of a small number of H-sensors and a large number of L-sensors [17]. H-sensors are allocated with more resources in terms of energy, computation power, storage capacity, and transmission power than that of L-sensors [12]. It enhances performance and scalability of the network.

Key management is essential for providing authentication and confidentiality to the network. It deals with the processes of key setup, key distribution and key revocation (removal of a compromised key) [14]. The key management scheme which we propose in this paper adopts the bilinear pairing to be implemented on heterogeneous sensor nodes. From this onwards, we call our proposed scheme as 'PKHSN' for convenience. The security of the protocol is verified by using the Strand Space model. PKHSN supports the dynamic behavior of the nodes. It ensures forward and backward secrecy. Moreover, it limits the impact of a compromised node. We implement the protocol using PBC [3], GMP [1], OpenSSL [2] library and evaluate the computation time of formation of one cluster. It is observed that the final result is better as compared to Yang et al. protocol [5].

The remainder of this paper is organized as follows: Sect. 2 presents background and some of the related works. In Sect. 3, we discuss our proposed scheme. We cover the security proof of the protocol in Sect. 4. In Sect. 5 we have done security analysis and in Sect. 6, we evaluate the performance of PKHSN using simulation. Section 7 concludes the paper.

2 Background and Related Work

2.1 Background

A. Bilinear Pairing

G_1 is a group of points on an elliptic curve over F_q of order p and G_2 is a subgroup of the multiplicative group of a finite field F_{q^k} of the same order for some $k \in Z_p^*$. We assume that a discrete logarithm problem is hard both in G_1 and G_2. A mapping $e : G_1 \times G_1 \to G_2$ satisfying the following properties is called a cryptographic bilinear map.

- Bilinearity:
  $e(aP, bQ) = e(P, Q)^{ab} = e(aP, Q)^b = e(P, bQ)^a, \forall\, P, Q \in G_1$ and $a, b \in Z_p^*$.
- Non-degeneracy: If G is generator of G_1, e(G, G) is generator of G_2 i.e. $e(G, G) \neq 1$.
- Computable: e(P, Q) can be computed in polynomial-time for $\forall\, P, Q \in G_1$.
  The conventional bilinear maps are Weil Pairing [4] and Tate Pairing.

B. Mathematical Problem

The following hard cryptographic problems are used in our proposed scheme.

- Discrete Logarithm Problem (DLP): Given $P, Q \in G_1$, find an integer n such that $P = nQ$ whenever such integer exists, for $n \in Z_p^*$.
- Computational Diffie-Hellman Problem (CDHP): Given a triple $(P, aP, bP) \in G_1$ for $a, b \in Z_p^*$, find the element abP.

2.2 Related Work

Different Researchers have proposed different key management schemes. In the present study five different key management protocols have been reviewed.

The key management scheme proposed by Eschenauer and Gligor [7] is based on a probabilistic key pre-distribution concept. Prior to node deployment, a sub-set of keys from a large key pool is kept in each node. Then, each node broadcasts its key identifiers to its neighbors. The nodes which have at least one in common will start communicating. This scheme will work only if the probability of key-sharing is high. Even though the scheme seems to be simple, it requires a large storage space and small sensor nodes cannot satisfy this requirement.

Du et al. [6] presents a routing-driven key management scheme where each node establishes shared keys only with its c-neighbors using elliptic curve cryptography. c-neighbor of a node includes those nodes that are found en route from its own to the Base station.

Yang et al. [5] proposes a clustering-based key management scheme which utilizes four keys for the enhancement of security.

Kodali et al. [13] provided a scheme which is a hybrid of Identity-based cryptography (IBC) and pairwise probabilistic key distribution. IBC is applied in higher level i.e. between cluster heads and Base Station (BS) whereas, pairwise probabilistic key distribution is applied in lower level i.e. within the cluster.

In Szczechowiak and Collier [15] scheme, they skip pairing for encryption and at the same time, they have hashed identities to elliptic curves.

3   Proposed Scheme

3.1   System Model

We consider a clustered heterogeneous sensor network. The network is composed of a Base Station and sensor nodes. The nodes are of two types: High-end sensor (H-sensor) and Low-end sensor (L-sensor). H-sensors have more memory, higher transmission range, more computational power and longer battery lifetime as compared to L-sensors. L-sensor selects one H-sensor as its cluster head (CH) on the basis of signal strength. L-sensors send their collected information to their own cluster heads directly or through other L-sensors. After compressing those information, H-sensors send directly to the BS or via other CHs. Table 1 displays the notations used in this paper.

Table 1. Notations used in the paper

Symbols	Meaning
$\rightarrow$	Unicast
$\Rightarrow$	Broadcast
$\parallel$	Concatenation operator
Z_p^*	The numbers which has multiplicative inverse and less than p
CH	Cluster head
CK_{H_i}	Cluster Key of ith H-sensor
$PK_{H_i L_j}$	Pairwise key generated between H_i and L_j using bilinear pairing
$E_k(M)$	Message M is encrypted using key k using symmetric cryptography
$MAC_K(M)$	MAC (Message authentication code) value of message M generated using key K
LOC_i	i^{th} node's location

3.2   Assumptions

We consider a dynamic sensor network. Nodes do not have prior knowledge about their neighbors (considering that nodes are deployed through aerial scattering). But, they can locate their positions. It is also assumed that the nodes may be prone to attacks. If somehow a node is compromised, all of its information may be revealed. The proposed scheme follows the following communication rules:

1. BS sends messages to L-sensors via H-sensor and vice-versa.
2. H-sensors can send messages to a specific L-sensor in the cluster.
3. H-sensor can broadcast messages to all L-sensors in the cluster.
4. Generally, L-sensors do not communicate with each other except when an L-sensor cannot directly send data to any H-sensor. The advantage is that compromisation of one L-sensor will not affect other sensors in the cluster.
5. In most cases, H-sensors directly communicate with BS and those nodes which can not communicate directly to BS, send messages via other H-sensors.

3.3   Description of Our Proposed Paring-Based Key Management Scheme 'PKHSN'

PKHSN consists of mainly three phases and each phase has its own responsibility.

(A) Initialization phase: In this phase, keys and system parameters are pre-deployed in each node.
(B) Cluster formation and Intra-cluster communication phase: This phase illustrates how a cluster is formed and how cluster key is shared among L-sensor nodes.
(C) Inter-cluster communication phase: This phase explains the information exchange between CH and BS.

In addition to these phases, we talk about node addition, transition and revocation process.

PKHSN uses four keys to support different levels of security similar to [5]. For example, a message which contains cryptographic keys needs the highest level of security.

- Global key: This key is shared globally in the whole network (pre-deployed). Whenever BS needs to broadcast a message to the whole network, it uses the global key for encryption. Another use of the global key is encryption of ID. Otherwise, an attacker can snoop the ID and insert a new malicious sensor and masquerade as an authentic sensor.
- Cluster key: It is a common key which is shared among all members within a cluster. It is used to secure H-sensor's broadcast messages.
- Pairwise key: This key is generated by using bilinear pairing. It is used for one to one communication and distribution of cluster keys.
- Individual key: This key deals with direct communication with BS. It is used by sensor nodes to send critical messages like a fire alarm (Fig. 1).

Table 2. Preloaded information in each sensor node

Arguments	Description
$<q, p, G_1, G_2, Q_{BS}, e, n, H, H_1>$	System parameters
ID_i	Unique ID of ith sensor node
$IDlist$	List of all legitimate node IDs deployed in the network
S_i, Q_i	Private key and public key of ith node (Used in calculation of shared pairwise key)
GK	Global key
IK_i	Individual Key of ith node
$(r, S)_i$	Signature certificate of ith node

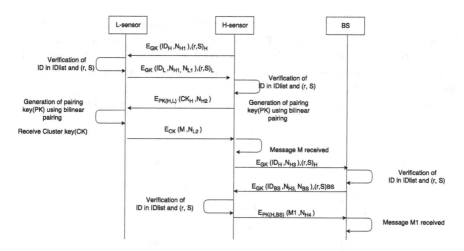

Fig. 1. Proposed protocol (PKHSN)

(A) Initialization Phase

During this initialization phase, BS performs the following operations:

Step 1: BS selects the system parameters $<q, p, G_1, G_2, Q_{BS}, e, n, H, H_1>$ and preloads in each sensor node. q and p are two large prime numbers. G is a generator of G_1. $s \in Z_p^*$ is BS's master secret and $Q_{BS} = sG \in G_1$ is BS's public key. H and H_1 are two cryptographic hash functions.

$$H: \{0,1\}^* \to G_1, H_1: G_2 \to \{0,1\}^n.$$

Step 2: BS computes private and public key for each node. For example, for a node A, $Q_A = H(ID_A)$ and private key $S_A = sQ_A$.

Step 3: BS generates an individual key (IK) with the help of a pseudo-random function. For example, for the node A, $IK_A = f_{K^I}(ID_A)$ where K^I is secret to BS. BS does not store individual keys, they are created only on demand. Due to the computational efficiency of the pseudo-random function, the computational overhead is negligible.

Step 4: BS deploys the global key and the signature certificate (r, S). (r, S) to provides authenticity. (r, S) is generated by Elliptic Curve Digital Signature Algorithm (ECDSA) [10]. ECDSA is described below:

BS selects a random integer $k \in Z_n^*$ and it generates $(r, S)_A$ as follows: $Q_A = H(ID_A), r = kG = (x_r, y_r), S = k^{-1}(Q_A + sx_r)(mod q)$

The verification process is like below:

$Q_A = H(ID_A), v_1 = r^{-1}Q_A(mod q)$ $v_2 = r^{-1}x_r(mod q), V = v_1 G + v_2 Q_{BS}$

To prove a node to be legitimate: $V = S$. From above, it is observed that the cost of verification is low. Hence, ECDSA can be implemented in sensor nodes.

Step 5: A list of all legitimate node IDs ($IDlist$) is stored each node (Assumption: node ID is of few bits). The primary reason for storing IDs is to save energy.

If some attackers target the network by sending messages too many with fake ID and wrong (r, S), the large part of the node's energy will be wasted in unnecessary verification and eventually, it will decrease the lifetime of the nodes. In that case, maintaining an $IDlist$ would help in saving energy only by matching the received ID with $IDlist$.

The preloaded information that are stored in each sensor node are shown in Table 2.

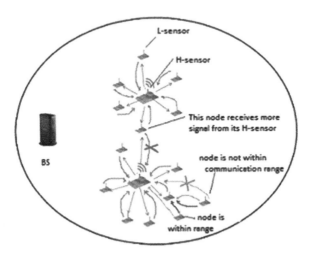

Fig. 2. Exchange of messages during cluster formation

(B) Cluster formation and Intra cluster communication Phase

The Cluster formation and Intra cluster communication Phase (Fig. 2) that is carried out between H-sensor and L-sensor is as follows.

Step 1: After deployment, H-sensor nodes initiate communication. They broadcast a HELLO message to their neighbors. HELLO message contains its own ID, a nonce which is encrypted with the global key (GK) and a signature certificate (r, S).

$$H_i \Rightarrow *: E_{GK}(ID_{H_i}, N_{H1}), (r, S)_{H_i}$$

Step 2: Upon receiving the HELLO message from H-sensor, the L-sensor first decrypts the message via Global key and check whether the node ID is in $IDlist$ or not. If the result is positive, then only it verifies the signature certificate. It may happen that one L-sensor may receive HELLO message from more than one H-sensor. In that case, it selects the one which has the highest signal strength and saves the next one for future. If the signal strengths are same, then the decision is made on the basis of battery power.

Step 3: After successful completion of decryption and verification, L-sensor encrypts its own ID, its nonce and nonce of the selected H-sensor using the global key and send to the H-sensor as an acknowledgment.

$$L_j \Rightarrow H_i: E_{GK}(ID_{L_j}, N_{H1}, N_{L1}), (r, S)_{L_j}$$

Step 4: After receiving the above message, H-sensor does similar verification like L-sensor. It generates the Cluster Key, $CK \epsilon Z_n^*$ and shares it to all its L-sensors using the pairwise key.

For example, H_i generates a pairwise key using bilinear pairing to communicate with its neighbor L_j

$$PK_{H_i L_j} = e(Q_{L_j}, S_{H_i}) = e(Q_{L_j}, sQ_{H_i}) = e(sQ_{L_j}, Q_{H_i}) = PK_{L_j H_i}$$

Suppose, H_i sends the CK to L_j using pairwise key $PK_{H_i L_j}$

$$H_i \rightarrow L_j: E_{PK_{H_i L_j}}(CK_{H_i} \| N_{H_i}) \| MAC_{E_{PK_{H_i L_j}}}(CK_{H_i} \| N_{H_i})$$

MAC is sent to ensure the integrity of the message.

Step 5: On receiving the message from CH, L-sensor decrypts by using the pairwise key and gets the cluster key. After that, they become a part of the CH easing sending of information to CH. On the event of missing a HELLO message from any of the H-sensors, an L-sensor L_M broadcasts an EXPLORE message after a fixed interval of time. The EXPLORE contains encrypted ID_M, its nonce and $(r, S)_M$.

$$L_M \Rightarrow *: E_{GK}(ID_M, N_M), (r, S)_M$$

Suppose L_K is the neighboring node receiving this message. First, it checks the authenticity of the message and sends an acknowledgment only if it possesses a Cluster key. This ACK basically contains its encrypted ID, its own nonce, nonce of the L-sensor and (r, S).

Similarly, L_M may get acknowledgments from various other neighbors. Let L_M receives the first acknowledgment from L_K. Then it authenticates L_K and sends its location to L_K using the Pairwise Key $PK_{L_M L_K}$. Now they can communicate by $PK_{L_M L_K}$ ignoring other acknowledgments. Now, L_K will send the ID list of the nodes similar to L_M to its CH using CK. It also sends locations of those nodes along with the ID list.

$$L_K \rightarrow CH: E_{CK}(ID_M, ID_N ..., LOC_M, LOC_N ...)$$

After receiving this message, H-sensor checks whether these nodes are in the communication range or not (The range is set prior to deployment and after testing). If yes, then H-sensor broadcasts its encrypted ID and (r, S) to those nodes. The receiving nodes verify the H-sensor and later the H-sensor send the CK using the pairwise key.

Even if EXPLORE message is sent to all neighbors, some nodes may fail to receive HELLO message from any of the H-sensors. Those nodes send its sensed information to the previous nearby L-sensor for which it has already created the pairwise key.

(C) Inter Cluster communication

After completion of cluster formation, each H-sensor broadcasts encrypted ID and (r, S). On receiving this message, BS verifies and sends ACK containing encrypted ID and (r, S). Now information exchange is possible between BS and H-sensor through the Pairwise key.

$$H_i \rightarrow BS: E_{PK_{BS,H}}(ID_{H_i}, M_{aggregated}, N_{H3})$$

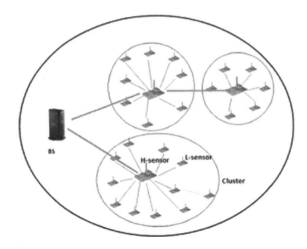

Fig. 3. CH sends messages to BS forwarded by L-sensor

For distantly located H-sensors, it is not possible to send the information directly to the BS. Those nodes send their locations to nearby H-sensors using pairwise key. Then BS tries to find a Shorted Path Tree (rooted at BS) by running Dijkstra's Algorithm. After finding, it sends the SPT to all H-sensors. So when H-sensor receives information from L-sensors, they aggregate and compress the data and send to BS by looking at SPT (Fig. 3).

Since many cryptanalytic attacks become easy if we send information using a specific key, that's why it is better to use a session key. So for communication between H-sensor and BS or between two H-sensors, first a session key is shared among them using the pairwise key. This session key is used to share information among them.

3.4   Joining of New Node

Sometimes to increase the lifetime of the network, new nodes are added in the network. All the required information (keys and system parameters) are preloaded in the nodes.

After the deployment of those new nodes, BS send an ADDITION message containing ID_{new} to all H-sensors using pairwise key.

$$BS \rightarrow H\colon E_{PK_{BS,H}}(ID_{new}), MAC_{PK_{BS,H}}(ID_{new})$$

Upon receiving this message, H-sensor adds the new ID to the $IDlist$. A new Cluster key is generated and broadcasts the new ID and new Cluster key to its L-sensors using old Cluster key.

$$H_i \rightarrow *\colon E_{CK_{H_i}}(ID_{new} \parallel CK_{new}), MAC_{CK_{H_i}}(ID_{new} \parallel CK_{new})$$

When an L-sensor receives the above message, it add the new ID to it's $IDlist$.

Since H-sensor broadcasts HELLO message periodically, so the new node will send an ACK or it will broadcast an EXPLORE message. This process is similar to Cluster formation and Intra cluster communication Phase.

3.5 Node Revocation

We assume that BS has an intrusion detection mechanism to detect malicious node [18]. When a compromised node is detected, BS will send a REVOCATION message containing node ID which is to be revoked and a new global key to all H-sensors using pairwise key.

$$BS \rightarrow CH \colon E_{PK_{BS,CH}}(ID_{revoked} \parallel GK_{new}), MAC_{PK_{BS,CH}}(ID_{revoked} \parallel GK_{new})$$

Upon receiving this message, H-sensor removes that ID from $IDlist$ and deletes the corresponding pairwise key. Then H-sensor checks if the node in its cluster. If yes, then generate a new Cluster key and send a REVOCATION message containing global key and Cluster key to all its L-sensors using pairwise key.

$$H_i \rightarrow L_j \colon E_{PK_{H_i,L_j}}(ID_{revoked} \parallel CK_{new} \parallel GK_{new}),$$
$$MAC_{PK_{H_i,L_j}}(ID_{revoked} \parallel CK_{new} \parallel GK_{new})$$

After receiving this message, L-sensor removes that ID from $IDlist$ and deletes the pairwise key generated for that ID (if present).

3.6 Node Transition

Since the nodes are mobile, a node may move from one cluster to another. In that case, its CH will not receive any message from it. After a fixed duration (which should be set previously depending on the information that the nodes collect), it will remove the ID of that node from the $IDlist$ and informs the same to its L-sensors. Moreover, the cluster key is also updated. Now, the departing node can not decrypt the earlier messages.

$$H \rightarrow L \colon E_{PK_{H,L}}(ID_{remove} \parallel CK_{new}), MAC(ID_{remove} \parallel CK_{new})$$

A departing node joins to a new CH similar to node addition.

3.7 Forward and Backward Secrecy

A new cluster key is generated and distributed after a new node joins the network. So the newly joined node cannot retrieve earlier messages and thus backward secrecy is attained. On the other way, whenever a node moves from the existing cluster or network, the rekeying process starts and new cluster key is generated and it helps to achieve forward secrecy as the outgoing node can't decipher new messages.

3.8   Re-keying Scheme

For better security, after some time interval global key and cluster key should be updated. BS sends new global key to all H-sensors using pairwise key. The H-sensors on receiving the new global key generates a new cluster key and send the new global key and cluster key using old cluster key.

$$BS \rightarrow CH\text{:} E_{PK_{BS,CH}}(GK_{new} \parallel MAC_{PK_{BS,CH}}(GK_{new}))$$

$$H_i \rightarrow *\text{:} E_{CK_{H_i}}(CK_{new} \parallel GK_{new}), MAC_{CK_{H_i}}(CK_{new} \parallel GK_{new})$$

4   Security Proof of PKHSN Using Strand Space Model

A security protocol needs to be verified. There are mainly two ways: ad-hoc analysis and formal analysis. In an ad-hoc analysis, all probable attacks are analyzed based on different scenarios. This is a tiresome task and not practicable. On the other hand, formal analysis is a way to systematically analyze the security protocol. It assures the correctness and helps to find out vulnerabilities. Different frameworks are available to verify the security of a protocol such as Model Checking, Strand Space model, and BAN Logic. Here we have adopted Strand space model as it is one of the most efficient and simple model to proof.

A strand is a series of message exchange between two or more participants in a security protocol. Participants may either be legitimate or intruder. The collection of strands are named as Strand space. A bundle is a portion of a strand space. It consists of a number of strands where one strand sends a message and another strand receives it. Each bundle must contain one strand for each legitimate parties which are participating in the session. Penetrator strands may also be entangled in the bundle. But they should not prevent legitimate parties to agree on data values, or from maintaining the secrecy of the chosen values. A Bundle is a collection of all activities during one run of the protocol [8].

For the clear understanding of formal analysis of the proposed scheme, some definitions and theorems related to strand space model are mentioned below:

4.1   Definitions

Definition (i) Let $\mathcal{M}$ is the set of messages that are exchanged between different participants in a protocol. The elements of $\mathcal{M}$ are called as terms. The set $\mathcal{M}$ is generated from two disjoint sets $\mathcal{N}$ and $\mathcal{K}$. $\mathcal{N}$ represents texts such as name or nonces. $\mathcal{K}$ represents keys. so $\mathcal{M}$ is the result of concatenation and encryption of messages from set $\mathcal{N}$ and $\mathcal{K}$. For example, the concatenation of terms p and q is expressed as $p \circ q$ and the encryption of q using key k is denoted $\{q\}_k$.

Definition (ii) If a term t' can be obtained from another term t by using repeated concatenation and encryption, then t' is called as subterm of t and expressed as $t \sqsubset t'$.

Definition (iii) The transmission and reception of a term t is represented as $+t$ and $-t$ respectively.

Definition (iv) A strand element is called a node. $<s, j>$ is the jth node on strand s.

Definition (v) Suppose, m and m' are two nodes on strand s. If $m = <s, j>$ and $m' = <s, j + 1>$, then we can express this relation as $m \Rightarrow m'$.

Definition (vi) A regular strand represents a strand of legitimate participants in the protocol and a penetrator strand represents a strand of attackers'.

Definition (vii) The set of keys that a penetrator can access is represented as $\mathcal{P}$. $\mathcal{P}$ includes penetrator's own private key and public keys of all the participants.

Definition (viii) The set of keys that penetrator has no access is called safe keys ($\mathcal{S}$). So set $\mathcal{P}$ and $\mathcal{S}$ are disjoint.

Definition (ix) A penetrator can participate in a protocol. They read and modify a transmitted message and can inject new messages. They have the ability to replay a message and initiate an instance of the protocol with any of the participants. Following are the capabilities of a penetrator:

C. Concatenation: $<-p, -q, +p \circ q>$
S. Separation: $<-p \circ q, +p, +q>$
K. Key: $<+K>$ where $K \in \mathcal{P}$
E. Encryption: $<-K, -m, +\{m\}_K>$
D. Decryption: $<-K^{-1}, -\{m\}_K, +m>$

Definition (x) A component is either an atomic value or encryption. A term is called component if it is not a concatenated value. For example, term t_1 is a component of t if $t_1 \sqsubset t$ and for each $t' \neq t_1$ satisfying $t_1 \sqsubset t' \sqsubset t$ is a concatenated term.

Definition (xi) If t is a component of node $n = <s, x>$ and if it does appear in any component of node $<s, y>$ for every $y < x$, then the component is new at $n = <s, x>$.

Definition (xii) The edge $n \Rightarrow n'$ is a ***transformed edge*** for $a \in A$ if n is positive and n' is negative, $a \sqsubset \text{term}(n)$ and there is a new component t' of n' such that $a \sqsubset t'$.

Definition (xiii) The edge $n \Rightarrow n'$ is a ***transforming edge*** for $a \in A$ if n is negative and n' is positive, $a \sqsubset \text{term}(n)$ and there is a new component t' of n' such that $a \sqsubset t'$.

Definition (xiv) $t = \{h\}_K$ is a *test component* for a in n if $a \sqsubset t$, is a component of n; t is not a proper subterm of a component of any regular node n'.

Definition (xv) A term t originates at a node $n = <s, i>$ if the sign of n is positive, $t \sqsubset \text{term}(n)$, and $t \not\sqsubset \text{term}(<s, j>)$ for every $j < i$. If a value originates on only one node in the strand space, it is called uniquely originating.

Definition (xvi) The edge $n \Rightarrow n'$ is a test for a if a uniquely originates at n and $n \Rightarrow n'$ is a transformed edge for a.

4.2   Authentication Tests

Thayer and Guttman [9] introduced the idea of authentication tests to proof the authentication goal of the security protocol. For that we have to identify the test components and verify whether they fulfill certain constraints or not. For the authentication of the participants, one of the following authentication tests must be satisfied.

Outgoing Test: In this test, participant sends a uniquely originating value e.g., a nonce in an encrypted form. The receiver is challenged to decrypt it and the result is sent back to the sender in another form.

Incoming Test: Here a participant sends a uniquely originating value. The receiver is challenged to generate its encrypted form and sends it back to the sender.

Unsolicited Test: Here a message is received without explicit request in a form that can only be produced by legitimate participants.

In the formal analysis of our proposed scheme, we use outgoing test and unsolicited test. The definitions and theorems for outgoing test and unsolicited test are stated below:

Definition 1. The edge $n \Rightarrow n'$ is an outgoing test for a in $t = \{h\}_K$ if it is a test for a in which $K^{-1} \notin \mathcal{P}$; a does not occur in any component of n other than t; and t is a test component for a in n.

Definition 2. A negative node n is an unsolicited test for $t = \{h\}_K$ if t is a test component for any a in n and $K \notin \mathcal{P}$.

Theorem 1. (Authentication Test 1) If $n \Rightarrow n'$ is an outgoing test for a in t, then there exist regular nodes m and m' such that t is a component of m and $m \Rightarrow m'$ is a transforming edge for a. If a occurs only in component $t_1 = \{h_1\}_{K_1}$ of m', t_1 is not a proper subterm of any regular component and $K_1^{-1} \notin \mathcal{P}$, then there is a negative regular node m'' with t_1 as a component.

Theorem 2. (Authentication Test 3) If n is an unsolicited test for $t = \{h\}_K$, then there exists a positive regular node m such that t is a component of m.

4.3   Formal Analysis

The interacting parties of the protocol are: Base Station (BS), H-sensor (H) and L-sensor (L).

GOAL: After completion of one instance of the protocol, a secure connection must be ensured among L-sensors and H-sensors. Similarly, H-sensor, and BS should also have a secure connection.

During the 1st run of the protocol, L-sensors receive cluster key from the H-sensors. Now, L-sensor and H-sensor are ready for message exchange. After 2nd run of the protocol, H-sensor and BS can interact with a pairwise key. Figures 4 and 6 demonstrate Bundle1 and 2. Figures 5 and 7 represent the regular strand traces for Bundle1 and 2.

A strand space for the protocol can be defined as a combination of a set of penetrator strands and regular strand traces. Each identifier has a unique value. $K_{CK} \neq N_H \neq N_{H1} \neq N_{H2} \neq N_{H3} \neq N_L \neq N_{BS} \neq N_{BS1}$.

Unlike the original protocol, strand space model is somewhat different from its predecessor due to its particular features.

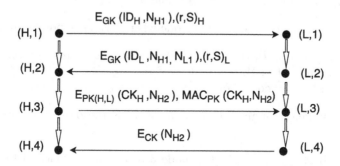

Fig. 4. Bundle1

$H\,[K_{GK}\,,\,ID_H\,,N_{H1}\,,K_{CK}\,,\,N_{H2},\,K_{PK(H,L)}\,]$ $L\,[K_{GK}\,,\,ID_{L1},N_{L1},\,K_{PK(H,L)}\,]$

1. $<+\{\,ID_H\,o\,\,N_{H1}\}K_{GK}$ $<-\{\,ID_H\,o\,\,N_{H1}\}K_{GK}$

2. $-\{\,ID_L\,o\,\,N_{H1}\,o\,N_{L1}\,\}K_{GK}$ $+\{\,ID_L\,o\,\,N_{H1}\,o\,N_{L1}\}K_{GK}$

3. $+\{\,K_{CK}\,o\,\,N_{H2}\,\}K_{PK(H,L)}$ $-\{\,K_{CK}\,o\,\,N_{H2}\,\}K_{PK(H,L)}$

4. $-\{\,N_{H2}\,\}K_{CK}\,>$ $+\{\,N_{H2}\,\}K_{CK}\,>$

Fig. 5. Strand Space format for Bundle 1

(i)   The global key (GK) is pre-stored in sensor nodes before deployment. Therefore, it is difficult to model it in terms of strand space model. Hence, we have considered it has already occurred.

(ii) Modeling of Pairwise key (PK) is hard because of limitations of Strand Space model which handle only ideal cryptography. Therefore, we model it as pre-shared secret key.

(iii) Due to high-security nature of ECDSA algorithm, signature (r, S) verification can be skipped in Strand space model.

(iv) Here, MAC only checks whether an encrypted message has been modified or not during transit. So they are excluded in Strand Space model.

Authentication Tests for Bundle1

Lemma 1. If $K_{GK} \notin \mathcal{P}$, then node 1 of L is an unsolicited test for $t = \{ID_H \circ N_{H1}\}_{K_{GK}}$ where m = node 1 of H and $a = N_{H1}$.

Proof. m is the only positive regular node where t is a component of m.

Lemma 2. If $K_{GK} \notin \mathcal{P}$, then node 2 of H is an unsolicited test for $t = \{ID_L \circ N_{H1} \circ N_{L1}\}_{K_{GK}}$ where m = node 2 of L and $a = N_{L1}$.

Proof. m is the only positive regular node where t is a component of m.

Lemma 3. If $K_{GK} \notin \mathcal{P}$, then $n \Rightarrow n'$ is an outgoing authentication test for a in t where n = node 1 of H, n' = node 2 of H, $a = N_{H1}$, $t = \{ID_H \circ N_{H1}\}_{K_{GK}}$ m = node 1 of L, m' = node 2 of L.

Proof. N_{H1} uniquely originates at n. $m \Rightarrow m'$ is the only transforming edge for a.

Lemma 4. If $K_{PK(H,L)} \notin \mathcal{P}$, then node 3 of L is an unsolicited test for $t = \{K_{CK} \circ N_{H2}\}_{K_{PK(H,L)}}$ where m = node 3 of H and $a = K_{CK}$.

Proof. m is the only positive regular node where t is a component of m.

Lemma 5. If $K_{PK(H,L)} \notin \mathcal{P}$, then $n \Rightarrow n'$ is an outgoing authentication test for a in t where n = node 3 of H, n' = node 4 of H, $a = N_{H2}$, $t = \{K_{CK} \circ N_{H2}\}_{K_{PK(H,L)}}$ where m = node 3 of L, m' = node 4 of L.

Proof. N_{H2} uniquely originates at n. $m \Rightarrow m'$ is the only transforming edge for a.

Authentication Tests for Bundle2

Lemma 6. If $K_{GK} \notin \mathcal{P}$, then node 1 of BS is an unsolicited test for $t = \{ID_H \circ N_{H3}\}_{K_{GK}}$ where m = node 1 of H and $a = N_{H3}$.

Proof. m is the only positive regular node where t is a component of m.

Lemma 7. If $K_{GK} \notin \mathcal{P}$, then node 2 of H is an unsolicited test for $t = \{ID_{BS} \circ N_{H3} \circ N_{BS}\}_{K_{GK}}$ where m = node 2 of BS and $a = N_{BS}$.

Proof. m is the only positive regular node where t is a component of m.

Lemma 8. If $K_{GK} \notin \mathcal{P}$, then $n \Rightarrow n'$ is an outgoing authentication test for a in t where n = node 1 of H, n' = node 2 of H, $a = N_{H2}$, $t = \{ID_H \circ N_{H3}\}_{K_{GK}}$, m = node 1 of BS, m' = node 2 of BS.

Proof. N_{H2} uniquely originates at n. $m \Rightarrow m'$ is the only transforming edge for a.

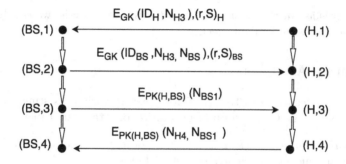

Fig. 6. Bundle2

BS [K_{GK}, ID_{BS}, N_{BS}, N_{BS1}, $K_{PK(H,BS)}$]   H [K_{GK}, ID_H, N_{H3}, N_{H4}, $K_{PK(H,BS)}$]

1.	$<-\{ ID_H \circ N_{H3} \}K_{GK}$	$<+\{ ID_H \circ N_{H3} \}K_{GK}$
2.	$+\{ ID_{BS} \circ N_{H3} \circ N_{BS} \}K_{GK}$	$-\{ ID_{BS} \circ N_{H3} \circ N_{BS} \}K_{GK}$
3.	$+\{ N_{BS1} \}K_{PK(H,BS)}$	$-\{ N_{BS1} \}K_{PK(H,BS)}$
4.	$-\{ N_{H4} \circ N_{BS1} \}K_{PK(H,BS)} >$	$+\{ N_{H4} \circ N_{BS1} \}K_{PK(H,BS)} >$

Fig. 7. Strand Space format for Bundle 2

Lemma 9. If $K_{PK(H,BS)} \notin \mathcal{P}$, then node 3 of H is an unsolicited test for $t = \{N_{BS1}\}_{K_{PK(H,BS)}}$ where m = node 3 of BS and $a = N_{BS1}$.

Proof. m is the only positive regular node where t is a component of m.

Lemma 10. If $K_{PK(H,BS)} \notin \mathcal{P}$, then $n \Rightarrow n'$ is an outgoing authentication test for a in t where n = node 3 of BS, n' = node 4 of BS, $a = N_{BS}$, $t = \{N_{BS1}\}_{K_{PK(H,BS)}}$, m = node 3 of H, m' = node 4 of H.

Proof. N_{BS1} uniquely originates at n. $m \Rightarrow m'$ is the only transforming edge for a.

Penetrator Analysis

The main goal of the penetrator is to impersonate H to L. The penetrator should able to produce every message that L expects from H.

But $K_{GK} \in \mathcal{S}$, $K_{PK(H,L)} \in \mathcal{S}$, $K_{CK} \in \mathcal{S}$ ($\mathcal{S}$ represents the set of Safe keys). These keys are not terms of any penetrator. Therefore, the penetrator cannot impersonate H to L, L to H, BS to H and H to BS.

Discussion

After the 1st protocol run, H will be authenticated to L (Lemma 1 satisfies). Similarly, L will be authenticated to H (Lemma 2 holds).

At the end of 2nd protocol run, H will be authenticated to BS (Lemma 6 holds). Similarly, BS will be authenticated to H (Lemma 7 holds). In both of the runs, secure key sharing is successful since Lemmas 5 and 10 holds true. So, secrecy is satisfied in this protocol. From the above analysis, we conclude that the proposed protocol is highly secure.

5   Security Analysis

We analyze the security of PKHSN with respect to various existing attacks.
    We also show the Comparison of prevention of attacks in Table 3.

- *Man-in-the-Middle-Attack:* This attack is not feasible since keys are generated without any message exchange except node ID.
- *Masquerade attack:* In this attack, attacker somehow able to sneak into the credentials of a sensor node. Later, the attacker acts as a legitimate user between the communicating parties inside the network. In PKHSN, the nodes are authenticated via signature certificate which makes the attack infeasible.
- *Replay attack:* Replay attack is prevented by sending a nonce along with the message.
- *Clone attack:* An attacker can retrieve all the secret information stored in a node by physically capturing. Then, the attacker can place replicas of that node in various locations. In order to sort out this problem, each H-sensor is required to send its member ID list to the BS along with another message after some fixed interval of time. BS performs the intersection of those lists sent by all H-sensors. If the result is not null, respective H-sensor is informed. After that global key and cluster key is updated.
- *Sinkhole attack:* In the sinkhole attack, a malicious node attracts traffic from its neighbors (by broadcasting forged data like high residual energy, high transmission power) and later drops it. In PKHSN, CHs are authenticated to BS or other CHs by signature certificate and exchange information using pairwise key. Moreover, L-sensor nodes only send their reading to trusted CHs, so sinkhole attack does not succeed.
- *Node Capture attack:* After the capture of a node, essential information like keys may be disclosed. A straightforward solution is to use tamper-resistant nodes. But, it will increase the network cost. Another approach is to use self-destructive mechanism. In that case, if some abnormal activities are detected, then RAM and flash memory are erased and node's radio service and measuring capabilities are destroyed. But, here we can't ignore the possibility of destruction of a genuine node (by mistake). One positive aspect is that PKHSN minimizes the impact of compromised nodes through its clustered design. Moreover, we can apply the following approaches:
  - (i) Relying on the reading of a single sensor should be avoided, rather waiting for other responses should be encouraged. CH can identify the malicious nodes after analyzing the reading of other authentic sensors.
  - (ii) SCADD proposed by Jokhio et al. [11] provides detection as well as defense against the node capture attack via carefully planned security strategies. We can apply SCADD as it is scalable, lightweight and has less processing overhead.

Table 3. The Comparison of prevention of attacks

Attack	Du et al. [6]	Yang et al. [5]	PKHSN
Man-in-the-middle-attack	Yes	Yes	Yes
Masquerade attack	No	No	Yes
Replay attack	No	Yes	Yes
Clone attack	No	No	Yes
Sinkhole attack	No	Yes	Yes
Node capture attack	No	No	Yes

6   Performance Analysis

In this section, we evaluate the performance of our proposed scheme PKHSN.

We also present a Point-wise Comparison between Yang et al. protocol [5] and PKHSN in Table 6.

6.1   Comparison of Computation Costs

Computation cost is the first measure of energy consumption by sensor nodes. To investigate the computation cost of PKHSN, we conduct our experiment on a machine having the following configuration: Fedora 16; Memory: 2 GB; Processor: Intel Core 2 Duo 2.10 GHz. The Libraries used in our experiment are: PBC (Pairing-based Cryptography) Library version 0.5.14 [3], GMP (GNU Multiple Precision Arithmetic) library version 6.0.0 [1] and OpenSSL (Open Source toolkit for SSL/TLS) version 1.0.1 [2]. We use AES-192 as the symmetric encryption algorithm. Type-A curve with default parameters is used for ECC and pairing.

Table 4 displays some operations used in PKHSN and their average computation cost.

Table 4. Time cost of different operations which are used in PKHSN

Parameters	Computation time (sec)
ECDSA signature generation	0.001733
ECDSA signature verification	0.00109
Encryption of ID and nonce using global key	0.0002328
Decryption of the message	0.000232

The reason for comparing PKHSN's computation cost only with [5] is that only Yang's work has addressed this issue pertaining to bilinear pairing for key generation. So, we have provided a detailed comparative performance analysis between Yang et al. scheme [5] and PKHSN.

In Yang's scheme [5], each node broadcasts the node ID and (r, S). From that, each node calculates its own neighbor list. H-sensor sends its neighbor list and a unique cluster key to its neighboring L-sensors. Every L-sensor compares its own neighbor list with the corresponding list sent by the CH. Then it forms a link list (*lklists*) by performing the following set operation: ($nblist_L - nblist_H$).

With the nodes of the generated lklists, L-sensor forms pairwise keys. The loophole of the scheme is that some of the nodes of the link list may also be the member of other H-sensors contributing to wastage of computation of pairwise keys. But in our proposed scheme, there is no need to calculate the neighbor list and link list. Moreover pairwise key formation and signature verification is much less in our case.

Suppose, each cluster in the network has 'n' number of L-sensor nodes. In PKHSN, within a cluster, total number of message exchange between H-sensor and L-sensor is $2n + 1$ (considering up to sending a cluster key). The total number of encryption and decryption are $2n + 1$, $3n$ respectively. But in [5], though there is same number of message exchange and encryption, the number of decryption scales up by a factor of 'd * n'. d is the connection degree of each L-sensor (expresses the density). So, in a densely connected network, the value of d is much higher. Decryption represents - (a) ID and nonce decryption and (b) Signature verification.

Table 5. Comparison of computation time of Yang et al. protocol [5] and PKHSN (Formation of one cluster)

Protocol	Computation time (sec)
Yang et al. protocol [5]	11.4958
PKHSN	11.21656

In our experiment, we have assumed that, there are 100 L-sensors in each cluster. They are uniformly distributed. We assume the connection degree of each node is 3. Table 5 presents the comparison of computation time required to form one cluster for both the schemes Yang et al. [5] and PKHSN.

Figure 8 demonstrates the density impact of the network on computation time. In PKHSN, computation time is observed to be constant even with increase of density but that is not the case with [5] which increases linearly with density.

6.2   Comparison in the Number of Pairwise Keys Generation

Generation of pairwise keys has a significant effect in energy consumption by sensor nodes. Because it involves high computation. In Yang's scheme [5], more pairwise keys are generated. It is due to the fact that L-sensor generates pairwise keys with more than one H-sensor. Because it generates pairwise keys before choosing CH. In a high density network, one L-sensor may get more HELLO messages from more than one H-sensor. Contrary to [5], in PKHSN, each

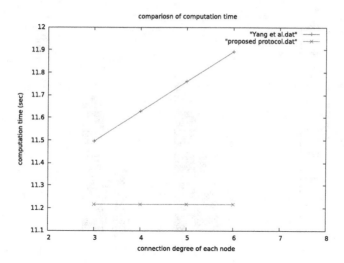

Fig. 8. Comparison of computation time

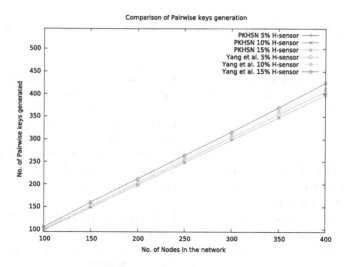

Fig. 9. Comparison in the number of generated pairwise keys

L-sensor generates pairwise keys for the H-sensor which it chooses as cluster head which in turn reduces the number of pairwise key formation. From Fig. 9, it is observed that, with the increase in the number of H-sensors, more number of pairwise keys are generated in Yang et al. scheme. On the other hand, the number of pairwise key remains constant in PKHSN even if there is an increase in H-sensors. This clearly indicates that the number of generated pairwise keys is less in PKHSN sets clear advantage over [5].

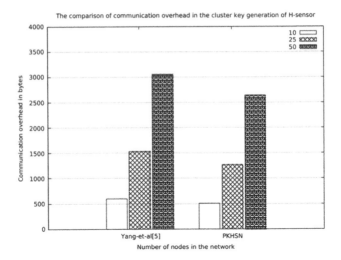

Fig. 10. Comparison of communication overhead in the cluster key generation of H-sensor

Table 6. Point-wise Comparison between Yang et al. protocol[5] and PKHSN

Yang et al. protocol [5]	PKHSN
Each L-sensor node needs to verify the signature certificate (r, S) of all of its neighboring nodes	Each L-sensor node has to verify only CH's (r, S). This results in less computation overhead. Though H-sensor verifies all the neighboring L-sensors, due to high resource availability it does not get affected
Due to the exchange of ID and (r, S) without encryption, masquerade attack can take place	We use the encrypted version of ID and (r, S) to avoid this attack
In case of large malicious requests from an attacker, the node's energy is wasted unnecessarily in verifying (r, S)	In PKHSN, ID is checked in IDlist and no need to go for further signature (r, S) verification reducing energy consumption
They have not stated how the message exchange will take place in case of H-sensor situated at the location directly unreachable to BS	PKHSN has the advantage of communication of H-sensor nodes which are far away from BS
H-sensor sends cluster key and the neighbor list to its L-sensors	Here, H-sensor only sends cluster key which infers less communication energy

6.3   Comparison of Communication Costs

Communication cost is another measure of energy consumed by sensor nodes. It is determined by the total length of messages exchanged among H-sensor, L-sensor and BS.

The Fig. 10 shows the communication overhead in the generation of cluster key for both the schemes (Yang et al. [5] and PKHSN). The simulation is performed by taking 10, 25 and 50 nodes at a time for both the schemes. It is observed that the communication overhead generated for PKHSN is lower than that of Yang et al. scheme for all the three cases. That infers PKHSN performs better in terms of communication overhead, thereby saving energy. This is because, PKHSN does not require to send neighbor list and *linklist* like that of [5].

6.4   Comparison of Storage Cost

Suppose, the number of H-sensors and L-sensors in the network are m and n respectively. Obviously m < n.

In E-G scheme [7], K keys are pre-loaded in each sensor. So, total number of pre-loaded keys in the whole network: $K * (m + n)$.

The value K depends on key pool size S and the probability of key sharing (at least one key) between two sensors. If we want to achieve the key-sharing probability of 0.9 and if $S = 10000$, m must be greater than 150 [7].

In Du et al. [6], one private key and public keys of all H-sensors are pre-deployed in each L-sensor. On the other hand, each H-sensor is pre-loaded with public keys of all L-sensors. Along with that, a pair of private-public key pair, a key K_H for the new deployed sensor are also pre-loaded in H-sensor. Thus, the total number of keys that are pre-loaded in a network: $m * (n + 3) + 2 * n = (m + 2) * n + 3 * m$.

In the case of PKHSN, each L-sensor node is preloaded with 3 keys (global key, private key, and public key). Each H-sensor also stores the same 3 keys as L-sensor. So, total pre-deployed keys in the entire network having $m + n$ nodes: $m * 3 + n * 3 = 3 * (m + n)$.

Suppose, n = 1000 and m = 20. Figure 11 shows the comparison of pre-deployed keys in all the schemes [5–7] and PKHSN. The x-axis represents the number of L-sensor nodes(n) in the network. We fix the number of H-sensor nodes (m = 20). The y-axis represents the number of pre-deployed keys.

From the graph above, we can see that PKHSN and Yang et al. [5] has same number of pre-deployed keys. But, after the execution of the protocols, the storage space required in case of Yang et al. will be more than PKHSN. The reason is that Yang et al. scheme needs to store more pairwise keys as each L-sensor generates pairwise key for all reachable H-sensors.

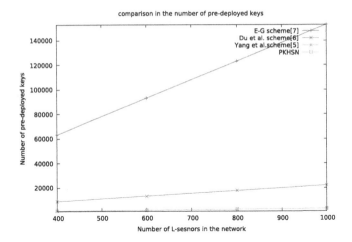

Fig. 11. Comparison of communication overhead in the cluster key generation of H-sensor

7 Conclusion

In this paper, we have proposed a key management scheme for heterogeneous sensor networks based on bilinear pairing and Identity-based cryptography. The proposed protocol can be used in low power sensor nodes due to lower consumption of energy (due to lower communication overhead and lower computation cost). It is also applicable in mobile node scenario. The robustness of the proposed scheme is analyzed and security is verified using Strand Space model. In future, we have plan to evaluate the energy consumption of our proposed scheme and compare with the existing schemes.

Acknowledgments. Authors would like to thank Nazatul Haque Sultan for his valuable suggestion.

References

1. gmp library. https://www.gmplib.org/. Accessed 10 May 2017
2. The openssl project. https://www.openssl.org/. Accessed 10 May 2017
3. Pbc: Pairing based cryptography. https://www.crypto.stanford.edu/pbc/. Accessed 10 May 2017
4. Boneh, D., Franklin, M.: Identity-based encryption from the weil pairing. In: Kilian, J. (ed.) CRYPTO 2001. LNCS, vol. 2139, pp. 213–229. Springer, Heidelberg (2001). https://doi.org/10.1007/3-540-44647-8_13
5. Yang, K., Zheng, K., Yang, Y., Guo, S.: Pairing-based key management scheme for heterogeneous sensor networks. In: 2010 6th International Conference on Wireless Communications Networking and Mobile Computing (WiCOM), p. 15. IEEE (2010)

6. Du, X., Xiao, Y., Ci, S., Guizani, M., Chen, H.-H.: A routing-driven key management scheme for heterogeneous sensor networks. In: IEEE International Conference on Communications, ICC 2007, pp. 3407–3412. IEEE (2007)

7. Eschenauer, L., Gligor, V.D.: A key-management scheme for distributed sensor networks. In: Proceedings of the 9th ACM Conference on Computer and Communications Security, pp. 41–47. ACM (2002)

8. Fabrega, F.J.T.H, Herzog, J.C., Guttman, J.D.: Strand spaces: why is a security protocol correct? In: Proceedings of 1998 IEEE Symposium on Security and Privacy, 1998 , pp. 160–171. IEEE (1998)

9. Guttman, J.D., Thayer, F.J.: Authentication tests. In: Proceedings of 2000 IEEE Symposium on Security and Privacy, 2000, pp. 96–109. IEEE (2000)

10. Johnson, D., Menezes, A., Vanstone, S.: The elliptic curve digital sig- nature algorithm (ECDSA). Int. J. Inf. Secur. 1(1), 36–63 (2001)

11. Jokhio, S.H., Jokhio, I.A., Kemp, A.H.: Node capture attack detection and defence in wireless sensor networks. IET Wirel. Sens. Syst. 2(3), 161–169 (2012)

12. Khan, S.U., Lavagno, L., Pastrone, C., Spirito, M.A.: Online authentication and key establishment scheme for heterogeneous sensor networks. Int. J. Distrib. Sens. Netw. 2014 (2014)

13. Kodali, R.K., Chougule, S., Agarwal, A.: Key management technique for heterogeneous wireless sensor networks. In: 2013 IEEE TENCON Spring Conference, pp. 183–187. IEEE (2013)

14. Lee, J.C., Leung, V.C.M., Wong, K.H., Cao, J., Chan, H.C.B.: Key management issues in wireless sensor networks: current proposals and future developments. IEEE Wirel. Commun. 14(5), 76–84 (2007)

15. Szczechowiak, P., Collier, M.: Tinyibe: identity-based encryption for heterogeneous sensor networks. In: 2009 5th International Conference on Intelligent Sensors, Sensor Networks and Information Processing (ISSNIP), pp. 319–354. IEEE (2009)

16. He, X., Niedermeier, M., De Meer, H.: Dynamic key management in wireless sensor networks: a survey. J. Netw. Comput. Appl. 36(2), 611–622 (2013)

17. Chen, C.-M., Zheng, X., Wu, T.-Y.: A complete hierarchical key management scheme for heterogeneous wireless sensor networks. Sci. World J. 2014 (2014)

18. Rassam, M.A., Maarof, M.A., Zainal, A.: A survey of intrusion detection schemes in wireless sensor networks. Am. J. Appl. Sci. 9(10), 1636–1652 (2012)

mINCARNATE: An Interference and Mobility Aware Spatial Scheme for Tightly Coupled LTE–Wi-Fi Networks

Sumanta Patro[⊠], Thomas Valerrian Pasca Santhappan,
Bheemarjuna Reddy Tamma, and A. Antony Franklin

Department of Computer Science and Engineering, IIT Hyderabad, Hyderabad, India
{cs15mtech01005,cs13p1002,tbr,antony.franklin}@iith.ac.in

Abstract. Stochastic geometry has clinched notability in the past several years. It is a robust mathematical tool for analyzing wireless systems due to its tractability in nature. In this work, a flexible and docile model has been proposed for heterogeneous wireless networks consisting of tightly coupled Long Term Evolution (LTE) Small cell eNodeBs (SeNBs) and Wireless Fidelity (Wi-Fi) Access Points (APs). By the assistance of stochastic geometry, the key performance metrics of LTE–Wi-Fi Aggregation (LWA) system have been analyzed in non co-located scenario. The positions of SeNBs and APs are modeled as two independent homogeneous Poisson Point Processes (PPPs). Enabling LWA operation with an arbitrary number of Wi-Fi APs in a given region may not ensure maximum rate and coverage for the mobile operators. A novel scheme, coined as, InterfereNCe Aware matéRN hArd-core poinT procEss (INCARNATE) has been proposed to increase the performance of LWA system by allowing LWA operation with a chosen subset of Wi-Fi APs available at the disposal. We derive Signal-to-Interference-plus-Noise Ratio (SINR) distribution of UEs which are associated with SeNB, AP or LWA node (*i.e.*, SeNB and AP). This further helps to find out the joint coverage probability and average data rate over the network. In addition to the density of APs, the velocity of UEs plays a vital role in analyzing Key Performance Indicators (KPIs) of the system. So, INCARNATE scheme has been further extended to mINCARNATE scheme wherein mobility of UEs is introduced in the LWA system. A handover model of LWA system has been proposed by considering the mobility of the UEs. Expected number of handovers and average data rate have been analytically measured. Average number of handovers observed per UE and throughput of UEs have been empirically evaluated by varying velocity of UE. Further, cost is defined as a function of velocity of UEs, number of handovers, and density of deployment. Capital Expenditures (CAPEX) and Operational Expenditures (OPEX) can be minimized for a given user velocity by operating at minimal cost value. INCARNATE scheme outperforms the traditional MHCPP scheme by 73% and 17% in terms of data rate and coverage probability, respectively. Similarly, LWA with INCARNATE scheme excels by 51% and 6.23% as compared to regular LWA in terms of data rate and coverage probability, respectively.

© Springer Nature Switzerland AG 2019
S. Biswas et al. (Eds.): COMSNETS 2018, LNCS 11227, pp. 126–149, 2019.
https://doi.org/10.1007/978-3-030-10659-1_6

The proposed cost function assists to obtain the optimal deployment of LWA nodes using mINCARNATE scheme. LWA with mINCARNATE scheme improves the throughput by 53% as compared to native LWA handover scheme.

1 Introduction

Due to profusion of wireless networks and immense growth of data traffic, heterogeneous networks (HetNet) are one of the salient facets of next generation wireless networks. Mobile operators can take advantage of the unlicensed band to cater the exponential traffic demand due to limited existence of licenced spectrum. Data offloading from the cellular network to wireless fidelity (Wi-Fi) network serves the data demand and facilitates an incessant access to the network by leveraging the heterogeneous connectivity. Offloading from cellular to Wi-Fi network has evolved from a coarse level of interworking at Packet Gateway (P-GW) to a finer level of interworking at radio level. The finer integration of long term evolution (LTE) along with Wi-Fi at radio level [18] is achieved by integrating them at the radio protocol stack, which is avowed as LTE–Wi-Fi Aggregation (LWA) [13].

Technical specifications for the realization of LWA are proposed by Third Generation Partnership Project (3GPP). The advantage that LWA facilitates over a P-GW based integration is the enhanced control which it offers over both the LTE and Wi-Fi radios. Also, the protocol stacks of LTE and Wi-Fi are coupled to provide a robust support for the link dynamics. LWA offers better Quality of Experience (QoE) with seamless flow mobility across LTE and Wi-Fi links. In LWA, LTE SeNB acts as the licensed anchor point for communication and LTE core network is unaware of the existence of Wi-Fi.

LWA could be realized in both co-located and non co-located scenarios. In a co-located scenario, SeNB and Wi-Fi AP are located in the same device (LWA node) and tightly integrated at radio level, which is driven by a finer control decision by combined intelligence. Unlike co-located LWA, in a non co-located LWA system, AP and SeNB are connected via a standardized interface referred as X_w [11] as shown in Fig. 1. It requires an intelligent decision-making scheme in steering the data across LTE and Wi-Fi as the round trip delay introduced by LTE and Wi-Fi links are different.

In LWA system, LTE operates in licensed bands and it is a centrally scheduled system. But Wi-Fi operates in the unlicensed spectrum which employs distributed carrier sense multiple access with collision avoidance (CSMA/CA) mechanism, wherein it allows transmissions when the sensed channel is found to be idle. Such a system with both licensed and unlicensed carriers exhibits significant potential in mitigating interference among LTE SeNBs, by serving cell edge users of LTE through Wi-Fi APs which could be configured to operate on orthogonal channels. In this work, we explore the above-mentioned potentials of LWA system in a spatial domain. In order to study the performance of LWA in a spatial domain, we have used stochastic geometry [6] to model and analyze

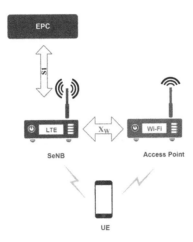

Fig. 1. Non co-located LWA system.

the system. Stochastic geometry has become a natural candidate and power-ful mathematical tool for analyzing wireless systems, due to its tractability in nature.

The locations of SeNBs and APs in non co-located scenarios are modeled using specific spatial point processes and key performance metrics such as cov-erage probability and data rate of the system can be obtained after diligent analysis of the system. In this work, a tractable framework has been proposed to analyze the downlink joint coverage probability and data rate of non co-located LWA system. With the assistance of stochastic geometry model, expressions for SINR, individual and joint coverage probabilities, and average data rate for a typical UE are obtained. The problem of modeling of interference has been addressed in [4,19,22,23] based on Poisson Point Process (PPP). In [7], authors have presented an extensive survey pertaining to stochastic geometry models for both single-tier and multi-tier cellular networks. Downlink performance of Dual Connectivity (DC) assisted HetNet has been analyzed in [21]. In [20], Wang *et al.* have used stochastic geometry to develop a framework for the co-existence between LTE-U and Wi-Fi in the unlicensed band. It also calculates retention probability and coverage probability of Wi-Fi and LTE-U networks. Authors in [15] have proposed a modified Matérn Hard-Core Point Process (MHCPP), wherein CSMA/CA nodes transmit simultaneously in a dense 802.11 network scenario. Similarly, in [1], authors have proposed a tractable technique which considers scenarios wherein APs are not distributed according to a PPP and have depicted an extension of stochastic geometry analysis to a dense CSMA network to estimate the throughput.

For mobile operators, accrediting LWA operation with an arbitrary number of Wi-Fi APs in a given region may not ensure maximum rate and coverage. A novel scheme, coined as, InterfereNCe Aware matéRN hArd-core poinT procEss (INCARNATE) has been proposed in [16] to increase the performance of LWA system by allowing LWA operation with a chosen subset of Wi-Fi APs at the disposal. Due to the dense and random deployment of SeNBs and APs in the terrain, mobility management has emanated as one of the most pivotal challenges, specifically when handling with variant speeds of UEs. Mobility management in wireless networks needs to be taken care to provide the best QoE to the mobile UEs by mitigating handover failures. Speed of UEs plays vital role on handover performance of UEs particularly when the density of radio access technologies (RATs) is high. Hence, in this work, INCARNATE scheme has been further extended to mINCARNATE scheme wherein mobility of UEs is factored in. A handover model of LWA system has been proposed by considering the mobility of the UEs. Further, cost is defined as a function of velocity of UEs, number of handovers, and density of deployment.

The rest of the paper is organized as follows. Mobility in LWA system is discussed in Sect. 2. LWA system model is described in Sect. 3, proposed modified MHCPP scheme is unfolded in Sect. 4, coverage probability and overall data rate of the network are derived in Sect. 5. Handover model of LWA system is illustrated in Sect. 6, wherein expected number of handovers and average data rate have been analytically modeled. Numerical simulation and analytical results are presented in Sect. 7. Finally, conclusions are drawn in Sect. 8.

2 Mobility in LWA System

Mobility management is inevitable in wireless networks, wherein roaming is a fact of life in this digital era. However, the QoE has not been aligned with users' requirement. We need to have persistent access to all types of communication services and most of the users have to alter a combination of cellular and WLAN connections while moving. Integrating LTE along with Wi-Fi at radio level will help mobile operators to satisfy users' need. A tighter coupling between LTE and Wi-Fi can be achieved by integrating both at their radio protocol stacks, which is avowed as LWA. In general, LTE seamlessly takes care of handovers (HO), however, after integrating LTE and Wi-Fi together, LWA system needs to take utmost care of Wi-Fi handovers.

There are several types of handover procedures. Hard handover follows "break before connect" policy, on contrary, soft handover uses "break after connecting". In case of hard handover, before the new radio link is established, old radio link breaks, and UE communicates with one of the RATs at any given time. Soft handover which follows the principle, connect-before-break, is a category of handover procedure wherein radio links are removed or added in such a fashion that there is always one radio link for the UE to communicate.

Dense deployment of HetNets leads to recurrent handovers, that result in a decline of user experience as well as extra signaling overhead in the network. Horizontal and vertical handovers have important ramifications for user mobility in multi-RAT networks. They directly impact the signaling overhead and QoE of flows. However, they are difficult to analyze due to the irregularly shaped network geometry introduced by multiple RATs of cells. In this work, a stochastic geometric analysis framework on user mobility has been proposed to capture the spatial randomness and various scales of cell sizes in multi-RAT system.

2.1 Handover Challenges

For providing a hassle-free connectivity, handover plays a vital role. When UEs enter or leave the coverage area of a base station, handover is triggered. When the UEs shift from more congested base station to less congested base station, handover is required for better QoE.

LTE uses various handover algorithms such as A2A4RSRQ and A3RSRP for handling handovers [9] and [17]. However, in LWA, while using Wi-Fi in addition to LTE, it may also need to consider other network related parameters. Handover can be triggered based on various parameters. Such network parameters include received signal strength indicator (RSSI), velocity of UE, signal to noise ratio (SNR), reference signal received power (RSRP), reference signal received quality (RSRQ), bandwidth, signal to interference plus noise ratio (SINR), traffic type, and cost function.

Mobility in a dense deployment of small cells in the indoor is a natural phenomenon in day-to-day life. When a UE moves in the interfering realm of small cells, ping pong effects can be observed. Similar effects can also be noticed in densely deployed LWA networks as well. However, not much work has not been done pertaining to handover analysis of LWA system in the literature. This has motivated us to address this issue by obtaining the expected number of handovers experienced by UEs in the highly interfering region and analyzing the system behaviour.

3 LWA System Model

A system model for a non co-located deployment scenario of LWA system is presented in this section. Notations used are given in Table 1.

3.1 Spatial Random Point Process

The most primitive objects which are studied in stochastic geometry are point processes. A point process (PP) can be delineated as a random collection of points in space. It is the crew of points in space, wherein the position of points are random variables. PP is said to be stationary if the relationship between the points does not change by translation. Homogeneous Poisson Point Process is identified by the parameter 'λ', known as density or intensity which is constant across space. The number of points in an area, say, '$\mathcal{A}$' is a Poisson random variable (RV) whose mean is $\lambda|\mathcal{A}|$ in a homogeneous PPP. In this work, the positions for SeNBs and APs are modeled as two independent homogeneous PPPs in case of non co-located LWA scenarios.

A stationary PPP Φ of density λ is characterized by, number of points in a bounded set $A \subset \mathbb{R}^2$ has a Poisson distribution with mean $\lambda|A|$, *i.e.*,

$$\mathbb{P}(\Phi(A) = n) = \exp(-\lambda|A|)\frac{(\lambda|A|)^n}{n!} \tag{1}$$

Table 1. Notations

Symbol	Definition
Φ_l	PPP of SeNBs
Φ_w	PPP of APs
Φ_{lwa}	PPP of LWA
λ_l	Density of SeNBs
λ_w	Density of APs
λ_u	Density of UEs
P_l	Transmit Power of LTE
P_w	Transmit Power of Wi-Fi
$h_{(0,l)}$	Shadowed fading coefficient of LTE
$h_{(0,w)}$	Shadowed fading coefficient of Wi-Fi
σ_l	Noise variance of LTE
σ_w	Noise variance of Wi-Fi
η	Path-loss exponent
Ψ_l	SINR Threshold of LTE
Ψ_w	SINR Threshold of Wi-Fi

Campbell's Theorem: Let $g : \mathbb{R}^d \rightarrow [0, \infty)$ be a function over a stationary point process Φ and $\lambda > 0$ is the density of it. Then average sum of a function evaluated at the points of Φ is given by,

$$\mathbb{E}\left[\sum_{x_i \in \Phi} g(x_i)\right] = \lambda \int_{\mathbb{R}^d} g(x)dx \qquad (2)$$

Probability Generating Functional (PGFL): The average of a product of a function over the PP, which is conditional probability generating functional (PGFL) of a PP Φ is given by,

$$\mathbb{E}\left[\prod_{x_i \in \Phi} g(x_i)\right] = \exp\left\{-\lambda \int_{\mathbb{R}^d} (1 - g(x))dx\right\} \qquad (3)$$

3.2 Radio Transmission Model

In [3], the authors have used a homogeneous Poisson distributed network and the power-law path loss model to calculate the coverage probability, which is the complementary cumulative distribution function (CCDF) of the SINR. In this work, we use standard power law path loss propagation model with path loss exponent $\eta > 2.0$, which depends on the environment [3]. Independent Rayleigh fading with unit mean is assumed between any pair of LWA node and UE with constant transmit power, say P_{tx}. This constant transmit power varies across different RATs such as, LTE, Wi-Fi, and LWA, denoted by P_l, P_w, and P_{lwa}, respectively. In general, received power of UE, which is at the origin, at distance r_0 from an LWA node is given by $P_u = P_i h_i r_0^{-\eta}$, where h_i follows an exponential distribution and $h_i \sim exp(1)$, where $i \in \{l, w, lwa\}$. Summation of signals stemmed from concurrent transmitters leads to interference, which directly depends on the transmitters' positions.

3.3 Wi-Fi MAC Model

Unlike LTE, Wi-Fi uses CSMA/CA protocol for accessing channel. IEEE 802.11 standard defines a Distributed Coordination Function (DCF) for sharing access to the medium based on the CSMA/CA protocol. This protocol comprises of Clear Channel Assessment (CCA) method and a random backoff mechanism to avoid collisions so that no two nearby nodes shall transmit simultaneously. The operation of Wi-Fi can be modeled using traditional MHCPP. Type II of MHCPP is generated by a dependent thinning of a parent stationary PPP. The following steps are followed for the traditional MHCPP scheme:

1. Based on density λ_w, generate a PPP Φ_w.
2. For each point, say $y_i \in \Phi_w$ associate a mark $m_{y_i} \in [0, 1]$ which is independent of any other points.
3. A point y_i is said to be retained in Φ_m if the assigned mark (m_{y_i}) is the lowest as compared to all other points in the ball $\mathcal{B}(y_i, r_h)$ of radius r_h.

The probability of an arbitrary point y_i is said to be retained in Φ_m can be obtained as following:

$$p_{ret} = \frac{1 - \exp(-\lambda_w \tilde{\mathcal{B}})}{\lambda_w \tilde{\mathcal{B}}} \tag{4}$$

Where, $\tilde{\mathcal{B}}$ is the Lebesgue measure of $\mathcal{B}$.

3.4 UE Association Model

UE associates with Wi-Fi and/or LTE RATs which are aggregated using a non co-located LWA node based on the shortest Euclidean distance from it. We will be using LTE UE and Wi-Fi STA interchangeably for representing a user depending on which RAT it is connected to. The distance distribution between a UE and its serving node (*i.e.*, SeNB, AP, or LWA node)can be obtained using the Probability Density Function (PDF).

The PDF of the distance r_w from STA to the associated AP is given by,

$$f_w(r_w) = 2\lambda_w \pi r_w e^{-\lambda_w \pi r_w^2}; \quad 0 < r_w < \infty \tag{5}$$

Similarly, the PDF of r_l from UE to the associated SeNB can be given as,

$$f_l(r_l) = 2\lambda_l \pi r_l e^{-\lambda_l \pi r_l^2}; \quad 0 < r_l < \infty \tag{6}$$

4   Proposed INCARNATE Scheme

Non co-located LWA system facilitates traffic to be steered across LTE and Wi-Fi networks where the deployment of SeNBs and APs are spatially distributed. Steering the traffic from SeNB to any AP in the given region may not yield better throughput. This is because each AP follows DCF which shares the channel equally, thus a UE receives lesser opportunity from the APs which would be better if a subset of APs transmissions is enabled. A better solution would be allowing SeNBs to steer the traffic to a selected subset of APs which includes the APs in the interference region of LTE and to a subset of APs which can transmit parallelly along with the chosen subset of APs in LTE interference region. Hence we propose a modified MHCPP known as InterfereNCe Aware matéRN hArdcore poinT procEss (INCARNATE) scheme, which models the operation of the chosen subset of APs and captures the performance improvement of the LWA system. The working mechanism of INCARNATE scheme is illustrated by a flowchart shown in Fig. 2.

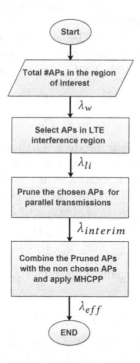

Fig. 2. Flowchart of INCARNATE scheme.

4.1   Procedures of INCARNATE Scheme

INCARNATE scheme involves a selected set of APs to perform LWA operation instead of allowing every AP to participate in. The steps of INCARNATE scheme as shown in Fig. 2 are detailed as below:

1. The density of Wi-Fi APs in the given region is denoted as λ_w.
2. Select a set of APs which are located in the LTE interference region. The density of the APs located in LTE interference region is represented as λ_{li}.
3. From the chosen set to APs, prune away those APs which do not involve in parallel transmissions. In other words, prune those APs which can listen to other AP's transmissions. This ensures no two APs can listen to each other in this environment, hence they can transmit in parallel. The density of pruned APs is represented by $\lambda_{interim}$.
4. Add a few more APs which are in the non-interfering region of LTE to the above set of pruned APs. Ensure that the newly added APs do transmit in parallel to the APs in the pruned set and also ensure that they transmit in parallel among themselves. The density of these APs is represented as λ_{eff}.

4.2 Modeling of INCARNATE Scheme

Expressions for INCARNATE scheme are obtained using various density parameters such as, λ_w, which is the density of the APs that are deployed using PPP, λ_{li} is the updated density which portrays the APs which are in the interfering region of LTE. A UE is said to be in outage (*i.e.*, coverage hole) if the SINR falls below some specified threshold. Outage probability ($\mathcal{O}_l$), which is the Cumulative Distribution Function (CDF) of SINR, can be found using coverage probability as given below.

$$\mathcal{O}_l = (1 - {}^l\mathcal{P}_c) \tag{7}$$

$$\lambda_{li} = \lambda_w \, \mathcal{O}_l \tag{8}$$

In the above, outage intensity product (OIP) signifies the average number of APs that are present in the interfering region of LTE. The probability p_{prune} assists for getting the number of simultaneous transmissions of APs in the LTE interference region.

$$p_{prune} = \frac{1 - \exp(-\lambda_{li} \, \tilde{\mathcal{B}})}{\lambda_{li} \, \tilde{\mathcal{B}}} \tag{9}$$

$$\lambda_{prune} = p_{prune} \, \lambda_{li} \tag{10}$$

$\lambda_{interim}$ signifies the intermediate density of APs as shown below, which is the candidate for λ_{eff}.

$$\lambda_{interim} = \lambda_{prune} + [\lambda_w - \lambda_{li}] \tag{11}$$

Proposed scheme prioritizes the APs which are in LTE interference region with less mark, say 0 and assigns a mark to the APs in the non-interfering region with mark $m_i \in (0, 1]$. p_{eff} is the Palm probability [8] of retaining APs of Φ_w after thinning procedure and it guarantees simultaneous transmissions of APs and λ_{eff} is the effective density which is used to obtain the maximum number of parallel transmissions of APs using p_{eff} in the LWA system.

$$p_{eff} = \frac{1 - \exp(-\lambda_{interim} \, \tilde{B})}{\lambda_{interim} \, \tilde{B}} \tag{12}$$

$$\lambda_{eff} = p_{eff} \, \lambda_{interim} \tag{13}$$

After thinning process, in Fig. 3, we show the Voronoi tessellation of LTE and updated Wi-Fi APs which are selected after applying INCARNATE scheme. Initially, all the APs are deployed using PPP, after applying traditional MHCPP scheme, the number of APs is reduced as it confirms the number of parallel transmissions among the APs. However, it does not guarantee high data rate to UEs which are suffering in LTE interfering region. Proposed INCARNATE scheme enables the APs that are in the interfering regime of LTE, which in turn revamps the data rate of UEs.

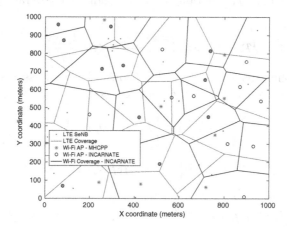

Fig. 3. Voronoi tessellation of LTE SeNBs, Wi-Fi APs after applying MHCPP, and selected Wi-Fi APs after applying INCARNATE scheme.

5   Coverage and Rate Analysis

By the assistance of stochastic geometry, we have analytically characterized the downlink coverage probability and data rate using INCARNATE scheme. Let λ_l be the density of SeNBs and λ_w be the density of APs. Without any loss of generality, we have assumed that the UE is at the origin. Coverage probability of LTE can be calculated as specified in [2]. Shadowed fading coefficients of LTE and Wi-Fi are $h_{(0,l)}$ and $h_{(0,w)}$, respectively, which are independent and identically distributed (i.i.d.), and exponential random variables with mean 1.

5.1   Coverage Probability of LTE SeNB

A UE is said to be in coverage of LTE, if the received SINR (S_l) by UE from SeNB is greater than the threshold Ψ_l and it disconnects from the network if S_l falls below Ψ_l. Coverage probability of LTE ($^l\mathcal{P}_c$) can be found as following,

$$^l\mathcal{P}_c = \mathbb{P}(S_l > \Psi_l) \tag{14}$$

where,

$$S_l = \left\{ \frac{P_l h_{(0,l)} r_{(0,l)}^{-\eta}}{I_l + \sigma_l^2} \right\},$$

and

$$I_l = \sum_{i \epsilon \Phi \backslash e_0} P_l h_{(i,l)} r_{(i,l)}^{-\eta}$$

Here, interference is calculated from other SeNBs excluding the SeNB (e_0) to which UE is connected to.

For notational simplicity, we denote $r_{(0,l)}$ as r_l and $h_{(0,l)}$ as h_l. Conditioning on r_l with exponential distribution of h_l, the conditional coverage probability of LTE is given by:

$$^l P_c(r_l) = \exp\left\{ \frac{-\Psi_l \sigma_l^2 r_l^\eta}{P_l} \right\} \mathscr{L}_{I_l}\left\{ \frac{\Psi_l r_l^\eta}{P_l} \right\} \tag{15}$$

Proof. Conditioning on r_l which is the distance between associated eNB and UE, the coverage probability can be obtained as,

$$^l P_c(r_l) = \mathbb{E}_{r_l}\left\{ \mathbb{P}\left\{ S_l > \Psi_l | r_l \right\} \right\}$$

$$= \int_0^\infty \mathbb{P}\left[S_l > \Psi_l | r_l \right] f_l(r_l) \, dr_l$$

$$= \int_0^\infty \mathbb{P}\left[\frac{P_l h_l r_l^{-\eta}}{I_l + \sigma_l^2} > \Psi_l \middle| r_l \right] \exp\left\{ -\pi\lambda_l r_l^2 \right\} 2\pi\lambda_l r_l \, dr_l$$

$$= \int_0^\infty \mathbb{P}\left[h_l > \frac{\Psi_l r_l^\eta (\sigma_l^2 + I_l)}{P_l} \middle| r_l \right] \exp\left\{ -\pi\lambda_l r_l^2 \right\} 2\pi\lambda_l r_l dr_l$$

where,

$$\mathbb{P}\left[h_l > \frac{\Psi_l r_l^\eta (\sigma_l^2 + I_l)}{P_l} \middle| r_l \right]$$

$$= \mathbb{E}_{I_l}\left[\mathbb{P}\left[h_l > \frac{\Psi_l r_l^\eta (\sigma_l^2 + I_l)}{P_l} \middle| r_l, I_l \right] \right]$$

$$= \mathbb{E}_{I_l}\left[\exp\left\{ \frac{-\mu\Psi_l r_l^\eta (\sigma_l^2 + I_l)}{P_l} \right\} \middle| r_l \right]$$

$$= \exp\left\{ \frac{-\mu\Psi_l r_l^\eta \sigma_l^2}{P_l} \right\} \mathscr{L}_{I_l}\left\{ \frac{\mu\Psi_l r_l^\eta}{P_l} \right\}$$

As mentioned above, h_l follows exponential distribution with unit mean, therefore the above expression can be written by applying $\mu = 1$ as below:

$$\exp\left\{ \frac{-\Psi_l r_l^\eta \sigma_l^2}{P_l} \right\} \mathscr{L}_{I_l}\left\{ \frac{\Psi_l r_l^\eta}{P_l} \right\}$$

The Laplace transform of I_l ($\mathscr{L}_{I_l}(s)$) can be obtained as,

$$\mathscr{L}_{I_l}(s) = \mathbb{E}\left\{\exp\left[-I_l s\right]\right\}$$

$$= \mathbb{E}\left\{\exp\left[-\left[\sum_{i\epsilon\Phi\backslash e_0} P_l h_{(i,l)} r_{(i,l)}^{-\eta}\right]s\right]\right\}$$

Due to the independence between fading and position of SeNBs, we can re-write the above expression as,

$$\mathscr{L}_{I_l}(s) = \mathbb{E}_\Phi\left\{\prod_{i\epsilon\Phi\backslash e_0} \mathbb{E}_{h_{(i,l)}}\left\{\exp\left[-P_l h_{(i,l)} r_{(i,l)}^{-\eta}\right]s\right\}\right\}$$

$$= \mathbb{E}_\Phi\left\{\prod_{i\epsilon\Phi\backslash e_0} \mathscr{L}_{h_{(i,l)}}\left\{P_l r_{(i,l)}^{-\eta} s\right\}\right\}$$

However, since $h_{(i,l)} \sim exp(1)$, we can express the above as the following,

$$\mathscr{L}_{I_l}(s) = \mathbb{E}_\Phi\left\{\prod_{i\epsilon\Phi\backslash e_0} \frac{1}{1 + P_l r_{(i,l)}^{-\eta} s}\right\}$$

According to PGFL of a homogeneous PPP, above expression can be represented as below:

$$\mathscr{L}_{I_l}(s) = \exp\left[-2\pi\lambda_l \int_{r_l}^{\infty} \left\{1 - \frac{1}{1 + P_l v^{-\eta} s}\right\} v dv\right]$$

$$= \exp\left[-2\pi\lambda_l \int_{r_l}^{\infty} \left\{\frac{P_l v^{-\eta} s}{1 + P_l v^{-\eta} s}\right\} v dv\right]$$

$$= \exp\left[-2\pi\lambda_l \int_{r_l}^{\infty} \left\{\frac{1}{\frac{1}{P_l v^{-\eta} s} + 1}\right\} v dv\right]$$

By substituting $s = \left(\frac{\Psi_l r_l^{\eta}}{P_l}\right)$, the above expression can be written as,

$$\mathscr{L}_{I_l}(s) = \exp\left[-2\pi\lambda_l \int_{r_l}^{\infty} \frac{1}{\frac{1}{\Psi_l r_l^{\eta} v^{-\eta}} + 1} v dv\right]$$

Let $u = \left(\frac{v^2}{\Psi_l^{2/\eta} r_l^2}\right)$, so that $du = \left(\frac{2v}{\Psi_l^{2/\eta} r_l^2}\right) dv$,

$$\mathscr{L}_{I_l}\left(\frac{\Psi_l r_l^{\eta}}{P_l}\right) = \exp\left[-\pi\lambda_l r_l^2 \Psi_l^{2/\eta} \int_{\Psi_l^{-2/\eta}}^{\infty} \frac{1}{1 + u^{\eta/2}} du\right]$$

$$= \exp\left[-\pi\lambda_l r_l^2 \, \theta(\Psi_l, \eta)\right]$$

where,

$$\theta(\Psi_l, \eta) = \Psi_l^{2/\eta} \int_{\Psi_l^{-2/\eta}}^{\infty} \frac{1}{1+u^{\eta/2}} du$$

After simplifying, the above expression pertaining to $^l\mathcal{P}_c$ can be found as in Eq. (16).

$$^l\mathcal{P}_c = \int_0^{\infty} 2\pi\lambda_l x \exp\left(-\frac{\Psi_l\sigma_l^2 x^{\eta}}{P_l} - \pi\lambda_l x^2 \left(1 + \Psi_l^{2/\eta} \int_{\Psi_l^{-2/\eta}}^{\infty} \frac{1}{1+u^{\eta/2}} du\right)\right) dx \tag{16}$$

It can also be represented using standard hyper-geometric function [5] as given below,

$$^l\mathcal{P}_c(r_l) = {}_2F_1\left[1, -\frac{2}{\eta}; 1 - \frac{2}{\eta}; -\Psi_l\right]^{-1} \tag{17}$$

where, ${}_2F_1[.]$ represents the hyper-geometric function.

By considering a PPP based LTE network in an interference limited environment with Rayleigh fading, the coverage probability for SeNB, when path loss exponent (η) is 4, which is a common pathloss exponent for outdoor environments, is given by:

$$^l\mathcal{P}_c\Big|_{\eta=4} = \left[\Psi_l^{0.5} \tan^{-1}(\Psi_l^{0.5}) + 1\right]^{-1} \tag{18}$$

5.2   Coverage Probability of Wi-Fi AP

A UE is said to be in the coverage of a Wi-Fi AP if the received SINR by the UE from Wi-Fi AP i.e., S_w is greater than the threshold Ψ_w, which can be denoted as,

$$^w\mathcal{P}_c = \mathbb{P}(S_w > \Psi_w) \tag{19}$$

where,

$$S_w = \left\{\frac{P_w h_{(0,w)} r_{(0,w)}^{-\eta}}{I_w + \sigma_w^2}\right\},$$

and

$$I_w = \sum_{i\epsilon\Phi\backslash a_0} P_w h_{(i,w)} r_{(i,w)}^{-\eta}$$

Here, the interference is calculated over other Wi-Fi APs excluding the serving AP (a_0) of the UE. For notational simplicity, we denote $r_{(0,w)}$ as r_w and $h_{(0,w)}$ as h_w.

Conditioning on r_w with exponential distribution of h_w, the conditional coverage probability ($^w\mathcal{P}_c(r_w)$) is given by:

$$^w\mathcal{P}_c(r_w) = \exp\left\{\frac{-\Psi_w\sigma_w^2 r_w^{\eta}}{P_w}\right\}\mathscr{L}_{I_w}\left\{\frac{\Psi_w r_w^{\eta}}{P_w}\right\} \tag{20}$$

where,

$$\mathscr{L}_{I_w}\left\{\frac{\Psi_w r_w^\eta}{P_w}\right\} = \exp(-\pi\lambda_w r_w^2 \theta(\Psi_w, \eta))$$

and

$$\theta(\Psi_w, \eta) = \Psi_w^{2/\eta} \int_{\Psi_w^{-2/\eta}}^{\infty} \frac{1}{1 + u^{\eta/2}} du$$

After simplifying, the above expression for $^w\mathcal{P}_c$ can be found as in Eq. (21).

$$^w\mathcal{P}_c = \int_0^\infty 2\pi\lambda_w y \exp\left(-\frac{\Psi_w \sigma_w^2 y^\eta}{P_w} - \pi\lambda_w y^2 \left(1 + \Psi_w^{2/\eta} \int_{\Psi_w^{-2/\eta}}^{\infty} \frac{1}{1 + u^{\eta/2}} du\right)\right) dy \tag{21}$$

5.3   Coverage Probability of LWA System with INCARNATE

The coverage probability of LWA is the probability that a user is in the coverage of an LWA node. The joint coverage probability involves two independent events viz., a user is in the coverage of LTE ($^l\mathcal{P}_c$) and coverage of Wi-Fi ($^w\mathcal{P}_c$). Coverage probability that a UE is in coverage of both LTE and Wi-Fi can be obtained if SINRs of both Wi-Fi and LTE are greater than the respective threshold values. Mathematically it can be found as given below,

$$^{lwa}\mathcal{P}_c = \mathbb{P}[(S_w > \Psi_w), (S_l > \Psi_l)]$$
$$= \mathbb{P}[(S_w > \Psi_w) \cap (S_l > \Psi_l)]$$

Conditioning on $r_{(0,lwa)}$ with exponential distribution of $h_{(0,lwa)}$, the conditional coverage probability $^{lwa}\mathcal{P}_c(r_{(0,lwa)})$ is given by:

$$\exp\left\{-\left[\frac{\Psi_l \sigma_l^2 r_l^\eta}{P_l} + \frac{\Psi_w \sigma_w^2 r_w^\eta}{P_w}\right]\right\} \mathscr{L}_{I_l}\left\{\frac{\Psi_l r_l^\eta}{P_l}\right\} \mathscr{L}_{I_w}\left\{\frac{\Psi_w r_w^\eta}{P_w}\right\}$$

where,

$$\mathscr{L}_{I_l}\left\{\frac{\Psi_l r_l^\eta}{P_l}\right\} = \exp(-\pi\lambda_l r_l^2 \theta(\Psi_l, \eta)),$$

$$\mathscr{L}_{I_w}\left\{\frac{\Psi_w r_w^\eta}{P_w}\right\} = \exp(-\pi\lambda_w r_w^2 \theta(\Psi_w, \eta)),$$

$$\theta(\Psi_l, \eta) = \Psi_l^{2/\eta} \int_{\Psi_l^{-2/\eta}}^{\infty} \frac{1}{1 + u^{\eta/2}} du,$$

and

$$\theta(\Psi_w, \eta) = \Psi_w^{2/\eta} \int_{\Psi_w^{-2/\eta}}^{\infty} \frac{1}{1 + u^{\eta/2}} du$$

5.4   Effective Data Rate of LWA System with INCARNATE

Analysis of coverage probability alone does not provide an intact characterization of the network performance. To envisage, we have further studied the data rate of both individual and overall networks. After obtaining the coverage probability, we derive the data rate of the LWA network. It captures the average number of bits that can be transmitted per unit time, assuming all LWA nodes transmit (*i.e.*, full buffer model). Wi-Fi data rate estimation is evaluated using MHCPP.

Let the data rate of LTE be R_l and Wi-Fi be R_w, which can be found as following:

Effective Data Rate Achieved Through LTE:
It is given by:
$$R_l(\Psi_l, \lambda_l) = B_w \ log_2(1 + \Psi_l) \ \lambda_l \ {}^l\mathcal{P}_c \tag{22}$$

where B_w denotes the bandwidth of LTE network and other terminologies have already been discussed in Sect. 5.1.

Effective Data Rate Achieved Through Wi-Fi:
As given in [15], approximate data rate for INCARNATE scheme with effective density λ_{eff} can be obtained as below:

$$R_w \approx \frac{\lambda_{eff}}{\lambda_u} \left[\int_0^\infty \sum_{n=1}^k \frac{p^r(\Psi_w)_n - p^r(\Psi_w)_{n+1}}{\rho_n} \frac{p_{eff}}{p_{ret}} f_w(r_w)dr \right]^{-1} \tag{23}$$

where $p^r(\Psi_w)_n$ represents the Palm probability for a UE to be potentially in the coverage with threshold Ψ_w by its nearest AP given that, this closest AP is located at distance 'r' at n^{th} instance and ρ_n signifies an auto-rate function which is a piecewise constant function w.r.t. SINR (in dB). It is equal to 0, if SINR falls below the specified threshold.

Effective Data Rate Achieved Through LWA System:
Effective data rate of LWA can be obtained using the sum of individual data rates of LTE and Wi-Fi.
$$\mathcal{R}_{lwa} = \mathcal{R}_l + \mathcal{R}_w \tag{24}$$

6   Handover Model of LWA System

LTE and Wi-Fi RATs are modeled as homogeneous PPP to capture their spatial randomness. Expressions for the rate of handover and average data rate experienced by an active user with arbitrary trajectory are presented. INCARNATE scheme is further extended to mINCARNATE scheme wherein mobility of UEs is introduced in the LWA system.

6.1 Handover Analysis of Native LWA System

A fibre is a sufficiently smooth simple curve of finite length in the plane. Fibre processes [6] model random collections of curves in the plane. The number of handovers which are experienced by a UE is same as the number of cell boundaries ($\mathcal{B}$) of LTE SeNB and Wi-Fi AP that it crosses while traversing from initial position to its end of trajectory ($\mathcal{T}$). The number of intersections between UE's trajectory '$\mathcal{T}$' and cell boundary '$\mathcal{B}$' can be denoted as $\mathcal{N}(\mathcal{B}, \mathcal{T})$. The term λ_{eff} (Eq. (13)) is the effective density which is used to obtain the maximum number of parallel transmissions of APs using p_{eff} in the LWA system as discussed in Sect. 4.2.

6.2 Handover Rate

Handover rate is defined as the probability that a UE crosses over to the next coverage of a cell in one movement period. The expected number of handovers $\mathbb{E}[\mathcal{N}]$ during one trajectory period is given by,

$$\mathbb{E}[\mathcal{N}] = \frac{2}{\pi}\sqrt{\frac{\lambda_{eff}}{\beta}}, \tag{25}$$

where β is a mobility parameter as in [12].

Let v denote the instantaneous velocity of an active UE, then handover rate i.e., $\mathcal{H}(v)$ can be evaluated as following,

$$\mathcal{H}(v) = \frac{4v}{\pi}\sqrt{\lambda_{eff}} \tag{26}$$

6.3 Average Data Rate

According to [10], control overhead consumes a fraction n_c of overall network capacity which is 0.3. Average data rate can be calculated as following:

$$\mathcal{R} = \mathcal{E}_s(1 - n_c)(1 - d\mathcal{H}(v))\mathcal{W}, \tag{27}$$

where $\mathcal{E}_s$ symbolizes the average spectral efficiency and $\mathcal{W}$ denotes the bandwidth of the channel and as per [14], handover delay 'd' for the IP-backhauled small cell is 2 s.

Mean spectral efficiency can be revealed in terms of the coverage probability as following,

$$\mathcal{E}_s = \int_0^\infty \mathbb{P}\{\ln(1 + \Psi) > x\}dx \tag{28}$$

In the above expression, the sub-expression $[ln(1 + \Psi) > x]$ can be expressed as below,

$$ln(1 + \Psi) > x$$
$$\implies \Psi > [\exp(x) - 1]$$

By substituting $[\exp(x) - 1]$ with y, in Eq. (28), it can be enunciated as,

$$\mathscr{E}_s = \int_0^\infty \frac{\mathbb{P}\{SINR > y\}}{[1+y]} dy \tag{29}$$

By solving Eq. (29) with pathloss exponent (η) as 4, it can be found as following,

$$\mathscr{E}_s = \int_0^\infty \frac{1}{[1 - \sqrt{y}\arctan(\sqrt{y})][y+1]} dy \tag{30}$$

6.4   Proposed Cost Function of LWA System

Cost function is a parameterized function which facilitates to analyze the system. As per [24], cost function is defined as,

$$M = \frac{M_o}{\log(n + ek)} NG \tag{31}$$

where, M_o is the value of traditional measurement such as RSRP and RSRQ, $e = 2.718$, n denotes the number of UEs which camp on the LTE/LTE-A cell or femtocell, k is the adjustment factor of different type of the cell, N is the maximal capacity of macrocell or femtocell, and G is the G-factor which used to adjust the value of M.

We have extended the cost function with an objective to obtain the optimal density of LWA nodes when UEs are moving. Cost function is defined as,

$$\mathcal{A}(r) = \mathscr{G} \cdot [\mathbb{E}[\mathscr{H}(r)]]^\gamma \cdot log(\mathscr{R}(r)) \tag{32}$$

where, $\mathscr{G}$ is a factor used to adjust the value of the cost function, $\mathbb{E}[\mathscr{H}(r)]$ denotes expected number of handover rate of RAT r, γ defines the trajectory exponent, and $\mathscr{R}(r)$ denotes the throughput of RAT r.

After substituting the value of $\mathbb{E}[\mathscr{H}(r)]$ and $\mathscr{R}(r)$, it can be found as below,

$$\mathcal{A}(r) = C_1 [\lambda_{eff}]^{\gamma/2} \cdot log \left[C_2 \left[1 - C_3 \sqrt{\lambda_{eff}} \right] \right] \tag{33}$$

where,

$$C_1 = \mathscr{G} \cdot \left[\frac{4v}{\pi} \right]^\gamma ,$$

$$C_2 = \mathscr{W}\mathscr{E}_s(1 - n_c),$$

and

$$C_3 = dC_1$$

Minimize $\mathcal{A}(r)$
where,

$$\mathcal{A}(r) = C_1 [\lambda_{eff}]^{\gamma/2} \cdot log \left[C_2 \left[1 - C_3 \sqrt{\lambda_{eff}} \right] \right] \tag{34}$$

subject to,

$$0 < \lambda_{min} \leq \lambda_{eff} \leq \lambda_{max} \tag{35}$$

where, 'v' is the input parameter which corresponds to the average velocity of the UE in the cell.

7 Performance Analysis

In this section, we present analytical and simulation results of non co-located LWA system using Monte-Carlo simulation experiments. We have focused on the persistent downlink traffic only without any uplink traffic for LTE, Wi-Fi, and LWA in this study.

Table 2. Simulation parameters

Parameter	Value
Network dimensions	$1000\,\mathrm{m} \times 1000\,\mathrm{m}$
LTE transmission power	$23\,\mathrm{dBm}$
Wi-Fi transmission power	$23\,\mathrm{dBm}$
Number of SeNBs	20
Number of APs	40
Number of UEs	1000
Path loss model	Power law model
LTE bandwidth	$20\,\mathrm{MHz}$
Wi-Fi bandwidth	$20\,\mathrm{MHz}$
Mobility model	Random WayPoint

Table 2 lists the simulation parameters that are used in the experiments. The calculation of the SINR of a user depends on its location and a user gets associated with the best serving cell in its vicinity.

The scenario includes deployment of LTE small cells and Wi-Fi APs in the two dimension region according to PPP. We have conducted experiments to observe the performance in various categories.

1. LTE: The performance of LTE small cells is analyzed in terms of rate and coverage.
2. Wi-Fi: The performance of Wi-Fi in the scenario is analyzed in terms of rate and coverage. At any given time the number of Wi-Fi APs that can transmit in parallel is given by MHCPP.
3. Wi-Fi with INCARNATE: The performance analysis, in this case, is done by choosing a subset of Wi-Fi APs in the interference region of LTE. At any given time the number of Wi-Fi APs that can transmit in parallel is given by INCARNATE scheme.

4. LWA: In case of LWA, LTE small cell can steer the traffic to any Wi-Fi AP in the region to serve a UE. At any given time the number of Wi-Fi APs that can transmit follows MHCPP.

5. LWA with INCARNATE: This method includes steering LTE traffic on to a confined set of APs chosen by INCARNATE scheme to perform LWA operation.

6. LWA with mINCARNATE: This method enables an enhanced handover mechanism which intents to achieve improved throughput as compared to a regular LWA handover.

7.1   Number of Parallel Transmissions in INCARNATE Scheme

The INCARNATE scheme not only chooses the APs in the interference region of LTE to transmit but also improves the number of parallel transmissions. Figure 4 captures the number of APs that can transmit in parallel at any given instance. When Matérn threshold is low (*i.e.*, when the detection threshold is very high), the number of APs that can transmit in parallel in a given region is same in both traditional Wi-Fi and Wi-Fi with INCARNATE scheme. As the detection threshold decreases, the number of APs that can transmit in parallel increases in Wi-Fi with INCARNATE scheme as compared to traditional Wi-Fi.

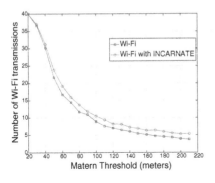

Fig. 4. Number of Wi-Fi transmissions at any given time instance.

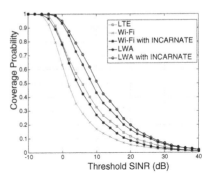

Fig. 5. Coverage probability of LTE, Wi-Fi, Wi-Fi with INCARNATE scheme, LWA, and LWA with INCARNATE scheme.

7.2   Coverage Probability of LWA System

In this section, we have validated the simulation results of coverage probability of LWA system with our analytical model. Coverage probability of INCARNATE scheme outperforms the traditional MHCPP scheme which uses only Wi-Fi by 17% as depicted in Fig. 5. Likewise, LWA with INCARNATE scheme excels by

6.23% as compared to LWA system. Figure 6 depicts the coverage probability of non co-located LWA using the proposed analytical framework and simulation experiment. SINR thresholds for coverage of LTE and Wi-Fi are varied on the X-axis, and the number of users prevailing in the coverage of LTE or Wi-Fi in a given region is captured on the Y-axis. As the SINR threshold increases, the probability that a user will be in the coverage of LTE or Wi-Fi decreases.

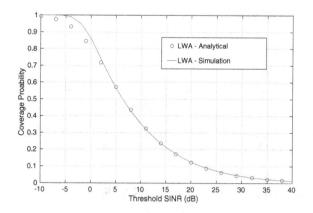

Fig. 6. Coverage probability of non co-located LWA system.

7.3   CDF of Data Rates of LTE, Wi-Fi, and LWA Systems

UE data rate is captured in case of (i) LTE, (ii) Wi-Fi, (iii) Wi-Fi with INCAR-NATE scheme, (iv) Non co-located LWA, and (v) Non co-located LWA with INCARNATE scheme. Data rate observed by the proposed Wi-Fi with INCAR-NATE scheme is better than the data rate observed in regular Wi-Fi, this is because the number of parallel transmissions in case of proposed INCARNATE scheme is more than the traditional Wi-Fi. Figure 7 depicts the performance of LTE, Wi-Fi, Wi-Fi with INCARNATE scheme, LWA without INCARNATE scheme (*i.e.*, LWA), and LWA with INCARNATE scheme. The LWA users in the proposed LWA with INCARNATE scheme outperforms the regular LWA significantly. This is because those UEs which are suffering from high interference from LTE are chosen as the target to be served through Wi-Fi in order to improve their data rates. Hence, our proposed scheme selectively enables those Wi-Fi APs in LTE interference region and provides high data rates for those UEs. The data rate of Wi-Fi with INCARNATE scheme is better compared to the traditional MHCPP scheme which uses only Wi-Fi by 73% as illustrated in Fig. 7. Similarly, LWA which involves INCARNATE scheme excels by 51% as compared to regular LWA system.

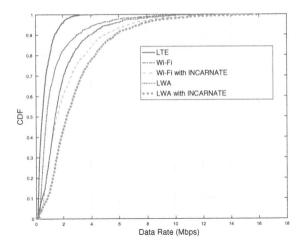

Fig. 7. CDF of data rates of LTE, Wi-Fi, Wi-Fi with INCARNATE scheme, LWA, and LWA with INCARNATE scheme.

7.4   Handover Analysis of mINCARNATE

In the handover experiment, UEs follow Random WayPoint (RWP) mobility model and initially all the SeNBs and APs are deployed using PPP. Handovers are counted based on the number of intersections of boundaries during the trajectory of UE movement. The term, trajectory exponent 'γ' is used as unity for simplicity.

The number of handovers in native LWA and proposed mINCARNATE are compared w.r.t. the simulation time as depicted in Fig. 8. Mean number of handovers of LTE in both the cases remain almost same. However, in mINCARNATE scheme, the number of handovers of Wi-Fi are reduced when the velocity of the users is low. In case of very high velocity, mINCARNATE leads to increase in the number of handovers to serve the UEs better.

7.5   Throughput Analysis of mINCARNATE

Figure 9 compares throughputs of native LWA and LWA with mINCARNATE under varying velocities. mINCARNATE enables more Wi-Fi nodes positioned at the interfering region of LTE, thus leading to improvement in throughput. In Fig. 9, the density of deployment is 40 SeNBs and 40 APs in the given region. The user stays connected to the older LWA node unless it finds a new LWA node to which it can associate with. In case of lower velocity, the user takes a longer time to find the new LWA node with higher SINR compared to moderate velocity. In case of moderate velocity, the user frequently finds a new LWA node and gets associated with it. It leads to significant improvement in the throughput. mINCARNATE improves the throughput by 53% as compared to native LWA handover.

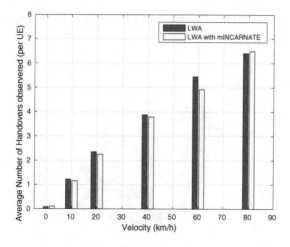

Fig. 8. Number of handovers observed for varying user velocity.

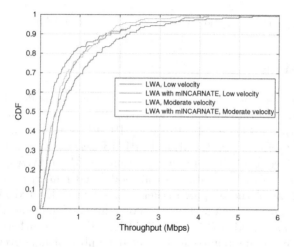

Fig. 9. CDF of throughput observed by users with low and moderate velocity where LWA deployment density $\lambda_l = \lambda_w = 40$.

7.6   Optimal Density of LWA Nodes for mINCARNATE

The proposed cost function is derived considering the density of LWA nodes and user velocity as major factors. Figure 10 illustrates the variation in proposed cost function with respect to user velocity and the density of LWA node deployment. The objective is to minimize the cost function in order to find the number of LWA nodes that have to be enabled. As the velocity increases the number of handovers increases and hence it leads to increase in the cost. But contrarily, the cost fluctuates as the density of LWA node deployment increases, which can be clearly seen from the figure. The optimal number of LWA nodes that can be enabled in the given region of interest can be obtained by minimizing the cost function with input as variable UE velocity.

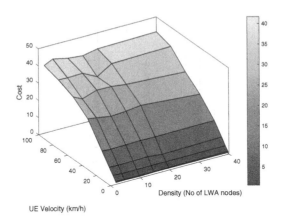

Fig. 10. Proposed cost function with varying density of LWA nodes and velocity.

8   Conclusions

In this paper, we have presented a tractable mathematical model for the coverage probability and data rate for non co-located LWA system. We have proposed a modified Matérn Hard-Core Point Process (MHCPP) scheme *i.e.*, INCARNATE scheme that outperforms the traditional MHCPP scheme as UEs that are in the high interfering region of LTE are served through Wi-Fi in LWA system in order to revamp their data rate. Mathematical model and numerical results demonstrated the merits of the proposed scheme in a non co-located LWA scenario. Further, to analyze the LWA system in a non-static environment, INCARNATE scheme is further extended to the mINCARNATE scheme, wherein UEs move in a Random WayPoint approach. Expected number of handover and rate of handover have been analyzed using fibre process. Expected number of handovers and average data rate have been analytically modeled. Proposed cost function facilitates to obtain the optimal density of LWA nodes using mINCAR-NATE scheme. Optimal deployment of LWA nodes can lead to improved cost efficiency for mobile operators. In terms of data rate and coverage probability, we have depicted that Wi-Fi with INCARNATE scheme outperforms the traditional MHCPP scheme that uses only Wi-Fi by 73% and 17% in terms of data rate and coverage probability, respectively. LWA with INCARNATE scheme excels by 51% and 6.23% as compared to regular LWA, in terms of data rate and coverage probability, respectively. Similarly, LWA with mINCARNATE scheme improves the throughput by 53% as compared to native LWA handover.

Acknowledgement. This work was supported by the project "Converged Cloud Communication Technologies", MeitY, Govt. of India.

References

1. Alfano, G., et al.: New insights into the stochastic geometry analysis of dense CSMA networks. In: IEEE INFOCOM, pp. 2642–2650 (2011)
2. Andrews, J.G., Gupta, A.K., Dhillon, H.S.: A primer on cellular network analysis using stochastic geometry. CoRR (2016)
3. Andrews, J.G., et al.: A tractable approach to coverage and rate in cellular networks. IEEE Trans. Commun. **59**(11), 3122–3134 (2011)
4. Baccelli, F., et al.: Stochastic geometry and wireless networks: volume ii applications. Found. Trends® Network. **4**(1–2), 1–312 (2010)
5. Buchholz, H.: The Confluent Hypergeometric Function: With Special Emphasis on Its Applications, vol. 15. Springer Science & Business Media, Heidelberg (2013)
6. Chiu, S.N., et al.: Stochastic Geometry and Its Applications. John Wiley & Sons, Singapore (2013)
7. ElSawy, H., et al.: Stochastic geometry for modeling, analysis, and design of multitier and cognitive cellular wireless networks: a survey. IEEE Commun. Surv. Tutorials **15**(3), 996–1019 (2013)
8. Haenggi, M.: Stochastic Geometry for Wireless Networks. Cambridge University Press, New York (2012)
9. Herman, B., et al.: Extensions to LTE mobility functions for ns-3. In: Proceedings of the 2014 Workshop on Ns-3, pp. 2:1–2:8. ACM, New York (2014)
10. Hoymann, C., Larsson, D., Koorapaty, H., Cheng, J.F.: A lean carrier for LTE. IEEE Commun. Mag. **51**(2), 74–80 (2013)
11. Intel, China, Qualcomm: LTE-WLAN Radio Level Integration and Interworking Enhancement (2015). https://goo.gl/n3euVC
12. Lin, X., et al.: Towards understanding the fundamentals of mobility in cellular networks. IEEE Trans. Wireless Commun. **12**(4), 1686–1698 (2013)
13. Ling, J., et al.: Enhanced capacity and coverage by Wi-Fi LTE integration. IEEE Commun. Mag. **53**(3), 165–171 (2015)
14. Mahmoodi, T., Seetharaman, S.: On using a SDN-based control plane in 5G mobile networks. In: Wireless World Research Forum, Meeting, vol. 32 (2014)
15. Nguyen, H.Q., et al.: A stochastic geometry analysis of dense IEEE 802.11 networks. In: IEEE INFOCOM, pp. 1199–1207 (2007)
16. Sumanta, P., et al.: INCARNATE: an interference aware spatial scheme for tightly coupled LTE-Wi-Fi networks. In: Proceedings of IEEE COMSNETS (2018)
17. Thakkar, M.K., et al.: Reducing ping-pong handovers in LTE by using A1-based measurements. In: Proceedings of NCC (2017)
18. Thomas Valerrian Pasca, S., et al.: Tightly coupled LTE Wi-Fi radio access networks: a demo of LWIP. In: Proceedings of IEEE COMSNETS (2017)
19. Venkataraman, J., et al.: Shot noise models for outage and throughput analyses in wireless ad hoc networks. In: IEEE MILCOM, pp. 1–7 (2006)
20. Wang, X., Quek, T.Q.S., Sheng, M., Li, J.: On the coexistence of Wi-Fi and LTE-U in unlicensed spectrum. In: IEEE ICC, pp. 1–6, May 2017
21. Wang, X., et al.: On the performance analysis of downlink heterogeneous networks with dual connectivity. In: IEEE WCSP (2016)
22. Weber, S.P., et al.: Transmission capacity of wireless ad hoc networks with outage constraints. IEEE Trans. Inf. Theor. **51**(12), 4091–4102 (2005)
23. Win, M.Z., et al.: A mathematical theory of network interference and its applications. Proce. IEEE **97**(2), 205–230 (2009)
24. Zhang, H., et al.: A novel handover mechanism between femtocell and macrocell for LTE based networks. In: ICCSN, pp. 228–231. IEEE (2010)

A Directional Medium Access Control Protocol for 5G Millimeter-Wave Local Area Networks

Bharadwaj Satchidanandan[1]([✉]), Simon Yau[1], Siva Santosh Ganji[1],
P. R. Kumar[1], Ahsan Aziz[2], Amal Ekbal[2], and Nikhil Kundargi[2]

[1] Texas A&M University, College Station, USA
bharadwaj.s1990@tamu.edu
[2] National Instruments, Austin, USA

Abstract. The vast amount of spectrum available at millimeter-wave bands has made millimeter-wave communications one of the key enabling technologies of the fifth-generation cellular network. The high directionality of the transmitter and the receivers operating at millimeter-wave frequencies introduces certain novel challenges for medium access control. Specifically, in a scenario where there is relative motion between the transmitter and the receivers, the transmitter must keep track of the direction in which each received signal is, and the receivers must keep track of where the transmitter is, so that they can orient their antenna boresight towards each other, or in a non-line-of-sight environment, in directions that optimize the link gain, in order to establish a physical link. In this paper, we propose TrackMAC, a directional medium access control protocol for millimeter-wave local area networks, that allows an access point to efficiently track every station associated with it at small overheads. The proposed protocol can be implemented squarely within the specifications of the IEEE 802.11ad standard for millimeter-wave local area networking.

1 Introduction

Frequency bands between 30 GHz and 300 GHz, also known as the millimeter-wave (mm-wave) bands, offer an unprecedented amount of spectrum for wireless communications. In the year 2016, the United States' Federal Communications Commission released 10.85 GHz of spectrum in the mm-wave band, 7 GHz of which is unlicensed, for the development of 5G technologies to meet the increasing demands of wireless networks [1]. Since then, many other countries have also released spectrum in mm-wave bands for field trials [2].

This material is based upon work partially supported by NSF under Contract Nos. CNS-1719384, CCF-1619085, CNS-1646449, and Science & Technology Center Grant CCF-0939370, Office of Naval Research under Contract N00014-18-1-2048, and the U.S. Army Research Office under Contract Nos. W911NF-18-10331 and W911NF-15-1-0279.

© Springer Nature Switzerland AG 2019
S. Biswas et al. (Eds.): COMSNETS 2018, LNCS 11227, pp. 150–171, 2019.
https://doi.org/10.1007/978-3-030-10659-1_7

While mm-wave bands provide large amounts of bandwidth, they also pose certain novel challenges that have to be addressed in order to use these bands effectively. The first is the significantly higher path loss of mm-wave frequencies as compared to sub-6 GHz frequencies that are in use today. It follows from the Friis equation

$$P_R = P_T G_R G_T (\frac{\lambda}{4\pi r})^2,$$

that the path loss of a signal scales as $\frac{1}{f^2}$, where f is the frequency of the signal. Here, P_T denotes the transmitted power, P_R the received power, G_T the transmit antenna gain, G_R the receive antenna gain, r the distance between the transmitter and the receiver, and $\lambda = \frac{c}{f}$ the wavelength of the transmitted signal. This implies that at frequencies close to 60 GHz, which is the frequency band that is of interest in this paper, the path loss of the signal is about 27 dB higher than that at 2.5 GHz.

A standard approach to combat this path loss is to use tens or even hundreds of antennae at the transmitter and perform transmit beamforming so that most of the power is transmitted in the direction of the receiver. The receiver, similarly, performs receive beamforming so that the signal received from a particular direction, viz., the direction in which the transmitter is present, is amplified. Since the antenna dimensions are inversely proportional to the operating frequency, it becomes possible, when operating at 60 GHz, to embed tens or even hundreds of antennae in the form factor of a mobile device and increase the antenna gain in certain directions [3–11]. In fact, the antenna gains G_R and G_T for a given antenna aperture scales as f^2, so that the net attenuation between the transmitter and the receiver is 27 dB *lower* at 60 GHz as compared to 2.5 GHz. The large amount of spectrum available at mm-wave bands, combined with the lower net attenuation, makes mm-wave communications an enticing prospect for improving the performance of wireless networks by several orders of magnitude. This in turn could enable applications such as virtual reality and wireless backhauling that may not be efficient on current wireless networks.

The use of highly directional beams for transmission and reception introduces certain novel challenges for Medium Access Control (MAC) design. One such challenge is the issue of "deafness" described in [12]. Existing MAC protocols such as CSMA/CA rely on the omni-directional nature of transmissions and receptions, and consequently, are not well suited for orchestrating the medium access of directional nodes. Another challenge that stems from directionality is the necessity for the transmitter to track the location of each station (STA) associated with it, assumed to be mobile, and similarly for the STAs to track the location of the Access Point (AP) in their frame of reference. In addition to translational motion of an STA, its rotational motion also affects the link gain. This requires the transmitter to track the net effect of the rotational and translational motion of each associated station and accordingly adapt its antenna configuration in order to establish a physical link. Similarly, each station must adapt its antenna configuration to its own movements so as to maintain the physical link with the transmitter.

Another distinguishing feature of mm-wave signals is that they are susceptible to blockages by commonly occurring objects in offices and other indoor environments. The human body, for example, attenuates a mm-wave signal power by a factor of about 30 dB, and links can be broken when an object ends up in between two nodes, either due to the movement of the nodes or objects.

The aforementioned challenges are unique to mm-wave networks, and it is clear that new directional MAC protocols need to be developed that take into account the unique aspects of mm-wave links so that efficient networks can be designed. In particular, it is essential for mm-wave MAC protocols to overcome the challenges of deafness, mobility and blockages in mm-wave networks. In this paper, we present TrackMAC, a directional MAC protocol designed to address these challenges.

Firstly, TrackMAC allows for both contention-based and scheduling-based service periods for channel access, while keeping track of the movements of all associated STAs. It does this based on a conservative estimate of how rapidly nodes in the network can move and rotate. To capture this quantity succinctly, we introduce the notion of *topological coherence time* of a network. Intuitively, the topological coherence time is the maximum duration that the topology of the network remains approximately constant. This does not mean that all STAs remain in a fixed position and orientation during the whole period, but rather that within this period, the configurations of the antennae do not need to change in order for them to communicate. This duration is primarily influenced by the mobility (both translational and rotational speeds) of the nodes in the network, but can also be affected by other factors such as the beamwidths of the antennae, the properties of the environment, etc. We discuss this in more detail in Sect. 3.2.

Secondly, TrackMAC overcomes one of the key bottlenecks which limits the performance of a mm-wave network. The high directionality of transmissions introduces a significant delay for initial access and association of STAs with the AP. With a small overhead, TrackMAC eliminates the need for constant rediscovery and re-association and allows the AP to track the STAs effectively.

Thirdly, we show in Sect. 4 that TrackMAC can be implemented squarely within the specifications of IEEE 802.11ad standard for mm-wave local area networks. In particular, TrackMAC can be realized by reprogramming only the scheduling layer of the 802.11ad network stack.

The rest of this paper is organized as follows. Section 2 presents an overview of related work in this area. Section 3 describes the TrackMAC protocol and analyzes its throughput performance. Section 4 highlights the key features of the IEEE 802.11ad standard, and details how TrackMAC can be implemented within the framework of the standard by reprogramming only the scheduling layer of the network stack. Section 5 presents simulation results demonstrating the tracking performance of the proposed MAC protocol. Section 6 concludes the paper.

2   Related Work

Prior to the advent of mm-wave communications and networks, directional medium access control protocols were studied in the context of increasing the network capacity since directional links result in reduced interference and increased spatial reuse. One of the earliest works in directional MAC is [13], which considers an ad hoc wireless network, and derives analytically the average progress of a packet for two directional MAC protocols, viz., the slotted ALOHA and the non-persistent CSMA. Evaluating the average progress of a packet requires the knowledge of the routing policy used in the transport layer, for which two particular routing policies are considered, viz., the Most-Forward-Routing (MFR) policy and the Point-to-Destination (PTD) routing policy. The parameters of the MAC protocols are consequently optimized to maximize the average progress of packets. All results are derived under the assumption that the nodes in the network are stationary, and that each node knows the direction in which any other node lies, so that the direction in which a node has to point its beam in order to communicate with another node is time-invariant. Also, while the transmissions are directional, the receptions are assumed to be omni-directional, which alleviates the problem of deafness.

Another early work on directional MAC is [14], where an ad hoc network with directional transmission and omni-directional reception is considered. As in [13], the location of the nodes are assumed to be known and time-invariant. A variant of the slotted ALOHA protocol that takes the directionality of the nodes into account is presented, and its performance is evaluated.

The transport capacity of an arbitrary network is derived in [15] under the protocol model and the physical model. The fundamental idea is to derive bounds for regions known as the exclusion region of a transmission, and use it to bound the transport capacity. In [16], the exclusion region for arbitrary antenna patterns is derived under the protocol model, which in turn can be used to derive the transport capacity of ad hoc directional wireless networks with arbitrary antenna patterns. As in most such works, mobility and tracking are not considered in this paper.

In [17], two directional MAC protocols are presented, namely, the Basic Directional MAC (DMAC) and the Multihop RTS MAC. Legacy 802.11 protocols designed for omni-directional transmitters and receivers employ the well-known RTS/CTS mechanism to alleviate the hidden terminal problem. A CTS message informs an otherwise hidden terminal about a scheduled transmission that it may be unable to sense. The node then updates its Network Allocation Vector (NAV) table to include this transmission, which allows it to perform virtual carrier sensing, in addition to physical carrier sensing, before attempting transmission. The Basic DMAC protocol presented in [17] extends this idea to a directional network. Similar in spirit to legacy 802.11 protocols, in Basic DMAC, each node maintains an NAV table corresponding to each direction for the purpose of virtual carrier sensing. Before transmitting in a certain direction, a node performs physical channel sensing, and then checks the directional NAV table to see if there is any scheduled transmission in that direction that it could interfere with.

If not, then it transmits an RTS message to initiate a connection. Also presented in [17] are certain drawbacks of the Basic DMAC protocol, and a variation of the Basic DMAC protocol, called the multihop RTS MAC protocol. Both of these protocols, however, assume that every node knows the position of each of its neighbor, and that it knows the beamforming weights to be used to communicate with any particular neighbor. It is also assumed that nodes have access to two antenna modes, viz., the omni-directional mode and the directional mode. When a node is idle, it switches its antenna pattern to the omni-directional mode so that it can receive signals from any of its neighbors, which alleviates the problem of deafness.

Reference [18] improves upon the Basic DMAC protocol presented in [17] by employing tones, or sinusoids of a certain frequency, which are transmitted omni-directionally so that the neighbors of a node can be informed regarding periods of deafness, and the transmissions of the neighbors intended to that node are accordingly adapted.

In addition to the aforementioned papers, several other works such as [19–21] also present directional MAC protocols for ad hoc directional wireless networks, but they too do not address the issue of mobility, assume that the directions of each node's neighbors are known, and most assume that the receivers, when idle, perform omni-directional sensing, so that the problem of deafness is alleviated.

To the best of our knowledge, only few papers deal with the problem of designing directional MAC protocols in the presence of mobility. Reference [22] presents one such protocol. It is assumed here that each node partitions its neighboring area into M sectors or directions, and that the node is equipped with M antenna arrays, one for transmitting and receiving in each direction. A transmitter that wishes to send packets to a certain node transmits an RTS signal in all directions simultaneously. Based on the received signal, the receiver identifies the direction of the transmitter. The receiver then sends a CTS packet, again in all directions simultaneously, and the transmitter notes the direction in which it receives the maximum power. This essentially amounts to an omni-directional transmission of RTS and CTS packets. At the end of this procedure, the transmitter and receiver know the beams to use to communicate during the data exchange phase. This process is repeated every time one node wishes to communicate with another node, which results in a rather high overhead. The Circular Directional RTS MAC (CDR-MAC) protocol presented in [23] employs a similar scheme to discover the directions of its neighbors, but in addition, also allows the nodes to remember the location of the nodes by means of a "location table" which each node maintains. A node that wishes to transmit broadcasts an RTS message in all directions sequentially. The receiver, based on the direction in which the RTS was received, updates its location table with the identity of the transmitter and its direction, and transmits a CTS in that direction. The transmitter then computes the direction of the receiver based on the CTS message and updates its location table accordingly. Mobility of the nodes is handled by updating this table as and when new information is received. However, a major drawback of this scheme is that it is only a best-effort scheme, in that there is no mechanism to guarantee that the location tables of the nodes do not become outdated.

Reference [24] presents a tracking scheme for mobile nodes wherein the base station points its beam in directions adjacent to the current antenna boresight to recalibrate its beam towards a mobile station. However, this tracking mechanism is presented as a standalone procedure for tracking a single mobile station, and the larger problem of how this mechanism is integrated with the MAC protocol so as to continuously track and serve multiple mobile stations over an extended period of time is not studied. This is one of the main issues that is addressed in this paper.

Certain papers also address the problem of directional MAC in the context of mm-wave networks. The main difference between a mm-wave network and a sub-6 GHz directional wireless network is that mm-wave frequencies are more susceptible to blockage by commonly occurring objects in an environment, especially an indoor environment, and consequently, the statistics of the channel between the transmitter and the receiver are vastly different in the two cases.

Among the earliest works on the topic of mm-wave MAC are [25] and [26] where interference analysis for mm-wave networks is carried out taking into account the high directivity of the individual links. It is shown that unlike in omni-directional networks where majority of the packet losses is due to collisions arising from simultaneous transmissions, in the case of mm-wave networks, the majority of the packet losses is due to misalignments between the boresights of the transmit antenna and the receive antenna. This leads to the pseudo-wired abstraction which is used in some subsequent papers for MAC design for mm-wave networks. One of these is [27], where it is assumed that both the AP as well as the STAs are fixed and that the topology of the network is known to all nodes, and in particular, the AP. A protocol to obtain the topology during network initialization is also outlined. The AP, therefore, points its beam in the direction of the intended receiver whenever it wishes to communicate. If the line-of-sight path is blocked, say due to a human being arriving in between the two nodes, the AP, based on its knowledge of the network topology, requests some other STA to act as a relay between itself and the STA that is blocked. It is assumed that all STAs sense omni-directionally, and once they sense a signal, steer their beams to receive directionally, so that the problem of deafness does not arise when setting up the relay path. Reference [12] presents a learning-based protocol using which an efficient TDM schedule can be converged upon by the nodes in the network. Here again, all nodes are assumed to be directional and stationary, and each node is assumed to know the direction of each of its neighbors.

A three-stage process to find the optimal beamforming weights by two nodes is presented in [28]. The first stage finds the optimal quasi-omni sector in which the receiver lies, the second stage the optimal sector within the quasi-omni sector, and the third stage the optimal beam weights within the sector. The problem of medium access control is not addressed in this paper. References [29–37] are some of the other papers dealing with the problem of directional MAC for mm-wave networks.

To the best of our knowledge, except for our own initial conference paper [38] on this topic upon which this paper is based, there exists *no* prior work on the design of MAC protocols for mm-wave wireless networks where the nodes are (i) mobile, (ii) at unknown locations to begin with, and are (iii) discovered, and (iv) tracked efficiently by the access point at small overheads, thereby removing the need for constant rediscovery. In this paper, we expand upon [38] along three specific directions:

1. We introduce a precise definition for topological coherence time, a notion which is of central importance in the proposed MAC protocol,
2. We outline a scheme that allows for increased duration for contention-based channel access, a feature that is desirable in situations where the traffic pattern is unpredictable or bursty, and
3. We test the performance of the proposed MAC protocol in the presence of a physical channel, modeled using the indoor millimeter-wave channel model agreed upon in the Third Generation Partnership Project (3GPP) 5G standards.

3 TrackMAC: A Directional MAC Protocol for Millimeter-Wave Indoor Local Area Networks

This section describes the TrackMAC protocol for mm-wave wireless indoor local area networks. TrackMAC contains many parameters that have to be chosen based on system specifications, such as the maximum translational speed of the stations, their maximum rotational speeds, the beamwidths of the nodes, the maximum number of stations that are to be supported by the AP, etc. For the sake of exposition, we describe TrackMAC and the process of determining its parameters using a running example which assumes specific numerical values for these quantities. The running example presents a worst-case design in that the values chosen for the system parameters are conservative for an indoor environment. While a design based on more realistic values of system parameters would undoubtedly yield a more efficient MAC, our primary goal here is not to optimize the efficiency of our design for specific scenarios. Rather, our aim is to describe the methodology that maps the system parameters to TrackMAC's parameters. As will be clear later, the methodology that is described applies to a broad range of realistic system parameters, and the parameters of TrackMAC can be tuned to optimize its performance.

3.1 System Specifications

Consider an infrastructure wireless network with an AP and n associated STAs operating in an indoor environment as shown in Fig. 1. Both the AP as well as the STAs communicate in the mm-wave band. Specifically, in adherence to the

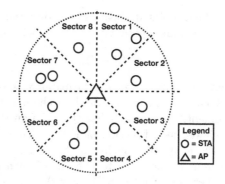

Fig. 1. An infrastructure wireless network

IEEE 802.11ad standard, they are assumed to communicate at a center frequency of 60.48 GHz, and a bandwidth of 2.16 GHz.

We assume that the AP is fixed and that the STAs are mobile. The STAs move and rotate in an arbitrary fashion subject only to the constraints that their maximum translational speed is $v_{max} = 2$ m/s and their maximum rotational speed is $\omega_{max} = 2\pi$ rad/s. Note that these are conservative bounds for these parameters in an indoor environment. We also assume that the AP and the STAs are separated by a distance of at least $d_{min} = 1m$ at all times. This is typical of indoor environments such as office spaces, airports, etc., where the APs are usually mounted on the ceiling and the STAs are distributed on the floor. We assume that both the AP as well as the STAs have an antenna beamwidth of $\theta = 10°$, both for transmission as well as reception. Finally, we suppose that the maximum number of STAs that the AP has to support at any time is $k = 25$.

3.2 Topological Coherence Time

Of central importance to the proposed MAC protocol is the notion of $(d, q)-topological\ coherence\ time$. The mobility of STAs in the network causes its topology to vary with time. The topological coherence time of a network, roughly speaking, is the time duration until which the network topology remains "approximately constant." To make this more precise, let $\phi_0(t)$ and $\psi_0(t)$ denote, respectively, the azimuth angle and the elevation angle of the AP's antenna boresight at time t, and let $\phi_i(t)$ and $\psi_i(t)$ denote those of STA i at time t. Suppose that at time $t = 0$, the AP's antenna boresight and a STA's, say STA 1's, antenna boresight are oriented in such a manner that a minimum specified link gain G_* dB required to establish a physical link is exceeded by at least d dB, where $d > 0$ is some fixed constant. Let $G(t)$ denote the link gain between the AP and STA 1 at time t. We therefore have that $G(0) \geq G_* + d$. Suppose now that at time $t = 0^+$, the AP orients its beam in some other direction, say to serve some other STA. Then, the $(d, q)-topological$ coherence time T_{TC} is defined as the maximum time T at which the AP can point its beam in the direction $(\phi_0(0), \psi_0(0))$, the last known orientation to communicate with STA 1, such that

$$\mathbb{P}(G(T) \geq G(0) - d) \geq 1 - q,$$

where $q > 0$ is a fixed constant. Here, the probability is taken over the random mobility of the STA as well as the random channel fluctuations due to changes in the environment. We assume that the term on the left hand side of the above inequality, viewed as a function of T for a fixed d, is nonincreasing. We also assume that the channel is such that for any $d > 0$ and $q > 0$, the (d, q)−topological coherence time is finite. The case when it is infinite corresponds to a scenario where neither the STAs nor the environment exhibit any mobility, and is of limited interest.

Once the constants d and q are fixed, we drop the qualifier (d, q) and refer to the above quantity as simply the topological coherence time.

3.3   The Protocol

TrackMAC slots time into intervals of duration $T_{TC}/2$. The rationale for slotting time in this fashion will be clear shortly. These time slots are referred to as "macroslots." Following [38], in our running example, we assume the topological coherence time to be 10 ms, which yields a macroslot duration of 5 ms.

Depending on the maximum number of STAs that are to be served by the AP, each macroslot is further divided into several intervals known as "microslots." Specifically, if a maximum of k STAs are to be served by an AP, then each macroslot is divided into k microslots. In our running example, we fix $k = 25$, which yields a microslot duration of 200 μs. The slotting of time into macroslots and microslots is illustrated in Fig. 2.

Suppose now that n STAs are associated with the AP, where $n \leq k$. Track-MAC schedules each STA i, $i \in \{1, \ldots, n\}$, in at least one microslot in every

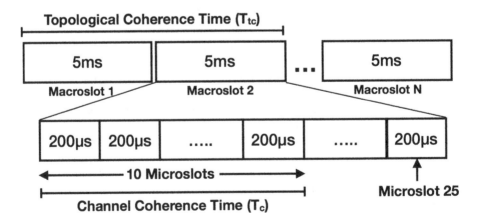

Fig. 2. Division of time into macroslots, and of macroslots into microslots

macroslot. If $n = k$, then each STA is scheduled in exactly one microslot. Suppose that in a microslot, the AP communicates with STA i. During that microslot, the AP informs the STA as a part of control information the microslot in which the STA is next scheduled. This microslot could either belong to the same macroslot or to the next macroslot. Since the time duration between any two microslots belonging to consecutive (or the same) macroslots is at most T_{TC}, it follows from the definition of topological coherence time that when the AP and STA i communicate next, with "high" probability, i.e., with probability at least $1 - q$, their antenna boresights would be oriented in such a manner that the resulting link gain is higher than the minimum required link gain G_* to establish the link. If and once the link is established, the AP and the STA use pilot symbols to recalibrate their antenna orientations and optimize the link gain, a process known as beam refinement. In the event that the AP and the STA are unable to establish the link due to insufficient link gain, the STA terminates the connection and attempts to reconnect with the AP in the following "Initial Access (IA) phase" - a period during which new nodes that wish to join the network are discovered and associated with the AP. The procedure for IA is described in Sect. 3.5.

3.4 Throughput Analysis

We assume throughout that the physical layer employs single-carrier modulation. Similar analysis can be carried out for other popular modulation formats such as Orthogonal Frequency Division Multiplexing (OFDM), and would yield similar throughput results.

We first derive the MAC overhead required for the functioning of TrackMAC. In order to enable the demodulation of the received signal, in the beginning of each microslot, the AP and the STA have to perform the functions of timing recovery, frame synchronization, beam refinement, and channel estimation. In addition, they may also have to exchange certain control information such as MAC schedule. In order to perform these functions, certain pilot symbols have to be allocated in each microslot. In what follows, we estimate the amount of pilot symbols required to perform each of the aforementioned operations.

Symbol timing recovery and frame synchronization are typically performed using standard sequences such as the Zadoff-Chu sequence or the Golay sequence of various possible lengths, owing to certain autocorrelation properties that they possess. As shown in [39], a pilot length of 2048 symbols provides robust timing recovery. Following [38], we assume in our running example that 2048 symbols are allocated in each microslot for timing recovery. A channel bandwidth of 2.16 GHz translates to a symbol duration T_S of $\frac{1}{W} = 0.46$ ns. This implies that timing recovery consumes about 1 μs in each microslot.

The pilot duration required for Channel Estimation (CE) is dictated by the channel delay spread. Prior channel measurement studies [40] have shown that for millimeter-wave indoor channels, the channel delay spread is at most 500 ns. While CE pilots extending for the duration of the channel delay spread are sufficient to estimate the impulse response, allocating more pilot symbols, thereby extending the duration of CE pilots, allows the receiver to smoothen the impulse response estimate of the channel in the presence of noise. In our example, we allocate a pilot duration of 5 μs for channel estimation, which is an order of magnitude larger than the maximum delay spread.

We next examine how often within a microslot channel estimation has to be performed. This depends upon the coherence time T_C of the channel. Recall that the channel coherence time has the operational meaning as the amount of time that the channel impulse response remains "significantly correlated," so that it is sufficient to perform channel estimation just once every T_C time units. The coherence time of a channel is given by $T_C = \frac{1}{\Delta f}$, where Δf is the doppler spread introduced by the channel. The doppler spread, in turn, depends on the translational speed of the receiver, and is given by $\Delta f = \frac{fv}{c}$, where f is the operating frequency, v is relative velocity between the transmitter and the receiver in the radial direction, and c is the speed of light. For the mobility parameters assumed, we obtain the value $\Delta f = 400\,\mathrm{Hz}$, and $T_C = 2.5\,\mathrm{ms}$. Since the channel coherence time is an order of magnitude higher than the microslot duration, the channel impulse response remains significantly correlated over a microslot, and it is sufficient to estimate the channel just once in a microslot. Therefore, the total time consumed by channel estimation pilots in each microslot is 5 μs.

The pilot duration for beam refinement is estimated next. Algorithms such as the Least Mean Squares (LMS) algorithm can be used in conjunction with pilot sequences to converge on the optimal beam orientations. The number of pilots to be allocated depends upon the convergence properties of the underlying algorithm. In our running example, in adherence to the IEEE 802.11ad standard, we allocate 10 μs for beam refinement.

Finally, a certain duration $t_{control}$ is reserved in every microslot for the AP and the STA to exchange necessary control information such the microslot in which the STA is scheduled next, the microslots that are reserved for contention, etc. We allocate $t_{control} = 5\,\mu s$ for this purpose, allowing the nodes to exchange about 10000 symbols of control information every microslot. With 16-QAM signaling, this translates to an uncoded bit rate of 40 kilobits per microslot.

Adding all of the above overheads, we obtain a total MAC overhead of 21 μs per microslot. Since a microslot duration in our example is 200 μs, it follows that the required MAC overhead is about 10%. We reiterate at this juncture that this is a conservative estimate of the pilot duration in each microslot, and the typical overheads required are likely to be much lower than this quantity.

We now estimate the throughput of the proposed MAC protocol. Note that in each microslot in which the AP and a STA communicate, they have about 180 μs to exchange payload data. For a symbol duration of 0.46 ns, this translates to a data rate of about 360000 symbols per microslot. Assuming a 16−QAM signal constellation and a rate-1/2 channel code, we obtain a coded data rate of 720 kilobits per microslot. If each associated STA is scheduled exactly once in each macroslot (the case $n = k$), we obtain a per STA throughput of 144 Mbps. This, of course, is assuming that the STA does not get disconnected from the AP. Multiplying the per-STA throughput by k yields a network throughput of 3.6 Gbps.

3.5   Initial Access

The Initial Access (IA) phase discovers new nodes that wish to join the network and associates them with the AP. In order to perform IA, TrackMAC periodically designates certain macroslots as IA macroslots. Suppose that in the beginning of an IA macroslot, there are $n < k$ STAs associated with the AP. Note that this is a necessary condition for the AP to associate new nodes with itself. During the IA macroslot, the n associated STAs are scheduled exactly once, and the remaining $k - n$ microslots are reserved for node discovery. During these microslots, the AP chooses a direction at random and transmits a beacon in that direction using a low-rate modulation and coding scheme. A new node that wishes to join the network configures its antenna in the quasi-omnidirectional mode, as defined in the IEEE 802.11ad standard, and awaits the reception of a beacon. Though a quasi-omnidirectional pattern results in reduced link gain, the fact that the beacon is transmitted at low rate enables the receiver to decode it despite the SNR being small. Once an STA decodes the beacon, the AP and the STA perform the association-beamforming training procedure specified in 802.11ad [41] to orient their beams in an optimal fashion and thereby establish a high SNR link.

3.6   Incorporating Contention-Based Channel Access

TrackMAC can also be configured to provide contention-based channel access. Consider a situation where the number of STAs n associated with the AP is lesser than k. Scheduling each STA exactly once in a macroslot, thereby ensuring that all STAs are tracked, leaves $k - n$ microslots unassigned to any STA. These microslots can be assigned for contention-based channel access, and any contention scheme can be used by the STAs during these periods for channel access. This framework is also in adherence to the IEEE 802.11ad standard, as described in the next section.

In systems where the traffic pattern is bursty, TrackMAC can be modified to provide additional time for contention-based channel access. The macroslots can be partitioned in a non-uniform fashion into microslots, and the STAs can be scheduled in microslots that have shorter durations. These scheduled microslots only serve the purposes of (i) tracking the STAs, and (ii) exchanging control information such as the next microslot in which the STA is scheduled, the microslots that are assigned for contention, etc. Consequently, these microslots can be of duration as low as $21\,\mu s$ in our running example. The larger microslots can then be allocated for contention.

4   IEEE 802.11ad-Based Implementation of TrackMAC

The IEEE 802.11ad standard has been developed specifically for mm-wave local area networks. Similar to legacy 802.11 standards, the 802.11ad slots time into intervals known as "beacon intervals (BIs)." While the duration of a beacon

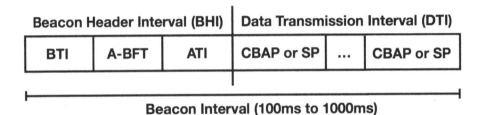

Fig. 3. Structure of a beacon interval

interval can range from 100 ms to 1 s, practical deployments typically choose the BI to be of duration 100 ms.

The structure of a beacon interval is illustrated in Fig. 3. Each BI is divided into two intervals, namely, the Beacon Header Interval (BHI) and Data Transmission Interval (DTI). The BHI in turn is composed of three phases, viz., the Beacon Transmission interval (BTI), the Association-Beamforming Training interval (A-BFT), and the Announcement Time Interval (ATI). During the BTI, the AP chooses a certain sector and transmits the beacon in that sector using the Modulation and Coding Scheme 0 (MCS) specified in the standard [41]. This is the lowest rate MCS defined in the 802.11ad, and provides the maximum error protection. New nodes in that sector that wish to join the network listen for this beacon and if and once they decode it, the STA and the AP perform beamforming training to determine the optimal antenna orientations. This process occurs during the A-BFT phase. The final phase of BHI, the ATI phase, is used to exchange control information with the new nodes. The AP, for example, can inform during the ATI the schedule during the DTI, i.e., the time periods during the DTI when the transmissions are scheduled and those that are open for contention. A more detailed description of the standard can be found in [42], and the standard itself can be found in [41].

We now outline, using our running example, how TrackMAC can be implemented within the framework of 802.11ad. Consider the case when the BI is of duration 100 ms. Since one macroslot is of duration 5 ms, each BI must be composed of 20 macroslots. The fact that the beginning of each BI is allotted for neighbor discovery implies that one in every twenty macroslots must be assigned to be an IA macroslot. The BHI typically extends for about 2 ms, following which we allocate the first ten microslots of the IA macroslot for neighbor discovery. This, of course, assumes that fewer than 15 STAs are associated with the AP in the beginning of the IA macroslot. Non-uniform partitioning of the IA macroslot along the lines mentioned in Sect. 3.6 allows for a higher number of STAs to be associated with the AP during the IA macroslot.

Figure 4 shows the format of an 802.11ad physical layer (PHY) packet. The Short Training Field (STF) is composed of training symbols that are meant to be used for packet detection and symbol timing recovery. The Channel Estimation Field (CEF), as the name suggests, contains training symbols that can be used

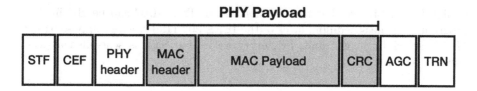

Fig. 4. The format of an IEEE 802.11ad PHY packet

by the receiver for channel estimation. The actual sequences that can be used in these fields are specified in the standard and can be found in [41]. The PHY header contains all the information necessary for the receiver to decode the PHY payload. This includes information such as the MCS scheme used to encode the data, the modulation scheme used (single-carrier or OFDM), etc.

Finally, the Automatic Gain Control (AGC) field contains training symbols that allow the receiver to adjust its gain, and the beamforming training (TRN) field contains pilot symbols that allow the AP and the STA to perform beam refinement. During the TRN phase, the transmitter transmits pilot symbols in a few sectors adjacent to the sector in which the PHY payload was transmitted. From the received signal, the sector that maximizes the received signal power can be determined, and optimal beam directions can be computed.

Note that an 802.11ad PHY packet supports the functions of timing recovery, channel estimation, and beam refinement, that are performed by TrackMAC in each microslot. This allows one to embed a PHY packet in each microslot and attain the desired functionality of TrackMAC. Figure 5 encapsulates the mapping between the 802.11ad parameters and the TrackMAC parameters. In particular, it overlays the macroslot structure of TrackMAC on the beacon intervals of 802.11ad, and the 802.11ad PHY packets on TrackMAC's microslots. It is now

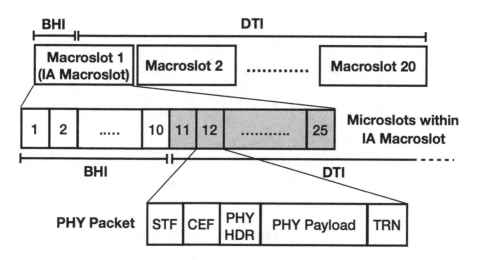

Fig. 5. Implementation of TrackMAC within IEEE 802.11ad specifications

straightforward to see that the functionality of TrackMAC can be obtained by programming the scheduling layer of the IEEE 802.11ad stack to impose Track-MAC's scheduling constraint, i.e., every associated STA is scheduled at least once in each macroslot.

5   Simulation Results

This section presents simulation results demonstrating the tracking performance of the proposed protocol. We simulate a "fully loaded" system, where there are $n = k = 25$ STAs associated with the AP. Both the AP as well as the STAs are equipped with a 64-element uniform linear array with an inter-element spacing of $\lambda/2$, where λ is the operating wavelength. The frequency of operation is set to 60.48 GHz. The antenna pattern of this array in the azimuth plane is shown in Fig. 6. We simulate the network for a duration of ten macroslots, which amounts to 50 ms. Each macroslot, following our running example, consists of 25 microslots.

We evaluate the performance of TrackMac in a typical indoor Line-of-Sight (LoS) environment. While multiple channel models have been proposed [43–47] to capture the propagation characteristics of mm-wave signals, a consensus is yet to be reached regarding the most accurate model. We consider in our simulations the channel model that has been agreed in the Third Generation Partnership

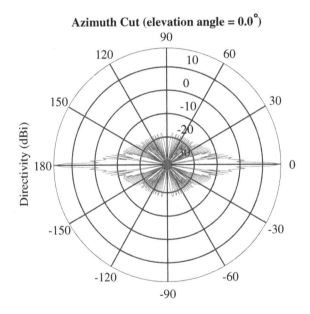

Azimuth Cut (elevation angle = 0.0°)

Directivity (dBi), Broadside at 0.00 degrees

Fig. 6. Azimuth pattern of a $\lambda/2$-spaced ULA at 60.48 GHz

Project (3GPP) 5G standards. Tapped Delay Line - D model [43] with a single LoS path and a short delay profile has been proposed to model indoor office environments at 60 GHz. The power delay profile specified by the model is as given in the following table.

Tap index	Delay ($\times 16$ ns)	Power (dB)
1	0	-0.2
1	0	-13.5
2	0.035	-18.8
3	0.612	-21
4	1.363	-22.8
5	1.405	-17.9
6	1.804	-20.1
7	2.596	-21.9
8	1.775	-22.9
9	4.042	-27.8
10	7.937	-23.6
11	9.424	-24.8
12	9.708	-30.0
13	12.525	-27.7

The first tap in the above table, of power -0.2 dB, corresponds to a LoS component, and follows a Rician distribution. All other taps correspond to reflections and follow a Rayleigh distribution. Note that the first tap is the sum of two random variables, one corresponding to a LoS component and another arising from multipath. Note also that the power of the strongest reflected component is more than 10 dB lower than that of the LoS component, suggesting that at mm-wave frequencies, the link quality is determined to a significant extent by whether or not a direct LoS path exists between the transmitter and the receiver.

Figure 7 shows the tracking performance of TrackMAC for different values of translational speeds of the STAs. In this setup, the STA moves randomly with an average speed of (i) 1 m/s, and (ii) 10 m/s, on a unit circle centered at the AP. The ordinate in the figure specifies a point on the unit circle in terms of the angle it makes with respect to the positive-x direction. The blue-colored curve plots the position of a randomly chosen STA across time when the STA moves at an average speed of 1 m/s, and the orange-colored curve plots the orientation of the AP's antenna boresight. At the lower translational speed, the AP tracks the STA closely, whereas as the STA speed increases, the tracking performance degrades. Figure 8 plots the average misalignment between the antenna boresights of the AP and the STAs.

Figures 9 and 10 plot similar results for the case when the STAs exhibit rotational motion. Specifically, Fig. 9 plots the received power, averaged over the

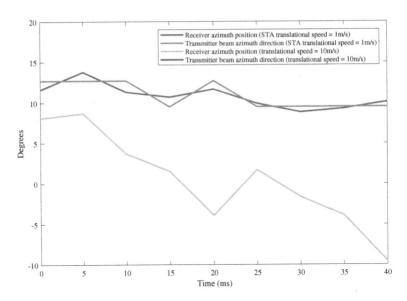

Fig. 7. Tracking of a randomly chosen STA by the AP across time (Color figure online)

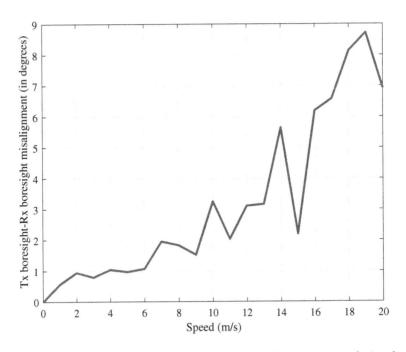

Fig. 8. Tracking performance of the AP as a function of the average translational speed of the STAs

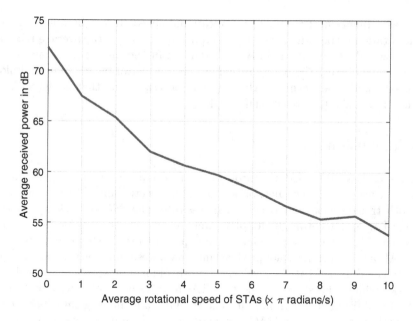

Fig. 9. Average received power vs. average rotational speed of the STAs

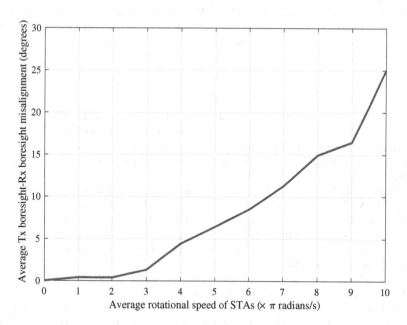

Fig. 10. Tracking performance of the AP as a function of the average translational speed of the STAs

STAs, as a function of their average rotational speed. It can be observed that as the rotational speed increases from 0 rad/s to 2π rad/s, the average received signal power drops by about 7 dB. This reduces further as the rotational speed increases, illustrating the deterioration of tracking performance. Figure 10 plots the misalignment between the AP's antenna boresight and that of the STAs as a function of the STAs' rotational speed.

6 Conclusion

This paper has addressed the problem of medium access control design for millimeter-wave local area networks. The high directionality of the nodes during both transmission and reception necessitates the AP to track the motion of the STAs and accordingly adapt its antenna boresight in order to maintain a physical link. The STAs, similarly, are required to track the relative position of the AP and accordingly adapt their antenna boresights. For this purpose, we have proposed TrackMAC, a novel MAC protocol for mm-wave indoor local area networks, which allows the AP and the STAs to track each other with little overheads. In addition to providing efficient tracking and multi-gigabit-per-second network throughputs, TrackMAC also lends itself to be implementable within the specifications of the IEEE 802.11ad standard for mm-wave local area networks. Specifically, TrackMAC can be realized by reprogramming just the scheduling layer of an IEEE 802.11ad network stack. Future work includes prototyping TrackMAC and evaluating its performance on a mm-wave testbed.

References

1. FCC takes steps to facilitate mobile broadband and next generation wireless technologies in spectrum above 24 GHz. https://apps.fcc.gov/edocs_public/attachmatch/DOC-340301A1.pdf. Accessed 13 Apr 2018
2. 5G spectrum bands. https://gsacom.com/5g-spectrum-bands/. Accessed 13 Apr 2018
3. Gilbert, J.M., Doan, C.H., Emami, S., Shung, C.B.: A 4-Gbps uncompressed wireless HD A/V transceiver chipset. IEEE Micro **28**(2), 56–64 (2008)
4. Piersanti, S., Annoni, L.A., Cassioli, D.: Millimeter waves channel measurements and path loss models. In: 2012 IEEE International Conference on Communications (ICC), pp. 4552–4556 (2012). http://ieeexplore.ieee.org/lpdocs/epic03/wrapper.htm?arnumber=6363950
5. Pi, Z., Khan, F.: An introduction to millimeter-wave mobile broadband systems. IEEE Commun. Mag. **49**(6), 101–107 (2011)
6. Ben-Dor, E., Rappaport, T.S., Qiao, Y., Lauffenburger, S.J.: Millimeter-wave 60 GHz outdoor and vehicle AOA propagation measurements using a broadband channel sounder. In: GLOBECOM - IEEE Global Telecommunications Conference (2011)
7. Rappaport, T.S., Ben-Dor, E., Murdock, J.N., Qiao, Y.: 38 GHz and 60 GHz angle-dependent propagation for cellular & peer-to-peer wireless communications. In: IEEE International Conference on Communications, pp. 4568–4573 (2012)

8. Rappaport, T.S., et al.: Millimeter wave mobile communications for 5G cellular: it will work!. IEEE Access **1**, 335–349 (2013)
9. Bogale, T.E., Le, L.B.: Massive MIMO and mmWave for 5G wireless HetNet: potential benefits and challenges. IEEE Veh. Technol. Mag. **11**(1), 64–75 (2016)
10. Maccartney, G.R., Rappaport, T.S.: 73 GHz millimeter wave propagation measurements for outdoor urban mobile and backhaul communications in New York City. In: 2014 IEEE International Conference on Communications, ICC 2014, pp. 4862–4867 (2014)
11. Rappaport, T.S., MacCartney, G.R., Samimi, M.K., Sun, S.: Wideband millimeter-wave propagation measurements and channel models for future wireless communication system design. IEEE Trans. Commun. **63**(9), 3029–3056 (2015)
12. Singh, S., Mudumbai, S., Madhow, U.: Distributed coordination with deaf neighbors: efficient medium access for 60 GHz mesh networks. In: Proceedings - IEEE INFOCOM (2010)
13. Chang, C.-J., Chang, J.-F.: Optimal design parameters in a multihop packet radio network using random access techniques. Comput. Netw. ISDN Syst. **11**(5), 337–351 (1986)
14. Zander, J.: Slotted aloha multihop packet radio networks with directional antennas. Electron. Lett. **26**(25), 2098–2100 (1990)
15. Gupta, P., Kumar, P.R.: The capacity of wireless networks. IEEE Trans. Inf. Theory **46**(2), 388–404 (2000)
16. Agarwal, A., Kumar, P.: Improved capacity bounds for wireless networks. Wirel. Commun. Mob. Comput. **4**(3), 251–261 (2004)
17. Choudhury, R.R., Yang, X., Ramanathan, R., Vaidya, N.H.: Using directional antennas for medium access control in ad hoc networks. In: Proceedings of the 8th Annual International Conference on Mobile Computing and Networking, pp. 59–70. ACM (2002)
18. Choudhury, R.R., Vaidya, N.H.: Deafness: a MAC problem in ad hoc networks when using directional antennas. In: Proceedings of the 12th IEEE International Conference on Network Protocols, ICNP 2004, pp. 283–292. IEEE (2004)
19. Takata, M., Bandai, M., Watanabe, T.: A receiver-initiated directional MAC protocol for handling deafness in ad hoc networks. In: IEEE International Conference on Communications, ICC 2006, vol. 9, pp. 4089–4095. IEEE (2006)
20. Takata, M., Bandai, M., Watanabe, T.: A MAC protocol with directional antennas for deafness avoidance in ad hoc networks. In: Global Telecommunications Conference, GLOBECOM 2007, pp. 620–625. IEEE (2007)
21. Gossain, H., Cordeiro, C., Agrawal, D.P.: MDA: an efficient directional MAC scheme for wireless ad hoc networks. In: Global Telecommunications Conference, GLOBECOM 2005, vol. 6, p. 5. IEEE (2005)
22. Nasipuri, A., Ye, S., You, J., Hiromoto, R.E.: A MAC protocol for mobile ad hoc networks using directional antennas. In: Wireless Communications and Networking Conference, WCNC 2000, vol. 3, pp. 1214–1219. IEEE (2000)
23. Korakis, T., Jakllari, G., Tassiulas, L.: CDR-MAC: a protocol for full exploitation of directional antennas in ad hoc wireless networks. IEEE Trans. Mob. Comput. **7**(2), 145–155 (2008)
24. Horneffer, M., Plassmann, D.: Directed antennas in the mobile broadband system. In: INFOCOM 1996. Proceedings of the Fifteenth Annual Joint Conference of the IEEE Computer Societies. Networking the Next Generation, vol. 2, pp. 704–712. IEEE (1996)

25. Mudumbai, R., Singh, S., Madhow, U.: Medium access control for 60 GHz outdoor mesh networks with highly directional links. In: INFOCOM 2009, pp. 2871–2875. IEEE (2009)

26. Singh, S., Mudumbai, R., Madhow, U.: Interference analysis for highly directional 60-GHz mesh networks: the case for rethinking medium access control. IEEE/ACM Trans. Netw. (TON) 19(5), 1513–1527 (2011)

27. Singh, S., Ziliotto, F., Madhow, U., Belding, E.M., Rodwell, M.: Blockage and directivity in 60 GHz wireless personal area networks: from cross-layer model to multihop MAC design. IEEE J. Sel. Areas Commun. 27(8), 1400–1413 (2009)

28. Wang, J.: Beam codebook based beamforming protocol for multi-Gbps millimeter-wave WPAN systems. IEEE J. Sel. Areas Commun. 27(8), 1390–1399 (2009)

29. Chen, Q., Tang, J., Wong, D., Peng, X., Zhang, Y.: Directional cooperative MAC protocol design and performance analysis for IEEE 802.11ad WLANs. IEEE Trans. Veh. Technol. 62(6), 2667–2677 (2013). https://www.scopus.com/inward/record.uri?eid=2-s2.0-84880527026&partnerID=40&md5=41429be7907ab8765148632b07e2ee30

30. Ramanathan, R., Redi, J., Santivanez, C., Wiggins, D., Polit, S.: Ad hoc networking with directional antennas: a complete system solution. IEEE J. Sel. Areas Commun. 23(3), 496–506 (2005)

31. Shokri-Ghadikolaei, H., Fischione, C., Fodor, G., Popovski, P., Zorzi, M.: Millimeter wave cellular networks: a MAC layer perspective. IEEE Trans. Commun. 63(10), 3437–3458 (2015)

32. Shihab, E., Member, S., Cai, L., Pan, J., Member, S.: A distributed asnchronous directional-to-directional MAC protocol for wireless ad hoc networks. IEEE TVT 58(9), 5124–5134 (2009)

33. Sum, C.S., et al.: Virtual time-slot allocation scheme for throughput enhancement in a millimeter-wave multi-Gbps WPAN system. IEEE J. Sel. Areas Commun. 27(8), 1379–1389 (2009)

34. Gong, M., Stacey, R.: A directional CSMA/CA protocol for mmWave wireless PANs. In: Wireless Communications and Networking Conference (WCNC), pp. 1–6 (2010). http://ieeexplore.ieee.org/lpdocs/epic03/wrapper.htm?arnumber=5506128

35. Chen, Q., Peng, X., Yang, J., Chin, F.: Spatial reuse strategy in mmWave WPANs with directional antennas. In: GLOBECOM - IEEE Global Telecommunications Conference, pp. 5392–5397 (2012)

36. Son, I.K., Mao, S., Gong, M.X., Li, Y.: On frame-based scheduling for directional mmWave WPANs. In: Proceedings - IEEE INFOCOM, pp. 2149–2157 (2012)

37. Niu, Y., Li, Y., Jin, D., Su, L., Wu, D.: Blockage robust and efficient scheduling for directional mmWave WPANs. IEEE Trans. Veh. Technol. 64(2), 728–742 (2015)

38. Satchidanandan, B., Yau, S., Kumar, P.R., Aziz, A., Ekbal, A., Kundargi, N.: TrackMAC: an IEEE 802.11ad-compatible beam tracking-based MAC protocol for 5G millimeter-wave local area networks. In: 2018 10th International Conference on Communication Systems Networks (COMSNETS), pp. 185–182, January 2018

39. Kimura, R., et al.: Golay sequence aided channel estimation for millimeter-wave WPAN systems. In: 2008 IEEE 19th International Symposium on Personal, Indoor and Mobile Radio Communications, pp. 1–5, September 2008

40. Smulders, P.F.M., Wagemans, A.G.: Frequency-domain measurement of the millimeter wave indoor radio channel. IEEE Trans. Instrum. Meas. 44(6), 1017–1022 (1995)

41. ISO/IEC/IEEE International Standard for Information technology–Telecommunications and information exchange between systems–Local and metropolitan area networks–Specific requirements-Part 11: Wireless LAN Medium Access Control (MAC) and Physical Layer (PHY) Specifications, pp. 1–634 (2014)

42. Nitsche, T., Cordeiro, C., Flores, A.B., Knightly, E.W., Perahia, E., Widmer, J.C.: IEEE 802.11ad: directional 60 GHz communication for multi-Gigabit-per-second Wi-Fi [Invited Paper]. IEEE Commun. Mag. **52**(12), 132–141 (2014)

43. Study on channel model for frequencies from 0.5 to 100 GHz. https://etsi.org/deliver/etsi_tr/138900_138999/138901/14.00.00_60/tr_138901v140000p.pdf. Accessed 13 Apr 2018

44. Maccartney, G.R., Rappaport, T.S., Sun, S., Deng, S.: Indoor office wideband millimeter-wave propagation measurements and channel models at 28 and 73 GHz for ultra-dense 5G wireless networks. IEEE Access **3**, 2388–2424 (2015)

45. Raschkowski, L., et al.: METIS channel models (D1.4), July 2015

46. Jaeckel, S., Peter, M., Sakaguchi, K., Keusgen, W., Medbo, J.: 5G channel models in mm-wave frequency bands. In: European Wireless 2016; Proceedings of 22nd European Wireless Conference, pp. 1–6. VDE (2016)

47. Maltsev, A., et al.: Channel models for 60 GHz WLAN systems. Doc.: IEEE 802.11-09/0334r8. IEEE 802.11 document 09/0334r8 (2010)

Pricing and Commission in Two-Sided Markets with Free Upgrades

Mansi Sood, Sharayu Moharir, and Ankur A. Kulkarni[✉]

Indian Institute of Technology Bombay, Mumbai 400076, India
sharayum@ee.iitb.ac.in, kulkarni.ankur@iitb.ac.in

Abstract. We address the problem of optimal pricing in two-sided markets with platforms that facilitate the exchange of services between freelance workers and customers. Often, such platforms offer multiple variants of the same service and in cases when the cheaper service variant witnesses a shortage of supply and the more expensive variant sees a surplus, the platform offers free upgrades to the customers of the cheaper service variant. In this work, we explore the impact of such free upgrades on the platform's revenue and throughput. In addition, for the setting where the demand and supply are unknown to the platform and the platform has to perform the joint task of supply/demand estimation and pricing, we devise an algorithm based on a strategic division of the search space that enables the platform to efficiently determine throughput and revenue optimal prices. Further, we ascertain the optimal value of the commission retained by the platform per transaction to maximize its revenue.

1 Introduction

In recent years, we have witnessed tremendous growth in the sharing economy, primarily facilitated by online marketplaces. The sharing economy has emerged in diverse areas including ride-sharing, food delivery, online tutoring, text translation, photo editing, and web development. Sharing economies are two-sided markets with customers on one side and workers on the other. Typically, a central platform facilitates transactions between customers and workers.

Motivated by this, we study a platform-driven two-sided market which functions as follows. The platform decides and advertises the price of service to all the potential workers and customers. Based on this price, a subset of the potential workers and customers enter the market. The platform matches the interested customers and workers in a suitable manner. In return for these services, the platform retains a fixed fraction of the price paid by each customer. For example, Uber charges a commission fee of 20% [12]. This process is repeated periodically, and in each iteration, the platform's pricing decisions are informed by its pricing history and the corresponding market reactions.

Ankur's work was supported in part by the grant SB/S3/EECE/0182/2014 of the Science and Engineering Research Board, Government of India.

S. Biswas et al. (Eds.): COMSNETS 2018, LNCS 11227, pp. 172–195, 2019.
https://doi.org/10.1007/978-3-030-10659-1_8

We consider the setting where demand and supply are unknown to the platform a-priori, and the platform has to perform the joint task of pricing and supply/demand estimation. This distinguishes this work from the existing body of literature on pricing in two-sided markets with known supply/demand [1,3,11,13,14,20]. Our setting is motivated by the ephemeral nature of supply/demand in many sharing economies due to, among other things, frequent changes in the incentive structure offered by competitors. The joint task of demand learning and pricing has been widely studied in traditional (one-sided) markets [7,8], however, to the best of our knowledge, pricing under unknown supply/demand in two-sided markets has not received much attention.

The pricing strategy of the platform is driven by its performance metric. In this work, we consider two such metrics. The first is *revenue maximization* which is the most natural goal for any business. In each transaction that the platform makes, the flow of money is as follows. A customer makes a payment to the platform, which then retains a fraction of the payment and passes on the remaining amount to the worker who serves the customer. We refer to this amount retained by the platform while facilitating exchange of services between workers and customers as the *revenue* generated by the platform. The second objective we consider is *throughput maximization*, i.e., maximizing the number of transactions made via the platform. This is a common objective for start-ups and impact-sourcing platforms like Samasource [4,18] whose goal is to generate employment in developing economies.

Many platforms offer multiple variants of the same service. For instance, ride-share platforms differentiate the workers based on their car type and each customer request is for a specific type of car. In situations where a customer requests for a compact car, but only full-size cars are available, the platform can offer the customer a *free upgrade* by allocating a full-size car at the price of a compact car. Motivated by this, our platform offers two variants of the same service, and is allowed to give free upgrades. This added flexibility can potentially increase throughput/revenue, but it couples the markets for the two service variants, thus complicating the task of pricing. A key objective of this work is to characterize the cost and benefits of allowing free upgrades in the setting where supply/demand are unknown to the platform. Once a platform receives a payment from a customer, it has control over the fraction of payment it retains and the fraction it passes on to the worker who serves the customer. In this work, we also determine the optimal value of the commission which maximizes the platform's revenue in the presence of potential free upgrades.

1.1 Main Contributions

The main contributions of this work can be summarized as follows.

Characterization and Search for Optimal Prices Given Fixed Commission: We show that at the throughput optimal price, the cumulative supply of the two types of services matches the cumulative demand. We show that the revenue optimal price corresponds to a demand-limited market in which no customers are left unserved. We also show that free upgrades can increase the platform's revenue even though the platform provides the more expensive service at the cost of the cheaper service. In the setting where the supply/demand are a-priori unknown to the platform, we show that revenue/throughput optimal prices can be found by sampling the supply/demand curves at $O(p_m \log p_m)$ carefully chosen prices, where p_m is an upper limit on the price of a single transaction. This is a vanishing fraction of the total number of admissible prices (p_m^2). Compared to this, if free upgrades are not allowed, the optimal prices can be found using $O(\log p_m)$ samples. This characterizes the overheads due to coupling the markets for the two service variants.

Characterization and Search for Optimal Commission Given Fixed Prices: We show that for a fixed price, the optimal commission corresponds to a supply-limited market where no workers are left unserved. Further, when the commission takes values in multiples of Δ, where $0 < \Delta < 1$, we propose an algorithm to arrive at the optimal commission in $O\left(\frac{1}{\Delta} \log(\frac{1}{\Delta})\right)$ steps. When free upgrades are not facilitated by the platform, the proposed algorithm converges to the optimal commission in $O\left(\log(\frac{1}{\Delta})\right)$ steps.

1.2 Related Work

Two-sided markets have been widely studied in the economics community. An overview of these studies can be found in [10, 16, 17, 21] and the references therein. Since in most two-sided markets, players on either side benefit from the presence of players on the other side, the goal of the platform is often to increase the population on both sides of the market.

There is a growing body of work which looks at the task of pricing in two-sided markets when the supply and demand of are known to the platform. For example, [11] focuses on the trade-offs between profit maximization and social welfare in two-sided markets. Pricing in ride-sharing markets is the focus in [1, 3, 13, 20]. In [3], the authors conclude that while dynamic pricing does not lead to an increase in revenue, it outperforms static pricing strategies in terms of its robustness to fluctuations in supply and demand. In [13, 20], the focus is on maximizing the number of customers served. An approximation framework to design pricing strategies in ride-sharing systems is proposed in [1]. Using pricing for market segmentation is one of the issues addressed in [2]. In [14], authors use a game-theoretic framework to compare three pricing strategies, namely, membership-based pricing, transaction-based pricing and cross-subsidization. The key difference between our work and the works discussed above is that in our setting, the platform does not know the supply/demand.

The joint challenge of demand estimation and pricing has been widely studied in the classical single-sided market setting (see [7, 8] and the references therein). Since we focus on two-sided markets, the estimation challenge is two-fold as both supply and demand are functions of price and unknown to the platform. The variation of supply and demand with price in two-sided markets has been studied in [5, 6]. In [6], the focus is on studying the impact of prices on the labor supply and [5] shows that demand decreases with surge-pricing in ride-share platforms.

2   Setting

We study a two-sided market with freelance workers on one side and customers on the other side. There are two types of services on offer. The second type of service (Type 2) is more expensive than the other type (Type 1) of service. Each customer/worker requests/offers one of the two types of services. For example, ride-share platforms like Uber offer multiple types of services based on the type of cars and customers make requests for a specific type of service.

A platform facilitates transactions between the potential workers and customers as follows. Time is divided into slots. In each time-slot, the platform first advertises the price of service for both types of services. Based on these prices, a subset of the potential workers and customers enter the market. We refer to these workers and customers as active workers and customers, respectively. The platform then matches the active workers and customers, i.e., each worker is allocated to serve at most one customer and each customer is matched to at most one worker. The matched workers serve the corresponding customers and the unmatched workers/customers leave the system. At the end of the time-slot, the platform retains a fraction (γ, $0 < \gamma < 1$) of the price paid by each matched customer and gives the rest to the corresponding worker. For analysing the throughput and revenue optimal prices in Sects. 3 and 4, we assume that the commission (γ) is fixed and identical for both the services. In Sect. 5, we consider the more general case in which the platform can charge different values of commission γ_1 and γ_2 respectively for the Type 1 and Type 2 services.

2.1   Types of Transactions

The platform facilitates two types of transactions:

- *Regular transactions*: The platform matches customers requesting for a specific type of service to workers offering that type of service, i.e., Type i customers are matched to Type i workers for $i = 1, 2$ (Fig. 1(a)).
- *Free upgrades*: The platform matches customers of Type 1 service to workers of Type 2 service (Fig. 1(b)).

2.2   Supply and Demand Curves

We assume that supply/demand are deterministic functions of price. Admittedly, this is a strong assumption and our rationale for studying this simplified model is to develop some understanding of two-sided markets with unknown supply/demand in the presence of free-upgrades before exploring more realistic/complicated scenarios with stochastic supply/demand. We make some more assumptions on the nature of supply/demand curves. We use the following notation to elucidate these assumptions.

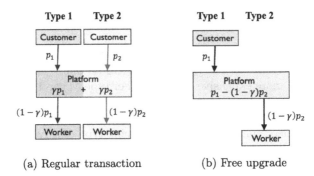

(a) Regular transaction   (b) Free upgrade

Fig. 1. Types of transactions facilitated by the platform– (a) Regular transactions: Type i workers serve Type i customers for $i = 1, 2$, (b) Free upgrades: Type 2 workers serve Type 1 customers.

1. p_i: Price paid by a customer to the platform for Type i service,
2. $w_i(p_i)$: Number of active Type i workers at p_i and at a fixed commission γ,
3. $c_i(p_i)$: Number of active Type i customers at p_i,

where $i = 1, 2$. A key point to note here is that that workers see the price $(1-\gamma)p_i$ which is in fact the argument of the supply curve. However, for the purposes of finding the optimal price for a fixed commission $(\gamma, 0 < \gamma < 1)$ in Sects. 3 and 4, we absorb γ and denote the supply for Type i as $w_i(p_i)$ instead of $w_i((1-\gamma)p_i)$. We make this dependence more explicit in Sect. 5 where we ascertain the value of the commission which maximizes the revenue for a fixed price (p_1, p_2).

Assumption 1 (Supply and demand)

a. *The range of values p_1 and p_2 are allowed to take is finite. In addition, since the Type 2 service is the costlier service, p_1 does not exceed p_2, i.e., $\exists\, p_m < \infty$ such that $0 \leq p_1 \leq p_2 \leq p_m$.*
b. *Demand is a decreasing function of price, i.e, $c_1(p_1)$ and $c_2(p_2)$ are decreasing in their arguments p_1 and p_2 respectively.*
c. *Supply is an increasing function of price, i.e., $w_1(p_1)$ and $w_2(p_2)$ are increasing in their arguments p_1 and p_2 respectively.*
d. *Many two-sided freelance markets are oligopolies with a few players accounting for a large fraction of the market share. Motivated by this and the fact that the demand curves in oligopolies are known to be concave (e.g. the kinked demand curve [9, 15, 19]), we make the assumption that*

$$\frac{d^2 c_1}{dp_1^2} \leq 0, \ \forall p_1 > p_{1\text{bal}}, \ and \ \frac{d^2 c_2}{dp_2^2} \leq 0, \ \forall p_2 > p_{2\text{bal}}.$$

e. *We assume that there is surplus demand when service is offered at zero cost, i.e., $w_1(0) < c_1(0)$, $w_2(0) < c_2(0)$.*

f. *Finally, we assume the existence of equilibrium prices p_{1bal}, p_{2bal} for the two service types which are found by sampling the individual markets. The platform defines expensive service as the one with the higher equilibrium price and announces higher prices for this service. WLOG $p_{1bal} \leq p_{2bal}$. Thus, we assume that*

$$\exists\ p_{1bal} \in (0, p_m]\ s.t.\ w_1(p_{1bal}) = c_1(p_{1bal}),\ and$$
$$\exists\ p_{2bal} \in (0, p_m]\ s.t.\ w_2(p_{2bal}) = c_2(p_{2bal}), where,\ p_{1bal} \leq p_{2bal}.$$

2.3   Platform's Objective

There are multiple potential performance metrics for such platforms. In this work, we consider two objectives.

- *Throughput maximization*: The goal is to maximize the number of customers served by the platform in each time-slot. Recall that this includes customers that are matched to workers of the type they have requested for as well as customers who receive free upgrades. Most start-ups in their initial phase focus on throughput maximization to increase their market presence.
- *Revenue maximization*: The goal is to maximize the platform's revenue in each time-slot. This includes revenue generated from regular transactions as well as free upgrades. This is very likely to be the objective of an established platform.

2.4   Algorithmic Challenge

The algorithmic challenge is to determine the optimal prices for the two type of services in the setting where the supply and demand curves are unknown to the platform. The way the platform finds the optimal prices by fixing the prices to certain values and observing the market's reaction. This information can then be used to choose appropriate prices in subsequent time-slots. The goal is to converge to the optimal prices in as few time-slots as possible.

2.5   Definitions

Regular Transactions: We first define the regular throughput $N_B(p_1, p_2)$ and revenue $R_B(p_1, p_2)$ generated at price (p_1, p_2),

$$N_B(p_1, p_2) := \min\{c_1(p_1), w_1(p_1)\} + \min\{c_2(p_2), w_2(p_2)\},$$
$$R_B(p_1, p_2) := \gamma p_1 \min\{c_1(p_1), w_1(p_1)\} + \gamma p_2 \min\{c_2(p_2), w_2(p_2)\}.$$

Note that the function $R_1(p_1) = \gamma p_1 \min\{c_1(p_1), w_1(p_1)\}$ is unimodal, i.e., it increases till its unique maximum and subsequently decreases. This is because for $p_1 < p_{1bal}$, it becomes $p_1 w_1(p_1)$, which increases with p_1 and beyond p_{1bal} it becomes $p_1 c_1(p_1)$, which is a concave function as $p_1 c_1''(p_1) + 2c_1'(p_1) \leq 0$ from Assumption 1.

Free Upgrades: After matching customers and workers of each service type at price (p_1, p_2), if there are some unmatched Type 1 customers and Type 2 workers, then the platform upgrades the unmatched $c_1(p_1) - w_1(p_1)$ customers to the costlier service offered by remaining $w_2(p_2) - c_2(p_2)$ workers, such that the unmatched customers still pay p_1 and workers still get $(1 - \gamma)p_2$.

For modelling free upgrades, we define upgrade throughput $N_U(p_1, p_2)$ and upgrade revenue, $R_U(p_1, p_2)$

$$N_U(p_1, p_2) := \max\{\min\{c_1(p_1) - w_1(p_1), w_2(p_2) - c_2(p_2)\}, 0\},$$
$$R_U(p_1, p_2) := \max\{(p_1 - (1 - \gamma)p_2) \max\{\min\{c_1(p_1) - w_1(p_1),$$
$$w_2(p_2) - c_2(p_2)\}, 0\}, 0\}.$$

Total Revenue and Throughput: The total throughput $N(p_1, p_2)$ and revenue $R(p_1, p_2)$ are given as follows

$$N(p_1, p_2) := N_B(p_1, p_2) + N_U(p_1, p_2), R(p_1, p_2) := R_B(p_1, p_2) + R_U(p_1, p_2).$$

3   Throughput Maximization

3.1   Problem Formulation

The following is the throughput optimization problem in the presence of free upgrades,

$$\max_{p_1, p_2} \quad \min\{c_1(p_1), w_1(p_1)\} + \min\{c_2(p_2), w_2(p_2)\}$$
$$+ \max\{\min\{c_1(p_1) - w_1(p_1), w_2(p_2) - c_2(p_2)\}, 0\}$$
$$\text{s.t.} \quad 0 \le p_1 \le p_m, \ 0 \le p_2 \le p_m, \ p_1 \le p_2.$$

3.2   Feasible Region

For the analysis of this problem, we define subsets of the feasible region (Fig. 2) based on the arguments of the max and min functions in the objective function as follows,

$$\text{I} := \{(p_1, p_2) \mid p_2 \le p_{2\text{bal}}, \ p_1 \le p_{1\text{bal}}, \ p_1 \le p_2\},$$
$$\text{II} := \{(p_1, p_2) \mid p_2 \le p_{2\text{bal}}, \ p_{1\text{bal}} \le p_1 \le p_m, \ p_1 \le p_2\},$$
$$\text{III} := \{(p_1, p_2) \mid p_{2\text{bal}} \le p_2 \le p_m, \ p_{1\text{bal}} \le p_1 \le p_m, \ p_1 \le p_2\},$$
$$A := \{(p_1, p_2) \mid w_1(p_1) + w_2(p_2) < c_1(p_1) + c_2(p_2), \ p_{2\text{bal}} \le p_2 \le p_m, \ p_1 \le p_{1\text{bal}}\},$$
$$B := \{(p_1, p_2) \mid w_1(p_1) + w_2(p_2) > c_1(p_1) + c_2(p_2), \ p_{2\text{bal}} \le p_2 \le p_m, \ p_1 \le p_{1\text{bal}}\},$$
$$C := \{(p_1, p_2) \mid w_1(p_1) + w_2(p_2) = c_1(p_1) + c_2(p_2), \ p_{2\text{bal}} \le p_2 \le p_m, \ p_1 \le p_{1\text{bal}}\}.$$

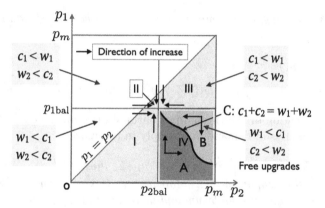

Fig. 2. Subsets I, II, III, A, B and C of feasible region for throughput optimization problem. Arrows point towards increase in throughput.

The curve C plays a crucial role in the subsequent analysis. Notice that it passes through (p_{1bal}, p_{2bal}) which is the equilibrium price of individual markets. The function $c_1(p_1) - w_1(p_1)$ is a strictly decreasing function of p_1 and therefore invertible. Hence, we know that on the curve C, $p_2 = (w_2 - c_2)^{-1}(c_1(p_1) - w_1(p_1))$. Also, $w_2(p_2) - c_2(p_2)$ is an increasing function of p_2. Consequently, for the point (p_1, p_2) to remain on the curve C, if p_1 increases, $c_1(p_1) - w_1(p_1)$ decreases and therefore, p_2 must decrease to bear an equivalent decrease in $w_2(p_2) - c_2(p_2)$. Lastly, from Assumption 1, that there is a demand surplus at zero price, we have $w_1(0) + w_2(0) < c_1(0) + c_2(0)$. Thus, the set A lies on the same side of curve C as the origin. Note that in Fig. 2, the curve C could also intersect the p_2 axis at a $p_2 \leq p_m$; the precise point of intersection does not affect the analysis.

3.3 Location of Optimal Prices

Note that free upgrades take place in the region $A \cup B \cup C$ with $p_1 \leq p_{1bal}$ and $p_2 \geq p_{2bal}$, as this region sees a supply shortage for Type 1 service and a simultaneous supply surplus for Type 2 service.

Theorem 1 (Throughput maximization). *Throughput optimal prices must lie on curve C which is the set $\{(p_1, p_2) \mid w_1(p_1) + w_2(p_2) = c_1(p_1) + c_2(p_2), \ p_{2bal} \leq p_2 \leq p_m, \ p_1 \leq p_{1bal}\}$.*

This theorem states that the platform can attain optimal throughput only when all the customers and workers get served. This situation would also be desirable to the workers and customers since every individual would be serviced by a throughput maximizing platform. Furthermore, if there was an additional cost incurred on the platform due to idle customers or workers, the optimal price would still continue to be on curve C.

Corollary 1. *Throughput optimization problem can be equivalently represented as follows,*

$$\max_{p_1, p_2} \quad w_1(p_1) + w_2(p_2)$$

$$s.t. \quad c_1(p_1) + c_2(p_2) = w_1(p_1) + w_2(p_2), \ p_{2\text{bal}} \le p_2 \le p_m, \ p_1 \le p_2.$$

The exact location of the throughput optimal price on the curve C depends on the characteristics of demand and supply in the market.

Proposition 1. *If* $\left|\frac{w_1'(p_1)}{c_1'(p_1)}\right| \ge \left|\frac{w_2'(p_2)}{c_2'(p_2)}\right| \ \forall p_1 \le p_{1\text{bal}}$ *and* $p_2 \ge p_{2\text{bal}}$, *then,* $(p_{1\text{bal}}, p_{2\text{bal}})$ *is throughput optimal. Moreover, in this situation, markets for the individual services are in equilibrium and there are no free upgrades. Conversely, if* $\left|\frac{w_1'(p_1)}{c_1'(p_1)}\right| < \left|\frac{w_2'(p_2)}{c_2'(p_2)}\right| \ \forall p_1 \le p_{1\text{bal}}$ *and* $p_2 \ge p_{2\text{bal}}$, *then the throughput is optimal at the least allowed value of* p_1 *or equivalently the greatest allowed* p_2 *along curve* C. *In this case, the platform in fact benefits from free upgrades.*

We illustrate this proposition using linear supply and demand curves as follows:

$$w_1(p_1) = \bar{w}_1 p_1, \ w_2(p_2) = \bar{w}_2 p_2, \ c_1(p_1) = \bar{c}_1 p_1 + k_1, \ c_2(p_2) = \bar{c}_2 p_2 + k_2,$$

where $\bar{w}_1, \bar{w}_2 > 0$, $\bar{c}_1, \bar{c}_2 < 0$ and $\bar{k}_1, \bar{k}_2 > 0$. It follows that $p_{1\text{bal}} = \frac{k_1}{\bar{w}_1 - \bar{c}_1}$, $p_{2\text{bal}} = \frac{k_2}{\bar{w}_2 - \bar{c}_2}$. The curve C becomes the line $L = \{(p_1, p_2)|(\bar{w}_1 - \bar{c}_1)p_1 + (\bar{w}_2 - \bar{c}_2)p_2 = k_1 + k_2\}$. Using Proposition 1, we note that the throughput optimization problem becomes a linear program with the following maxima,

– If $\dfrac{\bar{w}_1}{\bar{c}_1} < \dfrac{\bar{w}_2}{\bar{c}_2}$, then $(p_{1\text{bal}}, p_{2\text{bal}})$ is throughput optimal.

– If $\dfrac{\bar{w}_1}{\bar{c}_1} = \dfrac{\bar{w}_2}{\bar{c}_2}$, then all points on L are optimal.

– If $\dfrac{\bar{w}_1}{\bar{c}_1} > \dfrac{\bar{w}_2}{\bar{c}_2}$, then the point on L with maximum allowed feasible value of p_2 or equivalently the minimum allowed feasible vale of p_1 is optimal.

An interesting consequence of Proposition 1 arises when Type 2 workers saturate beyond the equilibrium price, i.e., $w_2'(p_2) = \epsilon \ \forall p_2 > p_{2\text{bal}}$, where ϵ is small and positive. In this case, the throughput is optimal at $(p_{1\text{bal}}, p_{2\text{bal}})$. Likewise, if Type 2 customers fall sharply beyond the equilibrium price, i.e., $|c_2'(p_2)| \ge \lambda$ $\forall p_2 > p_{2\text{bal}}$, where λ is large, then throughput is again optimal at $(p_{1\text{bal}}, p_{2\text{bal}})$. Thus, free upgrades can both increase or decrease the throughput depending on the market conditions, namely the price derivatives of demand and supply.

3.4 Our Policy

We work with the assumption that prices are multiples of a smallest allowed denomination in the economy and these form the set of allowed increments for the platform. Time is divided into slots. When the platform enters the market, it has no prior knowledge of demand and supply. In subsequent time-slots, it announces a price to which customers and workers respond. While facilitating transactions between the customers and workers, it keeps a track of the number of active workers and customers. It then uses these observations to set a new price in a manner which speeds up its search for the optimal price. In our policy, we first find p_{1bal} and p_{2bal} using a modified binary search and then use this information to eliminate regions I, II and III from the search space. In the remaining region, $p_1 \leq p_{1bal}, p_2 \geq p_{2bal}$, and throughput is unimodal along each row, increasing till the curve C and subsequently decreasing. This enables us to repeatedly use a modified binary search (Algorithm 1) to compute the optimal price. Algorithm 2 summarizes these steps.

Algorithm 1. MODIFIED BINARY SEARCH (MBS)

Input: domain $x \in [L, U]$, and unimodal function $f(x)$.
Output: x^*, which is argmax $f(x)$.

1 **while** $L < U$ **do**
2 $\quad$ $M \leftarrow \dfrac{L+U}{2}$
3 $\quad$ **if** $f(M) > f(M+1)$ **then**
4 $\quad\quad$ $U \leftarrow M$
5 $\quad$ **else**
6 $\quad\quad$ $L \leftarrow M + 1$

7 **return** L

3.5 Computational Complexity of Our Policy

Note that only one amongst the lines 5 and 9 of Algorithm 2 would be executed (calculations of the complexity are detailed in Table 1). Thus the total complexity becomes $O\big(3 \log p_m + p_{1bal} \log(p_m - p_{2bal})\big) = O\big(p_m \log p_m\big)$. Had the platform instead blindly sampled all the feasible values, it would have costed it $p_m{}^2$ time steps to reach the optimal price. Thus, our algorithm outperforms this approach by a factor $(\log p_m)/p_m$, performing even better as price range p_m rises.

4 Revenue Maximization

4.1 Problem Formulation

Following is the revenue optimization problem for the platform,

$$\max_{p_1, p_2} \; \gamma p_1 \min\{c_1(p_1), w_1(p_1)\} + \gamma p_2 \min\{c_2(p_2), w_2(p_2)\}$$

$$+ \max\{(p_1 - (1-\gamma)p_2) \max\{\min\{c_1(p_1) - w_1(p_1), w_2(p_2) - c_2(p_2)\}, 0\}, 0\}$$

$$\text{s.t.} \quad 0 \leq p_1 \leq p_m, \; 0 \leq p_2 \leq p_m, \; p_1 \leq p_2.$$

Algorithm 2. FINDING THROUGHPUT OPTIMAL PRICE

Input: γ, p_m.
Output: p_{N1}^*, p_{N2}^*, N^*.
1 STEP 1 : *Find p_{1bal} and p_{2bal}.*
2 $p_{1bal} \leftarrow \text{MBS}(p_1 \in [0, p_m]; \min\{w_1(p_1), c_1(p_1)\})$
3 $p_{2bal} \leftarrow \text{MBS}(p_2 \in [0, p_m]; \min\{w_2(p_2), c_2(p_2)\})$
4 STEP 2 : *Find curve $w_1(p_1) + w_2(p_2) = c_1(p_1) + c_2(p_2)$.* **if**
   $w_1(0) + w_2(p_m) < c_1(0) + c_2(p_m)$ **then**
5 | $\bar{p}_1 \leftarrow \text{MBS}(p_1 \in [0, p_{1bal}]; N(p_1, p_m)), \ \bar{p}_2 \leftarrow p_m$
6 **else if** $w_1(0) + w_2(p_m) = c_1(0) + c_2(p_m)$ **then**
7 | $\bar{p}_1 \leftarrow 0, \ \bar{p}_2 \leftarrow p_m$
8 **else**
9 | $\bar{p}_1 \leftarrow 0, \ \bar{p}_2 \leftarrow \text{MBS}(p_2 \in [p_{2bal}, p_m]; N(0, p_2))$

10 STEP 3 : *Find and store $N(p_1, p_2)$ on the curve.*
11 $L \leftarrow \bar{p}_2$
12 **for** p_1 *in* $[\bar{p}_1, p_{1bal}]$ **do**
13 | $\hat{p}_2 \leftarrow \text{MBS}(p_2 \in [p_{2bal}, L]; N(p_1, p_2))$
14 | Add $(p_1, \hat{p}_2), N(p_1, \hat{p}_2), R(p_1, \hat{p}_2)$ to $\widehat{P}, \widehat{N}, \widehat{R}$
15 | $L \leftarrow \hat{p}_2$

16 STEP 4 : *Compute throughput optimal price.*
17 $p_{N1}^*, p_{N2}^* \leftarrow \text{argmax} \ \widehat{N}, \quad N^* \leftarrow \widehat{N}(p_{N1}^*, p_{N2}^*)$
18 **return** p_{N1}^*, p_{N2}^*, N^*

4.2 Feasible Region

We define subsets of the feasible region (Fig. 3) based on the arguments of the max and min functions in the objective function. We divide the feasible region into sets I, II and III as defined in Sect. 3 and introduce new subsets $\bar{A}, \bar{B}, \bar{C}, D$:

$$\bar{A} := \{(p_1, p_2) \mid p_1 \geq (1 - \gamma)p_2\} \cap A,$$
$$\bar{B} := \{(p_1, p_2) \mid p_1 \geq (1 - \gamma)p_2\} \cap B,$$
$$\bar{C} := \{(p_1, p_2) \mid p_1 \geq (1 - \gamma)p_2\} \cap C,$$
$$D := \{(p_1, p_2) \mid p_1 < (1 - \gamma)p_2\} \cap (A \cup B \cup C).$$

In our model, the platform can upgrade unmatched Type 1 customers to Type 2 workers, generating a revenue $p_1 - (1 - \gamma)p_2$ per customer in the process. Thus, free upgrades can only take place when there is a supply shortage for Type 1 service and a simultaneous supply surplus for Type 2 service, under the additional condition that the revenue from these upgrades is positive. This corresponds to the set $\bar{A} \cup \bar{B} \cup \bar{C}$. For there to be a possibility of profitable upgrades, γ needs to be chosen such that this set is non empty, i.e., $1 - \gamma \leq \dfrac{p_{1bal}}{p_{2bal}}$.
Note that in Fig. 3, the line $\{(p_1, p_2) \mid p_1 = (1 - \gamma)p_2\}$ could possibly intersect the line $\{(p_1, p_2) \mid p_2 = p_m\}$ at a value of $p_1 > p_{1bal}$. Next, we define the revenue

Table 1. Calculation of the computational complexity of Algorithm 2.

Lines	Number of MBS calls	MBS domain	Complexity
2,3	2	p_m	$2\log p_m$
5	1	$p_{1\mathrm{bal}}$	$\log p_{1\mathrm{bal}}$
9	1	$p_m - p_{2\mathrm{bal}}$	$\log(p_m - p_{2\mathrm{bal}})$
13	$\leq p_{1\mathrm{bal}}$	$\leq p_m - p_{2\mathrm{bal}}$	$\leq p_{1\mathrm{bal}}\log(p_m - p_{2\mathrm{bal}})$

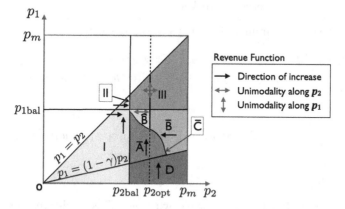

Fig. 3. Subsets I, II, III, $\bar{A}, \bar{B}, \widehat{B}, \bar{C}$ and D of feasible region for revenue optimization problem. Here, the black arrows points towards increase in revenue and the red arrows indicate unimodality along a particular direction. (Color figure online)

optimal prices $p_{1\mathrm{opt}}$ and $p_{2\mathrm{opt}}$ for the markets of the individual service types in absence of free upgrades,

$$p_{1\mathrm{opt}} := \underset{p_1}{\arg\max}\, p_1 \min\{c_1(p_1), w_1(p_1)\},$$

$$p_{2\mathrm{opt}} := \underset{p_2}{\arg\max}\, p_2 \min\{c_2(p_2), w_2(p_2)\},$$

and let $\widehat{B} := \{(p_1, p_2) \mid p_2 \leq p_{2\mathrm{opt}}\} \cap \bar{B}$. Had the revenue generated from a free upgrade not been positive, i.e., $1 - \gamma > \dfrac{p_{1\mathrm{bal}}}{p_{2\mathrm{bal}}}$, then the platform would not provide these upgrades. In such a setting, the optimal price would simply be $(p_{1\mathrm{opt}}, p_{2\mathrm{opt}})$ which corresponds to the revenue optimal price for the individual markets of the two services. However, $p_{1\mathrm{opt}}$ may be greater than $p_{2\mathrm{opt}}$, in which case, the maximum feasible value of p_1 given that p_2 is $p_{2\mathrm{opt}}$, is optimal. Thus, the optimal price becomes $(\min\{p_{1\mathrm{opt}}, p_{2\mathrm{opt}}\}, p_{2\mathrm{opt}})$.

4.3   Location of Optimal Prices

Theorem 2 (Revenue maximization). *Revenue optimal prices lie in the set* $(\min\{p_{1\mathrm{opt}}, p_{2\mathrm{opt}}\}, p_{2\mathrm{opt}}) \cup \bar{C} \cup \widehat{B}$.

A consequence of this theorem is that at a revenue optimal price, the platform would be in one of the following operational regimes. The price $(\min\{p_{1\mathrm{opt}}, p_{2\mathrm{opt}}\}, p_{2\mathrm{opt}})$ corresponds to no free upgrades and the platform maximizes its revenue, separately for the individual services. In region $\bar{C}$, the free upgrades provided by the platform clear the market, i.e., all active customers and workers are served by the platform. In region $\widehat{B}$, unmatched Type 1 customers are fewer in number than unmatched Type 2 workers. Note that in all the three regimes mentioned above, the revenue maximizing platform serves all customers but may not serve all workers.

Remark 1. Revenue is unimodal w.r.t. p_2 in set $\widehat{B}$ where,

$$R(p_1, p_2) = \gamma p_1 w_1(p_1) + \gamma p_2 c_2(p_2)$$
$$+ (p_1 - (1-\gamma)p_2)(c_1(p_1) - w_1(p_1)).$$

Observe that,

$$\frac{\partial R}{\partial p_2} = \gamma c_2(p_2) + \gamma p_2 c_2'(p_2) - (1-\gamma)(c_1(p_1) - w_1(p_1)),$$
$$\frac{\partial^2 R}{\partial p_2^2} = 2\gamma c_2'(p_2) + \gamma p_2 c_2''(p_2) \le 0.$$

Thus, the revenue function is concave w.r.t p_2. This facilitates the use of a modified binary search based technique (Algorithm 1) to arrive at the optimal price in this region.

Corollary 2. *If the demand of Type II goods is elastic beyond $p_{2\mathrm{bal}}$, i.e.,* $\left|\frac{dc_2}{c_2}\right| / \left|\frac{dp_2}{p_2}\right| \ge 1$ $\forall p_2 \ge p_{2\mathrm{bal}}$, *then revenue optimal prices can only lie on the curve $\bar{C}$ or at the point $(\min\{p_{1\mathrm{opt}}, p_{2\mathrm{opt}}\}, p_{2\mathrm{opt}})$.*

This follows from the fact that for an elastic demand $|\frac{dc_2}{c_2} / \frac{dp_2}{p_2}| \ge 1$, which implies $R_2'(p_2) = p_2 c_2'(p_2) + c_2(p_2) \le 0, \forall p_2 \ge p_{2\mathrm{bal}}$. Hence, if demand is elastic $\forall p_2 \ge p_{2\mathrm{bal}}$, then $p_{2\mathrm{opt}} = p_{2\mathrm{bal}}$. Consequently, the set $\widehat{B}$ reduces to the point $(p_{1\mathrm{bal}}, p_{2\mathrm{bal}})$. If the demand for both service types is elastic beyond $(p_{1\mathrm{bal}}, p_{2\mathrm{bal}})$, i.e., $\forall p_1 \ge p_{1\mathrm{bal}}, \forall p_2 \ge p_{2\mathrm{bal}}$ we get $p_{1\mathrm{opt}}$ is $p_{1\mathrm{bal}}$ and $p_{2\mathrm{opt}}$ is $p_{2\mathrm{bal}}$. Using Corollary 2, the optimal revenue occurs on the curve $\bar{C}$.

Remark 2. Consider the optimization of $\alpha N + (1-\alpha)R$ where $\alpha \in (0,1)$, assuming the elasticity of demand of both services beyond $(p_{1\mathrm{bal}}, p_{2\mathrm{bal}})$. In this case, in region $\bar{A}$, $\frac{\partial R}{\partial p_1} > 0$, $\frac{\partial N}{\partial p_1} > 0$ whereas in region $\bar{B}$, $\frac{\partial R}{\partial p_2} < 0$, $\frac{\partial N}{\partial p_2} < 0$. Therefore the solution of the optimization of $\alpha N + (1-\alpha)R$ also lies on $\bar{C}$. Note, however, that the optimal (p_1, p_2) may lie in region D. A scheme similar to Algorithm 3 can then be used to find the optimal prices.

4.4   Our Policy

As for the policy proposed for throughput, the platform samples the market behaviour in discrete steps to discover revenue optimal price. From Theorem 2, the curve $\bar{C}$, the region $\hat{B}$ and the point $(\min\{p_{1opt}, p_{2opt}\}, p_{2opt})$ emerge as the only candidates for revenue optima. We first find p_{1opt} and p_{2opt}. If there are no profitable upgrades, then we declare $(\min\{p_{1opt}, p_{2opt}\}, p_{2opt})$ as the optimal price. Else, we sample the revenue on curve $\bar{C}$ by invoking Algorithm 2 and find the optimal price on it. If, $p_{2bal} = p_{2opt}$, then we declare the optimal revenue as the maximum of observed value of revenue on curve $\bar{C}$ and that obtained at $(\min\{p_{1opt}, p_{2opt}\}, p_{2opt})$. Next, we check the remaining region $\hat{B}$ in which revenue is unimodal along each row (Remark 4). This enables us to repeatedly use modified binary search (Algorithm 1) to compute the revenue optimal price. Algorithm 3 summarizes these steps.

4.5   Computational Complexity of Our Policy

Note that Algorithm 3 uses the outputs from Algorithm 2. The complexity is calculated in Table 2. The total complexity becomes $\mathrm{O}\big(5 \log p_m + 2 p_{1bal} \log(p_m - p_{2bal})\big) = \mathrm{O}\big(p_m \log p_m\big)$.

5   Revenue Optimal Commission

Given a pair of operational prices (p_1, p_2) announced by the platform to the customers, we characterize the revenue optimal commission, i.e., the fraction of the price paid by the customer that is retained by the platform. For a Type i transaction, each Type i customer pays a price p_i to the platform. The platform retains an amount $\gamma_i p_i$ and passes on the rest to the worker who serves the customer. Thus, a worker of Type i responds to the price $(1-\gamma_i)p_i$. Consequently, the supply for the Type i service when the platform announces a price p_i to the customers is given by $w_i((1 - \gamma_i)p_i)$. In this section, we study the effect of varying γ_i and thus retain γ_i in the notation for the supply and denote it by $w_i((1 - \gamma_i)p_i)$. Note that the analysis in this section considers the general case where the platform independently sets the commission γ_1 and γ_2 for the two services. For the purpose of analysing the revenue optimal commission, we make the following assumption on the nature of the supply curves.

Assumption 2. *The supply curves are concave and thus $w_i''(p_i) \leq 0$ for $i = 1, 2$.*

We work with Assumption 2 for the remainder of this section.

5.1   Market Without Upgrades

We first consider the case in which no upgrades are provided by the platform. When the platform operates at a price (p_1, p_2), the goal is to find the commission (γ_1, γ_2) which maximizes the revenue. The revenue optimization problem is given by,

$$\max_{\gamma_1, \gamma_2} \quad \gamma_1 p_1 \min\{c_1(p_1), w_1((1 - \gamma_1)p_1)\} + \gamma_2 p_2 \min\{c_2(p_2), w_2((1 - \gamma_2)p_2)\}$$

$$\text{s.t.} \quad 0 < \gamma_1, \gamma_2 < 1.$$

Algorithm 3. FINDING REVENUE OPTIMAL PRICE

Input: γ, p_m, and $p_{1bal}, p_{2bal}, \widehat{P}, \widehat{R}$ from Algorithm 2
Output: Outputs: p_{R1}^*, p_{R2}^*, R^*
1 STEP 1 : *Find p_{1opt} and p_{2opt}.*
2 $p_{1opt} \leftarrow$ MBS$(p_1 \in [p_{1bal}, p_m]; p_1 \min\{w_1(p_1), c_1(p_1)\})$
3 $p_{2opt} \leftarrow$ MBS$(p_2 \in [p_{2bal}, p_m]; p_2 \min\{w_2(p_2), c_2(p_2)\})$
4 STEP 2 : *Compute maxima amongst sampled prices.*
5 $r_a \leftarrow \max\limits_{p_1 \geq (1-\gamma)p_2} \widehat{R}$
6 $r_b \leftarrow R(\min\{p_{1opt}, p_{2opt}\}, p_{2opt})$
7 **if** $(1 - \gamma) > \frac{p_{1bal}}{p_{2bal}}$ **then**
8    $R^* \leftarrow r_b$
9    $p_{R1}^*, p_{R2}^* \leftarrow (\min\{p_{1opt}, p_{2opt}\}, p_{2opt})$, QUIT
10 **else if** $p_{2opt} = p_{2bal}$ **then**
11    $R^* \leftarrow \max\{r_a, r_b\}$
12    $p_{R1}^*, p_{R2}^* \leftarrow$ argmax $\max\{r_a, r_b\}$, QUIT
13 STEP 3 : *Find revenue in region $\widehat{B}$.*
14 Search for p_{1o} s.t. (p_{1o}, p_m) in $\widehat{P}$
15 **if** *not found* **then**
16    $p_{1o} \leftarrow -\infty$
17 Search for $p_1^\dagger$ s.t. $(p_1^\dagger, \frac{p_1^\dagger}{1-\gamma})$ in $\widehat{P}$
18 **if** *not found* **then**
19    $p_1^\dagger \leftarrow -\infty$
20 $p_1' \leftarrow \max\{p_{1o}, p_1^\dagger\}$
21 **for** p_1 *in* $[p_1', p_{1bal}]$ **do**
22   Search for L s.t. (p_1, L) in $\widehat{P}$
23    $p_2' \leftarrow \min\{p_{2opt}, \frac{p_1}{1-\gamma}\}$
24    $\tilde{p}_2 \leftarrow$ MBS$(p_2 \in [L, p_2']; R(p_1, p_2))$
25   Add $(p_1, \tilde{p}_2)$ to $\widetilde{P}, R(p_1, \tilde{p}_2)$ to $\widetilde{R}$
26 STEP 4 : *Compute revenue optimal price.*
27 $p_{1c}, p_{2c} \leftarrow \text{argmax}\limits_{p_1 \geq (1-\gamma)p_2} \widetilde{R}, \ r_c \leftarrow \widetilde{R}(p_{1c}, p_{2c})$
28 $R^* \leftarrow \max\{r_a, r_b, r_c\}$
29 $p_{R1}^*, p_{R2}^* \leftarrow$ argmax $\max\{r_a, r_b, r_c\}$
30 **return** p_{R1}^*, p_{R2}^*, R^*

Let $R_i(\gamma_i) := \gamma_i p_i \min\{c_i(p_i), w_i((1 - \gamma_i)p_i)\}$, for $i = 1, 2$. We can solve the above optimization problem separately for γ_1 and γ_2 as,

$$\max_{0 < \gamma_1 < 1} R_1(\gamma_1) + \max_{0 < \gamma_2 < 1} R_2(\gamma_2) \tag{1}$$

Proposition 2. *$R_i(\gamma_i)$ is a unimodal function of γ_i for $i = 1, 2$.*

Table 2. Calculation of the computational complexity of Algorithm 3.

Lines	Number of MBS calls	MBS domain	Complexity
2	1	$p_m - p_{1\text{bal}}$	$\log(p_m - p_{1\text{bal}})$
3	1	$p_m - p_{2\text{bal}}$	$\log(p_m - p_{2\text{bal}})$
24	$\leq p_{1\text{bal}}$	$\leq p_m - p_{2\text{bal}}$	$\leq p_{1\text{bal}} \log(p_m - p_{2\text{bal}})$

Proof. Observe that given a price p_i for the Type i service, the number of customers $c_i(p_i)$ is a fixed value. Depending on the relative magnitudes of the demand and supply levels at price p_i, the following cases can arise.

– *Case 1:* $c_i(p_i) > w_i(p_i)$ – If the demand is higher than the supply when the platform charges zero commission ($\gamma_i = 0$), i.e., $c_i(p_i) > w_i(p_i)$, then no matter what value of γ_i is set by the platform, the service stays supply-limited since $w_i((1 - \gamma_i)p_i) < w_i(p_i) < c_i(p_i)$ for $0 < \gamma_i < 1$. We get,

$$R_i(\gamma_i) = \gamma_i p_i w_i((1 - \gamma_i)p_i) \quad 0 < \gamma_i < 1.$$

Next, we establish the unimodality of $R_i(\gamma_i)$,

$$R_i'(\gamma_i) = p_i w_i((1 - \gamma_i)p_i) - \gamma_i p_i^2 w_i'((1 - \gamma_i)p_i),$$
$$R_i''(\gamma_i) = -2p_i^2 w_i'((1 - \gamma_i)p_i) + \gamma_i p_i^3 w_i''((1 - \gamma_i)p_i).$$

From Assumptions 1 and 2, it follows that $R_i''(\gamma_i) \leq 0$ for $0 < \gamma_i < 1$ and hence $R_i(\gamma_i)$ is a unimodal function of γ_i.

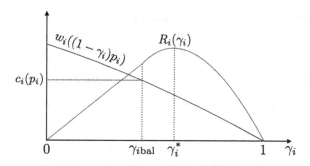

Fig. 4. Variation of supply $w_i((1 - \gamma_i)p_i)$, demand $c_i(p_i)$ and revenue $R_i(p_i)$ for Type i service at price p_i in absence of upgrades. Supply ($w_i((1 - \gamma_i)p_i)$) decreases in γ_i, demand ($c_i(p_i)$) does not depend on γ_i and revenue ($R_i(p_i)$) is a unimodal function in γ_i with peak at γ_i^*.

– *Case 2:* $c_i(p_i) \leq w_i(p_i)$ – This case corresponds to a market which is demand-limited when platform charges zero commission. As γ_i is increased, the supply decreases and let γ_{ibal} denote the value of γ_i at which the supply matches the demand, i.e., $c_i(p_i) = w_i((1-\gamma_{ibal})p_i)$ (Fig. 4). Observe that such a $\gamma_{ibal} \in (0,1)$ exists when $0 < c_i(p_i) \leq w_i(p_i)$. This is because with increasing γ_i, $w_i((1-\gamma_{ibal})p_i)$ decreases and admits all intermediate values between 0 and $w_i(p_i)$. Therefore, there exists γ_{ibal} such that $w_i((1-\gamma_{ibal})p_i)$ is equal to $c_i(p_i)$. When γ_i is less than γ_{ibal}, there is a dearth of customers and as γ_i is raised beyond γ_{ibal}, workers become fewer in number than the customers. Using the monotonicity of the supply curve, we can write, $\gamma_{ibal} = 1 - \frac{w_i^{-1}(c_i(p_i))}{p_i}$, $i = 1, 2$. Observe that fixing a value for p_i such that $c_i(p_i) \leq w_i(p_i)$ gives a unique value of γ_{ibal}. Moreover, it can be argued that γ_{ibal} is an increasing function of p_i. It follows that when $c_i(p_i) \leq w_i(p_i)$, the revenue is given by

$$R_i(\gamma_i) = \begin{cases} \gamma_i p_i c_i(p_i) & 0 < \gamma_i \leq \gamma_{ibal}, \\ \gamma_i p_i w_i((1-\gamma_i)p_i) & \gamma_{ibal} < \gamma_i < 1. \end{cases}$$

In this case $R_i(\gamma_i)$ increases linearly until γ_{ibal}. When $\gamma_i \in (\gamma_{ibal}, 1)$, the service is supply-limited and as in the previous case, $R_i(\gamma_i)$ is concave. This results in the unimodal nature of the revenue $R_i(\gamma_i)$ (Fig. 4).

Notice that given a fixed price, the optimal commission corresponds to a supply-limited service. This is in contrast to the optimal price problem where the revenue optimal prices were shown to correspond to a demand-limited service (Sect. 4).

Example 1. Let the demand and supply curves be linear, given by

$$w_i((1-\gamma_i)p_i) = \bar{w}_i(1-\gamma_i)p_i, \ c_i(p_i) = \bar{c}_i p_i + k_i,$$

where $\bar{w}_i, k_i > 0$, $\bar{c}_i < 0$ and $\bar{c}_i, k_i$ are such that $\bar{c}_i p_m + k_i > 0$ for $i = 1, 2$. Let γ_i^* denote the optimal value of commission (γ_i) for linear demand and supply curves. Then, if $c_i(p_i) > w_i(p_i)$, then $\gamma_i^* = \frac{1}{2}$ or else, if $c_i(p_i) \leq w_i(p_i)$, then $\gamma_i^* = \max\left\{\frac{1}{2}, \gamma_{ibal}\right\}$. When $c_i(p_i) > w_i(p_i)$, $R_i(p_i) = \gamma_i p_i \bar{w}_i (1-\gamma_i)p_i$ which is maximum when $\gamma_i = \frac{1}{2}$. On the other hand, when $c_i(p_i) \leq w_i(p_i)$, solving $\bar{w}_i(1-\gamma_{ibal})p_i = \bar{c}_i p_i + k_i$, we get $\gamma_{ibal} = 1 - \dfrac{k_i + \bar{c}_i p_i}{\bar{w}_i p_i}$. Now,

$$R_i(\gamma_i) = \begin{cases} (p_i(\bar{c}_i p_i + k_i))\gamma_i & 0 < \gamma_i \leq \gamma_{ibal}, \\ (p_i \bar{w}_i p_i)\gamma_i(1-\gamma_i) & \gamma_{ibal} < \gamma_i < 1. \end{cases}$$

$R_i(\gamma_i)$ grows linearly till γ_{ibal}, following which it is quadratic in γ_i with a peak at $\frac{1}{2}$ and thus $\gamma_i^* = \max\left\{\frac{1}{2}, \gamma_{ibal}\right\}$. It follows that a revenue maximizing platform retains at least half of the payment made by the customer in case of linear demand and supply. Furthermore, if a service has excess supply, the platform can keep raising its commission for that service as long as the supply continues to meet the demand.

5.2   Market with Upgrades

If the platform can facilitate *free upgrades*, then it generates additional revenue from upgrades $R_U(\gamma_1, \gamma_2)$ given by,

$$R_U(\gamma_1, \gamma_2) = \max\{(p_1 - (1 - \gamma_2)p_2)\max\{\min\{c_1(p_1) - w_1((1 - \gamma_1)p_1),$$
$$w_2((1 - \gamma_2)p_2) - c_2(p_2)\}, 0\}, 0\}.$$

We define the total revenue, $R(\gamma_1, \gamma_2) := R_1(\gamma_1) + R_2(\gamma_2) + R_U(\gamma_1, \gamma_2)$. The revenue optimization problem now becomes coupled in γ_1, γ_2 as,

$$\max_{\gamma_1, \gamma_2} \quad R_1(\gamma_1) + R_2(\gamma_2) + R_U(\gamma_1, \gamma_2) \tag{2}$$
$$\text{s.t.} \quad 0 < \gamma_1, \gamma_2 < 1.$$

Note that if the Type 2 service is supply-limited at price p_2 at 0 commission, i.e., $c_2(p_2) > w_2(p_2)$, then for all values of $\gamma_2 \in (0, 1)$, there are fewer Type 2 workers than Type 2 customers. Consequently, upgrades are not possible and problem (2) is equivalent to problem (1).

Next, we analyse the case $c_2(p_2) \leq w_2(p_2)$. For an upgrade transaction to be profitable, $(p_1 - (1 - \gamma_2)p_2)$ must be positive or equivalently $\gamma_2 > 1 - \frac{p_1}{p_2}$. Also, note that for potential free upgrades, the number of Type 2 workers must be more than the number of Type 2 customers which is true only if $\gamma_2 < \gamma_{2bal}$ (Fig. 4). Thus, profitable free upgrades may take place only if $\gamma_{2bal} > 1 - \frac{p_1}{p_2}$ and further γ_2 is chosen such that $1 - \frac{p_1}{p_2} < \gamma_2 < \gamma_{2bal}$. In addition to this, free upgrades are possible only when the Type 1 workers are fewer in number than the Type 1 customers. Thus, either $c_1(p_1) > w_1(p_1)$, or else if $c_1(p_1) \leq w_1(p_1)$ then γ_1 must be greater than γ_{1bal} or equivalently $w_1((1 - \gamma_1)p_1) \leq c_1(p_1)$ (Fig. 4).

Remark 3. The preceding arguments together imply that free upgrades can be facilitated by the platform only when all of the following conditions are satisfied.

1. $c_2(p_2) \leq w_2(p_2)$,
2. $1 - \frac{p_1}{p_2} < \gamma_2 < \gamma_{2bal}$, and
3. $c_1(p_1) > w_1(p_1)$ or, $c_1(p_1) \leq w_1(p_1)$ and $\gamma_{1bal} < \gamma_1 < 1$.

In all other cases, there are no potential free upgrades and optimization problem (2) is analogous to the case of market with no upgrades (Problem (1)) and the parameters γ_1 and γ_2 can be optimized separately.

We now study the revenue optimal commission (γ_1, γ_2) when the above mentioned conditions are satisfied and the platform may provide free upgrades in order to increase its revenue. We separately analyse the two cases $c_1(p_1) \leq w_1(p_1)$ along with $\gamma_{1bal} < \gamma_1 < 1$, and $c_1(p_1) > w_1(p_1)$.

− **Case 1:** $c_1(p_1) \leq w_1(p_1)$ and $\gamma_{1bal} < \gamma_1 < 1$ −To ascertain the optimal commission (γ_1, γ_2), we follow an approach similar to that in Sects. 3 and 4. We define curve C as $\{(\gamma_1, \gamma_2) \mid c_2(p_2) + c_1(p_1) = w_2((1 - \gamma_2)p_2) + w_1((1 - \gamma_1)p_1)\}$ which is key to the analysis. Observe that it passes through the point $(\gamma_{1bal}, \gamma_{2bal})$ at which demand matches supply for each service type. Furthermore, for (γ_1, γ_2)

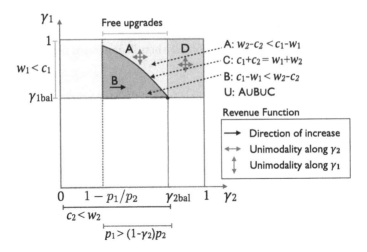

Fig. 5. Subsets A, B, C, D and U for the optimal commission problem (2) for the case $c_1(p_1) \leq w_1(p_1)$ and $\gamma_{1\mathrm{bal}} < \gamma_1 < 1$. In absence of free upgrades, the optimal commission lies in set D while in the presence of upgrades, the optima can also occur in set A where free upgrades are possible and unmatched Type 2 workers are fewer than unmatched Type 1 customers.

to lie on curve C, as γ_1 is increased, γ_2 must decrease. This is because on the curve C, $\gamma_2 = 1 - \frac{w_2^{-1}(c_2(p_2)+c_1(p_1)-w_1((1-\gamma_1)p_1))}{p_2}$ which is decreasing in γ_1. Let D denote the region where the optima lies in the absence of upgrades and let U denote the set of values of (γ_1, γ_2) for which upgrades are possible. Thus,

$$D = \{(\gamma_1, \gamma_2) \mid \gamma_{2\mathrm{bal}} \leq \gamma_2 < 1, \gamma_{1\mathrm{bal}} \leq \gamma_1 < 1\},$$

$$U = \{(\gamma_1, \gamma_2) \mid 1 - \frac{p_1}{p_2} < \gamma_2 < \gamma_{2\mathrm{bal}}, \gamma_{1\mathrm{bal}} < \gamma_1 < 1\}.$$

Depending on whether there are fewer unmatched Type 2 workers or unmatched Type 1 customers, we further divide U into subsets A and B as defined below.

$$A := \{(\gamma_1, \gamma_2) \mid w_2((1-\gamma_2)p_2) - c_2(p_2) \leq c_1(p_1) - w_1((1-\gamma_1)p_1)\} \cap U,$$

$$B := \{(\gamma_1, \gamma_2) \mid w_2((1-\gamma_2)p_2) - c_2(p_2) > c_1(p_1) - w_1((1-\gamma_1)p_1)\} \cap U.$$

Now, since $0 < \gamma_{1\mathrm{bal}}, \gamma_{2\mathrm{bal}}$ and consequently $c_1(p_1) + c_2(p_2) < w_2(p_2) + w_1(p_1)$, it follows that $(0,0)$ lies on the same side of curve C as the set B. Observe that curve C divides set U into subsets A and B. Figure 5 illustrates this case. For (γ_1, γ_2) in U, the revenue from regular transaction and free upgrades is given by,

$$R_1(\gamma_1) = \gamma_1 p_1 w_1((1-\gamma_1)p_1), \quad R_2(\gamma_2) = \gamma_2 p_2 c_2(p_2),$$

$$R_U(\gamma_1, \gamma_2) = (p_1 - (1-\gamma_2)p_2) \min\{c_1(p_1) - w_1((1-\gamma_1)p_1),$$

$$w_2((1-\gamma_2)p_2) - c_2(p_2)\}.$$

Next, we separately analyse regions A and B for the optimal commission.

Theorem 3 (Revenue optimal commission). *The revenue optimal commission lies in the set $A \cup D$.*

Proof. In the absence of upgrades, problem (2) is equivalent to problem (1) and the maxima lies in the set D. Free upgrades can take place in the sets B and A which we analyse below.

– *Region B:* In this region, there are fewer unmatched Type 1 customers than unmatched Type 2 workers and the upgrade revenue is given by, $R_U(\gamma_1, \gamma_2) = (p_1 - (1-\gamma_2)p_2)(c_1(p_1) - w_1((1-\gamma_1)p_1))$. Note that, $\frac{\partial R_U}{\partial \gamma_2} = p_2(c_1(p_1) - w_1((1-\gamma_1)p_1)) \geq 0$. $R_2(\gamma_2)$ also increases until $\gamma_{2\text{bal}}$ with $R_2'(\gamma_2) = p_2 c_2(p_2)$ and

$$\frac{\partial R(\gamma_1, \gamma_2)}{\partial \gamma_2} = p_2(c_1(p_1) - w_1((1-\gamma_1)p_1)) + p_2 c_2(p_2) + 0 > 0.$$

Since $\frac{\partial R(\gamma_1, \gamma_2)}{\partial \gamma_2} > 0$, the maxima is pushed to set A (Fig. 5).

This theorem also implies that a revenue maximizing platform always charges at least a commission $\gamma_{1\text{bal}}$ and $1 - \frac{p_1}{p_2}$ respectively from the Type 1 and Type 2 services. Observe that sets A and B correspond to a supply-limited market and thus at the revenue optimal commission the cumulative demand is greater than the cumulative supply.

Remark 4. Revenue is a unimodal function of γ_2 in set A.

In set A, there are fewer unmatched Type 2 workers than unmatched Type 1 customers and the revenue from free upgrades is given by

$$R_U = (p_1 - (1-\gamma_2)p_2)(w_2((1-\gamma_2)p_2) - c_2(p_2)),$$
$$\frac{\partial R_U}{\partial \gamma_2} = p_2 w_2((1-\gamma_2)p_2) - p_2 c_2(p_2) - p_2 w_2'((1-\gamma_2)p_2)(p_1 - (1-\gamma_2)p_2),$$
$$\frac{\partial^2 R_U}{\partial \gamma_2^2} = -2p_2^2 w_2'((1-\gamma_2)p_2) + p_2^2 w_2''((1-\gamma_2)p_2)(p_1 - (1-\gamma_2)p_2).$$

Observe that $\frac{\partial^2 R}{\partial \gamma_2^2} \leq 0$. Thus, the revenue is concave and consequently a unimodal function in γ_2. Therefore, for a fixed γ_1, a modified binary search algorithm (Algorithm 1) can be used to arrive at the optimal commission γ_2.

– **Case 2:** $c_1(p_1) > w_1(p_1)$ – For this case, Type 1 service is always supply-limited since $c_1(p_1) > w_1((1-\gamma_1)p_1)$ and upgrades are possible for $0 < \gamma_1 < 1$ and $1 - \frac{p_1}{p_2} < \gamma_2 < \gamma_{2\text{bal}}$. The optimal solution can be argued as in the previous case.

5.3   Search for Optimal Commission

Let the interval $(0, 1)$ be divided into uniformly spaced steps of size Δ and let γ_1 and γ_2 take values in multiples of Δ. The platform can sample the market for different values for (γ_1, γ_2) and thus arrive at the optimal commission by repeatedly invoking modified binary search algorithm (Algorithm 1) as in Sects. 3 and 4. Due to space constraints, we present only a brief outline of our algorithm to search for the revenue optimal commission. In Fig. 4, notice that the curve $w_i((1-\gamma_i)p_i) - c_i(p_i)$ is a decreasing function of γ_i which is positive for $\gamma_i < \gamma_{ibal}$ and negative for $\gamma_i > \gamma_{ibal}$. Hence, by checking the sign of $w_i((1-\gamma_i)p_i) - c_i(p_i)$ at the midpoint of the search space in every step, one can arrive at γ_{ibal} in $O\left(\log(\frac{1}{\Delta})\right)$ steps. Also, for the case of no upgrades, the revenue is unimodal and by running a modified binary search, one can ascertain the optimal commission γ_1^* and γ_2^* in $O\left(\log(\frac{1}{\Delta})\right)$ steps. Next, by observing the value of the demand and supply at zero commission, one can check whether all the conditions in Remark 3 hold. If any of these conditions is false, then no upgrades are possible and the optimal commission is (γ_1^*, γ_2^*). When upgrades are possible, we first find the locus of curve C using modified binary search by noting that for a fixed γ_1 in U, the revenue is unimodal along γ_2. This is because within region B, the revenue increases with γ_2 until it hits curve C and is unimodal along γ_2 in region A (Fig. 5). Next we check set A where revenue is unimodal along γ_2 (Remark 4). Consequently, the search complexity for this case is $O\left(\frac{1}{\Delta}\log(\frac{1}{\Delta})\right)$.

6　Conclusions

This work focuses on the task of pricing in platform-aided two-sided markets where the platform facilitates transactions between workers and customers. The platform offers two variants of the same service and is allowed to offer free-upgrades to the customers of the cheaper service variant. We characterize the impact of free upgrades on the platform's revenue and throughput and show that depending on the market conditions, in some cases, free upgrades lead to an increase in revenue/throughput, while in others the best revenue/throughput can be obtained without any free upgrades.

We also study the setting where demand and supply are unknown to the platform a-priori, and the platform has to perform the joint task of pricing and supply/demand estimation. For two objectives, namely, throughput maximization and revenue maximization, we propose algorithms which find the optimal price efficiently, i.e., by sampling the supply/demand curves at a vanishing fraction of the entire space of allowed prices. Lastly, for a given pair of prices that the platform announces to the customers, we characterize the optimal value of the commission charged by a revenue maximizing platform. These results could be improved if we assume that the platform has some a-priori knowledge of the supply/demand curves.

7　Appendix

7.1　Proof of Theorem 1

We separately analyse the throughput function in subsets I, II, III, A and B of the feasible region defined in Sect. 3 (Fig. 2), first arriving at the optima within individual subsets and later finding the global optima. We additionally define region IV as $A \cup B \cup C$.

Region I. Here, $w_1(p_1) \leq c_1(p_1)$, $w_2(p_2) \leq c_2(p_2)$. Thus, $N(p_1, p_2) = w_1(p_1) + w_2(p_2)$. Now, $\frac{\partial N}{\partial p_1} > 0$, $\frac{\partial N}{\partial p_2} > 0$. From the sign of partial derivatives, the optimal price occurs at maximum feasible value of both p_1 and p_2 which is (p_{1bal}, p_{2bal}).

Region II. Here, $c_1(p_1) \leq w_1(p_1)$, $w_2(p_2) \leq c_2(p_2)$. Thus, $N(p_1, p_2) = c_1(p_1) + w_2(p_2)$. Now, $\frac{\partial N}{\partial p_1} < 0$, $\frac{\partial N}{\partial p_2} > 0$. The optimal price occurs at minimum feasible value of p_1 and maximum feasible value of p_2 which is (p_{1bal}, p_{2bal}).

Region III. Here, $c_1(p_1) \leq w_1(p_1)$, $c_2(p_2) \leq w_2(p_2)$ and $N(p_1, p_2) = c_1(p_1) + c_2(p_2)$. Now, $\frac{\partial N}{\partial p_1} < 0$, $\frac{\partial N}{\partial p_2} < 0$. The optimal price occurs at minimum feasible value of p_1 and p_2 which is again (p_{1bal}, p_{2bal}).

Region IV. This is perhaps the most interesting region as there's a possibility of free upgrades. Here, $w_1(p_1) \leq c_1(p_1)$, $c_2(p_2) \leq w_2(p_2)$. For the purpose of analyzing the throughput, we separately analyze the following 2 regions,

– *Region A:* Here, $w_2(p_2) - c_2(p_2) \leq c_1(p_1) - w_1(p_1)$, and $N(p_1, p_2) = w_1(p_1) + w_2(p_2)$. Moreover, $\frac{\partial N}{\partial p_1} > 0$, $\frac{\partial N}{\partial p_2} > 0$. Thus, the optimal price occurs at maximum allowed feasible values of p_1 and p_2 which pushes the optimal price to curve C.

– *Region B:* Here, $c_1(p_1) - w_1(p_1) \leq w_2(p_2) - c_2(p_2)$, and $N(p_1, p_2) = c_1(p_1) + c_2(p_2)$. Now, $\frac{\partial N}{\partial p_1} < 0$, $\frac{\partial N}{\partial p_2} < 0$. As above, the optimal price occurs at minimum allowed feasible values of p_1 and p_2 which correspond to curve C.

7.2   Proof of Proposition 1

In Sect. 3, we have shown that throughput must lie on the curve C. The function $c_2(p_2) - w_2(p_2)$ is a strictly decreasing function of p_2 and therefore invertible. Hence, we can parameterize C as $p_1 = (w_1 - c_1)^{-1}(c_2(p_2) - w_2(p_2))$. Denote, $\eta(p_2) := w_1((w_1 - c_1)^{-1}(c_2(p_2) - w_2(p_2))) + w_2(p_2)$. It can be verified that,

$$\frac{d\eta(p_2)}{dp_2} = \frac{w_1'(p_1)c_2'(p_2) - w_2'(p_2)c_1'(p_1)}{w_1'(p_1) - c_1'(p_1)}.$$

Note that $w_1'(p_1) - c_1'(p_1) > 0 \; \forall p_1$. Consequently, the sign of $w_1'(p_1)c_2'(p_2) - w_2'(p_2)c_1'(p_1)$ determines the sign of $\frac{d\eta}{dp_2}$. If $w_1'(p_1)c_2'(p_2) < w_2'(p_2)c_1'(p_1)$ along curve C, then throughput is optimal at the least feasible value p_2 which in fact corresponds to the equilibrium price (p_{1bal}, p_{2bal}). On the other hand, if $w_1'(p_1)c_2'(p_2) > w_2'(p_2)c_1'(p_1)$, then the throughput is optimal at the least allowed value of p_1 or equivalently the greatest allowed p_2 along curve C. Noting that $|c_1'(p_1)| = -c_1'(p_1)$, $|c_2'(p_2)| = -c_2'(p_2)$, and that $w_1'(p_1), w_2'(p_2) > 0$ we get the required result.

7.3   Proof of Theorem 2

We separately analyse the revenue function in regions I, II, III, $\bar{A}, \bar{B}$ and D of the feasible region as defined in Sect. 4 (Fig. 3). We additionally define region IV as $\bar{A} \cup \bar{B} \cup \bar{C} \cup D$.

Region I. Here, $w_1(p_1) \leq c_1(p_1)$, $w_2(p_2) \leq c_2(p_2)$. Thus, $R(p_1, p_2) = \gamma p_1 w_1(p_1) + \gamma p_2 w_2(p_2)$ whereby, $\frac{\partial R}{\partial p_1} > 0$, $\frac{\partial R}{\partial p_2} > 0$. From the sign of partial derivatives, the optimal price occurs at maximum feasible value of both p_1 and p_2 which is (p_{1bal}, p_{2bal}).

Region II. Here, $c_1(p_1) \leq w_1(p_1)$, $w_2(p_2) \leq c_2(p_2)$. Thus, $R(p_1, p_2) = \gamma p_1 c_1(p_1) + \gamma p_2 w_2(p_2)$. Now, $\frac{\partial R}{\partial p_2} > 0$. Thus, $\forall p_1$, p_2 takes the maximum feasible value. Hence, optimal price occurs on line $\{(p_1, p_2)|p_2 = p_{2bal}\}$.

Region III. Here, $c_1(p_1) \leq w_1(p_1)$, $c_2(p_2) \leq w_2(p_2)$ and consequently there are no free upgrades. As discussed in Sect. 4, the optimal price becomes $(\min\{p_{1opt}, p_{2opt}\}, p_{2opt})$.

Region IV. Here, $w_1(p_1) \leq c_1(p_1)$, $c_2(p_2) \leq w_2(p_2)$ and there's a possibility of free upgrades if the transaction price of an upgrade $p_1 - (1 - \gamma)p_2$ is positive. We separately analyze regions $\bar{A}, \bar{B} \setminus \hat{B}$ and D.

- *Region D*: Here, $w_1(p_1) \leq c_1(p_1)$, $c_2(p_2) \leq w_2(p_2)$ but there are no free upgrades as $p_1 < (1 - \gamma)p_2$. Thus, $R(p_1, p_2) = \gamma p_1 w_1(p_1) + \gamma p_2 c_2(p_2)$. Now, $\frac{\partial R}{\partial p_1} > 0$. Thus, $\forall p_2$, p_1 takes the maximum feasible value. Hence, the optimal prices cannot lie in interior of region D.

- *Region $\bar{A}$*: Here, $w_2(p_2) - c_2(p_2) \leq c_1(p_1) - w_1(p_1)$, $p_1 \geq (1 - \gamma)p_2$. In this region, all unmatched Type 2 workers serve Type 1 customers, whereby,

$$R(p_1, p_2) = \gamma p_1 w_1(p_1) + \gamma p_2 c_2(p_2) + (p_1 - (1 - \gamma)p_2)(w_2(p_2) - c_2(p_2)).$$

It is easy to see that $\frac{\partial R}{\partial p_1} > 0$. Thus, $\forall p_2$, p_1 takes the maximum feasible value. Hence, the optimal prices cannot lie in the interior of this region and are pushed to curve $\bar{C}$.

- *Region $\bar{B} \setminus \hat{B}$*: Here, $p_2 \geq p_{2opt}$, $p_1 \geq (1 - \gamma)p_2$, $c_1(p_1) - w_1(p_1) \leq w_2(p_2) - c_2(p_2)$. In this region, all unmatched Type 1 customers are provided a free upgrade to Type 2 service. Consequently, $R(p_1, p_2) = \gamma p_1 w_1(p_1) + \gamma p_2 c_2(p_2) + (p_1 - (1 - \gamma)p_2)(c_1(p_1) - w_1(p_1))$. Observe that,

$$\frac{\partial R}{\partial p_2} = \gamma c_2(p_2) + \gamma p_2 c_2'(p_2) - (1 - \gamma)(c_1(p_1) - w_1(p_1)).$$

Since the function $p_2 c_2(p_2)$ has its maxima at p_{2opt} after which it decreases. Thus, $\forall p_2 > p_{2opt}, (p_2 c_2(p_2))' = c_2(p_2) + p_2 c_2'(p_2) < 0$. Hence, $\frac{\partial R}{\partial p_2} < 0$. Thus $\forall p_1$, p_2 takes the minimum feasible value in this region. Thus, the optimal price is pushed to region $\hat{B} \cup C$. Therefore, revenue optimal prices lie in $(\min\{p_{1opt}, p_{2opt}\}, p_{2opt}) \cup \bar{C} \cup \hat{B}$.

References

1. Banerjee, S., Freund, D., Lykouris, T.: Pricing and optimization in shared vehicle systems: an approximation framework. CoRR abs/1608.06819 (2016)
2. Banerjee, S., Gollapudi, S., Kollias, K., Munagala, K.: Segmenting two-sided markets. In: Proceedings of the 26th International Conference on World Wide Web, International World Wide Web Conferences Steering Committee, pp. 63–72 (2017)
3. Banerjee, S., Johari, R., Riquelme, C.: Pricing in ride-sharing platforms: a queueing-theoretic approach. In: Proceedings of the Sixteenth ACM Conference on Economics and Computation, p. 639. ACM (2015)
4. Borokhovich, M., Chatterjee, A., Rogers, J., Varshney, L.R., Vishwanath, S.: Improving impact sourcing via efficient global service delivery. In: Proceedings of Data for Good Exchange (D4GX) (2015)
5. Chen, L., Mislove, A., Wilson, C.: Peeking beneath the hood of Uber. In: Proceedings of the 2015 ACM Conference on Internet Measurement Conference, pp. 495–508. ACM (2015)
6. Chen, M.K., Sheldon, M.: Dynamic pricing in a labor market: surge pricing and flexible work on the Uber platform. In: EC, p. 455 (2016)
7. Cheung, W.C., Simchi-Levi, D., Wang, H.: Dynamic pricing and demand learning with limited price experimentation. Oper. Res. **65**, 1722–1731 (2017)
8. den Boer, A.V.: Dynamic pricing and learning: historical origins, current research, and new directions. Surv. Oper. Res. Manag. Sci. **20**(1), 1–18 (2015)
9. Efroymson, C.W.: A note on kinked demand curves. Am. Econ. Rev. **33**(1), 98–109 (1943)
10. Evans, D.S.: Some empirical aspects of multi-sided platform industries. Rev. Netw. Econ. **2**(3), 191–209 (2003)
11. Fang, Z., Huang, L., Wierman, A.: Prices and subsidies in the sharing economy. In: Proceedings of the 26th International Conference on World Wide Web, International World Wide Web Conferences Steering Committee, pp. 53–62 (2017)
12. Huet, E.: Uber raises uberx commission to 25 percent in five more markets. Forbes
13. Jia, Y., Xu, W., Liu, X.: An optimization framework for online ride-sharing markets. In: 2017 IEEE 37th International Conference on Distributed Computing Systems (ICDCS), pp. 826–835. IEEE (2017)
14. Kung, L.C., Zhong, G.Y.: The optimal pricing strategy for two-sided platform delivery in the sharing economy. Transp. Res. Part E Logist. Transp. Rev. **101**, 1–12 (2017)
15. Maskin, E., Tirole, J.: A theory of dynamic oligopoly, II: price competition, kinked demand curves, and edgeworth cycles. Econ. J. Econ. Soc. **56**, 571–599 (1988)
16. Rochet, J.C., Tirole, J.: Two-sided markets: a progress report. RAND J. Econ. **37**(3), 645–667 (2006)
17. Rysman, M.: The economics of two-sided markets. J. Econ. Perspect. **23**(3), 125–143 (2009)
18. Samasource. https://www.samasource.org/
19. Stigler, G.J.: The literature of economics: the case of the kinked oligopoly demand curve. Econ. Inq. **16**(2), 185–204 (1978)
20. Waserhole, A., Jost, V.: Pricing in vehicle sharing systems: optimization in queuing networks with product forms. EURO J. Transp. Logist. **5**(3), 293–320 (2016)
21. Weyl, E.G.: A price theory of multi-sided platforms. Am. Econ. Rev. **100**(4), 1642–1672 (2010)

On the Impact of Duty Cycled LTE-U on Wi-Fi Users: An Experimental Study

Anand M. Baswade[1($\boxtimes$)], Touheed Anwar Atif[2], Bheemarjuna Reddy Tamma[1], and A. Antony Franklin[1]

[1] Indian Institute of Technology Hyderabad, Sangareddy, India
{cs14resch11002,tbr,antony.franklin}@iith.ac.in
[2] University of Michigan, Ann Arbor, USA
touheed@umich.edu

Abstract. The deployment of LTE in unlicensed spectrum is a plausible solution to meet explosive traffic demand from mobile users. However, fair coexistence with the existing unlicensed technologies, mainly Wi-Fi, needs to be ensured before any such deployment. Duty cycled LTE (LTE-U) is a simple and an easily adaptable scheme which helps in fair coexistence with the Wi-Fi. Nonetheless, the immense deployment of Wi-Fi necessitates a user-oriented study to find the effects of LTE-U operation, primarily in scenarios where the LTE-U eNB remains hidden from Wi-Fi Access Point. To delineate these effects, we perform a user-level Transmission Control Protocol (TCP) and User Datagram Protocol (UDP) throughputs study of Wi-Fi in the presence of LTE-U using a testbed. Since, TCP is a more complicated protocol, we analyzed the Congestion Window and Round Trip Time data to comprehend the throughput results. This further explains the unfairness in throughput distribution among Wi-Fi users. Furthermore, we also notice inability among the disadvantaged users to receive the periodic Wi-Fi beacon frames successfully. The reasons and the subsequent consequences of throughput unfairness and beacon losses, are carefully elaborated. Also, to validate the beacon loss results, we present a beacon loss analysis which provides a mathematical expression to find the beacon loss percentage. Finally, we examine the results and highlight a need for incorporating additional functionalities in either LTE-U or Wi-Fi to overcome the present challenges.

Keywords: Inter-RAT hidden terminal
LTE in Unlicensed (LTE-U) · IEEE 802.11 (Wi-Fi)
LTE-U and Wi-Fi coexistence

1 Introduction

The last few years have seen a rapid increase in cellular data traffic demand [24] due to a sudden surge in the usage of smart phones and tablets [15]. To manage such high user data demands, the telecom industry is keen on utilizing

© Springer Nature Switzerland AG 2019
S. Biswas et al. (Eds.): COMSNETS 2018, LNCS 11227, pp. 196–219, 2019.
https://doi.org/10.1007/978-3-030-10659-1_9

Non-Victim user

Access Point

-62dBm

Victim user

LTE-U eNB

Fig. 1. Scenario shows a Wi-Fi AP with two users and an LTE-U eNB both operating on the same unlicensed channel. The victim Wi-Fi user is inside the influence zone of LTE-U; and the non-victim Wi-Fi user along with Wi-Fi AP are outside the influence zone of LTE-U.

the unlicensed spectrum [4,6]. Although LTE in unlicensed might fulfill these demands, along with improving the spectral efficiency of unlicensed spectrum—it must ensure fair coexistence with other technologies in unlicensed spectrum, mainly IEEE 802.11 (a.k.a. Wi-Fi)—before being widely accepted. Some of the approaches like Licensed Assisted Access (LAA) which follows Listen Before Talk (LBT) [6], a similar channel access mechanism like Wi-Fi; and duty cycled discontinuous transmission with LTE eNB following an ON-OFF cycle pattern (called as LTE-U) [4,18–21]; claims to fairly coexist with Wi-Fi. However, discontinuous and duty cycled transmission approach, due to its simplicity of requiring minimal changes in the existing LTE protocol, is being pushed to the markets. One such example is Carrier Sense Adaptive Transmission (CSAT) [2], where eNB follows an ON-OFF cycle pattern, with ON and OFF durations corresponding to LTE transmissions and muting duration, respectively.

Furthermore, [13] shows both LTE-U CSAT scheme and LBT to be equally fair with Wi-Fi and leaves it on the operator to decide which scheme to deploy. But, due to the current ubiquitous deployment of Wi-Fi, there are scenarios where very intricate challenges can prevail. We consider one such class of scenarios and delineate thoroughly the complications involved in achieving fair throughput distribution among the Wi-Fi users and the difficulties arrived in attaining consistent beacon reception by these Wi-Fi users in such scenarios.

The class of scenarios which we consider is in fact, very similar to the Wi-Fi hidden terminal problem, with LTE-U eNB required to be hidden from the Wi-Fi Access Point (AP) while the AP may or may not be hidden from the LTE-U eNB. The scenario essentially consists of a Wi-Fi network partially overlapped with the LTE-U network as shown in Fig. 1; with the Wi-Fi AP outside the influence zone of LTE-U, and thus can transmit or receive data even during the LTE-U ON period. We define the influence zone of LTE-U as the region around LTE-U eNB where a Wi-Fi device cannot transmit or receive successfully when LTE-U is ON because of the following two reasons. Firstly, the signal strength received by the Wi-Fi user from the LTE-U transmissions is high enough compared to the Clear Channel Assessment (CCA) Threshold [9] of the Wi-Fi device, causing it to sense the channel as busy and halt from any transmission. Secondly, the interference caused by the LTE-U transmissions to the Wi-Fi user is substantial and thereby decreases the Signal-to-Interference-plus-Noise-Ratio (SINR) below the minimum SINR required for successful reception. Now, we consider some of the Wi-Fi users to be present within the influence region of LTE-U and call them as victim users. Consequently, the remaining Wi-Fi users which are outside the influence region are called as non-victim users.

The main contributions of the paper can be summarized as follows:

- We analyze the considered hidden terminal scenario on a testbed setup, and study the performance of Wi-Fi users in the presence of duty cycled LTE-U for both UDP and TCP traffic cases.
- We observe the unfairness caused to the victim users in terms of throughput and study the effect of the presence of these victim users on the Wi-Fi network. The lack of comprehensive literature for such scenario using real hardware makes our study novel.
- We also study the beacon lost phenomena of victim users and present the effects of beacon losses. We also propose beacon loss analysis and provide a mathematical expression to calculate the beacon loss percentage. Finally, we validate the analytical results using simulation and testbed.

The rest of the chapter is organized as follows. In Sect. 2, the related work is discussed. Experimental setup and results are shown in Sects. 3 and 4, respectively. In Sect. 5, beacon loss analysis for victim users is proposed. Finally, conclusions and future work are given in Sect. 6.

2   Related Work

Though the telecom industry is very keen to make LTE to operate in unlicensed spectrum [4,6], the research community is concerned about LTE-U fairly sharing the spectrum with other unlicensed technologies. Hence, most of the work in the literature focuses on the fair coexistence of LTE-U/LAA with Wi-Fi [7,10]. The foremost claim made is that the deployment of LTE in unlicensed spectrum without changing LTE protocol will significantly degrade the performance of Wi-Fi. This was shown in [14] using a system-level simulator. In [23], the performance of LTE and Wi-Fi in a shared frequency band was presented which again showed that LTE degrades the performance of Wi-Fi, but to improve the performance of Wi-Fi a muting technique was introduced within LTE, while maintaining fairly good performance of LTE.

In [8], the authors apart from evaluating through simulations the impact of LTE on the performance of Wi-Fi when both the networks operate in the same frequency, suggested a modified almost blank subframe approach in LTE for fair coexistence with Wi-Fi. In fact, most of the works in literature are focused on simulation and/or mathematical modeling [10–12,17,25]. On the other hand, in [22] the performance degradation of Wi-Fi was studied using a testbed when a traditional LTE network operates in the same unlicensed channel. However, a Wi-Fi user oriented performance study using a testbed is unprecedented. In this paper, we focus on the class of scenarios where the effect of LTE is dissimilar for different set of Wi-Fi users. Furthermore, to make our study more realistic, we consider a more justifiable LTE operation enabled with discontinuous duty cycled transmissions, and study the effect of LTE-U on Wi-Fi users using a testbed. We study the effect of LTE-U on Wi-Fi users for both UDP and TCP traffic cases. We also propose a beacon loss analysis for the so called victim users and validate the results using the testbed.

3   Experimental Testbed Setup

The experimental testbed setup consists of an LTE-U network partially over-lapped with a Wi-Fi network—with one user as victim and another as non-victim—as shown in Fig. 2. The center frequency for LTE-U and Wi-Fi is set to 2.442 GHz (*i.e., Wi-Fi channel 7*).

Fig. 2. Experimental testbed setup demonstrating the Wi-Fi network partially over-lapped with the LTE-U network, with additional two Desktops used for sending and receiving iPerf traffic to/from the Wi-Fi users.

In [5], National Instruments (NI) demonstrated a real-time LTE-U and Wi-Fi coexistence testbed and provided an application framework for LTE-U/LAA. This framework was developed by modifying the existing NI LTE application framework [3]. We have employed the USRP RIO board with the same NI LTE-U/LAA application framework [5] to create an LTE-U eNB and an LTE-U user. Furthermore, a Wi-Fi network is setup using a commercial "Netgear N600 wireless dual band router WNDR3400v3" as an AP. The equipments used for Wi-Fi AP and LTE-U eNB are shown in Fig. 3. The Wi-Fi AP is operating in 802.11n mode with two Laptops (Ubuntu 14.04 LTS with Intel wireless 8260 chipset and Realtek drivers) as two Wi-Fi stations. The two Laptops along with two Desktops are used for a client-server application each installed with iPerf [1], with Desktops being connected to the switch using 1 Gb/s Ethernet cables as shown in Fig. 2. For the traffic flow in the network, we configured LTE-U eNB to be transmitting only in downlink (as LTE in unlicensed is used only in down-link [4,6]) and studied Wi-Fi performance for the following two scenarios. First, Downlink (DL) only, containing solely the DL traffic. Second, Uplink (UL) and DL containing both UL and DL traffic. To direct the DL traffic of the Wi-Fi network to its stations for both the scenarios, we configured the Wi-Fi network in infrastructure mode with AP as the primary entity, responsible for all DL transmissions.

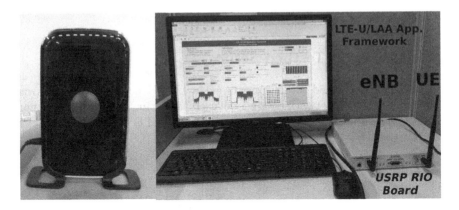

Fig. 3. Equipment used in the testbed: (i) Netgear N600 wireless dual band router WNDR3400v3 used as Wi-Fi AP. (ii) USRP RIO board with LTE-U eNB and LTE-U user operated using LTE-U/LAA application framework.

For coexistence of LTE-U with Wi-Fi, the LTE-U follows a ON and OFF patterns, where it transmits for few milliseconds during the ON period and becomes silent in the OFF period. The experiments are conducted to study the throughput and beacon loss percentage of Wi-Fi users with different LTE-U ON periods. This variation in ON period is achieved by identically varying the ON-OFF periods in such a way that the complete duty cycle period (LTE ON + LTE-U OFF) is always 10 ms. Each experiment is performed several times in order to remove the undesirable randomness and understand the average behavior of the network.

4   Experimental Results

The performance of the deployed Wi-Fi stations is observed while varying the LTE-U ON fraction where, LTE-U ON fraction is a fraction of time LTE-U is ON in a given duty cycle period. As discussed earlier, the two main issues are highlighted—degradation in throughput and losses in beacon reception. The effect of LTE-U on throughput of Wi-Fi users is showed for both the UDP and TCP traffic cases.

4.1   Throughput Results for UDP Traffic

For the throughput measurement of Wi-Fi network, a client-server application named iPerf [1] is installed and is used for generating UDP traffic at a rate of 10 Mb/s per user. The throughput performance of Wi-Fi stations is measured for both DL only and UL+DL traffic scenarios.

DL Only Scenario: In the DL only scenario, client applications are set up in the Desktops which transmit UDP packets to the servers listening at the victim and non-victim users, via the Wi-Fi AP. Throughput calculations are made after every iteration, with each iteration running for 40 s, by varying the LTE-U ON period. Furthermore, the same experiment is performed with two different packet sizes to observe the effect of packet size on the performance of Wi-Fi users, mainly the victim user. In addition, the performance of non-victim user without victim user is also shown to highlight the effect of the presence of victim user on the non-victim user and the Wi-Fi network.

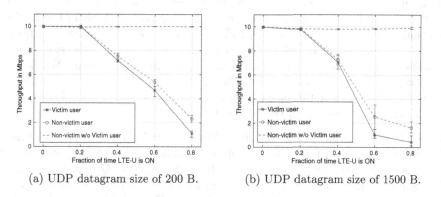

(a) UDP datagram size of 200 B.   (b) UDP datagram size of 1500 B.

Fig. 4. Throughput of victim user, non-victim user, and non-victim user without the presence of victim user with varying LTE-U ON fraction.

Following observations can be made from the experiments:

1. Substantial Retransmission Losses Leading to a Decrease in Throughput of Victim as Well the Non-victim Users: From Figs. 4a and b, it can be observed that the performance of non-victim user, with victim user being muted, is independent of LTE-U ON period and remains at the maximum possible throughput of 10 Mb/s. However, with the introduction of victim user traffic, not just the achievable throughput of victim descends with increasing LTE-U ON period but also the presence of victim user wrenches the throughput of non-victim user. The decrease in the throughput of victim user with ON period is quite anticipated—with the decrease in duration where victim user can receive packets successfully the throughput of victim user is expected to decrease. However, the decrease in non-victim users throughput is unexpected and can be explained as follows. During the LTE-U ON period, the transmissions to non-victim user would be successful, but the transmissions to the victim user, due to high interference, would result in a packet loss. Wi-Fi AP regards this transmission to be a collision and re-transmits the same packet, but by exponentially incrementing its Contention Window (CW) and in turn selecting a higher Back-Off (BO) value. This leads to a profuse increase in the total retransmissions in the Wi-Fi network. As the non-victim user is also served by the same

AP, which is all but wasting most of the ON period doing retransmissions, the non-victim user also gets starved and eventually receives a decreased throughput. In [11], we have provided an analytical model to study the effect of duty cycled LTE-U on throughputs of victim and non-victim users in the network.

2. Disproportionate Throughput Distribution Among Victim and Non-victim Users: Distributed Coordination Function (DCF) of Wi-Fi ensures equal throughput distribution among its users which can be seen from Figs. 4a and b at low LTE-U ON fraction. But as the ON fraction increases, an imbalance is created among the throughput distribution to victim and non-victim users. This is because victim users can receive packets only in the LTE-U OFF period, whereas non-victim users can receive packets both in the LTE-U ON and OFF periods. In principle, LTE-U ceases to access the channel, during its OFF cycle, so that the victim users get channel access and thereby achieve a proportionate share of the channel and hence the throughput. Non-victim users access to the channel–during this (LTE-U OFF) period–engenders lower throughput to these victim users. This results in unfairness among Wi-Fi users which further increases with the LTE-U ON period.

3. Restriction on the Packet Size Meant for Victim Users: The final observation which can be made from Figs. 4a and b is the dependence of packet size on victim users throughput. Although higher packet sizes give higher throughputs, but if the size of packet meant for victim user is considerably large, such that the air time of the packet exceeds the LTE-U OFF period, the packet would merely be lost. Moreover, if the packet air time is less but still significant compared to the OFF period, the probability that the packet would occur at the transition from an OFF to ON period would be high and would again result in a packet loss.

In addition, since the Wi-Fi AP was unable to serve the victim users during the LTE-U ON period, after receiving an opportunity in the LTE-U OFF period, it tries serving these victim users with minimal rates (due to the rate control algorithm), consequently increasing the packet air-time by multitudes. This unnecessary increase in the air-time and the limited OFF period, restricts the packet size and eventually becomes a compromise with the throughput. From the above figures, a comparable performance among victim and non-victim users can be observed with 200 B (in Fig. 4a) and 1500 B (in Fig. 4b) packet sizes for low ON periods, but as ON period ascends the throughput of transmissions involving 1500 B packets noticeably descends and reaches very low.

UL + DL Scenario: For a UL + DL scenario, the client and server applications (using iPerf) are setup in the Desktops as well as in the Laptops, so as to transmit packets in both UL and DL, via the Wi-Fi AP. Throughput measurements are made while varying the LTE-U ON period, with each flow having a rate of 10 Mb/s and a UDP datagram size of 200 B.

The key observations for the UL + DL scenario are enumerated as follows:

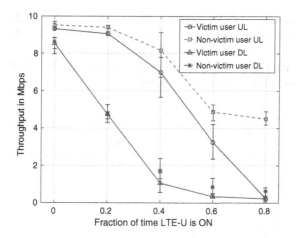

Fig. 5. Throughput of victim and non-victim users with varying LTE-U ON fraction in UL and DL scenario.

1. Preferential UL Transmissions over DL Transmissions: Figure 5 shows the variation in UL and DL throughputs of victim and non-victim users, with increasing LTE-U ON fraction. It can be seen that the UL throughputs of both the users are greater than their DL throughputs. As discussed earlier, the Wi-Fi AP being completely unaware of the fact that the packets meant to victim users are lost because of ongoing LTE-U ON period, tries re-transmitting packets to the victim users. Since every retransmission escalates the CW exponentially, multiple retransmissions would mean a sudden inflation in average BO value of the Wi-Fi AP, thus reducing the channel access ability of the AP. This results in a decrease in the DL throughputs of both the victim and non-victim users. While on the other hand, the non-victim users being distanced from the effect of LTE-U, gain an advantage to the channel in comparison with Wi-Fi AP. This can lead to a considerable increase in UL throughput in contrast to DL throughput.

2. Decrease in UL Throughput for All Users with Increasing LTE-U ON Period: From Fig. 5, the decrease in UL throughput of victim user is quite expected—with increase in LTE-U ON fraction, the channel available for the victim user to contend and transmit data decreases, and thereby reduces its throughput. However, a decrease in non-victim users UL throughput is astonishing. The fact to be perceived here is that the LTE-U transmissions not just affect the victim users but also decrease the UL SINR of the non-victim users (though not less than the minimum required). This causes the non-victim users to choose lower Modulation and Coding Schemes and consequently decrease their throughput.

3. A Proportional Effect on DL Throughput for All Users: From Fig. 5, it can be seen that the effect of LTE-U on DL throughputs is commensurate for both the victim and non-victim user. Although Wi-Fi AP can communicate with the non-victim user during the LTE-U ON period, the AP's convention of performing re-transmissions to the victim user, leaves the AP with very less ON period in which it can successfully transmit to non-victim and provide a perquisite over victim user. Therefore, with the increase of LTE-U ON time, the DL throughputs of all the users decreases.

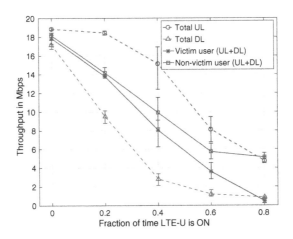

Fig. 6. Total UL and DL throughputs and total victim and non-victim users throughputs with varying LTE-U ON fraction.

Figure 6 shows the total throughput of Wi-Fi network in UL and DL as well as the individual total throughput of victim and non-victim users with varying LTE-U ON fraction. Again the total DL throughput is lower than the total UL throughput. As the individual DL throughputs are less than the individual UL throughputs, it is certain that the total DL throughput of the network would be less than the total UL throughput of the network. In addition, the unfairness in the performance among the victim and non-victim users can also be observed. Moreover, this unfairness further increases with increasing LTE-U ON fraction.

Although the hidden terminal class of scenarios are discussed above in the perspective of duty cycled LTE-U scheme, the impact on Wi-Fi victim users holds true even for the case of LAA. The LBT mechanism of LAA may reduce the overall impact on the Wi-Fi network, but unfairness among users would still remain unjustified.

4.2   Throughput Results for TCP Traffic

TCP is a connection oriented Internet protocol aiming to provide a reliable and ordered delivery between applications running at sources. This is primarily achieved by embedding a retransmission mechanism within the protocol which ensures successful delivery of packets to the receiver. However, with the presence of LTE-U, the performance of TCP (*i.e.,* the performance of the TCP based

Wi-Fi user) is impacted, with the impact exponentiating in the considered hidden terminal scenario.

Thus, we extend our study on the TCP performance in the considered LTE-U and Wi-Fi hidden terminal scenario, in terms of throughput and fairness among the victim and non-victim users. To measure the throughput of the Wi-Fi network, we used iPerf [1] and generated TCP traffic using it. We set the Maximum Segment Size (MSS) to 1448 B and receiver window size to 85 KB. For TCP, we use TCP CUBIC as the congestion control algorithm. The iPerf client applications are set up in the Desktops (Scenario shown in Fig. 2) which transmit TCP packets. The iPerf server applications are running on victim and non-victim users. The victim and non-victim users are receiving TCP traffic from Desktop via the Wi-Fi AP. Throughput calculations are made after every iteration, with each iteration running for 60 s, while varying the LTE-U ON period.

What Is Different About TCP and Does It Manifest Here?: Unlike UDP, TCP performance is heavily dependent on the packet losses that occur in its flow. Every packet loss decreases the congestion window of TCP, and in-turn the transmission rate is reduced by half. This behavior of TCP has been well-suited and in fact proved to be very promising in most of the network settings. However, the considered scenario of the Wi-Fi network partially hampered by the operation of a nearby LTE-U, creates a very unique situation to understand and analyze.

Figure 7a shows the instability caused to the TCP performance of the Wi-Fi users, as the ON fraction of the LTE-U is increased. Furthermore, very dissimilar results for victim and non-victim users are observed, requiring a separate approach to understand the performance of different users of the same Wi-Fi network. It can be seen from the Fig. 7a, as the LTE-U ON fraction is increased, the throughput of victim, as anticipated, decreases but in no-time reaches almost zero. On the other hand, the non-victim user's throughput very surprisingly increases. In the following sections, we explore more of such behavior, and to rationalize the results, we investigate the Congestion Window and Round Trip Time (RTT) variation for these TCP flows provide insights using these. In addition, to quantify the throughput unfairness among victim and non-victim users, we used Jain's fairness index [16]. The throughput fairness index among victim and non-victim users is shown in Fig. 7b. We can clearly see that as the duty cycle increases the fairness among victim and non-victim users decreases drastically. In the following section, we explain the throughput behavior of victim and non-victim users and provide reasons for the same.

Near Zero Throughput for Victim Users at Moderately High LTE-U ON Fractions: The decrease in throughput of the victim user with gradually increasing LTE-U ON period is quite anticipated—the smaller the duration available to access the channel and to transmit a data packet, the lesser the throughput. However, compared to UDP throughput, the TCP throughput of victim user decreases rapidly (Fig. 7a). The primarily reason behind this is the distinct architecture of TCP and UDP. As discussed earlier, TCP reacts to packet losses profusely, assuming that packet losses are due to network congestion and its

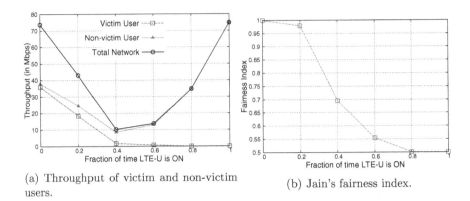

(a) Throughput of victim and non-victim users.

(b) Jain's fairness index.

Fig. 7. Victim and non-victim users TCP throughput and fairness.

reaction (of multiplicative decrease) could solve the network congestion. However, the packet losses here are not because of network congestion. In fact, adopting such a decrease is further hindering the victim user to access the channel in the upcoming ON duration, where it could have send the packets successfully. Now, owing to decrease in the transmission rate of TCP has made the victim user to not just suffer from the LTE-U operation, but has also hinged its performance from its core. Further discussion on this behavior is provided with the results demonstrating congestion window and the smoothed RTT variation.

Table 1. Average smoothed RTT.

η	Non-victim sRTT	Victim sRTT
0	252.591 ms	285.475 ms
0.2	397.982 ms	60.431 ms
0.4	580.623 ms	149.123 ms
0.6	131.621 ms	124.066 ms
0.8	125.169 ms	NA

An Interesting Decrease Followed by an Increase Is Observed for the Non-victim User: To explain this unique trend, we bank upon two factors which establish a trade-off in the throughput. One of the factor increases the throughput and the other decreases it, but finally both relate to the channel access opportunity of the non-victim user. They are as follows,

1. As discussed in the UDP behavior, the victim user packets transmitted in the LTE-U ON period cannot be successfully decoded, resulting in packet loss and requiring a need for retransmission at the Medium Access Control (MAC) layer. These retransmissions are not just a humongous channel

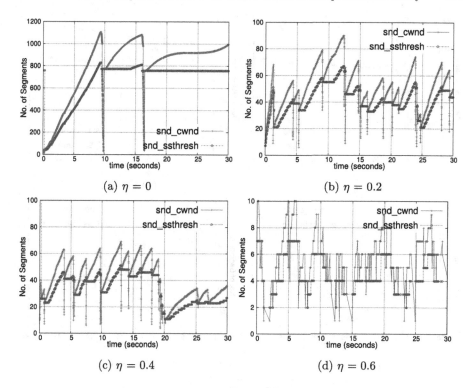

Fig. 8. Victim user congestion window variation over time.

wastage, but at the same time deprive the non-victim users packets waiting in the queue to be transmitted, which could have been a successful transmission. Further discussion on these retransmissions is presented in the UDP performance evaluation section where we explained how the retransmission losses can potentially lead to decrease in throughput for both the users.

2. This factor is very unique to TCP. When the MAC layer is unable to transmit a packet meant for the victim user (primarily during the LTE-U ON period), or even if the ACK from the victim user to the AP is unable to be received within the stipulated time-out interval, TCP regards this packet as a packet loss and decreases its rate by a multiplicative factor (β). This causes a decreased TCP flow of the victim user in the network. Now, if one of the flows does not use the channel, TCP algorithm allows the other flows (non-victim user) to extract the best it can by using an additive increase. This component is more pronounced at high LTE-U ON fractions when the victim user traffic is almost zero.

Using the above factors, we conclude the following. The decrease in the non-victim user throughput until LTE-U ON fraction (η) can be ascribed to component 1. This is because, at such low η values, the victim user is able to achieve a noteworthy throughput (though less than the non-victim) and hence would

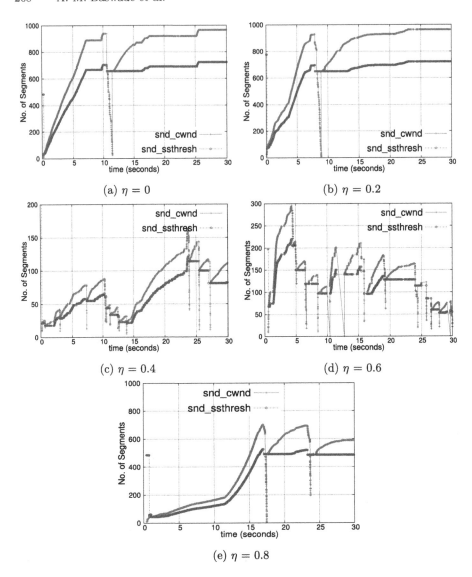

Fig. 9. Non-victim user congestion window variation over time.

consume a significant portion of the channel. From 0 to 0.4 as η is increased, the retransmissions starts to consume a crucial amount of the channel access and thus causes a decrease in the non-victim user throughput However, as η is further increased, the victim user's TCP algorithm drops its rate drastically (also confirmed later through the Contention Window plots) and hence cause the victim user packets to pass onto the MAC layer at a very decreased rate. Although this is dreadful for the victim user, but nonetheless helps the non-victim user gain its lost authority over the network.

Congestion Window Study of Victim and Non-victim Users with Varying LTE-U ON Fraction: To validate our claims about the throughput variation made above, we perform a study on the congestion window and RTT variation. In TCP, every packet loss event can potentially reduce the transmission window size, as the transmission window size is defined as the minimum of congestion window and the receiver window size. Hence, this dropping of congestion window due to packet losses, is one of the major reasons for TCP throughput degradation. Furthermore, the main reason for these packet losses is not the network congestion, which the TCP assumes is solving by decreasing its congestion window. Instead, in the presence of LTE-U, this decrease results in a complete reversal of what was intended from the TCP algorithm, at least for the victim user. Figure 8 shows the victim user's congestion window for $\eta = 0, 0.2, 0.4$, and 0.6. Figure 9 shows the non-victim user's congestion window for $\eta = 0, 0.2, 0.4, 0.6$ and 0.8. For $\eta = 0.8$ and 1 the AP was unable to serve the victim user so we were unable to find any traces for the victim user flow at the sender.

Following observations can be made from the experiments:

- At $\eta = 0$, both victim and non-victim users perform similar. This confirms the TCP's appropriateness as both the TCP connections fairly utilize the channel. The behavior of victim and the non-victim user is mostly the same, except for some random packet losses at both the users due to the channel condition, that caused the contention window to drop multiplicatively. Figures 8a and 9a demonstrates the contention window variation with time. Nonetheless, the average throughput remains same for both the users.

- At $\eta = 0.2$, Figs. 8b and 9b show the extent to which the flow of victim user gets effected as compared to the non-victim user. A small value of LTE-U ON period causes a profuse number of packets to be dropped at the TCP layer, while we still have the MAC layer beneath the TCP trying its best to successfully transmit the packet, by retransmitting the lost TCP packets many times. One can now imagine the monstrous impact this leaves on the objective to efficiently utilize the channel.

  Moreover, the retransmission at the MAC layer increases the Smoothed Round Trip Time (SRTT) of the packets waiting in the buffer queue (especially meant for the non-victim user). An increase of more than 50% in the average SRTT, compared to that at $\eta = 0$, for the non-victim user can be observed in Table 1. However, since retransmissions or failure of the packets do not contribute to SRTT calculation, the SRTT of the victim remains low compared to that of non-victim user. So, the non-victim user's performance comes down along with the victim user.

- At $\eta = 0.4$, (similar to earlier ($\eta = 0.2$)), the throughput of non-victim continues to decrease. Congestion window goes down for both the users (shown in Figs. 8c and 9c) and SRTT increases, but still, the SRTT for non-victim user is more compared to that of victim user as discussed above.

- At $\eta = 0.6$, the victim user's performance decreases drastically, and its congestion window reaches to extreme low values (*i.e.,* in the range of 1 to 10 MSS as shown in Fig. 8d). The lower values of congestion window reduces the channel access and hence incurs less wastage of channel resources. Therefore, non-victim user's performance at $\eta = 0.6$ is improved compared to $\eta = 0.4$. The increase in the congestion window of non-victim user at $\eta = 0.6$ compared to at $\eta = 0.4$ (in Fig. 9c) can be seen in Fig. 9d.
- At $\eta = 0.8$, victim users throughput is almost reached to zero, and hence more opportunity to the non-victim user. Consequently, the non-victim users throughput is further increased compared to $\eta = 0.4$ and 0.6. The non-victim user's congestion window at $\eta = 0.8$ is shown in Fig. 9e.
- At $\eta = 1$, the LTE-U is entirely ON and hence victim user cannot respond which gives the entire opportunity to non-victim user. Every packet that the AP transmits to victim user is a loss and thus, at transport layer TCP sender doubles the timeout and retransmit the same packet. The continuous increase in timeout of victim user reduces the packet transmissions as it waits for the timeout to happen. Hence, the opportunity of the victim user is negligible compared to non-victim user which gives maximum throughput to the non-victim user.

4.3 Beacon Loss Results

According to the IEEE 802.11 standard, APs are typically configured to periodically send out beacon frames. The purpose of a beacon frame is to advertise the presence of an AP; its capabilities; encryption protocol being used and also flags meant for the stations which convey them the information on presence of any packets in the buffer to be transmitted in the upcoming beacon interval—an essential feature for station operating in power saving mode.

Although beacon reception is indeed very crucial, LTE-U transmissions in the scenarios presented above can engender many beacons to be lost in-succession by the victim users. For evaluating the average beacon loss percentage, we used the same setup described in Sect. 3. With the help of Wireshark (an open source Wi-Fi packet analyzer) [26], we captured the beacon frames on the victim user's laptop. Using the time stamp of the beacon frame provided by Wireshark, we were able to identify the number of missed beacons between two successfully received beacons. Consequently, the fraction of losses were calculated using these missed beacons and then averaged over many iterations for different LTE-U ON fractions. Figure 10 shows one such instance for LTE-U ON fractions of 0.2, 0.4, 0.6. As the beacon interval was 102.4 ms, the presence of a peak at an interval of every 102.4 ms indicates a successful beacon reception, and the absence denotes a beacon loss. It can be seen from the same figure that the beacon losses increase with increasing LTE-U ON fraction.

Furthermore, Table 2 shows a significant observation regarding the percentage of continuous beacon losses. The reason behind these consecutive beacon losses is the simultaneous periodicity in the beacon interval and the LTE-U duty cycle period. For instance, if the beacon interval is 102.4 ms with LTE-U ON and

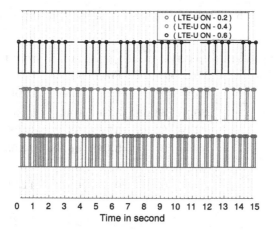

Fig. 10. Beacons received over time for different LTE-U ON fraction. The presence of a peak at every 102.4 ms indicates successful reception of a beacon and absence indicates loss of beacon by the victim user.

OFF periods as 6 ms and 4 ms, respectively (*i.e.,* LTE-U ON fraction of 0.6); any beacon occurring at 0.8 ms from the start of LTE-U ON period would lead to a loss of 8 successive beacons. The obtained results were verified using MAT-LAB simulations. A slight mismatch in the experimental and simulated results is because of the fact that any extra beacons lost or received in the experiment apart from those in simulations, would result in generation of a new sequence of beacons lost.

Such beacon losses create the following problems.

Increased Association Delay. Since a victim user loses beacons transmitted by the AP, its association gets delayed. This delay is more pronounced with passive scanning where the Wi-Fi station has to wait for a beacon to get connected with the network [9]. When two or three beacons are lost in succession, the association delay will increase by the same multitude. However, the effect with active scanning is less serious unless if the probe response overlaps with the LTE-U ON period. In such cases another probe request needs to be transmitted.

Increased Disassociation Frequency as a Result of Losing Channel Switch Information. Channel Switch Announcement (CSA) [9] is an important information which the Wi-Fi AP shares with its users before switching to a new channel. It sends out this information using beacons. If a user loses beacons containing CSA—in succession, then it may get disassociated and has to follow all the procedures again to re-associate itself.

Increased Awake Time and Data Latency for Power-Saving Stations. Users with power saving mode enabled, wake up periodically at the correct

Table 2. Consecutive beacon Loss (%) for victim users in Experiment (Expt) and Simulation (Simu).

No. of consecutive beacon losses	LTE-U ON Fraction = 0.2		LTE-U ON Fraction = 0.4		LTE-U ON Fraction = 0.6	
-	Expt	Simu	Expt	Simu	Expt	Simu
1	**30.84**	**33.65**	3.65	0.47	0	0
2	**66.08**	**66.35**	**37.89**	**33.17**	10.98	0
3	1.76	0	**53.88**	**66.35**	74.05	**80.00**
4	0.88	0	1.82	0	2.0	0
8	0	0	0	0	**11.39**	**19.43**

beacon period and stay awake until they receive the beacon [9]. Transmission of beacons in an LTE-U ON period would cause the victim users to miss the beacon and remain awake for the entire beacon interval or some preset duration. Also, by losing beacons, these users would not be able to send PS-Poll frames (requesting the AP to transmit their data), thus increasing the delay in data received.

To mitigate the above effects, a quantification of beacon losses is necessary. Therefore, in the following section, we develop an analytical framework to determine the percentage of beacon losses and finally provide a mathematical expression for the same. This proposed expression also validates the results obtained using the testbed and simulations.

5   Beacon Loss Analysis

Let B and $B_{air-time}$ be the beacon interval (defined as the duration between two successive beacons) and beacon air-time (defined as the duration required to transmit a complete beacon frame), respectively. Let T denote the LTE-U duty cycle period with T_{on} and T_{off} as the ON and OFF periods of the LTE-U. For finding the average beacon loss percentage, we define Beacon Start Time (BST) as the instant at which the beacon frame is transmitted with respect to the LTE-U duty cycle period. For example, i_1 in Fig. 11 denotes the first BST and

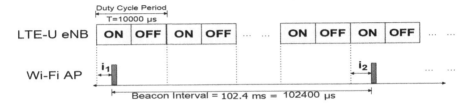

Fig. 11. Illustration of beacon arrival with respect to LTE-U duty cycle period.

i_2 denotes the second BST. Using these variables (*i.e.*, $i_1, i_2, i_3, \ldots$), we calculate the beacon loss ratio and average it for all possible values of first BSTs. This gives the average beacon loss percentage. In addition, we make an assumption that the delay in beacon frames is negligible (*i.e.*, the beacons arrive exactly at the start of beacon interval which is true for most of the cases). The definitions of the notations in this paper are provided in Table 3.

Table 3. Glossary of terms

Notation	Definition
η	Fraction of time LTE-U is ON in a duty cycle period
B	Beacon interval
$B_{air-time}$	Beacon air time
T_{on}	LTE-U ON duration
T_{off}	LTE-U OFF duration
T	Duty cycle period $(T_{on} + T_{off})$
L_{frac}	Beacon loss fraction

If i_1 is the first BST, then the time at which the second beacon would arrive with respect to LTE-U duty cycle period will be $i_2 = (i_1 + B) \bmod T$, and similarly the third beacon would arrive at

$$i_3 = ((i_1 + B) \bmod T + B) \bmod T = (i_2 + B) \bmod T$$

and hence the nth beacon arrival would arrive at

$$i_n = (i_{n-1} + B) \bmod T \tag{1}$$

For example, if i_1 is $10\,\mu s$ in Fig. 11, i_2 and i_3 would be

$$i_2 = (10 + 102400) \bmod 10000 = 2410\,\mu s$$
$$i_3 = (2410 + 102400) \bmod 10000 = 4810\,\mu s$$

Claim: The BST returns to the first BST (i_1) after every T beacon intervals, i.e., $i_{T+1} = i_1$.

Proof: We know that $i_k = (i_{k-1} + B) \bmod T$.

$$\implies i_k = ((i_{k-2} + B) \bmod T + B) \bmod T \tag{2}$$

Using the addition property of modular arithmetic, we get

$$i_k = (i_{k-2} \bmod T + B \bmod T) \bmod T + B \bmod T$$
$$= ((i_{k-2} \bmod T + B \bmod T) \bmod T$$
$$+ B \bmod T) \bmod T \tag{3}$$

Using the fact that i_k's are less than T, we get

$$i_k = ((i_{k-2} + B \bmod T) + B \bmod T) \bmod T$$
$$= ((i_{k-2} + 2 \cdot B \bmod T)) \bmod T$$
$$= ((i_1 + (k-1)B) \bmod T) \bmod T \tag{4}$$
$$\text{Finally,} \quad i_{T+1} = ((i_1 + T \cdot B) \bmod T) \bmod T \tag{5}$$

Assuming $B \bmod T = k$, for some $k < T$

$$\implies i_{T+1} = (i_1 + T \cdot k) \bmod T = i_1 \tag{6}$$

Now, we need to find the fraction of beacon losses, given the first BST was i_1. We know that, given i_1, the BSTs will follow a pattern as shown

$$\{i_1, i_2, \ldots, i_{T-1}, i_T, i_1, i_2, \ldots, i_T, i_1, i_2, \ldots, i_T, i_1, \ldots\} \tag{7}$$

As the duration of operation of Wi-Fi network tends to a large number, the pattern shown above repeats itself. Now, we need to use the fact that a beacon would be lost if its transmission overlaps with the LTE-U ON period (the ON period does not allow victim users to decode beacons successfully). This implies that if the BST occurs to be in one of the following two intervals, the beacons would be lost. Firstly, if the BST lies anywhere in the LTE-U ON period (*i.e.*, $(0, T_{on})$). Secondly, if the BST is in OFF period, but a part of beacon transmission overlaps with the upcoming ON period (due to the non-zero beacon air-time $- B_{air-time}$). Therefore, if the BSTs lie in $(0, T_{on})$ or $(T - B_{air-time}, T)$, the beacons can be considered as lost.

Now these BSTs from i_1 to i_T can be divided into two sets, those lying in $(0, T_{on}) \cup (T - B_{air-time}, T)$, called the lost set and others lying between $(T_{on}, T - B_{air-time})$, called the capture set. Let m_i and n_i denote the number of distinct BSTs from the set $\{i_1, i_2, \ldots, i_T\}$ belonging to the lost and capture sets, respectively. Note that, $m_i + n_i$ need not always be equal to T. In fact, many times the period of Eq. (7) can be much smaller than T, however the upper bound is guaranteed to be T. Hence, the fraction of beacons lost with first BST as i_1 is

$$L_{frac}(i_1) = \frac{m_i}{m_i + n_i} \tag{8}$$

In addition, for first BSTs from $\{i_2, i_3, \ldots, i_T\}$, the set $\{i_1, i_2, \ldots, i_T\}$ will remain same, but the order in which the BSTs occur, would be slided. For example, if the first BST is i_3, the subsequent BSTs would follow a pattern as

$$\{i_3, i_4, \ldots, i_T, i_1, i_2, i_3, \ldots, i_T, i_1, i_2, \ldots, i_T, i_1, i_2, \ldots\} \tag{9}$$

This would imply that m_i and n_i would remain same, and consequently L_{frac} would also remain same.

$$\text{Therefore,} \quad L_{frac}(i_1) = L_{frac}(i_2) = \ldots = L_{frac}(i_T) \tag{10}$$

Now, consider any other first BST j_1, such that $j_1 \notin \{i_1, i_2, \ldots, i_T\}$. This would imply that j_1 would produce a new set $\{j_1, j_2, \ldots, j_T\}$ with new m_j and n_j. Consequently, the beacon loss fraction for these BSTs would be

$$L_{frac}(j_1) = L_{frac}(j_2) = \ldots = L_{frac}(j_T) = \frac{m_j}{m_j + n_j} \tag{11}$$

Similarly, consider any other first BST k_1, such that $k_1 \notin \{i_1, i_2, \ldots i_T\} \cup \{j_1, j_2, \ldots j_T\}$. This would again produce m_k and n_k with the beacon loss fraction to be

$$L_{frac}(k_1) = L_{frac}(k_2) = \ldots = L_{frac}(k_T) = \frac{m_k}{m_k + n_k} \tag{12}$$

After exhausting the complete duty cycle period T, the average beacon loss fraction can be computed as

$$L_{frac} = \frac{\sum\limits_{i=1}^{T} L_{frac}(i)}{T} = \frac{\sum\limits_{p=\{i,j,k,\ldots\}} \sum\limits_{x=1}^{m_p+n_p} L_{frac}(p_x)}{T} \tag{13}$$

Since $L_{frac}(p_x)$ is constant for all $x \in$ either $\{i_1, i_2, \ldots, i_T\}$, or $\{j_1, j_2, \ldots, j_T\}$ and so on, L_{frac} will reduce to

$$L_{frac} = \frac{\sum\limits_{p=\{i,j,k,\ldots\}} \frac{m_p}{m_p + n_p} \cdot (m_p + n_p)}{T} = \frac{\sum\limits_{p=\{i,j,k,\ldots\}} m_p}{T} \tag{14}$$

Since, the complete duration from $(0, T]$ was exhausted by selecting appropriate first BSTs, the sum of all $m_{p's}$ should be equal to the size of lost set.

$$\implies \sum\limits_{p=\{i,j,k,\ldots\}} m_p = T_{on} + B_{air-time} \tag{15}$$

Therefore, the average beacon loss fraction is given by

$$L_{frac} = \frac{T_{on} + B_{air-time}}{T} \tag{16}$$

For a special case when $T_{on} > T - B_{air-time}$, the LTE-U OFF period would be insufficient for the victim users to receive any beacon successfully, making the lost set as $(0, T)$. Similarly, when $T_{on} = 0$, the scenario reduces to a simple only Wi-Fi scenario and thus the lost set would be a null set (ϕ). This implies the expression for L_{frac} considering all the conditions would be

$$L_{frac} = \begin{cases} 0 & if \quad T_{on} = 0 \\ 1 & if \quad T_{on} > T - B_{air-time} \\ \dfrac{T_{on} + B_{air-time}}{T} & otherwise \end{cases}$$

The above beacon loss analysis is validated using the testbed described in Sect. 3 and also using MATLAB simulations. For both the testbed and simulations the beacon interval was set to 102.4 ms. In general, AP uses the lowest rate to transmit beacons, hence the beacon rate in our setup was observed to be 1 Mb/s with a beacon size of 287 B. As a result, the beacon air-time of 2.3 ms was used in the simulations and analysis. Figure 12 validates the beacon loss percentage results collected for a duty cycle period of 10 ms with different LTE-U ON fractions. The simulation and analysis curves match closely with the testbed results, thus confirming their correctness. Moreover, it also shows an increase in beacon loss percentage of victim user with LTE-U ON period. This comes from the fact that the average beacon loss fraction (L_{frac}) is indeed a linear function of LTE-U ON fraction ($\frac{T_{on}}{T}$), and can be obtained by simplifying Eq. (16) as

$$L_{frac} = \text{LTE-U\_ON\_Fraction} + \frac{B_{air-time}}{T} \tag{17}$$

Figure 13 shows the variation in beacon loss percentage with increasing LTE-U duty cycle period. It shows that the beacon loss percentage decreases with increasing LTE-U duty cycle period, but finally saturates near the LTE-U ON percentage (for very high duty cycle periods), with the second term in Eq. (17) becoming negligible. However, an important consideration before increasing LTE-U duty cycle period is that higher periods become a bottleneck for satisfying Quality of Service (QoS) requirement of the Wi-Fi network.

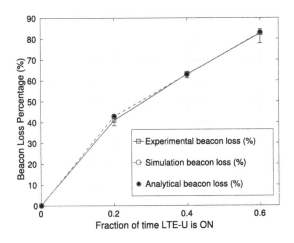

Fig. 12. Validation of analytical beacon loss percentage (%) of the victim user through testbed experiment and simulation results for an LTE-U duty cycle period of 10 ms with varying ON fraction.

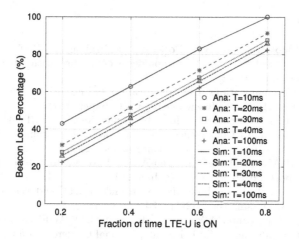

Fig. 13. Analytical (Ana) and Simulated (Sim) beacon loss percentage (%) of victim user for different LTE-U duty cycle periods with varying ON fraction.

6   Conclusions and Future Work

In this paper, we have shown the impact of duty cycled LTE-U on the performance of Wi-Fi users in the hidden terminal scenario, using testbed experiments. The throughput results are collected for both TCP and UDP traffic. The results demonstrate a surprising behavior, with the fairness among Wi-Fi users completely forfeited and a declination in the network throughput as well. In fact, the users in the considered scenario were divided into two groups, with one group, apart from receiving lower throughput, was also deprived from listening to periodic beacons. These beacon losses were quantified through a testbed experiment and then was throughly validated using simulations and mathematical analysis. In addition, issues related to successive beacon losses like delay in association, frequent disassociation, etc were also highlighted. Consequently, the paper shows that the channel access schemes for LTE in unlicensed, like duty cycled LTE-U or LBT based LAA need additional functionality to address these hidden terminal problems.

Although hidden terminal problem has been well studied for the Wi-Fi deployments, the presence of a different Radio Access Technology (RAT) utilizing the same unlicensed spectrum, *i.e.,* an LTE-U/LAA, makes this problem challenging. It requires a need to look into the complication created by presence of LTE-U, which we delineated extensively in our work, so as to find a solution. Hence, as a part of future work we intend to solve this issue to ensure a better and fair coexistence of LTE-U and Wi-Fi in the unlicensed spectrum.

Acknowledgment. This work was supported by the project "Converged Cloud Communication Technologies", Meity, Govt. of India.

References

1. Dugan, J., Elliott, S., Mah, B.A., Poskanzer, J., Prabhu, K.: iPerf. https://iperf.fr/
2. LTE in Unlicensed Spectrum: Harmonious Coexistence with Wi-Fi. Qualcomm White Paper, June 2014
3. LabVIEW Communications LTE Application Framework 1.1. National Instruments, March 2015. http://www.ni.com/white-paper/52524/en/
4. LTE-U SDL CSAT Procedure Technical Specifications V1.0. LTE-U Forum (2015)
5. Real-time LTE/Wi-Fi Coexistence Testbed. National Instruments White Paper, February 2016. http://www.ni.com/white-paper/52119/en/
6. 3GPP: TSGRAN; Study on Licensed-Assisted Access to Unlicensed Spectrum. Technical report TR 36.889 V13.0.0, June 2015
7. Abinader, F.M., et al.: Enabling the coexistence of LTE and Wi-Fi in unlicensed bands. IEEE Commun. Mag. **52**(11), 54–61 (2014)
8. Almeida, E., Cavalcante, A.M., et al.: Enabling LTE/WiFi coexistence by LTE blank subframe allocation. In: IEEE International Conference on Communications (ICC) (2013)
9. Association, I.S., et al.: 802.11-2012-IEEE Standard for Information Technology-Telecommunications and Information Exchange between Systems Local and Metropolitan Area Networks-Specific requirements Part 11: Wireless LAN Medium Access Control (MAC) and Physical Layer (PHY) Specifications (2012). http://standards.ieee.org/about/get/802/802.11.html
10. Babaei, A., Andreoli-Fang, J., Pang, Y., Hamzeh, B.: On the impact of LTE-U on Wi-Fi performance. Int. J. Wirel. Inf. Netw. **22**(4), 336–344 (2015)
11. Baswade, A.M., Atif, T.A., Tamma, B.R., Franklin, A.: A novel coexistence scheme for IEEE 802.11 for user fairness and efficient spectrum utilization in the presence of LTE-U, vol. 139, pp. 1–18. Elsevier (2018)
12. Baswade, A.M., Atif, T.A., Tamma, B.R., et al.: LAW: a novel mechanism for addressing hidden terminal problem in LTE-U and Wi-Fi networks, vol. 22, pp. 1280–1283. IEEE (2018)
13. Cano, C., Leith, D.J.: Unlicensed LTE/WiFi coexistence: is LBT inherently fairer than CSAT? In: IEEE International Conference on Communications (ICC), July 2016
14. Cavalcante, A.M., Almeida, E., et al.: Performance evaluation of LTE and Wi-Fi coexistence in unlicensed bands. In: IEEE 77th Vehicular Technology Conference (VTC Spring) (2013)
15. Ericsson: Ericsson mobility report, June 2017
16. Jain, R., Chiu, D.M., Hawe, W.: A quantitative measure of fairness and discrimination for resource allocation in shared computer systems (1998)
17. Jeon, J., Niu, H., Li, Q.C., Papathanassiou, A., Wu, G.: LTE in the unlicensed spectrum: evaluating coexistence mechanisms. In: Globecom Workshops (GC Wkshps), pp. 740–745. IEEE (2014)
18. LTE-U Forum: eNB Minimum Requirements for LTE-U SDL (2015). http://www.lteuforum.org/documents.html
19. LTE-U Forum: LTE-U Forum online (2015). http://www.lteuforum.org
20. LTE-U Forum: LTE-U Technical report (2015). http://www.lteuforum.org/documents.html
21. LTE-U Forum: UE Minimum Requirements for LTE-U SDL (2015)
22. Maglogiannis, V., Naudts, D., et al.: Impact of LTE operating in unlicensed spectrum on Wi-Fi using real equipment. In: IEEE Global Communications Conference (GLOBECOM) (2016)

23. Nihtilä, T., Tykhomyrov, V., Alanen, O., et al.: System performance of LTE and IEEE 802.11 coexisting on a shared frequency band. In: IEEE Wireless Communications and Networking Conference (WCNC) (2013)
24. White paper: Cisco visual networking index: global mobile data traffic forecast update, 2016–2021, February 2017
25. Wang, X., Quek, T.Q., Sheng, M., Li, J.: Throughput and fairness analysis of Wi-Fi and LTE-U in unlicensed band. IEEE J. Sel. Areas Commun. **35**(1), 63–78 (2017)
26. Wireshark. https://www.wireshark.org

NeMoI: Network Mobility in ICN

Sripriya Adhatarao[1]([✉]), Mayutan Arumaithurai[1], Dirk Kutscher[2],
and Xiaoming Fu[1]

[1] University of Göttingen, Göttingen, Germany
{adhatarao,arumaithurai,fu}@cs.uni-goettingen.de
[2] Huawei's German Research Center, Munich, Germany
dku@dkutscher.net

Abstract. With the advancement in technology mobility has become
a norm. Recent trend towards 5G and increasing popularity of IoT is
expected to demand increased mobility support in the network. Information Centric Networking (ICN) treats content as the first class entity
and nodes exchange information based on the identity of the content
rather than the location of the content. ICN inherently supports consumer mobility and there are many recent works on producer mobility.
However, an untouched area of work is ICN's support for network mobility. Network-segments/domains comprising of various networking nodes,
consumers and producers can also experience mobility and can aggravate
the problems associated with supporting mobility.

In this paper, we propose *NeMoI: Network Mobility in ICN*, a full
fledged ICN based mobility solution with a special focus on network
mobility including the case of producers and consumers present within
such mobile networks. With evaluations using the RocketFuel1221 topology we show that NeMoI significantly reduces the amount of signalling
traffic, routing updates and path inflation compared to existing solutions
while ensuring connectivity for mobile nodes with minimum packet loss
for users during mobility.

Keywords: ICN · Mobility · Mobile agent · Binding Interest

1 Introduction

Nowadays, mobile Internet access is prevalent with 3.6 billion mobile broadband
subscriptions in 2016 [29]. Recent advancements in technology has allowed the
hand-held/portable devices to dominate the market. These devices introduce
mobility that in turn raises challenges for the underlying network to support
them. The recent advancements in IoT and trend towards 5G [3] is expected
to increase the demand and challenges for supporting mobility. Further, Billions
(50 Billion by 2020 [11]) of IoT devices are expected to be connected in the
near future to realize many future applications including smart cities, smart
industries, etc., and many of these nodes could be mobile. Hence, mobile traffic
will soon dominate majority of traffic in the Internet.

© Springer Nature Switzerland AG 2019
S. Biswas et al. (Eds.): COMSNETS 2018, LNCS 11227, pp. 220–244, 2019.
https://doi.org/10.1007/978-3-030-10659-1_10

This is further compounded with scenarios where the network/domain itself is in motion. E.g. a moving car equipped with numerous sensor/IoT nodes or a moving passenger train with WiFi connectivity for its passengers. In these scenario, the end-nodes/users within these networks could behave both as the producer and consumer of the content. The moving train/car constitutes a *network-on-the-move*[1]. We envision that domain mobility will be a norm in the near future. With *network-on-the-move*, the network will incur increased signalling traffic and global updates could consume a large portion of the network traffic. In Sect. 5 we show that global updates, anchor-based and anchorless solutions generate ~0.215B mobility update during deterministic network mobility for a dataset with 1M names and 243340 mobility update during non-deterministic mobility update with just 200 cars. The resulting global updates might be too slow for latency sensitive applications resulting in increased loss of connectivity and packets. Overall, increase in network mobility could lead to poor performance and below par user experience.

Many recent proposals have been made under the umbrella of Information Centric Networking (ICN) such as Content Centric Networking [15], Named *Data* Networking (NDN) [32], DONA [17], PSIRP [10], NetInf [8] and COPSS [7]. ICN approaches shifts the focus from "location-based" network towards "content/name-centric" networking. Many recent works like [5,23,33] propose various solutions for addressing producer mobility in ICN. Nonetheless, support for *network-on-the-move* remains a largely untouched area of work. A *network-on-the-move* also differs from a mobile host that advertises multiple prefixes. The mobile host advertising multiple prefixes will produce the same content, but with many names. Hence, duplicate copies of the content will be stored in the caches but with different names, which is not exactly aligned with the ICN principles. Further, such solutions also affect aggregation in the network [2]. Although there exist IP based *network-on-the-move* solutions such as Nemo [9] and MobileIP [24], they cannot be directly adopted in content centric ICN [14].

In this paper, we extend our initial work titled *NeMoI: Network Mobility in ICN* [1], where we proposed a comprehensive ICN based solution to support end-points that are within *network-on-the-move*. These end-points could be producers and/or consumers. Moreover, NeMoI is designed to seamlessly support the mobility of consumers and producers not located inside a moving network to avoid the need for multiple protocols for different scenarios. NeMoI also encompasses several optimization strategies that makes it an efficient solution to support mobility in ICN. To the best of our knowledge, we believe that NeMoI is the first work to address network mobility in ICN. In this work, we refer to NDN as an exemplary ICN architecture. We perform extensive evaluations on the RocketFuel1221 Telstra Australia [20] topology with 1M names and show that with NeMoI, we reduce signalling traffic and routing updates from ~0.215B to ~4.6M in deterministic mobility scenario and 243,340 to 3767 in non-deterministic mobility scenario. We also minimize path inflation and packet

---

[1] *network-on-the-move* refers to a mobile network in this work.

loss in various scenarios and show effective route optimization strategies. Our results show that NeMoI significantly improves the overall performance and user experience in ICN. The key contributions in the paper includes:

- An enhanced architecture to support *network-on-the-move* in ICN.
- Distributed Mobility Agents service for name resolution.
- A distributed deployment model for realizing Mobility Agents.
- A new field "Time Stamp" in the Binding Interest Packet.
- Logically multi-layered Forwarding Information Base.
- Proactive and Reactive solutions to synchronize mobility updates.
- Enhanced Security features.
- Extended evaluations to include Deterministic and Non-deterministic mobility.

2   Scenario and Related Work

2.1   Mobility Scenario

Let's consider a scenario where a person P has a mobile phone and is walking to a train station. If P uses his phone to watch some video or read news, then he is a consumer. If P is uploading some photos/videos or any content then P is the producer of that content. P now boards a train and connects to the WiFi access point in the train. When the train starts to move, it represents a *network-on-the-move*. Further, P can change the train resulting in a shift from one *network-on-the-move* to another. Additionally, let's consider a nested *network-on-the-move* scenario where P is in a moving train and uses the WiFi in the train. P connects his laptop to the Internet via the mobile phone. In this scenario, mobility triggers updates from all these devices, increasing the scale of the problem. In future, especially with increasing popularity of IoT and 5G, we believe such mobility will most likely be a norm and is a matter of concern that demands attention.

2.2   Objectives

Based on the above scenario, we derive the following objectives to be met by a mobility solution in ICN.

Mobility Support: There are basically three kinds of mobility: consumer, producer and *network-on-the-move*. The solution should support all three kinds of mobility.

Synchronization: The solution should ensure that mobility updates are synchronized in the network especially with the previous location of the mobile entity.

Signalling Traffic: Increased mobility will cause signalling traffic to consume majority of the network traffic. The solution should try to minimize such signalling traffic.

Mobility Update: Mobility updates should be propagated throughout the network. However, the updates should not overwhelm the network especially with continuous mobility. The routers should not be overloaded to perform frequent updates to their tables instead of forwarding request/data.

Path Inflation: The solution should try to minimize the path inflation experienced by users due to mobility.

Packet Loss: The solution should try to minimize the packet loss experienced by consumers due to mobility.

2.3   Related Work

ICN inherently supports consumer mobility. However, producer mobility on the other hand is a rather hard challenge. Since all the nodes in the network maintain information in their routing tables about how to reach each producer/source, when a producer moves to a new location, every router in the network should be updated with this information. During this time any new requests for data cannot be satisfied until this information is propagated in the network. This is a major concern as it renders the network incapable of satisfying any requests until the update has reached all the nodes in the network, unless the content was cached in the routers. However, this is not always the case especially for real-time delivery of content. We broadly classify the relevant producer mobility literature into the following categories.

Anchor Based: In this method, a dedicated anchor is used to manage the mobility of the producer. The mobile producer notifies the anchor whenever it changes its point of attachment in the network. The request for content are re-directed to the anchor which then forwards it to the current location of the mobile producer. Mobile IP [24] and ICN solutions like [18] use this approach. Essentially a tunnel is established between the Home Access Router (HAR) of the mobile producer and the Foreign Access Router (FAR) where the producer currently resides. When the producer moves, the *Interests* are redirected towards the HAR which encapsulates the packets and forwards it to the producer. In [33], authors proposed a solution similar to an actual Kite. When producers move, they notify a dedicated immobile anchor about their new location using Traced *Interests* that are not deleted from the PIT.

Anchor based solutions are reactive and have minimal service interruption time. However, they increase the signalling traffic, path stretch and tunneling changes names and affects caching and aggregation in ICN.

Anchorless Based: In this method, every mobile node is responsible to notify the network about its mobility related information. In [5], authors use *Interest* Update (IU) and Temporary FIB (TFIB) to propagate mobility updates. The producer sends IU to the previous location when there is a change in its physical location. The intermediate routers that forward the IU update their TFIB. Similarly, authors in [16,31] proposed anchorless based approaches for supporting mobility in ICN.

Anchorless solutions are more reactive compared to anchor based solutions and also support frequent location changes. But, they may incur path stretch and signalling traffic as producers generate update for every prefix.

Resolution Based: In this method, several dedicated nodes in the network perform resolution of the names to their respective current locations. In IP, the traditional DNS is used to resolve URL's to their IP addresses which are then used to reach the producers. In IP, mobility results in a new IP address. In LISP [12], an additional resolution step is needed to resolve the identifiers to locators. In MobilityFirst [25], a 20-bit Globally Unique Identifier (GUID) is assigned to every entity. A distributed resolution architecture is used to resolve the GUIDs to the current location of the users. In [23], authors proposed *OPRA* where they place route resolvers at multiple points on the point to a content for reaching the source.

These solutions scale well and also produce less signalling traffic but incur path stretch and are not suitable for supporting frequent mobility especially, for latency-sensitive applications.

Survey: A survey of IP based mobility solutions is provided in RFC6301 [34] while [27,28] provides a survey of the mobility related challenges and potential research directions in ICN.

Many of the above mentioned solutions address only static producer mobility (i.e., nodes move from one point to another and remain there for a considerable time period [5]). The IP based network mobility solutions cannot be directly adopted in ICN. In NeMoI, we provide a comprehensive solution that support end points in *network-on-the-move* and mobile end points. NeMoI is dynamic and reactive to both micro and macro mobility and ensures reachability, reliability and connectivity during mobility.

3   NeMoI: Design

A mobility solution should meet certain objectives like, supporting consumer, producer and *network-on-the-move* mobility, synchronize mobility updates, minimize signalling traffic and updates in routers and reduce path inflation and packet loss experienced by consumers. In this section, we describe the design of NeMoI architecture with the topology in Fig. 1 and show how NeMoI meets these objectives.

3.1   NeMoI Components

End-Point: The term end-point is used to refer to any end-user/IoT node that attaches to the network. The end-point can be within *network-on-the-move* or static. It can represent consumers and producers. Figure 1 shows some end-points in a *network-on-the-move*.

Point of Attachment (*PoA*): They are the network nodes that the end points use to connect to the network *i.e.* the access routers. Figure 1a shows three such *PoA*s. In NeMoI, every *PoA* has an ICN routable name, e.g. *PoA*1.

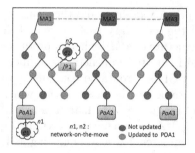
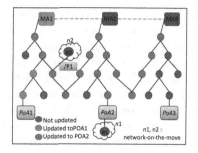

Fig. 1. First mobility update   **Fig. 2.** Second mobility update

Mobility Agent (*MA*): The network is composed of numerous Mobility Agents. Figure 1 shows three *MAs* in the sample topology. Every *MA* is responsible for maintaining information about the current location of the producer(s) associated with the *MA* and resolve the prefixes in the received *Interests*. Similar to *PoA* every *MA* also has an ICN routable name *e.g. MA*1.

Domain/Network Segment: A network segment[2] is basically a small part of the original network composed of numerous networking nodes, consumers and producers. E.g. the moving network *n1* with end-point *e1* in Fig. 1. Every domain is capable of mobility and must ensure connectivity to nodes located within with rest of the network.

Binding Interest: We introduce a logical packet type called *Binding Interest* (BI) shown in Fig. 3 to propagate mobility update information in the network. For implementation, *Interest* packets could be enhanced with the fields in Fig. 3 to function as mobility update packets.

3.2 NeMoI Architecture

Mobility Agents: Many anchor based (See Sect. 2.3) solutions [18,24,33] use Home Agents to support producer mobility. Similarly, NeMoI proposes Mobility Agents (*MAs*) to assist in both *network-on-the-move* and end-point mobility in ICN. Despite various anchorless proposals for source mobility, we realized that dedicated nodes to perform name resolution for mobile nodes can increase reliability and robustness of the network. We however, provide optimization techniques to increase the propagation of mobility updates and by pass the *MAs*. Therefore, NeMoI is in fact a hybrid solution. In NeMoI, a *MA* is a normal ICN forwarder with added functionality of NeMoI and has a routable name *e.g.* MA1. For reliability and robustness, the primary *MA* is a logical *MA*, and one or more physical *MAs* perform the tasks and they can be present in a distributed manner in the network. Each *MA* is responsible for resolving a set of primary prefixes and a set of secondary prefixes served by the producers. The *MAs* maintain

---

[2] *Domain & network segment* is used interchangeably in this work.

two tables, a primary table containing all the primary prefixes and their current location and a secondary table containing all the secondary prefixes and their current location. Figure 9 shows the internal structure of a *MA* where a producer p1 generates a content with the prefix /p and is located in a network-segment identified with the prefix /n1. Hence, /n1 is used as a routable component to reach p1. The figure also shows the secondary table for the prefix /a for which this *MA* is a secondary *MA*. As shown in the Fig. 1 the *MAs* maintain a logical one-hop connection with their neighbouring *MAs* in the network forming an overlay network for synchronizing the mobility updates. For load balancing *MAs* can drop some of their secondary prefixes.

The functionality of *MAs* is provided as a network service and is maintained by the network administrators. Based on our study, we provide two different options for realizing the *MAs* service. In the first option, we have numerous *MAs* in the network, each handling a set of dedicated prefixes. When a new *MA* needs to be added to this overlay, the network administrator identifies a network node and configures the *MA* on it. As part of the configuration, the network administrator assigns a name to the *MA*, its neighbouring *MA* and primary and secondary prefixes that this *MA* is responsible for resolving. The administrator also modifies the neighbours list of the respective *MAs* that are neighbours of the newly added *MA*. Similar to producers, the newly added *MA* will leverage NDN routing protocols such as NLSR to inform the routers of its presence. Every router that receives this update can check the number of hops to this *MA* and decide if it is in its shortest path and add it and forward to its neighbours, if not, then the update will be discarded. Similarly, when a *MA* is removed from a router, the network administrator assigns the prefixes (if required) to other *MAs* and update the neighbour list of the affected *MAs*. The affected *MAs* use the NDN routing protocols to inform the changes by indicating the name of the *MA* that has been removed. The routers that receive this information can check if their shortest path *MA* is in the list of removed *MA*, if yes then they update their routing information. In the second option, the *MAs* can be realized as a network service with a single *MA* that is implemented with distributed servers in the network. Where the network has numerous dedicated nodes configured to function as *MAs*. This is again a overlay network, where the *MAs* communicate with each other and synchronize the mobility update. The difference from the first option is that all the *MAs* will store the record for all the prefixes, similar to DNS servers. This type of service may incur influx of updates to some servers while others remain idle, and hence a load balancing mechanism needs to be in place, but this is out of scope of this paper. In this paper, we will refer to the first design while describing the functionality of NeMoI.

It is possible for the *MAs* to fail due to various reasons e.g., hardware failure, crash due to increased load, etc. However, since the *MA* is a service that is managed separately by the network administrator, there are several possibilities for recovery. Like instantiating the service on a new node in the network and updating the existing *MAs* with this information. However, there is a need to transfer the states from the crashed *MA* to the newly instantiated *MA*. One possible solution is for the *MAs* to periodically store a snapshot of their states in a server that is administered by the network administrator. The newly instantiated *MA* can then be initialized with the state information of the crashed *MA*.

The allocation of prefixes to *MAs* can be achieved by network administrators or a dedicated Registrar responsible for allocating unique prefixes to producers. At the time of allocating prefixes, the respective *MA* can also be allocated. The *MAs* can delegate prefixes to one another or decide to be in synchronization for a set of prefixes. We only provide some suggestion about the allocation of prefixes to *MAs* in this paper, while a complete solution supported with analysis is out of the scope of this paper.

Prefix (s)
Routable Component
Sequence No.
Time Stamp

Reverse Update	Reverse Update Received
Old Routable Component	
Signature	

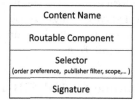

Content Name
Routable Component
Selector (order preference, publisher filter, scope,...)
Signature

Fig. 3. Binding *Interest* Packet

Fig. 4. CCN *Interest* with routable component

Binding Interest: We introduce a new packet type called the *Binding Interest* (*BI*) shown in Fig. 3 to carry mobility updates. The first field in the BI is used to specify one or more Prefixes served by the producer. The second field specifies the routable component that can be used to reach the producer at the new location. The *routable component* is basically the name of the new *PoA*. The third filed is the Sequence Number used to distinguish between multiple mobility updates generated due to continuous mobility. The mobile node increments the sequence number for every new BI sent. The fourth field is the Time Stamp, this indicates the duration for which the routable component is valid for routing. This is set by the mobile entity and stored in both the *MAs* tables and also in the FIB. This field is added to prevent the reuse of out-dated routing components and to maintain a clean FIB and *MAs* record. However, this necessitates that all the entities that use the time stamp should have an accurate clock for synchronization. In NeMoI we suggest these entities to utilize the Network Time Protocol [22] to synchronize their clocks. The next two fields namely, Reverse Update (*RU*) and Reverse Update Received (*RUR*) are used to update the old location about the new *PoA* while the following field contains the old *routable component* used to reach the old location. The last field contains the signature of the mobile node that generated the BI.

Every producer in the network is associated to at least one logical primary *MA* and many secondary *MAs*. Every *PoA* in the network has a routable name *e.g. PoA*1. Whenever a producer moves to a new location and attaches to a *PoA* in the network, the producer can obtain the name of the *PoA* similar to obtaining access point names in IP. The producer then sends a *Binding Interest* (*BI*) containing the prefixes served by the producer and the name of its *PoA*. The BI can be forwarded to any *MA* located on the shortest path from the producers current location. It should be noted that, non-NeMoI routers can simply forward the BI as an *Interest*. Once a BI reaches a *MA*, it updates its primary/secondary table accordingly. Since the *MAs* maintain a logical one hop connection with each other (overlay network), the receiving *MA* then forwards this BI to the router on the path to its neighbouring *MA*. This routing of BI continues till all the *MAs* are updated with the new location. The *MA* also sends an *Interest* to the producer with a special flag marked to acknowledge the receipt of the mobility update. During forwarding, the NeMoI aware routers update their routing information with the mobility update to widen the scope of propagation. Unlike a dedicated single resolver, in NeMoI the network uses a distributed set of *MAs*. A single prefix is maintained by many *MAs* for robustness and also to reduce path inflation.

3.3   Multiple Logical FIB Tables

In NeMoI, we made a design choice to use logically multi-level tables to represent FIB similar to the multi-level forwarding tables used in [6, 26]. This choice helps in reducing the number of updates required in the routers, especially when an entire network segment moves. Since the network is organized hierarchically into layers, each level in the FIB can represent the hierarchical layers in the network, with the lower layers pointing to entries in the higher layer tables for lookup. *i.e.* a prefix in a lower layer contains an indirection to a prefix in the next higher layer. E.g. the first level FIB contains prefixes served by the producers and the next *face* to reach the producer at their current *PoA* or the *routable component* located in the next level. The second level in the FIB contains prefixes associated with *PoA* in the network and other prefixes that can be used as the *routable component* by the first level.

Figures 5 and 6 illustrates the difference between current solutions and the advantage of using multi-level table like in NeMoI. Let's assume that there are 100 producers with prefix ranging from */p1* to */p100* in a train connected to *PoA*1. As shown in Fig. 5, the FIB entry for these 100 users would point to *face-1* which is the outgoing *face* for *PoA*1. When the train moves and connects to *PoA*2, all these 100 entries would have to be changed to point to *face-2* which is the outgoing *face* for *PoA*2. In NeMoI, due to logical multi-level tables, only the entry in the "level-2" table is changed from *face-1* to *face-2* as shown in Fig. 6. This is because the outgoing *face* of the prefix */p1* contains the prefix of the train */t1* as the *routable component*. When the prefix */p1* is looked up in the first level, it leads to an indirection to the level-2 table for the prefix */t1* and the outgoing *face* for */t1* is used for forwarding the *Interest* towards the producer.

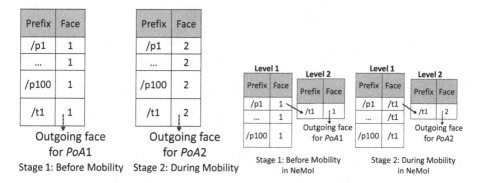

Fig. 5. FIB with no indirection   **Fig. 6.** Multi-level FIB in NeMoI

Therefore, this design choice for a multi-level table effectively reduces the number of updates required in routers especially during continuous mobility. Moreover, the producers/consumers within the *network-on-the-move* need not be informed of the different *PoA*'s that they attach to thereby limiting the signalling traffic and changes to the FIB tables.

The number of tables required is relative to the level of segregation desired in the network and the desired implementation strategy. Moreover, these are logical tables and can in fact be implemented as one table wherein an indirection entry points to another entry in the same table. Similar to [5], we also use a temporary FIB to store the mobility updates in the routers until the control plane synchronizes these update in the data plane of the router. The motivation to use a temporary FIB is similar to that of [5], i.e., only certain nodes with administrative access periodically verify and update the FIBs in the routers in their control. In theory, every change to any of the logical tables in the multi-level table would require a temporary FIB entry. However, in practice, temporary FIBs would exist only for nodes that are continuously moving. For instance, in case of the train scenario, as and when the train changes its *PoA*, it will create a temporary FIB entry for */t1* present in the "level-2" logical table depicted in Fig. 6. Only when the user with the prefix */p1* gets out of the train, a temporary FIB entry is created for */p1* in the "level-1" of logical table shown in Fig. 6.

3.4 Synchronization

In NeMoI the routers on the path from consumers to producers current location also get updated once an *Interest* flows through that path. However, there still remain the question about updating the old location and the non updated routers on the path to the old location of the mobile producer as shown in Fig. 7. In this section we describe the two approaches deigned in NeMoI to synchronize the old location and intermediate NeMoI aware routers on the path to old location of the mobile producers with the mobility update.

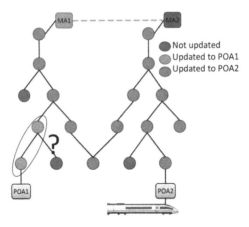

Fig. 7. Old location unsynchronized with the mobility update

Proactive Version: When a router receives a BI, it not only forwards the BI to the *MAs* but will also forward it to the old location. The router sets the *RU* flag to true in the original BI, in order to avoid the downstream routers from sending further updates to the old location. The router makes a copy of the original BI and adds the old *routable component* to the copy. The router then forwards the original BI towards the *MA* and the copied BI to the previous location of the mobile producer using the old *routable component*. As this BI is forwarded towards the old location, all the intermediate NeMoI aware routers on the path to the old location update their routing information. When the BI reaches the old location, the *RU* flag is flipped to false and *RUR* flag is set to true and forwarded towards the router that sent the update as an acknowledgement.

Reactive Version: When an *Interest* reaches the old location, the access router at the old location forwards the *Interest* towards the *MA* just like any other router in the network. The *PoA* at the old location also sets an error flag in the *Interest* to notify the *MA* and the routers on the path to *MA* that the producer has moved but mobility update is not yet synchronized. The intermediate NeMoI aware routers update their entries for the prefix and forward the *Interest* towards the *MA*. When the *MA* receives an *Interest* with error flag, it stores the *Interest* till the mobility update reaches the *MA* or the *Interest* times out. After receiving the BI with the mobility update, the *MA* sets the error flag in the *Interest* to false and adds the new *routable component* to the *Interest* and forwards the *Interest* towards the new location of the producer thus reducing packet loss. In order to not mistaken a sleeping producer for a mobile producer, we recommend the use of technologies like Wake-on-LAN [19], so the *PoA* can wake up a sleeping producer when an *Interest* is received.

3.5   Security

In NeMoI, we inherit the security features of ICN. Similar to RFC 2845 [30], a mobile entity can share secret keys with the *MAs* for authentication and use one way Hash for integrity. However, this implies that intermediate routers cannot update their routing tables. So in NeMoI, every BI is signed by the endpoint generating the BI *e.g.* by using the private key of the endpoint. Every intermediate NeMoI aware router and the *MAs* verify the BI using the public key of the endpoint before updating their tables. When the verification is unsuccessful, the BI is dropped to avoid forwarding malicious information and prevent attacks like DOS, FIB pollution.

Further, the *MAs* only forward the BI's to their neighbouring *MAs* for synchronizing the mobility updates, they do not modify them. Since the BI is actually signed by the private key of the endpoint, if a rouge *MA* tries to send false BI's or tries to modify and forward the BI, it can be detected during verification. Hence, the *MAs* don't add additional security risk. Further, any security measures designed for controlling *Interest* related attacks (*e.g. Interest* flooding) can be applied to prevent similar attacks using BI.

During synchronization of mobility updates, a *MA* can add its name in the list of *MAs* that are already updated and perform a one way hash of the list for security. This prevents any malicious user/node from modifying the BI and polluting the *MAs* tables. This ensures integrity of the BI and the synchronization can finish elegantly since no rouge BI's will be forwarded.

4   NeMoI: Support for Mobility Scenarios

We explain network mobility in NeMoI using the below scenarios with the example of a train travelling with passengers as *network-on-the-move* (see Figs. 1, 2 and 8). The passengers in the train can be both consumers and producers. The train itself can also be viewed as a producer associated with a prefix */t1*. When the train starts moving, the consumers and producers in the train are also under mobility. To ensure connectivity, the train, consumer and producer must propagate their mobility information. However, if all the entities under mobility start sending mobility updates for every prefix served by them, the resulting signalling traffic might overwhelm the network. Further, this will result in increasing the number of routing updates. With increased mobility, the signalling traffic might start competing with data traffic for bandwidth.

4.1   Producer in *Network-on-the-Move*

Let's consider the passengers in the train are producers generating contents like uploading images or video's of their surrounding. In NeMoI, to reduce the signalling traffic, when a producer enters the train and connects to the WiFi access point in the train, the producer sends only a single BI with all the prefixes served by the producer and the prefix of the train */t1* as the *routable component*.

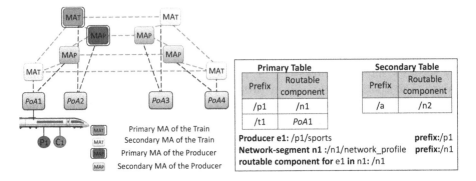

Fig. 8. Train mobility   **Fig. 9.** Mobility agent tables

This BI is forwarded to the nearest *MA* which in turn updates its neighbours and the network gets updated.

When the train starts moving, it propagates mobility updates by generating a BI at every new *PoA* that it attaches to and the *PoA* forwards this BI to its nearest *MA*. Please note, that none of the producers travelling inside the train will send further mobility updates as the train continues to move. During mobility, only the train's mobility update is propagated in the network even though there could be 1000's of producers travelling inside the train each with >=1 prefix. The *MAs* of the train and the intermediate NeMoI aware routers on their path get updated with the current location of the train. Due to our multi-level FIB, the number of updates also reduces as the routers only update the */t1* prefix and not all the prefixes that use it as a *routable component*. For any *Interest* generated for the producers travelling inside the train, the routers will use the *routable component /t1* and forward it to the current location of the producers. Since the train can be used as the *routable component* by other prefixes in the network, if multiple tables are used for representing FIB, then we recommend the prefix */t1* to be located in the second level FIB of the routers to minimize the updates required in the router. The prefixes of the producers travelling in the train can simply point to the prefix of the train in the next higher level in the FIB as shown in Fig. 6.

In Fig. 8, the train is travelling from *PoA1* to *PoA4*. The producer *P1* is a passenger seated in the train. *P1* sends a mobility update with BI containing */p1* as the prefix and */t1* as the *routable component*. This BI reaches the *MAs* of the producer. While the train sends multiple mobility updates one each at *PoA1*, *PoA2*, *PoA3* and *PoA4* with BI containing the prefix */t1* and *PoAx* as the *routable component*. This design choice of NeMoI, dramatically reduces the signalling traffic and the number of updates required in the routers. At the same time NeMoI propagates the mobility updates to majority of the routers, reduces the path inflation, packet loss and ensures connectivity. Further, since a single BI can carry all prefixes served by a producer, it significantly reduces the signalling traffic due to mobility.

4.2   Consumer in *Network-on-the-Move*

Let's consider the passengers in the train are consumers surfing the Internet and downloading news, images, videos, etc. When a consumer enters the train, they connect to the train's WiFi access point, hence its *PoA* is */t1*. When the train starts moving, it propagates the mobility updates by generating a BI at every new *PoA* it attaches to. The consumer continues to use the Internet. However, the train network is mobile and the network should be able to route the data towards the current location of the consumer. Since the network is updated with the current location of the train and the consumer is using train's WiFi as the *PoA*, the network simply forwards the data towards the train and the consumer receives it from the train's WiFi.

In Fig. 8, the train is travelling from *PoA*1 to *PoA*4. The consumer C1 is a passenger in the train. When C1 generates an *Interest*, the *Interest* is forwarded by the train's WiFi access router into the network. In NeMoI, since the train is already propagating the mobility update information and the consumers *PoA* is */t1*, the data is successfully re-routed towards the current location of the consumer in the train. The consumer experiences seamless data transfer while reducing the need for resending *Interest*s for unsatisfied content.

4.3   Consumer and Producer in *Network-on-the-Move*

Let's consider that producer and consumer of a content with the prefix */p1* are travelling in the same train as shown in Fig. 8. The producer and consumer connects to the WiFi access point in the train and the producer sends a BI with the prefix */p1* and */t1* as the *routable component*. The consumer generates an *Interest* with the prefix */p1* and sends it to the WiFi access router of the train. Since the train's router has already updated its entry for */p1* with the *routable component* as */t1*, the *Interest* is immediately forwarded to the producer in the train. In this scenario we see that in NeMoI we are able to eliminate the path inflation.

4.4   Nested *Network-on-the-Move*

Let's consider a nested network scenario where a passenger is a consumer and he connects his mobile phone to Internet using the WiFi of the train. Further, the consumer connects his laptop to the WiFi in the mobile phone to access the Internet forming a nested mobile network. When the train starts moving, it propagates the mobility update by generating a BI at every *PoA* it attaches to. When the train is moving, the consumer uses his mobile phone and generates an *Interest* to download some content from the Internet. The content is successfully routed back to the consumer using the mobility update generated by the train as discussed in earlier scenarios. When the consumer uses his laptop to access the Internet, the consumer uses the WiFi access point on the mobile phone. The *Interest* is forwarded by the mobile phone to the WiFi access router of the train which in turn forwards it to the network. Upon receiving the content, the WiFi access router in the train will forward it to the WiFi access point of the mobile phone which in turn forwards it to the consumer's laptop. Although the train and consumer's mobile and laptop are in mobility, in NeMoI the consumer's mobile phone and laptop are treated as stationary as the mobility update is taken care by the train.

4.5   Travelling from One to Another *Network-on-the-Move*

Let's consider a passenger in the train is the producer of the content with the prefix */p1*. The producer connects to the WiFi access point in the train and sends a BI with the prefix */p1* and */t1* as the *routable component*. When the train starts moving, it propagates the mobility update by generating a BI at every *PoA* it attaches to. These BI's are forwarded to the nearest *MA* which in turn updates its neighbours and the network gets updated. As the train continues to move, the producer does not send any further mobility updates. The network uses the prefix of the train */t1* as the *routable component* to forward any *Interest* to the producer. The producer now changes his train at a stop and enters another train with the prefix */t2*. The producer connects to the WiFi access router in the second train and generates a new BI with the prefix */p1* and *routable component* */t2* and forwards it to the network. In NeMoI, the old location i.e., the first train with the prefix */t1* is also notified with this change.

4.6   Continuous Requests

If a train is moving fast, consumers might not receive the content they request. According to ICN principle, the consumers have to re-initiate the requests, but since the train is changing its *PoA* so fast, the content might not reach the consumers in time. In NeMoI, we suggest to use proactive caching similar to PeRCeIVE [13]. Consumers can include route related information in the *Interest* like the train's current location, speed, etc. Using this information, the data source can pro-actively cache the data at the respective road side units on the path of the consumer.

5   Evaluation

In this section we demonstrate the benefits of NeMoI during deterministic and non-deterministic mobility. With the RocketFuel AS1221 topology using a C# simulator we measure five main network characteristics: signalling traffic, routing updates, effective route optimization, path inflation, and packet loss during network mobility.

5.1   Signalling Traffic and Routing Updates

Experimental Setup. To demonstrate the effectiveness of NeMoI, we evaluate two different kinds of network mobility patterns: deterministic and non-deterministic. For deterministic network mobility experiment, we introduced

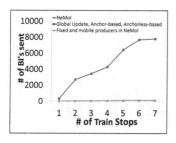

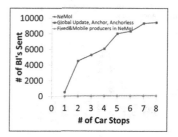

Fig. 10. Signalling traffic and routing updates in train

Fig. 11. Signalling traffic and routing updates in cars

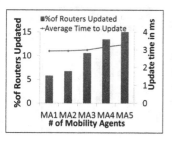

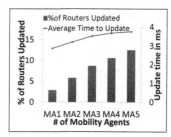

Fig. 12. Mobility updates with core MA placement strategies

Fig. 13. Mobility updates with edge MA placement strategies

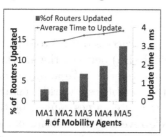

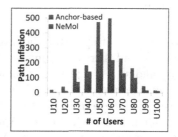

Fig. 14. Mobility updates with random MA placement strategies

Fig. 15. Path inflation in anchor and NeMoI with core strategy

network mobility by using the earlier example of a moving train that carried producers and consumers as passengers. To mimic a real train journey, we simulated the famous Australian Indian Pacific train route (the longest train route in Australia) for our evaluation. In the experiment, the train travels from *Perth* to *Sydney* covering a distance of 4,325 km. While for the non-deterministic network mobility experiment, we introduced network mobility with cars. We use around 200 cars, each with a capacity to seat 4 persons. In the experiment, the cars travel from *Perth* to *Sydney*. To make this journey non-deterministic, a random number of cars chose path1 that covered a distance of 3935 km while the rest chose path2 that covered 4135 km. In order to introduce some more randomness, the cars had several stops along the way.

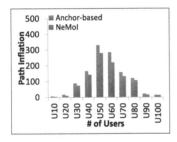

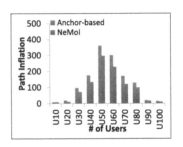

Fig. 16. Path inflation in anchor and NeMoI with edge strategy

Fig. 17. Path inflation in anchor and NeMoI with random strategy

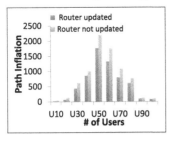

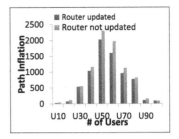

Fig. 18. Comparison of path inflation in NeMoI with/without router updates (Core)

Fig. 19. Comparison of path inflation in NeMoI with/without router updates (Edge)

We assume that at each stop the train and cars have access routers to connect to the Internet and there are numerous Base Stations (BS) between the intermediate cities and stops to provision connection to the Internet. We approximate the coverage area of each BS to 25 Miles (40 km) to resemble real world scenario.

For the *Data*set we used the top one Million web site names ranked by the Majestic million website [21] on 04 April 2017. We reversed the website names to resemble hierarchical names in NDN and replaced the '.' with '/'.

For the train and path1 in cars journey, there were seven stops between *Perth* and *Sydney* while for the path2 in cars journey there were eight stops. So, we placed seven access routers between the stations/stops in each city for train and path1 and eight access routers for path2. Based on the distance between these cities/stops we introduced 110 BS for the train and 98 BS for path1 and 103 BS for path2 for the cars. To mimic a real mobility scenario and to show the impact of mobility in it, for the train journey, at every stop, 0.16M producers board the train while a random number of producers exit the train. In the car scenario, at each stop in the car's journey 50 passengers enter the car while random number of passengers exit the car. This is similar to a Taxi service that picks up and drops off passengers along the journey but the stops and the route taken are not as deterministic as the train. Additionally, we also examined a scenario where a random number of producers were fixed while the rest were mobile. In all these

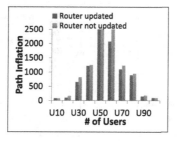

Fig. 20. Comparison of path inflation in NeMoI with/without router updates (Random)

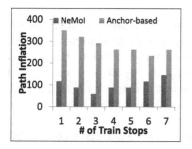

Fig. 21. Path inflation in train

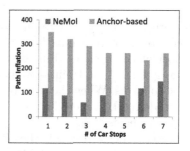

Fig. 22. Path inflation in car

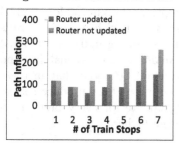

Fig. 23. Path inflation with optimization in NeMoI during network mobility

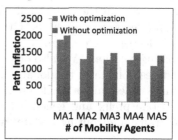

Fig. 24. Path inflation with increasing MA in NeMoI during network mobility

scenarios, during mobility, at every stop and at every BS there is a re-connection to the network.

Deterministic Mobility (Train Mobility). We measure the signalling traffic and number of updates in the routing tables incurred due to mobility of the train with three scenarios. In the first scenario, every producer along with train, produces a BI to notify the network with its mobility update, similar to the global updates, Anchor-based and Anchor-less solutions [5]. In the second scenario, we measure the signalling traffic with NeMoI where the producers notify the

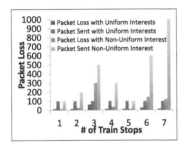 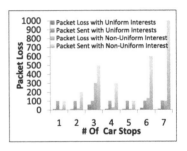

Fig. 25. Packet loss in train in NeMoI during network mobility

Fig. 26. Packet loss in car in NeMoI during network mobility

network with a mobility update only once when they board the train. In the third scenario, we have a mixed set of fixed and mobile producers in NeMoI. The number of BI's generated in these scenarios are equivalent to the number of routing updates. The train continues to notify the network at every point where it re-connects. When the train re-connects to the network through a *PoA*, the *PoA* sends the BI to any *MA* on the shortest path and the *MAs* route this update among themselves.

We observe from the results in the Fig. 10 that NeMoI generated ~4.6M mobility updates in scenario 2 and ~3.7M mobility updates in scenario 3. Whereas other standard solutions like global updates and Anchor and Anchor-less based solutions and without the logical multi-level FIB optimization in NeMoI ~0.215B mobility updates were generated. The results show that with NeMoI, there is a dramatic decrease in the signalling traffic and the routing updates compared to the existing solutions. We also observe that, NeMoI ensures reachability and faster updates compared to global updates. It should be noted that in these results, we assigned only a single prefix to each producer. If the producers serve more than one prefix and generated a mobility update for every prefix then signalling traffic and routing updates would be even higher.

Non-deterministic Mobility (Car Mobility). In this experiment, we measure the signalling traffic and number of updates in the routing tables incurred due to mobility of the 200 cars with a random number of cars travelling on path1 and the rest travelling on path2 with three scenarios. We treat all passengers and drivers in the cars as producers in this experiment. In the first scenario, every producer along with the cars, produce a BI to notify the network with their mobility update. This behaviour is similar to the current state of the art global updates, Anchor-based and Anchor-less solutions [5]. In the second scenario, we measure the signalling traffic with NeMoI where the producers notify the network with a mobility update only once when they enter the car. In the third scenario, we have a mixed set of fixed and mobile producers in NeMoI. Similar to the train scenario, the number of BI's generated in these scenarios are equivalent to the number of routing updates. The cars continue to notify the network at every point in the network where it re-connects to the network.

When a car re-connects to the network through a *PoA*, the *PoA* sends the BI to any MA on the shortest path and the MA's will synchronize this update among themselves.

We observe from the results in the Fig. 11 that NeMoI generated 3767 mobility updates in scenario 2 and 3245 mobility updates in scenario 3. Whereas other state of the art solutions like global updates and Anchor and Anchor-less based solutions and without the logical multi-level FIB optimization in NeMoI 243,340 mobility updates were generated. Similar to the train scenario, we see from the results that with NeMoI there is a significant decrease in the signalling traffic and routing updates compared to the existing solutions. We also observe that, NeMoI ensures reachability and faster updates compared to global updates. Similar to the train scenario, we assigned only a single prefix to each producer in these experiments. Since producers use a single Binding Interest packet for all of their prefixes (deterministic or non-deterministic), the number of packets is reduced to 1 for each producer in comparison to a design where each prefix has to be carried in a separate BI (i.e., no. of prefixes = no. of BI's sent).

5.2   Effective Route Optimization

We realized that with NeMoI, the effective placement of *MAs* is a key to achieve effective route optimization and to gain maximum performance benefit. So we used the network mobility with train as an example to evaluate the effect of *MA* placements, we choose three different placement strategies namely: Core, Edge and Random for placing the *MAs* respectively at the core, edge and random locations in the RocketFuel AS1221 topology. Placing the *MAs* at the edge of the network could result in reduced path inflation. However, it can affect the propagation of mobility updates and in turn contribute to increasing the overall path inflation. Placing the *MAs* at the core of the network seems to provide more promising results as it can increase the propagation of mobility updates. However, there is also a possibility that the placement of *MAs* might not be a significant factor so, even a random placement of *MAs* would be sufficient.

Hence, we investigated the behaviour of NeMoI with all three placement strategies and with different number of *MAs*. We started with one *MA* and gradually increased the number of *MAs* to five. We placed a single producer in *Adelaide*. The producer generated a BI after attaching to the router1737 in *Adelaide*. Further, we also measured for each placement, the percentage of intermediate routers that were updated and the time to update them. We observe from the results in the Figs. 12, 13 and 14 that Core *MA* placement performs the best out of the three choices and updates maximum number of routers in the network with the least amount of time. We also observed that the percentage of routers updated increased with increase in the number of *MAs*.

5.3   Path Inflation

Path inflation is an unavoidable consequence of indirection. In NeMoI, since *Interests* are redirected towards *MAs* for resolution, a concern emerges for path inflation experienced by the consumers. The design choices in NeMoI try to minimize path inflation if not eliminate it entirely. It is a trade-off we believe that has to be made to ensure connectivity and reachability with mobility. Since we use *MAs* similar to Anchor-based solutions, we compare the path inflation in NeMoI with that of Anchor-based solutions.

Experimental Setup. We placed a producer in *Adelaide* and associated 101 consumers, one each to every router in the topology (1:1). The consumer arrival process followed a normal distribution.

Experiment. First, we measured the path inflation experienced by consumers in NeMoI and compared it to Anchor-based solutions using the three different *MA* placement strategies described earlier with five *MAs*. The consumers arrived and generated *Interest*s accordingly. We then measured path inflation by counting the number of hops the *Interest* travels to reach the producer. For this experiment, in NeMoI, when the producer sent a BI, the *MAs* and intermediate routers that forward this BI were updated. We observe from the results in Figs. 15, 16 and 17 that path inflation in NeMoI is considerably lower compared to Anchor-based solutions. Further, consumers experienced the lowest path inflation with Core *MA* placement.

Second, we measured path inflation in NeMoI using two different scenarios. In the first scenario, we measured cumulative path inflation by counting the number of hops the *Interest* travels when the producer sends a BI and only *MAs* are updated. In the second scenario, we measured the same, but along with *MAs* the intermediate routers that forward this BI were updated.

We observe from the results in Figs. 18, 19 and 20 that NeMoI reduces path inflation by allowing the intermediate routers to update their routing information when they forward BI to the *MAs*. Again we observe that Core *MA* placement strategy outperforms Edge and Random placements. Further, NeMoI also allows rest of the network to gradually update reactively as they forward *Interest* towards the producer via the *MAs*.

Third, we analyzed the effect of increasing the number of *MAs* in NeMoI. We measured the cumulative path inflation in the Core placement strategy with two scenarios. In the first scenario, when the producer sends a BI, the intermediate routers are allowed to update their routing tables while in the second scenario the intermediate routers were not allowed to update their routing tables. For the same consumer arrival process described earlier, we increased the number of *MAs* from 1 to 5 and measured the cumulative path inflation for the consumers. We observe from the results in Fig. 24 that as we increase the number of *MAs*, the path inflation starts to decrease. Further, we observe that path inflation reduces when the intermediate routers are allowed to update their routing information. Hence, with the right number of *MAs*, we can minimize path inflation in NeMoI.

Last, we measure the path inflation experienced by consumers travelling in the train and the cars. At each stop, consumers travelling in the train and cars generate an *Interest* for content generated by an immobile producer located in

Adelaide. In the first scenario, we measure the cumulative path inflation experienced by the consumer in NeMoI and compare it to Anchor-based solutions. In the second scenario, we measure the cumulative path inflation experienced by the consumer in NeMoI when the intermediate routers were allowed to update their routing information with the mobility update and compare it to the case when the routers were not allowed to update.

We observe from the results in Figs. 21 and 22 that total path inflation experienced by consumers in NeMoI is only 24 hops, compared to 68 hops in Anchor-based solutions. Further, Fig. 23 shows that path inflation decreases considerably when intermediate routers are also updated.

5.4   Packet Loss

Since the producers in the train and cars are constantly moving during their journey from *Perth* to *Sydney* they are re-connecting to the internet at every access router and BS in the network. As a result during every re-connection the train and cars send a mobility update (BI) to the network to propagate the information of their current *PoA*. However, there is a delay involved as this information is propagated to all the nodes in the network. During this time, if any user sends an Interest for the data served by the train, cars or any producer travelling in these moving network, the Interest cannot be satisfied if there were no cached copies. This is a direct consequence of mobility, which is aggravated with the increasing number of mobility update as the network is unstable. Hence we measured the amount of packet loss in NeMoI.

Experimental Setup. During the journey from *Perth* to *Sydney* the train is reconnecting at 110 BS, similarly, the cars travelling in path1 reconnects at 98 BS while those on path2 reconnects at 103 BS and send BI during each reconnection. We configured the simulator to assume the delay of 1ms for propagating the mobility information to the nearest *MA*. We used five routers as *MAs* and assigned 101 consumers to each remaining router in the network.

Experiment. For the deterministic and non-deterministic scenarios, the train/cars started their journey from *Perth* to *Sydney*. The 101 consumers generated Interests according to a normal distribution and non-uniform arrival pattern. In the non-mobility case all the Interests would be satisfied by the network. However since during the mobility update information propagation the network is unstable, as a consequence, some Interests will be dropped and this leads to packet loss. Packet loss during this time is inevitable unless the Data was already cached in some routers. For this experiment, we turned off caching to measure the amount of packet loss. The results are shown in Figs. 25 and 26. We observed from the results that NeMoI tried to minimize packet loss with faster propagation of mobility update. Please note that at stop 3 we see maximum packet loss occurs this is because there are 48 reconnections (BS) between stop2 and stop3 compared to other stops where reconnections ranges between 8 to 22.

Due to space constraints, we could not include all the results for both deterministic (train) and non-deterministic(car) scenarios and however, since the results were similar, we show only the main results that were interesting in this paper. Through these evaluations we observe the effects of mobility in the network. We evaluated NeMoI with standard solutions and show that NeMoI significantly reduces the signalling traffic and path inflation. We also evaluated effective route optimizations with three placement strategies for *MA* and show that Core placement provides maximum benefits. In NeMoI, there is no need for a MA in every users Home Network like in Mobile IP, but the *MAs* are network nodes. With just 5 *MAs* we show a reduction in network update and increase in its propagation. With a careful design of the *MA* service it is possible to choose on suitable number of *MAs*. Intuitively, it can be seen that since NeMoI greatly reduces the signalling traffic w.r.to the state of the art solutions, the energy consumption in NeMoI is proportional to the signalling traffic. We observe from the evaluations that NeMoI reduced total traffic from 0.215B to 4.6M and total hops from 68 to 24. This also has energy related benefits [4].

6   Conclusion

In this paper, we focused on the need for ICN based architectures to support mobility of the network. We proposed NeMoI, which is an enhancement to our previous work NeMoI. NeMoI provides an efficient, robust, reliable and secure hybrid full fledged mobility architecture that is specifically designed to handle *network-on-the-move*. NeMoI is designed with distributed *MAs* and logical multi-level FIB tables to reduce routing updates. We optimized NeMoI to bypass *MAs* by reactively updating the routers in the path of request flow. We discussed proactive and reactive solutions for synchronizing mobility updates and also established an effective placement strategy for *MAs* to provide effective route optimization. We performed extensive evaluation on a real world topology with one million dataset and showed that NeMoI performs 47times better than global updates and other existing solutions. The results showed that NeMoI dramatically reduced the signalling traffic, routing updates, path inflation and minimized packet loss in both deterministic and non-deterministic mobility scenarios.

Acknowledgment. This work was supported by the joint EU H2020/NICT ICN2020 Project (Contract No. 723014. and NICT No. 184).

References

1. Adhatarao, S., Arumaithurai, M., Kutscher, D., Fu, X.: NeMoI: network mobility in ICN. In: 2018 10th International Conference on Communication Systems & Networks (COMSNETS), pp. 251–258. IEEE (2018)
2. Adhatarao, S.S., Chen, J., Arumaithurai, M., Fu, X., Ramakrishnan, K.: Comparison of naming schema in ICN. In: 2016 IEEE International Symposium on Local and Metropolitan Area Networks (LANMAN), pp. 1–6. IEEE (2016)

3. Alliance, N.: 5G white paper. Next generation mobile networks, white paper (2015)
4. Arumaithurai, M., Ramakrishnan, K.K., Hasegawa, T.: Information-centric networking: the case for an energy-efficient future internet architecture. In: Green Communications: Principles, Concepts and Practice, pp. 361–376 (2015)
5. Augé, J., Carofiglio, G., Grassi, G., Muscariello, L., Pau, G., Zeng, X.: Anchor-less producer mobility in ICN. In: Proceedings of the 2nd International Conference on Information-Centric Networking, pp. 189–190. ACM (2015)
6. Bakshi, K.: Considerations for software defined networking (SDN): approaches and use cases. In: 2013 IEEE Aerospace Conference, pp. 1–9. IEEE (2013)
7. Chen, J., Arumaithurai, M., Jiao, L., Fu, X., Ramakrishnan, K.K.: COPSS: an efficient content oriented pub/sub system. In: ANCS (2011)
8. Dannewitz, C., Kutscher, D., Ohlman, B., Farrell, S., Ahlgren, B., Karl, H.: Network of information (netinf) - an information-centric networking architecture. Comput. Commun. **36**(7), 721–735 (2013). https://doi.org/10.1016/j.comcom.2013.01.009
9. Devarapalli, V., Wakikawa, R., Petrescu, A., Thubert, P.: Network mobility (nemo) basic support protocol. Technical report (2004)
10. Esteve, C., Verdi, F., Magalhaes, M.: Towards a new generation of information-oriented Internetworking architectures. In: ReArch (2008)
11. Evans, D.: The Internet of Things: how the next evolution of the internet is changing everything. In: Cisco (2011)
12. Farinacci, D., Lewis, D., Meyer, D., Fuller, V.: The locator/ID separation protocol (LISP) (2013)
13. Grewe, D., Wagner, M., Frey, H.: PeRCeIVE: proactive caching in ICN-based VANETs. In: 2016 IEEE Vehicular Networking Conference (VNC), pp. 1–8. IEEE (2016)
14. Hermans, F., Ngai, E., Gunningberg, P.: Global source mobility in the content-centric networking architecture. In: Proceedings of the 1st ACM workshop on Emerging Name-Oriented Mobile Networking Design-Architecture, Algorithms, and Applications, pp. 13–18. ACM (2012)
15. Jacobson, V., Smetters, D.K., Thornton, J.D., Plass, M.F., Briggs, N.H., Braynard, R.L.: Networking named content. In: CoNEXT (2009)
16. Kim, D., Kim, J., Kim, Y., Yoon, H., Yeom, I.: Mobility support in content centric networks. In: Proceedings of the Second Edition of the ICN Workshop on Information-Centric Networking, pp. 13–18. ACM (2012)
17. Koponen, T., et al.: A data-oriented (and beyond) network architecture. In: SIGCOMM (2007)
18. Lee, J., Cho, S., Kim, D.: Device mobility management in content-centric networking. IEEE Commun. Mag. **50**(12), 28–34 (2012)
19. Lieberman, P.: Wake-on-LAN technology (2010)
20. Mahajan, R., Spring, N., Wetherall, D., Anderson, T.: Inferring link weights using end-to-end measurements. In: IMW (2002)
21. Majestic.com: Dataset (2017). https://blog.majestic.com/development/majestic-million-csv-daily/
22. Mills, D.L.: Internet time synchronization: the network time protocol. IEEE Trans. Commun. **39**(10), 1482–1493 (1991)
23. Nakazato, H., et al.: On-path resolver architecture for mobility support in information centric networking. In: 2015 IEEE Globecom Workshops (GC Wkshps), pp. 1–6. IEEE (2015)
24. Perkins, C.E.: Mobile IP. IEEE Commun. Mag. **35**(5), 84–99 (1997)

25. Raychaudhuri, D., Nagaraja, K., Venkataramani, A.: Mobilityfirst: a robust and trustworthy mobility-centric architecture for the future internet. ACM SIGMO-BILE Mob. Comput. Commun. Rev. **16**(3), 2–13 (2012)

26. Sgambelluri, A., Giorgetti, A., Cugini, F., Bruno, G., Lazzeri, F., Castoldi, P.: First demonstration of SDN-based segment routing in multi-layer networks. In: Optical Fiber Communications Conference and Exhibition (OFC), pp. 1–3. IEEE (2015)

27. Tyson, G., Sastry, N., Cuevas, R., Rimac, I., Mauthe, A.: A survey of mobility in information-centric networks. Commun. ACM **56**(12), 90–98 (2013)

28. Tyson, G., Sastry, N., Rimac, I., Cuevas, R., Mauthe, A.: A survey of mobility in information-centric networks: Challenges and research directions. In: Proceedings of the 1st ACM Workshop on Emerging Name-Oriented Mobile Networking Design-Architecture, Algorithms, and Applications, pp. 1–6. ACM (2012)

29. International Telecommunication Union: Ict facts and figures 2016 (2017). http://www.itu.int/en/ITU-D/Statistics/Pages/facts/default.aspx

30. Vixie, P., Gudmundsson, O., Eastlake, D., Wellington, B.: RFC 2845: secret key transaction authentication for DNS (TSIG) (2000)

31. Wang, L., Waltari, O., Kangasharju, J.: Mobiccn: Mobility support with greedy routing in content-centric networks. In: 2013 IEEE Global Communications Conference (GLOBECOM), pp. 2069–2075. IEEE (2013)

32. Zhang, L., Estrin, D., Burke, J., Jacobson, V., Thornton, J.: Named Data Networking (NDN) Project. Technical report ndn-0001, PARC (2010)

33. Zhang, Y., Zhang, H., Zhang, L.: Kite: A mobility support scheme for ndn. In: Proceedings of the 1st International Conference on Information-Centric Networking, pp. 179–180. ACM (2014)

34. Zhu, Z., Wakikawa, R., Zhang, L.: RFC 6301: a survey of mobility support in the internet (2011)

Game Theory Based Network Partitioning Approaches for Controller Placement in SDN

Bala Prakasa Rao Killi$^{(\boxtimes)}$, Ellore Akhil Reddy,
and Seela Veerabhadreswara Rao

Department of Computer Science and Engineering,
Indian Institute of Technology Guwahati, Guwahati, India
k.bala@iitg.ac.in

Abstract. Software Defined Networking decouples the control plane from the data plane and shifts the control plane to an external entity known as the controller. In large networks, the control plane is distributed among multiple controllers to satisfy fault tolerant and response time requirements. The network is divided into multiple domains, and one or more controllers are deployed in each of these domains. The naive approach for partitioning the network using the k-means algorithm with random initialization results in solutions that are far from optimal. In this paper, we propose a network partition based controller placement strategy by leveraging k-means algorithm with cooperative game theory initialization. The partitioning of the network into subnetworks is modeled as a cooperative game with the set of all switches as the players of the game. The switches try to form coalitions with other switches to maximize their value. It is referred as cooperative k-means for brevity. We also propose a variant of cooperative k-means strategy that tries to produce partitions that are balanced in size. Further, we propose a two step network partitioning strategy that considers both the load and latency. The performance of our proposed strategies are evaluated on networks from Internet 2 OS3E and Internet Topology Zoo. Results demonstrate that our cooperative k-means strategy generates solutions that are close to optimal in terms of the worst case switch to controller latency and outperforms the standard k-means algorithm. Evaluations also demonstrate that the variant of cooperative k-means produces balanced partitions. Furthermore, the load and latency aware partitioning approach reduces both partition imbalance and worst case latency.

Keywords: Cooperative game theory · Shapley value
Non cooperative game theory · Nash-equilibrium
Network partitioning · Controller placement
Software Defined Network

© Springer Nature Switzerland AG 2019
S. Biswas et al. (Eds.): COMSNETS 2018, LNCS 11227, pp. 245–267, 2019.
https://doi.org/10.1007/978-3-030-10659-1_11

1 Introduction

Software Defined Networking (SDN) decouples the control plane, responsible for routing and signaling, from the data plane, responsible for forwarding incoming packets. The data plane remains within the network element, and the control plane is shifted to an external entity known as the controller. The network element is a dumb entity which simply forward incoming packets based on the rules provided by the controller. SDN offers numerous benefits over the traditional networking architecture such as increased network infrastructure utilization, network management via software controlling and experimentation and deployment of new ideas and applications without disturbing the existing network. A single centralized controller may satisfy response time requirements of a small and medium scale network. However, a single controller does not satisfy the fault tolerant requirements of any network as it is the single point of failure. A potential solution is to divide the network into domains and assign a controller to each of these domains.

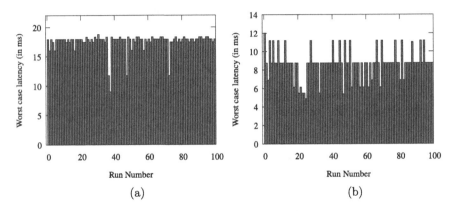

Fig. 1. Worst case latency of standard k-means for 100 different runs. (a) Chinanet topology with four partitions. (b) Interoute topology with six partitions.

The standard k-means strategy is used to partition the Chinanet and Interoute networks and the worst case latency for 100 different runs is depicted in Fig. 1. It can be observed from Fig. 1(a) that the worst case latency of Chinanet topology varied from 9 ms to 18.76 ms when the network is partitioned into four subnetworks. The worst case latency of Interoute topology varied from 4.9 ms to 12.1 ms when the network is partitioned into six subnetworks as shown in Fig. 1(b). Moreover, the average worst case latency computed over 100 runs, of Chinanet and Interoute network, is 17.45 ms and 8.7 ms respectively. However, the optimal worst-case latency obtained by solving the k-center problem [1] is 8.47 ms and 3.8 ms respectively. Therefore, we argue that k-means algorithm with random initialization results in solutions that are far from optimal. Since the players in cooperative game form coalitions to maximize their payoff, we argue that it can be used to partition the network into multiple domains.

Motivated by this, we propose various controller placement strategies for partitioning the network using the k-means algorithm with cooperative game theory based initialization. The major contributions of this paper are:

- We propose a latency aware controller placement strategy that partition the network using the k-means algorithm with cooperative game theory based initialization. Henceforth, we refer it as cooperative k-means for brevity. The partitioning of the network into subnetworks is modeled as a cooperative game with the set of all switches as the players of the game. The switches try to form coalitions with other switches to maximize their value.
- Although the cooperative k-means strategy produces partitions that are near optimal in terms of latency, it produces high imbalance among partitions in terms of size. Hence, we propose a variant of cooperative k-means strategy that tries to produce partitions that are balanced in size.
- Further, we propose a two step network partitioning strategy that considers both the load and latency. The cooperative k-means approach is used as the first step to obtain controller locations and switch to controller assignment. Then, we utilize a non cooperative game theory based clustering approach proposed in [2] to reduce the load imbalance among controllers obtained in the first step.
- The performance of our proposed strategies are evaluated on networks from Internet 2 OS3E topology and Internet Topology Zoo.

The remainder of the paper is organized as follows. Section 2 discusses the work related to the controller placement in SDN. We present the background concepts of cooperative game theory in Sect. 3 and introduce our cooperative game theory based k-means algorithm for controller placement in Sect. 4. Then, we report our evaluation results in Sect. 5. The last and final section concludes the paper.

2   Related Work

In this section, we discuss the related work on controller placement problem in SDN.

2.1   Controller Placement

Heller *et al.* initiated the study of controller placement problem in [3]. They analyzed the impact of placement on Internet 2 OS3E topology by considering various metrics such as the average latency, the worst case latency, and nodes with a bound on latency. An integer linear programming model for controller placement to minimize the cost of the network while ensuring that the latency is less than an upper bound, is presented in [4]. In [5], we proposed various hypervisor and controller placement schemes for minimizing the maximum latency in a virtualized SDN and modeled them as mixed integer linear programs.

2.2   Reliable Controller Placement

The works in [6–14] considered reliability aspects while deploying controllers in the network. [6] considers the fault tolerant controller placement problem that minimizes the cost of the network while maintaining an operational path between the switches and controllers with high probability. A framework that generates Pareto optimal controller placements with respect to the worst case latency, average latency, inter-controller latency, and controller imbalance is proposed in [9,10]. The authors of [7] modeled the reliability aware controller placement as an integer linear program towards minimizing the disconnections in the control network. A controller placement scheme for improving the connectivity and failover mechanism by considering multiple edge-disjoint paths and backup controllers is proposed in [8]. In [11–13], we proposed various controller placement schemes for minimizing the maximum latency in case of controller failures and modeled them as mixed integer linear programs. We also proposed a controller placement approach for minimizing the worst case latency in case of a single link failure [14].

2.3   Dynamic Controller Placement

The works in [15–17] adjusts the number and location of controllers according to the network traffic conditions. [15] considered a dynamic controller deployment scheme that minimizes the weighted sum of communication overhead between controllers, statistic collection cost, flow setup time, and switch reassignment cost. The problem is formulated as an integer linear program and proposed two heuristic methods. The authors in [16] proposed a controller placement scheme that detects the load imbalance of controllers and offloads switches from heavily loaded controllers to lightly loaded controllers. They also proposed a resizing algorithm that expands or reduces the controller pool with changing network conditions. In [17], Rath et al. utilized a Non-Zero-Sum game to solve the dynamic controller placement problem. Each controller decides whether to add/delete controllers instances or to migrate switches to other controllers using the payoff value.

2.4   Network Partitioning for Controller Placement

The works in [18–21] utilized network partitioning for deploying controllers in the network. In [18], Xiao et al. utilized the spectral clustering algorithm for partitioning the wider-area network into several subnetworks. A dedicated controller is deployed in each of the subnetworks at a location that minimized the average switch to controller latency. The authors in [19] proposed a hierarchical network optimization towards minimizing the overhead of the control plane. The idea is to partition the network into zones with a controller assigned to each zone. All these zone controllers are coordinated by a master controller. They formulated the problem as a binary integer linear program and proposed three heuristics namely clustering heuristic, partitioning heuristic, and assignment heuristic.

3   Background

In this section, we present the background concepts of the cooperative and non cooperative game theory that are used in formulating the problem.

3.1   Cooperative Game

A cooperative game is defined as a pair (N, v) where N is the set of all players in the game and v is value function or characteristic function. $v(F), F \subseteq N$ is known as the value of the coalition F and $v(N)$ is known as the value of the grand coalition A cooperative game can be analyzed using two solution concepts namely the core of the game and Shapley value.

3.2   Core of a Game

Let $x = (x_1, x_2, \ldots, x_n) \in \mathbb{R}^n$ be the payoff allocation with x_i being the payoff of switch i. A payoff allocation $x = (x_1, x_2, \ldots, x_n)$ is said to be individually rational if $x_i \geq v(\{i\})$, $\forall i \in N$. A payoff allocation x is said to be coalitionally rational if $\sum_{i \in F} x_i \geq v(F)$, $\forall F \subseteq N$. Additionally, a payoff allocation x is said to be collectively rational if $\sum_{i \in N} x_i = v(N)$. The core of a cooperative game is set of all payoff allocations that are individually rational, coalitionally rational, and collectively rational. Every coalitionally rational payoff allocation is an individually rational allocation. Thus, the set of all coalitionally rational and collectively rational payoff allocations constitutes the core of a cooperative game.

$$\mathbb{C}(N, v) = \Big\{ (x1, x2, \ldots, x_n) \in \mathbb{R}^n : \sum_{i \in N} x_i = v(N);$$

$$\sum_{i \in F} x_i \geq v(F), \forall F \subseteq N \Big\}$$

3.3   Shapley Value

The Shapley Value is a solution concept that fairly allocates the gains obtained by cooperation among the players while considering the relative importance of players in the game. Let $\phi(N, v) = (\phi_1(N, v), \phi_2(N, v), \ldots, \phi_n(N, v))$ and $\phi_i(N, v)$ be the Shapley value of the cooperative game and player i respectively. $\phi_i(N, v)$ specifies the expected payoff to player i and is given by,

$$\phi_i(N, v) = \sum_{F \subseteq N-i} \frac{|F|!(n - |F| - 1)!}{n!} \{v(F \cup \{i\}) - v(F)\}$$

3.4   Convex Game

A cooperative game (N, v) is said to be convex if the marginal contribution of a player is higher in larger coalitions.

$$v(H \cup \{i\})) - v(H) \geq v(F \cup \{i\})) - v(F),$$
$$\forall F \subseteq H \subseteq N \setminus \{i\}, \ i \in N$$

Here, $v(H \cup \{i\})) - v(H)$ and $v(F \cup \{i\})) - v(F)$ are the marginal contributions of player i with respect to the coalition H and F respectively.

Equivalently it can be written as follows:

$$v(H \cup \{i\})) - v(F \cup \{i\})) \geq v(H) - v(F),$$
$$\forall F \subseteq H \subseteq N \setminus \{i\}, \ i \in N$$

3.5   Shapley Value of a Convex Game

Let Π be the set of all orderings of $N = \{1, 2, \ldots, n\}$ and $\pi \in \Pi$ be a specific ordering of the players. The initial segments of the ordering π are given by,

$$R_{\pi,m} = \{i \in N : \pi(i) \leq m\}, \ m \in \{0, 1, 2, \ldots, n\}. \tag{1}$$

The core for a specific ordering π can be computed by solving the following equations.

$$s_i^\pi(R_{\pi,m}) = v(R_{\pi,m}), m \in \{1, 2, \ldots, n\} \tag{2}$$

The solution to (2) returns the coordinates of the intersection of the hyperplanes $H_{R_{\pi,m}}$.

$$s_i^\pi = v(R_{\pi,\pi(i)}) - v(R_{\pi,\pi(i)-1}), \ i \in \{1, 2, \ldots, n\} \tag{3}$$

The Shapley value of a convex game belongs to the core of the game and is the center of gravity of above intersection points s^π. Therefore, it is given by,

$$\phi_i = \frac{1}{n!} \sum_{\pi \in \Pi} s_i^\pi. \tag{4}$$

3.6   Non Cooperative Game

A non cooperative game is a game with competition between rational and self interested individual players. Each player has a strategy set and an utility/payoff function. It can be described using normal form representation as a tuple $(N, (\Delta_i)_{i \in N}, (P_i)_{i \in N})$, where

- N is the set of all players in the game.
- Δ_i is the strategy set of player i.
- $P_i : \Delta_1 \times \Delta_2 \times \ldots \Delta_{|N|} \to \mathbb{R}$ is the payoff function of player i.

A strategy profile is represented by $(\delta_i, \delta_2, \ldots, \delta_n)$ where $\delta_i \in \Delta_i$ is a strategy of player i. A non cooperative game can be analyzed using the solution concept namely the Nash-equilibrium.

3.7 Nash-equilibrium

A strategy profile $\delta^* = (\delta_1^*, \delta_2^*, \ldots, \delta_n^*)$ is said to be a Nash-equilibrium of a game if:

$$P_i(\delta_i^*, \delta_{-i}^*) \geq P_i(\delta_i, \delta_{-i}^*), \forall \delta_i \in \Delta_i, \forall i \in 1, 2, \ldots, n$$

where $\delta_{-i}^* \in \Delta_{-i}$ and $\Delta_{-i} = \Delta_1^* \times \Delta_2^* \times \ldots \Delta_{i-1}^* \times \Delta_{i+1}^* \times \ldots \Delta_n^*$ is the cartesian product of strategy sets of players other than i.

4 Problem Formulation

The physical network is denoted with the graph $G(S, E)$ where $S = \{s_1, s_2, \ldots, s_n\}$ is the set of switches and E is the set of edges between the switches. We denote all pairs shortest path latency matrix with D, where the entry $d(i, j)$ represents the shortest path latency between switch i and switch j. Let Q be the finite nonempty set of potential locations for deploying controllers in the network. We assume that every switch is a potential location for deploying a controller, i.e., $Q = N$. Table 1 lists all the notations used in problem formulation.

Table 1. Notations

Symbol	Description
C_0	Initial controller locations
$d(s_i, s_j) = D(i, j)$	Shortest path latency between switch i and switch j
D	All pairs shortest path matrix
D_{max}	Diameter of the network
E	Set of physical links
$G(S, E)$	Physical network
$G_i(S_i, E_i)$	i^{th} subnetwork
k	Number of partitions
N	Players of the game
P_i	Payoff function of player i
Q	Potential locations for installing controllers
S	Set of nodes/switches in the network
U	Similarity function
v	Value function
α	Threshold parameter
δ_i	A strategy of player i
ϕ_i	Shapley value of player i
Δ_i	Strategy set of player i
Δ_{-i}	Cartesian product of strategy sets of player other than i

4.1   Network Partitioning

The goal is to partition the network $G(S, E)$ into k subnetworks $G_i(S_i, E_i)$, $i = 1, 2, \ldots, k$, subject to the following:

$$\bigcup_{i=1}^{k} S_i = S, \quad \bigcup_{i=1}^{k} E_i = E \tag{5}$$

$$S_i \cap S_j = \emptyset, \quad \forall i, j \in \{1, 2, \ldots, k\}, i \neq j \tag{6}$$

$$G_i \text{ is a connected sub graph}, \quad \forall i \in \{1, 2, \ldots, k\} \tag{7}$$

(5) specifies that all the subnetworks together should cover the entire network. That is, the switches and edges of all the subnetworks together need to cover the switches and edges of the entire network respectively. (6) indicates that each switch is part of exactly one subnetwork. (7) specifies that the switches in a partition are connected.

4.2   Cooperative k-means Network Partitioning

We utilized the cooperative game theory based clustering method proposed in [22]. The partitioning of the network into subnetworks is modeled as a cooperative game (S, v) where the set of all switches $S = \{s_1, s_2, \ldots, s_n\}$ are the players of the game and $v : 2^{|S|} \to \mathbb{R}$ is the value function with $v(\phi) = 0$. The switches try to form coalitions with other switches to maximize their value. The value function that we employed is as follows:

$$v(F) = \frac{1}{2} \sum_{\substack{s_i, s_j \in F \\ s_i \neq s_j}} U(d(s_i, s_j)), \ F \subseteq S, F \neq \phi \tag{8}$$

where $U : \mathbb{R}^+ \cup \{0\} \to (0, 1]$ is a monotonically nonincreasing similarity function defined in (9). Note that D_{max} in (9) is the diameter of the network which is the maximum latency between any two switches.

$$U(d(s_i, s_j)) = 1 - \frac{d(s_i, s_j)}{1 + D_{max}} \tag{9}$$

Let F and H be any two coalitions with $F \subseteq H \subseteq S \setminus \{s_k\}, s_k \in S$. Then $v(H \cup \{s_k\}) - v(F \cup \{s_k\})$ is given by,

$$= \frac{1}{2} \sum_{\substack{s_i, s_j \in H \\ s_i \neq s_j}} U(d(s_i, s_j)) + \sum_{s_i \in H} U(d(s_i, s_k))$$

$$- \frac{1}{2} \sum_{\substack{s_i, s_j \in F \\ s_i \neq s_j}} U(d(s_i, s_j)) - \sum_{s_i \in F} U(d(s_i, s_k))$$

$$= \frac{1}{2} \sum_{\substack{s_i,s_j \in H \setminus F \\ s_i \neq s_j}} U(d(s_i,s_j)) + \sum_{\substack{s_i \in H \setminus F \\ s_j \in F}} U(d(s_i,s_j)) + \sum_{s_i \in H \setminus F} U(d(s_i,s_k))$$

$$= v(H) - v(F) + \sum_{s_i \in H \setminus F} U(d(s_i,s_k))$$

$$\geq v(H) - v(F)$$

Hence, the cooperative game (S,v) with the value function defined in (8) is convex. Consequently, the Shapley value can be computed using (4) as follows:

$$\phi_i = \frac{1}{n!} \sum_{\pi \in \Pi} s_i^\pi$$

it can be written, using (3), as

$$\phi_i = \frac{1}{n!} \sum_{\pi \in \Pi} v(R_{\pi,\pi(i)}) - v(R_{\pi,\pi(i)-1})$$

it can be written, using (1) and (8), as

$$= \frac{1}{n!} \sum_{\pi \in \Pi} \left[\frac{1}{2} \sum_{\substack{s_g,s_h \in R_{\pi,\pi(i)} \\ s_g \neq s_h}} U(d(s_g,s_h)) - \frac{1}{2} \sum_{\substack{s_g,s_h \in R_{\pi,\pi(i)-1} \\ s_g \neq s_h}} U(d(s_g,s_h)) \right]$$

avoiding duplicate pairs, gives us

$$= \frac{1}{n!} \sum_{\pi \in \Pi} \left[\sum_{\substack{\pi(g) \leq \pi(i) \\ \pi(h) < \pi(g)}} U(d(s_g,s_h)) - \sum_{\substack{\pi(g) \leq \pi(i)-1 \\ \pi(h) < \pi(g)}} U(d(s_g,s_h)) \right]$$

$$= \frac{1}{n!} \sum_{\pi \in \Pi} \sum_{\pi(j) < \pi(i)} U(d(s_i,s_j))$$

$$= \left[\frac{1}{n!} \sum_{\substack{\pi \in \Pi \\ \pi(i)=1 \\ \pi(j) < \pi(i)}} U(d(s_i,s_j)) + \frac{1}{n!} \sum_{\substack{\pi \in \Pi \\ \pi(i)=2 \\ \pi(j) < \pi(i)}} U(d(s_i,s_j)) + \ldots + \frac{1}{n!} \sum_{\substack{\pi \in \Pi \\ \pi(i)=n \\ \pi(j) < \pi(i)}} U(d(s_i,s_j)) \right]$$

There are total $(n-1)!$ orderings while fixing the position of the player i. In each of these orderings, every player other than i can occur in a position preceding i in $\frac{i-1}{n-1}$ ways. Therefore, summing over all orderings gives us:

$$\phi_i = \frac{1}{n!} \left(\sum_{i=1}^{n} \frac{i-1}{n-1} \right) (n-1)! \sum_{\substack{s_j \in S \\ j \neq i}} U(d(s_i,s_j))$$

$$\phi_i = \frac{1}{2} \sum_{\substack{s_j \in S \\ j \neq i}} U(d(s_i,s_j)) \tag{10}$$

The Shapley value of player i can be computed using (10). We present an algorithm for initializing the controller locations using the cooperative game theory in Algorithm 1. It takes as an input set of potential locations for deploying controllers, all pairs shortest path latency matrix and a threshold parameter, and returns an initial controller locations as output. Every switch is a potential location for deploying a controller, hence, step 1 of the algorithm initializes Q with S and starts with an empty set of initial controller locations C_0. The Shapley value of each location is computed in steps 2–4. Then, the algorithm iteratively does the following in steps 6–9 until the set Q is empty: selects a switch m from Q with the highest Shapley value (ties are broken in favor of the switch with the lower index), add m to the set of initial locations for deploying controllers, assign to m, all those switches T_m that are at least α similar to m, and updates the set Q. Note that the threshold parameter α determines the number of subnetworks.

Algorithm 1. Cooperative game theory initialization

    Input: Set of switches: $S = \{s_1, s_2, \ldots, s_n\}$
           All pairs shortest path matrix: D
           Threshold: $\alpha \in (0, 1]$
    Output: Initial controller locations: C_0

1 $Q = S$, $C_0 = \emptyset$
2 **for** $(i = 1, 2, \ldots, n)$ **do**
3      $\phi_i = \frac{1}{2} \sum\limits_{\substack{s_j \in S \\ s_j \neq s_i}} U(d(s_i, s_j))$

4 **end**
5 **while** $(Q \neq \emptyset)$ **do**
6      $m = \arg\max\limits_{i \in Q} \phi_i$
7      $C_0 = C_0 \cup \{m\}$
8      $T_m = \{i \in Q : U(d(s_i, s_k)) \geq \alpha\}$
9      $Q = Q \setminus T$
10 **end**

---

k-means algorithm for partitioning the nodes in a physical network is described in Algorithm 2. It takes as an input set of switches in the network, all pairs shortest path latency matrix and a threshold parameter and returns final locations for deploying controllers and switch to controller assignment. Step 1 of the algorithm initializes the locations for installing controllers using cooperative game theory initialization as shown in Algorithm 1. Step 2 of the algorithm initializes the updated controller locations C_{new} to empty. Then, the algorithm iteratively does the following until the current and updated controller locations are same: update the partitions in steps 4–7 by assigning switches to the nearest controller and update the controller location of each partition in steps 8–11.

Algorithm 2. Cooperative k-means for network topologies

Input: Set of switches: $S = \{1, 2, \ldots, n\}$
All pairs shortest path matrix: D
Threshold: $\alpha \in (0, 1]$
Output: Final locations for deploying controllers: C
Switch to controller assignment: $A_j, \forall c_j \in C$

1   C=Cooperative game theory based initialization (S,D,α)
2   $C_{new} = \emptyset$
3   **while** *(1)* **do**
4   **for** $(i = 1, 2, \ldots, n)$ **do**
5        $m = \underset{j:c_j \in C}{\arg\min}\, d(s_i, c_j)$
6        $A_m = A_m \cup \{i\}$
7   **end**
8   **for** $(j = 1, 2, \ldots, |C|)$ **do**
9        $m = \underset{i:i \in A_j}{\arg\min} \underset{l:l \in A_j}{\sum} d(s_i, s_l)$
10       $C_{new} = C_{new} \cup \{m\}$
11   **end**
12   **if** *(C and C_{new} are not equal)* **then**
13       $C = C_{new}$
14       $A_j = \emptyset,\ \forall c_j \in C$
15       $C_{new} = \emptyset$
16   **else**
17   exit
18
19 **end**

4.3   Load Aware Cooperative k-means Network Partitioning

Algorithm 2 presented in the previous section divides the network into partitions and then deploy a controller in each of the partitions. However, it results in high imbalance among partitions, i.e., the difference between the number of switches across partitions. Consequently, controllers deployed in large partitions are being overloaded and controllers deployed in smaller partitions are being lightly loaded. We present two metrics, namely maximum imbalance and average imbalance, for measuring the imbalance of a partitioning scheme. They are defined in (11) and (12) respectively.

$$Max\_Imbalance = \max_{c_j \in C} |A_j| - \min_{c_j \in C} |A_j| \tag{11}$$

$$Avg\_Imbalance = \frac{2}{k(k-1)} \sum_{c_i, c_j \in C} |A_j - A_i| \tag{12}$$

We present a network partitioning strategy in this section that takes into account the load imbalance.

Equipartition. We can circumvent the cluster imbalance by dividing the network into equal sized partitions. Henceforth, it is referred as equipartition cooperative k-means for brevity. We can implement this by replacing Step 5 of Algorithm 2 with the following step.

$$m = \underset{\substack{j:c_j \in C \\ |A_j| < \lceil \frac{|S|}{k} \rceil}}{\arg\min} \; d(s_i, c_j) \tag{13}$$

Here, $|S|$ is the total number of switches in the network, $|A_j|$ is the number of switches assigned to controller j and k is the number of partitions, i.e., the number of initial controllers returned by the Algorithm 1. (13) ensures that each switch is assigned to the nearest partition whose size is less than $\left\lceil \frac{|S|}{k} \right\rceil$.

4.4 Load and Latency Aware Network Partitioning

The load aware equipartition scheme presented in Sect. 4.3 is close to optimal in terms of load imbalance among controllers. However, it results in a significant degradation of performance in terms of latency between switches and controllers. The latency aware cooperative k-means scheme presented in Sect. 4.2 is near optimal in terms of switch to controller latency, but results in high imbalance among number of switches assigned to each controller. Hence, we present a network partitioning strategy, comprises of two steps, that considers both the load imbalance and the latency. In the first step, the cooperative k-means approach, presented in Algorithms 1 and 2, is used to obtain controller locations and switch to controller assignment. Then, we utilize the clustering approach proposed in [2] to reduce the load imbalance among controllers obtained in the first step. Figure 2 illustrates the flowchart describing the sequence of steps followed by the load and latency aware network partitioning.

Let C_l be the set of controllers, obtained in the first step, with a load less than the ideal load. Let C_h be the set of controllers, obtained in the first step, with a load greater than the ideal load. Note that load of a controller refers to the number of switches assigned to it. The ideal load of any controller is defined as follows:

$$Ideal\_Load = \left\lfloor \frac{|S|}{k} \right\rfloor$$

We refer the controllers in C_l and C_h as light and heavy controllers. The overhead associated with a heavy controller is the difference between the number of switches assigned to it and $Ideal\_Load$. The light controllers try to obtain switches from their nearest heavy controllers. But it may lead to a situation wherein some heavy controllers give away more than the overhead available with them. We refer such controllers as conflict controllers. A game is played, for each such conflict controller, with the light controllers that have requested switches from the conflict controller as players to maintain the ideal load at the conflict controller. The players try to receive switches from heavy controllers other than the conflict controller and release switches received from the conflict controller.

Algorithm 3. Payoff Matrix Generation for load and latency aware network partitioning

---

Input: Players={Light controllers}: C_p
Resources={Heavy controllers}: C_r
Conflict resource: cr
Strategy sets of players: $\{\Delta_i : \forall i \in C_p \}$
Ideal_Load:IL
Output: Payoff matrices of players: $\{ P_i, \forall i \in C_p \}$

1 **for** $(i = 1, 2, \ldots, |C_p|)$ **do**
2 $\quad$ Rows $X_i = |\delta_i|$
3 $\quad$ Columns $Y_i = \prod\limits_{\substack{h=1 \\ h \neq i}}^{C_p} |\Delta_h|$
4 $\quad$ **for** $(k = 1, 2, \ldots, Y_i)$ **do**
5 $\quad\quad$ **for** $(j = 1, 2, \ldots, X_i)$ **do**
6 $\quad\quad\quad$ $L = $ Cost incurred in terms of latency by controller i for receiving j switches from controllers $\{r \in C_r, r \neq cr, r.load \not< IL\}$
7 $\quad\quad\quad$ $\widetilde{L} = $ Cost incurred in terms of latency by controller i for receiving j switches from controllers $\{r \in C_r, r \neq cr, r.load \not< IL\}$ after remaining players $\{m \in C_p, m \neq i\}$ played their strategies
8 $\quad\quad\quad$ $\gamma = \widetilde{L} - L$
9 $\quad\quad\quad$ $\lambda(L) = $ Change in the load value of system when players other than i play their strategy combination corresponding to column k, and receive switches from controllers $\{r \in C_r, r \neq cr, r.load \not< IL \}$
10 $\quad\quad\quad$ $\mu = \left| Overhead(cr) - \lambda(L) - k \right|$
11 $\quad\quad\quad$ $P_i[j, k] = \sqrt{\gamma \mu}$
12 $\quad\quad$ **end**
13 $\quad$ **end**
14 **end**

Therefore, the strategies of a player comprises of the number of switches to be released to maintain the ideal load at the conflict controller.

We present an algorithm for computing the payoff matrices in Algorithm 3. It takes as an input a conflict controller, light controllers that have requested switches from the conflict controller as players of the game, heavy controllers, and strategy set of each player. The algorithm returns the payoff matrices of each player in the game as output. Steps 2–3 of the algorithm computes the payoff matrix size of player i in terms of the number of rows and columns. The strategy set size of a player i determines the number of rows in i's payoff matrix. However, the number of columns in player i's payoff matrix is the cartesian product of strategy set sizes of all players excluding i. The $(j, k)^{th}$ entry of payoff matrix corresponding to player i is computed using Steps 6–11 of the algorithm. Variable L in Step 6 of the algorithm maintains the cost incurred in terms of

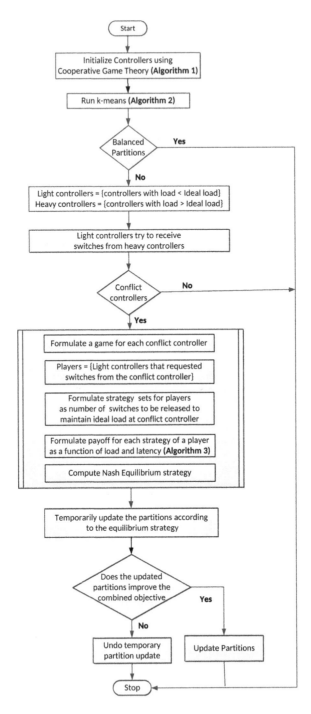

Fig. 2. Flow chart of load and latency aware network partitioning for controller placement

latency by a player i for receiving j switches from heavy controllers other than conflict controller. The cost incurred in terms of latency by a player i for receiving j switches from heavy controllers other than conflict controller when the remaining players play their strategies prior to player i is maintained in step 7 of the algorithm. The cost incurred in terms of latency by a player i for receiving switches from heavy controllers other than the conflict controller increases when remaining players play their strategies prior to player i. Because the heavy controllers closest to player i might have allocated the available overhead switches to other players. The increase in latency when the remaining players play their strategies prior to player i is captured in Step 8 of the algorithm. The load imbalance of a heavy controller decreases as the players try to receive some switches. Similarly, the load imbalance of a conflict controller cr decreases as the players try to release switches obtained from cr. However, as the total number of switches released by the players become greater than $Ideal\_Load$, the imbalance value for cr increases. The absolute change in load value of the players and a conflict controller is captured in Step 10 of the algorithm. Finally, the algorithm computes the payoff as a geometric mean of increase in latency and absolute change in load value of players and conflict controller. The Nash-equilibrium strategy set comprising of one strategy for each player in the game is computed from the payoff matrices of players.

5   Evaluation Results

The proposed cooperative k-means strategy is implemented in Python and evaluated its performance on both small scale and large scale network scenarios. We considered Internet 2 OS3E topology [23] with 34 nodes, BT North America network with 36 nodes and Chinanet [24] network with 42 nodes for a small network scenario, and Interoute network with 110 nodes for a large network scenario. Figure 3(a) and (b) illustrates the partitioning of the Internet 2 OS3E topology into four and five subnetworks using the cooperative k-means algorithm. Nodes within a subnetwork are depicted with the same symbol, and the controller of the subnetwork is highlighted by superimposing it with the same symbol multiple times. The maximum switch to controller latency path in each subnetwork is highlighted in blue color. The worst case latency path of the network is highlighted in red color. The cooperative k-means strategy resulted in a worst-case latency of 9.26 ms and 7.55 ms when the network is partitioned into four and five subnetworks respectively.

5.1   Switch to Controller Latency

k-means algorithm with random initialization, which is also known as standard k-means, is used as a baseline method for comparison with our proposed strategy. The objective of other placement solutions presented in [4,7] are different from our method, hence, not used as base line methods for comparison. Figure 4(a), (b) and (c) demonstrates the average worst case latency, computed over 100 runs,

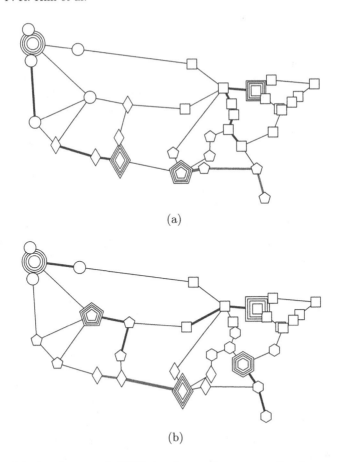

(a)

(b)

Fig. 3. Partitioning Internet 2 OS3E topology using cooperative k-means. (a) Four subnetworks. (b) Five subnetworks. (Color figure online)

of cooperative k-means, standard k-means and optimal k-center [1] strategies on BT North America, Chinanet, and Interoute networks respectively. We can observe that the worst case latency of the solution induced by cooperative k-means outperforms standard k-means and is very close to the optimal solution in all the networks.

5.2   Distribution

The average worst-case latency, computed over 100 runs, presented in Fig. 4 does not characterize the distribution of worst-case latencies over these 100 execution instances. Hence, the worst case latency distribution of cooperative k-means and standard k-means when evaluated on BT North America network for 100 times is presented in Fig. 5. The standard k-means algorithm randomly selects initial controller locations. Therefore, the solution produced by standard k-means algorithm varies with different execution instances. On the contrary, the only step

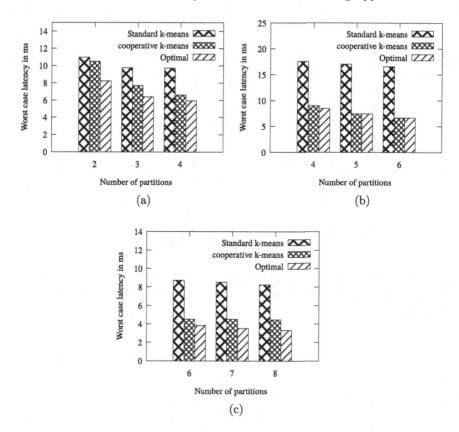

Fig. 4. Worst case latency of standard k-means and cooperative k-means strategies on various networks. (a) BT North America topology. (b) Chinanet topology. (c) Interoute topology

in the proposed cooperative k-means algorithm that involves some randomization is step 6. That is, selecting a switch m from P with the highest Shapley value. However, the ties are broken in favor of the switch with lower index. Hence, step 6 is also deterministic in nature. Since cooperative k-means algorithm does not involve any randomization or probability distribution, it is deterministic in nature. The solution produced by a deterministic algorithm remains same across different execution instances. Therefore, the distribution curve of the cooperative k-means approach is a deterministic line. We can observe that the worst case latency of the solution generated by cooperative k-means is equal to the best solution generated by the standard k-means in 100 runs. Figures 6 and 7 describes the distribution of worst-case latencies of cooperative k-means and standard k-means when evaluated for 100 times on Chinanet and Interoute networks respectively. Similar trends can be observed with respect to the distribution of worst-case latencies on Chinanet and Interoute networks.

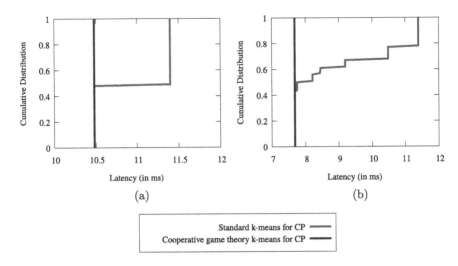

Fig. 5. Distribution of worst case latencies of cooperative k-means and standard k-means on BT North America topology when evaluated for 100 times (a) k = 2. (b) k = 3.

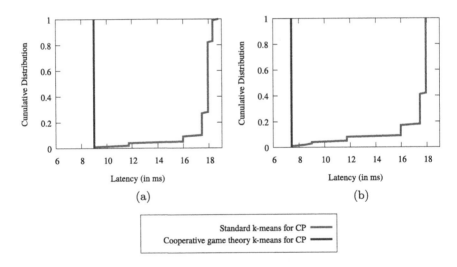

Fig. 6. Distribution of worst case latencies of cooperative k-means and standard k-means on Chinanet topology when evaluated for 100 times (a) k = 4. (b) k = 5.

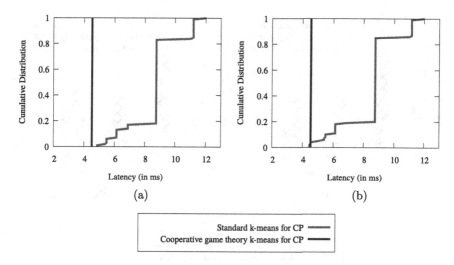

Fig. 7. Distribution of worst case latencies of cooperative k-means and standard k-means on Interoute topology when evaluated for 100 times (a) k = 6. (b) k = 7.

5.3   Partition Imbalance

We also evaluated the performance of load aware partitioning, and, load and latency aware partitioning approaches on BT North America, Chinanet, and Interoute networks. While evaluating these approaches, the demand of switches is set to 400 K/s [25, 26]. Figure 8 demonstrate the maximum partition imbalance (computed using Eq. 11) of latency aware partitioning, load aware partitioning, and load and latency aware partitioning approaches on different networks. We can observe from Fig. 8(a), (b) and (c) that the partitioning strategy that is aware of both load and latency performs better than the latency aware partitioning approach. We can also observe that the load aware partitioning approach performs better than the load and latency aware partitioning scheme. Further, the maximum load imbalance of the load aware partitioning approach is less than or equal to one because it divides the network into nearly equal sized sub-networks. The average partition imbalance (computed using Eq. 12) of latency aware partitioning, load aware partitioning, and load and latency aware partitioning approaches when evaluated on different networks is illustrated in Fig. 9. The load and latency aware partitioning strategy outperforms the latency aware partitioning approach and competes with the load aware partitioning approach.

Figure 10 demonstrates the worst case latency of latency aware partitioning, load aware partitioning, and load and latency aware partitioning approaches

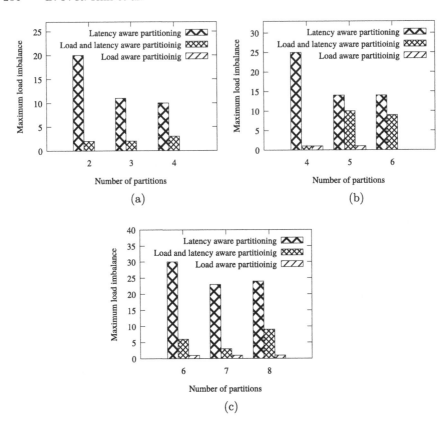

Fig. 8. Maximum partition imbalance of latency aware, load aware, and load and latency aware network partitioning strategies. (a) BT North America topology. (b) Chinanet topology. (c) Interoute topology

when evaluated on BTNA and Chinanet networks. The load and latency aware partitioning strategy performs better than load aware partitioning approach. Further, latency aware partitioning approach outperforms the load aware partitioning and load and latency aware strategies.

5.4   Running Time

The running time of the standard k-means and our cooperative k-means is less than one second for every network we evaluated including the interoute topology with 109 nodes. Hence, the proposed cooperative k-means algorithms quickly adapts to the change in network characteristics.

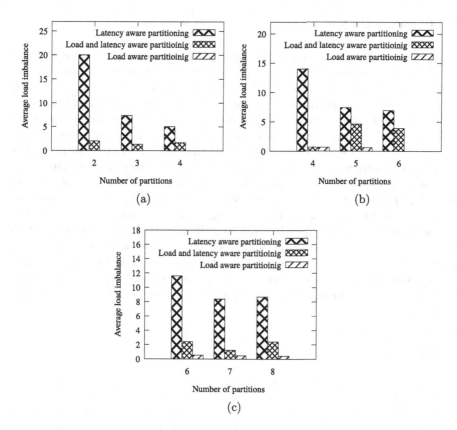

Fig. 9. Average partition imbalance of latency aware, load aware, and load and latency aware network partitioning strategies. (a) BT North America topology. (b) Chinanet topology. (c) Interoute topology

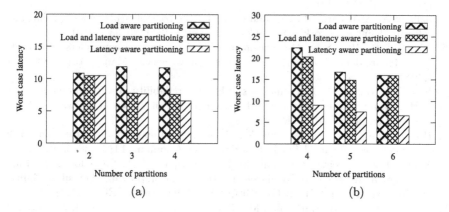

Fig. 10. Performance of latency aware, load aware, and load and latency aware network partitioning strategies. (a) BT North America topology. (b) Chinanet topology. (c) Interoute topology

6 Conclusion

We proposed a controller placement strategy that partitions the network using the k-means algorithm with the cooperative game theory based initialization and deploys a controller in each of the partitions. We also proposed a load aware cooperative k-means strategy to circumvent the partition imbalance in terms of size. Further, we proposed a two step network partitioning strategy that considers both the load and latency. The cooperative k-means approach is used as a first step to obtain controller locations and switch to controller assignment. Then, we utilized a non cooperative game theory based clustering approach to reduce the load imbalance among controllers obtained in the first step. The performance of our proposed strategies are evaluated on networks from Internet 2 OS3E and Internet Topology Zoo and compared it with the k-means algorithm with random initialization. Results show that our cooperative k-means strategy produces near-optimal solutions and outperforms the standard k-means for controller placement. Evaluations also demonstrated that the load aware cooperative k-means produces balanced partitions Further, the load and latency aware partitioning approach reduces both the partition imbalance and the worst case latency.

References

1. Vazirani, V.: Approximation Algorithms. Springer-Verlag, New York Inc., New York (2001)
2. Gupta, U., Ranganathan, N.: A game theoretic approach for simultaneous compaction and equipartitioning of spatial data sets. IEEE Trans. Knowl. Data Eng. **22**(4), 465–478 (2010)
3. Heller, B., Sherwood, R., McKeown, N.: The controller placement problem. In: Proceedings of the First Workshop on Hot Topics in Software Defined Networks, pp. 7–12. ACM (2012)
4. Sallahi, A., St-Hilaire, M.: Optimal model for the controller placement problem in software defined networks. IEEE Commun. Lett. **19**(1), 30–33 (2015)
5. Killi, B.P.R., Rao, S.V.: On placement of hypervisors and controllers in virtualized software defined network. IEEE Trans. Netw. Service Manag. **15**(2), 840–853 (2018)
6. Ros, F.J., Ruiz, P.M.: Five nines of southbound reliability in software-defined networks. In: Proceedings of the Third Workshop on Hot Topics in Software Defined Networking, pp. 31–36. ACM (2014)
7. Hu, Y., Wang, W., Gong, X., Que, X., Cheng, S.: On reliability-optimized controller placement for software-defined networks. China Commun. **11**(2), 38–54 (2014)
8. Muller, L.F., Oliveira, R.R., Luizelli, M.C., Gaspary, L.P., Barcellos, M.P.: Survivor: an enhanced controller placement strategy for improving SDN survivability. In: Proceedings of the IEEE GLOBECOM, pp. 1909–1915. IEEE (2014)
9. Hock, D., Gebert, S., Hartmann, M., Zinner, T., Tran-Gia, P.: Poco-framework for pareto-optimal resilient controller placement in SDN-based core networks. In: Proceedings of the IEEE Network Operations and Management Symposium (NOMS), pp. 1–2. IEEE (2014)

10. Lange, S., et al.: Heuristic approaches to the controller placement problem in large scale sdn networks. IEEE Trans. Netw. Service Manag. **12**(1), 4–17 (2015)
11. Killi, B.P.R., Rao, S.V.: Optimal model for failure foresight capacitated controller placement in software defined networks. IEEE Commun. Lett. **20**(6), 1108–1111 (2016)
12. Killi, B.P.R., Rao, S.V.: Controller placement with planning for failures in software defined networks. In: Proceedings of the IEEE International Conference on Advanced Networks and Telecommunications Systems (ANTS), pp. 1–6. IEEE (2016)
13. Killi, B.P.R., Rao, S.V.: Capacitated next controller placement in software defined networks. IEEE Trans. Netw. Service Manag. **14**(3), 514–527 (2017)
14. Killi, B.P.R., Rao, S.V.: Link failure aware capacitated controller placement in software defined networks. In: Proceedings of the International Conference on Information Networking (ICOIN) (2018)
15. Bari, M.F., et al.: Dynamic controller provisioning in software defined networks. In: Proceedings of the International Conference on Network and Service Management (CNSM 2013), pp. 18–25 (2013)
16. Dixit, A.A., Hao, F., Mukherjee, S., Lakshman, T., Kompella, R.: Elasticon: an elastic distributed SDN controller. In: Proceedings of the ACM/IEEE Symposium on Architectures for Networking and Communications Systems, pp. 17–28. ACM (2014)
17. Rath, H.K., Revoori, V., Nadaf, S.M., Simha, A.: Optimal controller placement in software defined networks (SDN) using a non-zero-sum game. In: Proceedings of the International Symposium on a World of Wireless, Mobile and Multimedia Networks (WoWMoM), pp. 1–6 (2014)
18. Xiao, P., Qu, W., Qi, H., Li, Z., Xu, Y.: The SDN controller placement problem for wan. In: Proceedings of the IEEE/CIC International Conference on Communications in China (ICCC), pp. 220–224. IEEE (2014)
19. Li, X., Djukic, P., Zhang, H.: Zoning for hierarchical network optimization in software defined networks. In: Proceedings of the Network Operations and Management Symposium (NOMS), pp. 1–8. IEEE (2014)
20. Wang, G., Zhao, Y., Huang, J., Duan, Q., Li, J.: A k-means-based network partition algorithm for controller placement in software defined network. In: Proceedings of the International Conference on Communications (ICC), pp. 1–6. IEEE (2016)
21. Killi, B.P.R., Reddy, E.A., Rao, S.V.: Cooperative game theory based network partitioning for controller placement in SDN. In: Proceedings of the International Conference on Communication Systems & NetworkS (COMSNETS) (2018)
22. Garg, V.K., Narahari, Y., Murty, M.N.: Novel biobjective clustering (BIGC) based on cooperative game theory. IEEE Trans. Knowl. Data Eng. **25**(5), 1070–1082 (2013)
23. Internet2 open science, scholarship and services exchange. http://www.internet2.edu/network/ose/
24. Knight, S., Nguyen, H.X., Falkner, N., Bowden, R., Roughan, M.: The internet topology zoo. IEEE J. Sel. Areas Commun. **29**, 1765–1775 (2011)
25. Kandula, S., Sengupta, S., Greenberg, A., Patel, P., Chaiken, R.: The nature of data center traffic: measurements & analysis. In: Proceedings of the Internet Measurement Conference, pp. 202–208. ACM (2009)
26. Yao, G., Bi, J., Li, Y., Guo, L.: On the capacitated controller placement problem in software defined networks. IEEE Commun. Lett. **18**(8), 1339–1342 (2014)

User Response Based Recommendations

Salman Memon[1]([⊠]), Veeraruna Kavitha[1], Manjesh K. Hanawal[1],
Eitan Altman[2,3], and R. Devanand[1]

[1] IEOR, IIT Bombay, Mumbai, India
1reachsalman@gmail.com
[2] Inria, University of Cote d'Azur, LINCS, Nice, France
[3] LIA, University of Avignon, Avignon, France

Abstract. In a recommendation system, users provide description of their interests through initial search keywords and the system recommends items based on these keywords. A user is satisfied if it finds the item of its choice and the system benefits, otherwise the user explores an item from the recommended list. Usually when the user explores an item, it picks an item that is nearest to its interest from the list. While the user explores an item, the system recommends new set of items. This continues till either the user finds the item of its interest or quits. In all, the user provides ample chances and feedback for the system to learn its interest. The aim of this paper is to efficiently utilize user responses to recommend items and find the item of user's interest quickly.

We first derive optimal policies in the continuous Euclidean space and adapt the same to the space of discrete items. We propose the notion of local angle in the space of discrete items and develop user response-local angle (UR-LA) based recommendation policies. We compare the performance of UR-LA with widely used collaborative filtering (CF) based policies on two real datasets and show that UR-LA performs better in majority of the test cases. We propose a hybrid scheme that combines the best features of both UR-LA and CF (and history) based policies, which outperforms them in most of the cases.

Towards the end, we propose alternate recommendation policies again utilizing the user responses, based on clustering techniques. These policies outperform the previous ones, and are computationally less intensive. Further, the clustering based policies perform close to theoretical limits.

1 Introduction

Recommendation systems (RS) became an active research area after the research on collaborative filtering in mid-1990s, (e.g., [1–5]). Over the past decade recommendation engines have become ubiquitous, and used for various purposes, e.g. e-commerce, social and professional networks, such as YouTube, Pandora, Amazon etc., (e.g., [2]). Even after plenty of work done by the industry and academia to develop new methods for RS in the last decade, this research area still has lots of scope to explore practical applications [4].

© Springer Nature Switzerland AG 2019
S. Biswas et al. (Eds.): COMSNETS 2018, LNCS 11227, pp. 268–291, 2019.
https://doi.org/10.1007/978-3-030-10659-1_12

In a RS, a user starts a session looking for an item (unknown to system) and its interest can vary drastically from one session to another. For example, a user might visit an online portal to buy a book at one time, while the same user might be interested in mobile phones the next time. However, the interest of the user during the same session would be consistent and the partial information about the same is available via the user responses. The objective is to satisfy the user's requirement at the earliest using the responses of the same user to the previous recommendations of the same session.

At every step system provides a recommendation list, and user chooses one among them to explore. It is natural for the user to explore an item, among the recommended list, which best matches the item of its interest. The exploration-recommendation continues till the user finds the item of its interest, or quits. We refer to the sequence of steps between a user entering and leaving the system as a session. The sequence of items that the user explores provides a useful feedback about the user's hidden (to the system) interest. In such scenarios it is better suited to recommend 'faraway' items (from each other as well as from the current item being explored) at least initially, as opposed to the traditional methods of recommending the 'nearby' items. We derive such policies using the policies of continuous Euclidean space, where the optimal policy (for e.g., for two recommendations) turns out to be recommending items at each time step that are at 180° from each other, while are at 90° with respect to the ones at the previous time step. We adapt the continuous-space policies to discrete space by proposing a new 'notion of angle' for a discrete set. While translating 180°, we would choose items among those which are at the same distance from a reference point, but whose sum of inter-distances is maximum. This results in recommending the 'faraway' items, however the distances reduce progressively. Basically this narrows down the system's belief of users interest geometrically faster.

We consider the similarity based distance between items obtained using the previous ratings (history) of different items (e.g., [6]). Most of the previous work focuses on finding the best one-shot recommendation and ignores the feedback generated within a session. However, we use the feedback provided by the users in the same session for further recommendations. In [7,8] authors consider prompting the new users for the purpose of learning them and for subsequent improved person based recommendations. They discuss the set of items which are optimal in certain information theoretic approach to learn the user, while ours uses the history as well as the user responses to learn the user of current session.

Our approach can also help cold start problems [8–10], in particular a new user problem, by using a non-history dependent distance measure, e.g., distance defined using the features of the items and we may consider this for future research.

We also propose a hybrid algorithm that combines the main ideas of UR-LA and CF policies. We tested our policies on two real datasets [11,12], and they outperform the CF policy in most of the cases. The improvement is significant, more than 30% in some, and at least 15% in many cases.

This work is an extended version of the results in [3]. The extensions include a new set of policies based on clustering approach. These policies again recommend 'faraway' items as discussed above and perform much better. We showed that they perform close to theoretical limits, based on some numerical results on the data sets. Further the new clustering algorithms require computation (and storage of centres) of 'nested clusters' at one time (offline), while the online part of the algorithm is significantly simplified. This simplification facilitated (fast) computation of optimal policies even with large (with any) number of recommendations per time.

2 System Dynamics

We consider a large (finite) database $\mathcal{S}$ where each item is described by a number of defining features. For example, in a music video, singer, composer, instruments etc., can be the features. For an item in an e-commerce portal like Amazon, Flipkart etc., type, make, category, price etc., are the features. The similarities/dis-similarities between the items can either be obtained by comparing these features and or by comparing the ratings provided by various users of the system. We assume there exists a distance metric $d(v_1, v_2)$ for any pair of items (v_1, v_2), which captures their similarity. It can be a well known similarity measure based distance between the two items [6], or can be proportional to the number of matching features between them, or can be a combination of the two.

When a user visits such a system, it is interested in one of the items referred by V_{ref}, which is unknown to the Content Provider (CP). We assume that V_{ref} is equally likely to be one of the items available with CP. The user specifies its interest by an initial search query and the system generates a set of recommendations based on this search query. User is satisfied if any one of the suggested recommendations (say a) is close to V_{ref}, i.e., if the distance $d(V_{ref}, a) \leq \underline{r}$ for some $\underline{r} \geq 0$ and then the CP derives benefit. For example, the user is satisfied if a has at least $\overline{F}$ number of matching features with V_{ref}. The satisfaction radius $\underline{r}$ can be zero, which implies the user is interested only in a particular product. The user starts a session with CP using an item X_0 (obtained after a search query) only if there is at least a slight match, i.e., only if the distance $d(X_0, V_{ref}) \leq \bar{R}$, where $\bar{R}$ is larger than $\underline{r}$. Threshold $\bar{R}$ can be the largest possible distance between any two items of the system, in which case the user always starts the session.

The CP displays a list of M recommendations (call it $\mathbf{a}_1 = (a_{1,1} \cdots, a_{1,M})$, a vector of length M) while displaying the item X_0. If the user is not satisfied in X_0, it explores one of the suggestions (call it X_1) from among $\mathbf{a}_1$. CP while displaying item X_1 also suggests new recommendation list $\mathbf{a}_2$. The user, if not satisfied in X_1, chooses one among $\mathbf{a}_2$ and this continues. That is, the user navigates through the recommendations of the CP and the user does this for a maximum T number of steps. We assume that at every step, the user chooses one of the items recommended by the CP which is closest to V_{ref}. That is,

$$X_k \in \arg\min_{a_{k,m}} d(V_{ref}, a_{k,m}). \tag{1}$$

In case an item recommended via initial/subsequent recommendations satisfies the user, the CP benefits and we assume the benefit is inversely proportional to the search time. The faster the user is satisfied, more is the benefit to the CP. Our aim is to minimize the time taken to suggest an item that satisfies the user.

3   Problem Formulation

We denote the space of items by $\mathcal{S}$, V_{ref} is one among $\mathcal{S}$ and a distance measure d is defined on this set. Our analysis is also applicable to the case when $\mathcal{S}$ is an (continuous) Euclidean subset. We could handle this generalization without extra effort and, more importantly, we derive recommendation policies for discrete content space by translating optimal policies of a continuous space.

A user can be interested in any item in $\mathcal{S}$. We consider that V_{ref} is selected uniformly at random from $\mathcal{S}$, i.e., the probability that V_{ref} lies in a subset $\Lambda \subset \mathcal{S}$ is given by:

$$P(V_{ref} \in \Lambda) = \frac{\mu(\Lambda)}{\mu(\mathcal{S})},$$

where μ is the Lebesgue measure (length, area respectively in one and two dimensional spaces) in the continuous case and is the cardinality (number of elements in a set) if $\mathcal{S}$ is discrete.

Distance Measures. One can define distance between two items in a discrete space using a similarity measure, which in turn is obtained by the ratings provided by different users to different items. The Cosine similarity measure between two items v, u is defined as [6]:

$$s_c(v, u) = s_{v,u} = \frac{\sum_{i\in I_{v,u}} r_{v,i} r_{u,i}}{\sqrt{\sum_{i\in I_{v,u}} (r_{v,i})^2} \sqrt{\sum_{i\in I_{v,u}} (r_{u,i})^2}}, \tag{2}$$

where $I_{v,u}$ is the set of users that rated both the items v and u, $r_{v,i}$ is the rating of item v by user i.

In continuous Euclidean spaces, d is either Euclidean or L^1 distance. In this paper we consider L^1 distance, i.e., $d(v_1, v_2) := \sum_i |v_{1,i} - v_{2,i}|$, where $\{v_{1,i}\}_i$ are components of the item defining vector v_1. One can now define the balls around an item/point v by:

$$\mathcal{B}(v, \underline{r}) := \{x \in \mathcal{S} : d(x, v) < \underline{r}\}.$$

We assume that any ball with a given satisfaction radius has the same measure, i.e., $\mu(\mathcal{B}(v, \underline{r}))$ is the same irrespective of the centre v.

Time to Satisfy the User
The user's interest lies in any item inside the ball $\mathcal{B}(V_{ref}, \underline{r})$ while the initial search X_0 lies inside $\mathcal{B}(V_{ref}, \overline{R})$. Recall that V_{ref} is unknown to CP, however, it is

known that $V_{ref} \in \mathcal{B}(X_0, \overline{R})$. The problem is to find a strategy that optimizes the time to satisfy the user. Let τ represent the first time a recommendation is within the ball $\mathcal{B}(V_{ref}, \underline{r})$, i.e., using (1) and using the notation $x \wedge y := \min\{x, y\}$,

$$\tau := \inf\left\{k \geq 1 : a_{k,i} \in \mathcal{B}(V_{ref}, \underline{r}) \text{ for some } i \leq M\right\} \wedge T$$
$$= \inf\left\{k \geq 1 : X_k \in \mathcal{B}(V_{ref}, \underline{r})\right\} \wedge T.$$

Note that we are only given T chances and are interested only if $\tau \leq T$ and hence the above definition is sufficient. Our aim is to minimize the expected value of the hitting time, $E[\tau]$, or equivalently maximize the time spent in the system, i.e. $E[T - \tau]$,

$$\arg\min_{\pi} E[\tau] \equiv \arg\max_{\pi} E[T - \tau],$$

where the optimization is over all possible recommendation policies π, that would be described shortly.

Recommendation Policies and Markov State

This problem is a fixed time horizon problem, and the time step is represented by the time epoch at which the user has chosen a new item to explore. The recommendations depend upon the user response to the previously recommended items. Thus policy would be an M-tuple of recommendations (actions), one for each time step k as below:

$$\pi = \{(a_{1,1}, \cdots, a_{1,M}), \cdots, (a_{T-1,1}, \cdots, a_{T-1,M})\}.$$

Here $a_{k,i}$ represents the i-th recommendation for the k-th step and this depends upon an appropriate state of the system. The state of the system at time k is given by (X_k, V_{ref}), where X_k defined in (1) is the choice of user at time k and V_{ref} is the interest of the user. Since V_{ref} is unknown to CP, we consider the alternate state $Z_k = (X_k, B_k)$, inspired by Partially Observable MDP (POMDP) framework. Here belief random variable B_k is the conditional distribution of V_{ref} given history H_k (previous states, actions and current observation) defined by:

$$H_k = \{(X_0, B_0), (X_1, B_1), ...(X_{k-1}, B_{k-1}), \mathbf{a_1}, ...\mathbf{a_k}, X_k\}.$$

The belief only improves with time, in the sense for all k, B_k is concentrated on certain sets $\mathcal{A}_k \subseteq \mathcal{A}_0$, in the following manner. We provide the proof and alongside introduce the required notations. To keep notations short, we present our results for $M = 2$. These can easily be extended for $M > 2$.

Lemma 1. *The belief random variable B_k at any time step k depends only upon the previous belief B_{k-1}, current recommendation $\mathbf{a_k}$ and current user choice X_k. For each k, $B_k \sim \mathcal{U}(\mathcal{A}_k)$, which implies that B_k is uniformly distributed over a subset $\mathcal{A}_k \subset \mathcal{S}$. Also the subsets $\{\mathcal{A}_k\}_{k \leq T}$ are nested:*

$$\mathcal{S} = \mathcal{A}_0 \supset \mathcal{A}_1 \cdots \supset \mathcal{A}_{T-1} \supset \mathcal{A}_T \quad \text{almost surely.}$$

Proof: Fix any deterministic policy π. We prove below (with $M = 2$) that the policy is represented by 'centres'

$$\mathcal{Q}_\pi := \{a_i^k, 1 \leq k \leq T \text{ and } i \leq 2^k\}.$$

For step $k = 1$, $a_{1,1} = a_1^1$ and $a_{1,2} = a_2^1$ represent the two recommendations provided by the system. If the user's interest V_{ref} lies in either one of the balls around the recommendations $\mathcal{B}_i^1 := \mathcal{B}(a_i^1, r)$ with $i = 1$ or 2, the user is satisfied in the first step itself. If not user chooses one among them (whichever is closer to V_{ref}), which is X_1, and we then have a partition of the area of the first belief, $\mathcal{A}_1^0 := \mathcal{A}_0 = \mathcal{S} \cap B(X_0, \bar{R})$:

$$X_1 = a_{1,1} 1_{\{V_{ref} \in \mathcal{A}_{11}\}} + a_{1,2} 1_{\{V_{ref} \in \mathcal{A}_{12}\}}, \text{ where}$$
$$\mathcal{A}_{11} = \{v \in \mathcal{A}_0 \mid d(v, a_{1,1}) < d(v, a_{1,2})\} \text{ and}$$
$$\mathcal{A}_{12} = \{v \in \mathcal{A}_0 \mid d(v, a_{1,2}) \leq d(v, a_{1,1})\}. \tag{3}$$

By Lemma 2 of Appendix A the new belief B_1 is uniformly distributed over $\mathcal{A}_1$ (i.e., $B_1 \sim \mathcal{U}(\mathcal{A}_1)$), which is either one of the above two mentioned partitions, i.e.,

$$\mathcal{A}_1 = \mathcal{A}_1^1 \text{ or } \mathcal{A}_2^1, \text{ where } \mathcal{A}_1^1 := \mathcal{A}_{11} \text{ and } \mathcal{A}_2^1 := \mathcal{A}_{12}.$$

Given the feedback by user, X_1, the system proposes two more recommendations $a_{2,1}(X_1, B_1)$ and $a_{2,2}(X_1, B_1)$. These two recommendations depend upon the current state (X_1, B_1) and since B_1 is fixed by X_1 and $\mathcal{A}_0$ (by Lemma 2) it is actually specified only by X_1. Let a_1^2, a_2^2 be these two recommendations if user choice $X_1 = a_{1,1}$, and let a_3^2, a_4^2 be the two recommendations if $X_1 = a_{1,2}$, i.e.,

$$(a_{2,1}(X_1),\ a_{2,2}(X_1)) = \begin{cases} (a_1^2, a_2^2) & \text{if } X_1 = a_{1,1} \\ (a_3^2, a_4^2) & \text{else.} \end{cases}$$

Again the user is satisfied, if V_{ref} lies in one among the two balls, $\mathcal{B}(a_{2,1}(X_1), r)$ or $\mathcal{B}(a_{2,2}(X_1), r)$. If not, user again chooses one among the two recommended items to explore further, whichever is closer to V_{ref}. This is X_2, and it equals

$$X_2 = a_{2,1}(X_1) 1_{\{V_{ref} \in \mathcal{A}_{21}\}} + a_{2,2}(X_1) 1_{\{V_{ref} \in \mathcal{A}_{22}\}}, \text{ where}$$
$$\mathcal{A}_{21}(X_1) = \left\{v \in \mathcal{A}_1 \mid d(v, a_{2,1}(X_1)) < d(v, a_{2,2}(X_1))\right\} \text{ and}$$
$$\mathcal{A}_{22}(X_1) = \left\{v \in \mathcal{A}_1 \mid d(v, a_{2,1}(X_1)) \geq d(v, a_{2,2}(X_1))\right\}. \tag{4}$$

By Lemma 3 of Appendix A the new belief B_2 is concentrated on $\mathcal{A}_2$ which is either one of the 4 choices based on (X_1, X_2):

$$\mathcal{A}_1^2 := \mathcal{A}_{21} \text{ with } X_1 = a_1^1, \mathcal{A}_2^2 := \mathcal{A}_{22} \text{ with } X_1 = a_1^1,$$
$$\mathcal{A}_3^2 := \mathcal{A}_{21} \text{ with } X_1 = a_2^1 \text{ or } \mathcal{A}_4^2 := \mathcal{A}_{22} \text{ with } X_1 = a_2^1.$$

Continuing this way, at any k we have 2^k centres given by $\mathcal{Q}_\pi$ and the corresponding 2^k nested-partition areas $\{\mathcal{A}_i^k, i \leq 2^k\}$ (see Fig. 1), by using Lemma 4 of Appendix A. $\qquad\square$

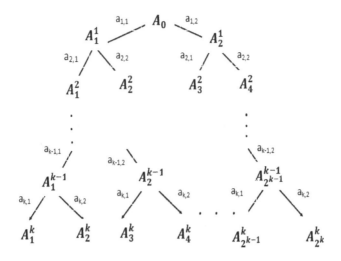

Fig. 1. Nested notations

To summarize, $a_{k,i}$, $i = 1, 2$ represent the two recommendations at step k. These two can be random, depend upon the recommendation history till time $k - 1$, $X_1, \cdots, X_{k-1}$. At any step, the user chooses one amongst the two recommendations, which is given by X_k. Overall, the random choice X_k can be one among the 2^k values $\{a_i^k, i \le 2^k\}$. Finally the belief B_k at time step k is uniformly distributed over (random) area $\mathcal{A}_k$, i.e., $B_k \sim \mathcal{U}(\mathcal{A}_k)$, which in turn can be one among 2^k areas $\{\mathcal{A}_i^k, i \le 2^k\}$ (see Fig. 1).

Further from the proof of Lemma 1, for any policy π and for any k, the sets $\{\mathcal{A}_j^k\}_{j \le 2^k}$ form a 2^k- partition of $\mathcal{S}$. And the 2^k partition is a finer division of 2^{k-1} partition, i.e.,

$$\mathcal{A}_i^{k-1} = \mathcal{A}_{2i-1}^k \cup \mathcal{A}_{2i}^k \text{ for each } i \le 2(k-1), k.$$

Objective

The sequence (X_k, B_k) is a controlled Markov Chain, controlled by sequence of state dependent actions/policy, π. The required cost $E[T - \tau]$ with any π and initial $X_0 = x$ equals

$$J(x, \pi) = E_x^\pi[T - \tau] = \sum_{k=0}^{T-2} P(T - \tau > k) = \sum_{k=0}^{T-2} P(\tau < T - k)$$

$$= \sum_{k=1}^{T-1} P(\tau \le k) = \sum_{k=1}^{T-1} P\left(V_{ref} \in \cup_{l=1}^k \mathcal{B}(X_l, \underline{r}) \cap \mathcal{A}_0\right), \tag{5}$$

and we are interested in maximizing the above cost.

4   Optimal Policies

The areas $\{\mathcal{A}_i^k\}_{i,k}$ and the recommendation choices $\mathcal{Q}_\pi$ depend upon the policy π, but given a policy π one can determine all of them. Fix any policy π and define $\mathcal{B}_i^k := \mathcal{B}(a_i^k, \underline{r})$ to represent the desired ball around the recommendation $a_i^k \in \mathcal{Q}_\pi$. It is clear to see that X_l at time l would be one among a_i^l for some $i \leq 2^l$, say it equals $a_{\bar{i}}^l$. This also implies $V_{ref} \notin \mathcal{B}_i^l$ for any $i \neq \bar{i}$. In all, user is satisfied on or before time slot k, i.e., $\tau \leq k$ if and only if

$$\{\tau \leq k\} = \left\{ V_{ref} \in \cup_{l=1}^k \cup_{i=1}^{2^l} \mathcal{B}_i^l \cap \mathcal{A}_0 \right\}.$$

Hence the Eq. (5) modifies as below:

$$J(x,\pi) = \sum_{k=1}^{T-1} P\left(V_{ref} \in \cup_{l=1}^k \cup_{i=1}^{2^l} \mathcal{B}_i^l \cap \mathcal{A}_0 \right)$$

$$\overset{b}{\leq} \sum_{k=1}^{T-1} \sum_{l=1}^k \sum_{i=1}^{2^l} P\left(V_{ref} \in \mathcal{B}_i^l \cap \mathcal{A}_0 \right)$$

$$= \sum_{k=1}^{T-1} \sum_{l=1}^k \sum_{i=1}^{2^l} \frac{\mu(\mathcal{B}_i^l \cap \mathcal{A}_i^l)}{\mu(\mathcal{A}_0)}, \text{ as } \mathcal{B}_i^l \subset \mathcal{A}_i^l \subset \mathcal{A}_0.$$

Using the above we state the first result, Theorem 1:

Theorem 1. *For any policy π, with $|\mathcal{B}| := \mu(\mathcal{B}(0,\underline{r}))$:*

(i) $J(x,\pi) = E[T - \tau](\pi) \overset{b}{\leq} \dfrac{\sum_{k=1}^{T-1} \sum_{l=1}^k \sum_{i=1}^{2^l} \mu(\mathcal{B}_i^l)}{\mu(\mathcal{A}_0)}$ (6)

$$= \frac{\sum_{k=1}^{T-1}(2^{k+1} - 2)|\mathcal{B}|}{\mu(\mathcal{A}_0)} = \frac{2\left(2^T - T - 1\right)|\mathcal{B}|}{\mu(\mathcal{A}_0)}.$$

(ii) For any π, (5) can directly be upper bounded ($P(A) \leq 1$):

$$E[T - \tau](\pi) \leq T - 1.$$

(iii) Further, $E[T - \tau](\pi) \leq \min_{1 \leq k \leq T} \left\{ \dfrac{2\left(2^k - k - 1\right)|\mathcal{B}|}{\mu(\mathcal{A}_0)} + T - k \right\}.$

Proof: Parts (i), (ii) are immediate. Part (iii) is obtained by using upper bounds of Part (i) and Part (ii) respectively for first and second terms of the following (for any k):

$$J(x,\pi) = \sum_{t=1}^{k-1} P\left(V_{ref} \in \cup_{l=1}^t \cup_{i=1}^{2^l} \mathcal{B}_i^l \cap \mathcal{A}_0 \right) + \sum_{t=k}^{T-1} P\left(V_{ref} \in \cup_{l=1}^t \cup_{i=1}^{2^l} \mathcal{B}_i^l \cap \mathcal{A}_0 \right).$$

$\square$

It is easy to see that the upper bound b of Eq. (6) can be achieved with equality if all the balls $\{\mathcal{B}_i^k\}_{k,i\leq 2^k}$ are disjoint and if all these balls lie completely in $\mathcal{A}_0$. And this would provide an optimal policy as below:

Corollary 1. *If there exists a policy π^* whose $(2^{T+1}-2)$-balls[1], $\{\mathcal{B}_i^{k*}\}_{k\leq T, i\leq 2^k}$, are disjoint and further if $\mathcal{B}_i^{k*} \subset \mathcal{A}_i^{k*}$ for every (k,i), then the inequality (b) in (6) is satisfied with equality and then π^* is an optimal policy because:*

$$E[T-\tau](\pi^*) \geq E[T-\tau](\pi) \text{ for any policy } \pi. \qquad \square$$

On the other hand, Part (ii) upper bound is useful to obtain:

Corollary 2. *If $\mathcal{A}_0 \subset \mathcal{B}(\mathbf{a}, \underline{r})$ for some $\mathbf{a}$ then π^* with $\pi_{k,i}^* = \mathbf{a}$ for all k, i is optimal achieving the upper bound $(T-1)$.* $\qquad \square$

Similarly one can have optimal policies that achieve the upper bound of Theorem 1(iii), via an $k \neq T$. This can be the case, for example, when $\mathcal{A}_0$ is union of L disjoint balls with $L < (2^{T+1}-2)$ (see in Appendix B). As another example, consider $\mathcal{S} = (v_1, v_2, \cdots, v_n) \subset \mathcal{R}$ with usual $d(v_1, v_2) = |v_1 - v_2|$. Say $\underline{r}$ is small such that $\mathcal{B}(v, \underline{r}) = \{v\}$ (a single element) for any $v \in \mathcal{S}$. Then the well known binary search method is an optimal policy when T is sufficiently large.

4.1 Optimal Policies in Continuous Space $(\mathcal{R}^2)$ with L^1 Metric

With L^1 metric on $\mathcal{R}^2$ any ball $\mathcal{B}(\mathbf{a}, r)$ is a rhombus, which on rotation becomes a square. So, user interest V_{ref} is uniformly distributed in a square of dimension, $\sqrt{2}\,\overline{R}$, with centre as the initial recommendation X_0. The user is satisfied with any item which lies inside a square of dimension $\sqrt{2}r$ with V_{ref} as the centre. If $(2^{T+1}-2) \leq \frac{\overline{R}^2}{r^2}$, we have sufficient disjoint balls and Corollary 1 is applicable. With $R := \sqrt{2}\,\overline{R}/2 = \overline{R}/\sqrt{2}$, one can easily verify that an optimal policy π^* is given by:

$$
\begin{aligned}
&a_{1,1}^* = (\tfrac{R}{2}, 0), &\qquad &a_{1,2}^* = (-\tfrac{R}{2}, 0), \\
&a_{2,1}^* = X_1 + (0, \tfrac{R}{2}), &\qquad &a_{2,2}^* = X_1 + (0, -\tfrac{R}{2}) \\
&a_{3,1}^* = X_2 + (\tfrac{R}{4}, 0), &\qquad &a_{3,2}^* = X_2 + (-\tfrac{R}{4}, 0),
\end{aligned}
$$

$$\vdots$$

$$
\begin{aligned}
&a_{2k-1,1}^* = X_{2k-1} + (0, \tfrac{R}{2^{2k-2}}), \\
&\quad a_{2k-1,2}^* = X_{2k-1} + (0, -\tfrac{R}{2^{2k-2}}).
\end{aligned}
$$

$$
\begin{aligned}
&a_{2k,1}^* = X_{2k} + (\tfrac{R}{2^{2k-2}}, 0), \\
&\quad a_{2k,2}^* = X_{2k} + (-\tfrac{R}{2^{2k-2}}, 0) \text{ for all } k,
\end{aligned}
$$

(7)

---

[1] We need 2 balls at step 1, 4 at step 2 and 2^k at step k and so on up to time $k = T$ (Fig. 1) and thus we need a total of $\sum_{k=1}^T 2^k = 2^{T+1} - 2$ disjoint balls. This is when the number of recommendations at a time step equals 2. Similarly for M recommendations we require $(M^{T+1} - M)/(M - 1)$ balls.

where user choice at any time step $k \geq 1$ is given by:

$$X_k = \begin{cases} a_{k,1}^* & \text{if } d(a_{k,1}^*, V_{ref}) < d(a_{k,2}^*, V_{ref}) \\ a_{k,2}^* & \text{if } d(a_{k,1}^*, V_{ref}) \geq d(a_{k,2}^*, V_{ref}). \end{cases} \tag{8}$$

Optimal policies for the case with $(2^{T+1} - 2) > \overline{R}^2/\underline{r}^2$ are obtained using Theorem 1(iii) in Appendix B.

L^1 **metric with 4 recommendations, i.e., with** $M = 4$: The above analysis can easily be extended. We will have 4^k partitions in Theorem 1 and the optimal policy for L^1 metric is ($r \angle \theta$ is representation in polar coordinates):

$$a_{k-1,i}^* = X_{k-1} + \frac{\overline{R}}{2^{k-2}} \angle((i-1)90° + 45°) \text{ for all } i \leq 4, k.$$

5   Algorithms for Continuous Space

Our ultimate aim is to provide algorithms that implement good recommendation policies on any item space $\mathcal{S}$. When S is discrete one can directly derive optimal policies through exhaustive search as discussed in Appendix C. However, this could be a restrictive procedure and probably works only for small T. To derive an algorithm for the general spaces, we first derive optimal policies for the continuous case and then adopt it to the discrete case. We do this by introducing a notion of local angle on discrete spaces. We first discuss the implementation of continuous policies.

5.1   Implementation

We refer the optimal policy discussed in Eq. (7) on $\mathcal{R}^2$ by π_{90}^*; the subscript indicates that 90° plays major role as explained below.

Policy π_{90}^*: From (7) at any time step k, CP recommends two items $(a_{k,1}, a_{k,2})$, equidistant $(R/2^{k/2})$ from X_{k-1} while maintaining the following angular separations:

$$\angle\{\overrightarrow{X_{k-1}a_{k,1}}, \overrightarrow{X_{k-1}a_{k,2}}\} = 180° \text{ while}$$

$$\angle\{\overrightarrow{X_{k-1}a_{k,1}}, \overrightarrow{X_{k-1}X_{k-2}}\} = 90°,$$

where $\overrightarrow{xy}$ implies the line joining points $\mathbf{x}, \mathbf{y}$.

One can obtain the estimate of $E[\tau]$, using the iterative procedure described in Algorithm 1. Repeating it for many samples and averaging gives an estimate for $E[\tau]$.

Remark: These results in continuous space are of independent interest. For example, they can be used in robotics: in rescue robot, robot navigation systems etc.

Policy π_{180}: The policy π_{90}^* needs 90°, and we notice that the implementation of 90° (after translation to discrete space) requires complicated logic. Hence we

---

Algorithm 1. Policy π_{90}^* Algorithm (for each sample)

Initialize: Generate V_{ref}, X_0 randomly (uniformly)
For steps: $k = 1, 2, \cdots$

  a CP provides two recommendation $a_{k,i}^*$, $i = 1, 2$
     as given by (7).
  b User chooses the best recommendation according
     to (8) and returns X_k.

If $k \geq T$ or $X_k \in \mathcal{B}(V_{ref}, \underline{r})$ **Then** Exit with $\tau = k$
Else return to (a) with $k = k + 1$

---

propose another policy π_{180} which only ensures 180° separation between the two recommendations ($a_{k,1}$ and $a_{k,2}$), but the angular separation with respect to the previous user choice X_{k-1} is chosen randomly, i.e., now

$$\angle\{\overrightarrow{X_{k-1}a_{k,1}}, \overrightarrow{X_{k-1}X_{k-2}}\} \text{ is random.}$$

Below, we study the loss of performance with this policy.

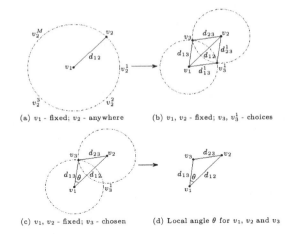

$\underline{r}$	$E[\tau]$	$E[\tau]$
	π_{90}^*	π_{180}
10	6.9	36.8
15	5.6	26.9
20	4.8	20.0
30	3.4	11.6
50	2.2	4.7
60	1.8	3.2
70	1.7	2.3
80	1.5	1.8

(a) v_1 - fixed; v_2 - anywhere   (b) v_1, v_2 - fixed; v_3, v_3^1 - choices

(c) v_1, v_2 - fixed; v_3 - chosen   (d) Local angle θ for v_1, v_2 and v_3

Fig. 2. $E[\tau]$ with L^1 metric, $\overline{R} = 100$

Fig. 3. Notion of 'Local' angle.

Simulation Results. We compare value of $E[\tau]$ for policies π_{180} and π_{90}^* (Fig. 2). The loss of performance with π_{180} in comparison to π_{90}^* increases with decrease in $\underline{r}$. This implies: (a) in continuous space with Euclidean distance one may use less complicated π_{180} in place of π_{90}^*, when $\underline{r}$ is not very small; (b) in other cases, it may be important to ensure 90° separation. We leave this topic for future research.

6 Algorithms for Discrete Database

We assume any dataset is specified by an item space $\mathcal{S}$ and a rating matrix $\mathbb{R}$. The (i,j)-th entry $r_{i,j}$ of matrix $\mathbb{R}$ is the rating given by user j to item i and it equals 0 when user has not rated it. Using this data and using the similarity measures of (2), we compute the distance matrix $\mathbb{D}$.

Notion of Distance. Distance is defined using similarity measure. The similarity measure takes values between 0 and 1, as it is a normalized measure (see (2)) and is inversely proportional to the distance. Hence we can say that distance between items i, j is $d(i,j) = 1 - s_c(i,j)$ and hence is the (i,j)-th element of matrix $\mathbb{D}$. It is clear that maximizing distance based functions is equivalent to minimizing the same functions with respect to similarity measure and vice versa.

The distance matrix is used to compute the neighbourhood matrix $\mathbb{N}$. Row j of matrix $\mathbb{N}$ has items arranged in the descending order of similarity with item j, i.e., $s_c(j, v_1) \geq s_c(j, v_2)$ if item v_1 is placed before item v_2 in row j.

Notion of Local Angle. We discuss the notion of $180°$ using the distance measure described above.

Consider a center in a continuous space and points on a given circumference. There are uncountable such points. The points might be at equidistant from the center, but their inter distances can vary based on their angular separations. This can be used to define the notion of $180°$. We begin with three items (v_1, v_2 and v_3) and let d_{12}, d_{23} and d_{13} be their inter distances. Fix the position of item v_1, then v_2 can be anywhere on the circumference of $\mathcal{B}(v_1, d_{12})$ (see Fig. 3). Fix one of these points as v_2 and now draw two circles, with respective centres as v_1 and v_2 and radii as d_{13} and d_{23}. Then item v_3 can be at one of the two intersecting points as shown (see Fig. 3). Choose any one of the two points as v_3 and form a triangle to obtain the required angle. For example, θ in Fig. 3 represents the 'local' angle between lines joining items v_1–v_2 and v_1–v_3. Note that, this angle is independent of the chosen points and depends only upon their inter distances, d_{12}, d_{23} and d_{13}.

Implementation of $180°$. An angular separation close to $180°$ is achieved if the inter distances between the pair of points (both at the same distance say R, from a reference point X_0) is maximized. We in fact suggest an algorithm for general M, which ensures maximum separation between the M-tuple in case their inter angular separations are at least $360/M°$. We extract the row corresponding to X_0 of the matrix $\mathbb{N}$, and list consequent n ($n > M$) items starting at a distance R from X_0. Out of these n we have to pick M items such that the sum of the inter similarity distances between the items is minimized. The following Integer

Linear Programme (ILP) exactly achieves this:

$$\text{minimize} \sum_{i \in S} \sum_{j \in S:i>j} s_c(i,j)x_{ij}$$

$$\text{subject to} \sum_{i \in S} \sum_{j \in S:i>j} x_{ij} = \frac{M(M-1)}{2},$$

$$x_{ij} + 1 \geq y_i + y_j, \forall i \in S, j \in S, i > j \qquad (9)$$

$$\sum_{i \in S} y_i = M$$

$$x_{ij} \in \{0,1\}, y_i \in \{0,1\}, i,j \in S.$$

The required set of M-items are those i, for which the solution of (9) has $y_i = 1$.

Brief Details of ILP (9): The objective function to be minimized equals the sum of inter similarity measures of the items. The aim is to chose M 'least similar' items (among the given set S) as recommendations and hence this objective function. Here x_{ij} equals 1 if pair of items i,j are both in the solution set. Thus we have constraint 1, as we need $M(M-1)/2$ such pairs. A pair is to be considered in solution, as it precisely accounts for the inter similarity measures in the objective function. Further y_i equals 1 if node i is in the solution and 0 otherwise. Constraint 2 ensures that both y_i and y_j equal 1, if their pair x_{ij} is in the solution. Constraint 3 ensures that we have M recommendations.

UR-LA Algorithm. We now adapt the algorithm (7) to propose a recommendation policy that can be implemented on any discrete dataset and call it as *UR-LA (User Response and Local Angle based) Algorithm*.

We assume that user is interested in a particular item V_{ref}, unknown to the recommender. The recommender starts the recommendation with a randomly selected item X_0 where $d(V_{ref}, X_0) \leq \bar{R}$. For each V_{ref} we run the algorithm for 300 different initial points picked uniformly at random. We initially tested the algorithm with $M = 2$. At every step k we choose n items using $\mathbb{N}$ starting at distance R_k from X_k (where R_k is as in (7) and $R_1 = \bar{R}/\sqrt{2}$), from previous user choice X_{k-1}, and then use program (9) to recommend two items. We set $n = 4$. The user chooses one among them, which is X_k. The algorithm terminates when a recommendation is within ball $B(V_{ref}, \underline{r})$ or after T steps.

The UR-LA Algorithm is compared with the widely used item based Collaborative Filtering (CF) Algorithms of [6]. The CF algorithm also uses rating matrix $\mathbb{R}$ to generate the similarity based distance matrix $\mathbb{D}$. At every step k it recommends M items that are nearest to X_k. We also propose the following hybrid policy which combines the best features of both the UR-LA and CF algorithms:

Algorithm 2. UR-LA Algorithm - Given $\overline{R}, \underline{r}, n, M, \mathbb{R}, \mathcal{S}$

Initialize:

- Generate $s_c(i,j)$ between all items i and j using (2) and store in distance matrix $\mathbb{D}$.
- Generate neighbourhood matrix $\mathbb{N}$ using $\mathbb{D}$:
- Generate V_{ref}, X_0 randomly (uniformly), such that $d(V_{ref}, X_0) \leq \overline{R}$. Set $R_1 = \overline{R}/\sqrt{2}$.

For steps $k = 1, 2, \ldots$

  a Choose n consequent items from a row of $\mathbb{N}$, that
     start at distance R_k from X_k.
  b CP provides M recommendations out of n as in (9).
  c User chooses the best recommendation according to (8) and returns X_k.

If $k \geq T$ or $X_k \in \mathcal{B}(V_{ref}, \underline{r})$ **Then** Exit with $\tau = k$
Else return to (a) with $k = k + 1$ and set
$R_k = R_{k-1}/2$ if $k\%2 = 0$ else $R_k = R_{k-1}$.

Hybrid Recommendation (Hybrid): We found that UR-LA performs significantly better for the cases for which start radius $\overline{R}$ is large, i.e., if X_0 is often far away from V_{ref}. If X_0 is close to V_{ref} then the performance is poor. UR-LA basically recommends 'faraway' items (from say X_k), with the reasoning that user is not yet satisfied and has chosen to explore further. This is the main reason for improvement over CF. However, exactly the same reason deteriorates the performance if start-radius is small. Thus we propose an Hybrid Algorithm which uses ideas from both *CF* and *UR-LA* algorithms. One can define this algorithm for any $M \geq 3$ and we describe it here for $M = 3$. In each round, one of the recommendation is the most similar item to the previously selected item as in CF and the other two items are selected as in UR-LA. We will show that the Hybrid algorithm outperforms in most of the cases.

6.1   Numerical Experiments

In this section we test the performance of the algorithms on two real datasets. The first one [12] has 285 music bands rated by 1257 users. In the rating matrix, each column corresponds to a unique band and each row to a unique user. The ratings are binary–each user gives a rating 1 if he likes the band and 0 if he does not like. If no entry exists then it is considered as 0.

The second one is the MovieLens dataset [11]. We again constructed the rating matrix after appropriate conversion of the data. Each column again represents a movie and each row a user. Each entry here corresponds to the rating given by the user to a particular movie on a scale of 0 and 5. If the user has not seen/not rated the movie then the rating is set to zero. We have ratings of 1682 movies given by 943 users.

For both the datasets we set $T = 20$. Table 1 summarizes the simulation results of the UR-LA compared to CF on various settings. We consider the following two settings. (1) Start Anywhere (SA): in this setting we selected

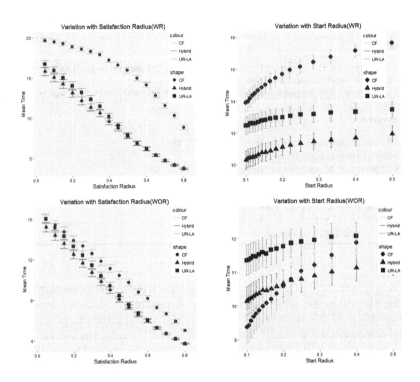

Fig. 4. Variations around the expected time to satisfy the user

Table 1. $E[\tau]$ (in terms of Steps) for different algorithms with $\overline{R} = 1, \underline{r} = 0.25, n = 4$ and $M = 2$.

Music	CF	UR-LA	%Imp	Movie	CF	UR-LA	%Imp
SA-WR	19.5	13.9	33.9	SA-WR	20.4	17.6	14.4
SA-WOR	16.0	13.5	17.0	SA-WOR	18.2	17.2	5.5
SF-WR	20.6	14.2	36.5	SF-WR	20.8	17.8	15.7
SF-WOR	17.4	13.8	23.2	SF-WOR	18.9	17.2	9.2

Table 2. $E[\tau]$ (in terms of Steps), including hybrid algorithm, $\overline{R} = 1, \underline{r} = 0.25$, $n = 4, M = 3$ and 'Start Anywhere'.

Settings		CF	UR-LA	Hybrid	%Imp
Music	WR	18.61	13.25	12.10	42.42
Music	WOR	13.04	11.94	11.31	14.26
Movie	WR	19.70	17.94	17.40	12.39
Movie	WOR	16.53	16.41	15.87	4.04

initial point uniformly at random. (2) Start Far (SF): in this setting an initial point is selected uniformly at random but at a fixed distance from the V_{ref}. In addition to the above, we also considered recommendations With Replacement (WR) and Without Replacement (WOR). In WR, an item once recommended can be recommended again, whereas in the WOR it is not recommended again. The values in the table correspond to the average steps taken by the algorithm to satisfy the user for various settings. In Table 2 we included the Hybrid policy, and provided a comparative study of all the three algorithms CF, UR-LA and Hybrid with $M = 3$ (for all policies).

One can observe from the tables that UR-LA algorithm has significant improvement over CF algorithm and Hybrid algorithm performs even better.

In Tables 3 and 4 we provide the variance around $E[\tau]$ with varying satisfaction radius r and start radius $\bar{R}$, respectively. We have also plotted the corresponding graphs in Fig. 4, WR setting is in sub-figures 1–2 while WOR setting is in sub-figures 3–4. As seen, UR-LA and Hybrid algorithms perform way better than the CF algorithm (even with respect to the variance) for the WR setting. With WOR setting, UR-LA and Hybrid algorithms perform better when $\bar{R}$ is large. However, when $\bar{R}$ is small, CF performs better, the performance of Hybrid algorithm is comparable to that of CF.

Table 3. Variance around $E[\tau]$ (in terms of Steps) versus Satisfaction Radius (r): Music dataset, 'WR' Condition and $\bar{R} = 1, n = 4, M = 3$

	0.75	0.65	0.55	0.45	0.35	0.25
Hybrid	4.13	5.34	6.81	8.69	10.58	12.15
UR-LA	4.08	5.33	6.83	8.99	11.44	13.18
CF	10.24	12.79	14.91	16.56	17.85	18.58
%Imp	85.03	82.17	74.56	62.32	51.11	41.8

Table 4. Variance around $E[\tau]$ (in terms of Steps) versus Start Radius ($\bar{R}$): Music dataset, 'WR' condition and $r = 0.25, n = 4, M = 3$

	0.5	0.4	0.25	0.2	0.11	0.1
Hybrid	11.91	11.67	11.34	11.1	10.46	10.30
UR-LA	13.42	13.3	13.13	12.96	12.6	12.46
CF	17.61	17.14	16.15	15.67	14.17	13.9
%Imp	38.63	38	35.01	34.13	30.11	29.8

7   Recommendation Tree Based Approach (UR-RT)

Our aim has been to derive optimal (user response based) recommendation policies, based on the results of Theorem 1 and its Corollaries. It was to construct the 'nested partition' of the dataset according to Fig. 1, which results in optimal policies. Recall that we require $(M^{T+1} - M)/(M - 1)$ (see the footnote of the Corollary 1) disjoint balls (if the database is sufficiently large) to construct the partition. If the database is small (for a given T), one again requires the nested partition which possibly ends early (i.e., at level/depth less than T). And if such a partition is possible the user can definitely be satisfied in fewer steps than T, to be precise, in as many steps as the depth of the nested partition. In the previous section, we proposed a heuristic notion of local angle to provide the required partition and UR-LA is based on this approach.

We now use clustering based approach to propose a new heuristic. We basically construct a recommendation tree (RT), and call the resulting policies as UR-RT policies. One way of achieving the nested partition of Fig. 1 for M recommendations is as follows: (a) at first level divide the dataset into M equal partitions; (b) subsets corresponding to every node in the second level are again partitioned into M equal partitions; and (c) this should continue till we are left with at maximum one ball (of radius $\underline{r}$) in the subsets corresponding to the nodes of the last level. If one can achieve such a nested partition[2], we have an optimal policy.

We propose to achieve a similar partition using clustering based approach. Towards this, we add two extra constrains to the well known k-means clustering algorithm: (a) the number of clusters should be M and (b) the resulting clusters should be of equal size. We refer this policy as UR-RTe, where 'e' stands for equal clusters. However, with the addition of extra constraints, the clustering algorithm may not be efficient: nearby points may get partitioned into different clusters. Thus one may finish the search within d steps, where d is the depth of the nested partition (so constructed), however one may have misses.

We propose a second policy, referred to as UR-RTu (u for unequal partitions), where clustering is considered without the second constraint. The depth of the resulting tree will be different at different nodes, and hence is not an optimal division. However, one may have fewer misses and this heuristic may outperform the other. We first begin with detailed description of the policies, followed by their numerical evaluations. *For large data sets and finite number of trials T (as in practical scenarios), we anticipate our second heuristic UR-RTu to be near optimal.*

UR-RTe

We divide the dataset into equal partitions at every step and the center of the partitions are given as recommendations to the user. As before, the user selects the center closer to V_{ref} out of all the recommendations, and further

---

[2] In Appendix C some such example partitions are explained.

recommendations are provided from within the partition corresponding to the centres chosen by user. This method will reach V_{ref} in the least possible steps, provided the nested partitions are efficient. However, because of the extra 'equal size clusters' constraint, the clustering might not be optimal which may lead to inefficiencies. Due to inefficient clustering (for example), V_{ref} might be in the first cluster, but is closer to the center of the second cluster. This will lead to divergence and the session will never reach the desired V_{ref} leading to a miss.

UR-RTu

We relax the 'equal size clusters' constraints while deriving the nested clusters. This may lead to sub optimal tree but might significantly reduce the number of misses.

Implementation

We will use clustering techniques to divide the dataset into partitions. Towards this, we first describe an Integer linear Programming (ILP) model, that can implement the general k-means clustering:

$$\text{minimize} \quad \sum_{i \in S} \sum_{j \in S} x_{ij} d(i, j)$$

$$\text{subject to (i)} \quad \sum_{i \in S} y_i \leq M,$$

$$\text{(ii)} \quad \sum_{j \in S} x_{ij} = 1, \forall i \in S \tag{10}$$

$$\text{(iii)} \quad x_{ij} \leq y_j, \forall i, j \in S$$

$$\text{(iv)} \quad x_{ij} \in \{0, 1\}, i, j \in S$$

$$\text{(v)} \quad y_i \in \{0, 1\}, i \in S.$$

Recall $d(i, j)$ is the distance measure between items i, j of data set S. The variable x_{ij} is binary and its value is 1 if item i is in the cluster with center as item j. The variable y_i is also binary and is set to 1 if item i is acting as a center and 0 otherwise. Here M is the upper bound on the number of centres. The objective function minimizes the inter distances between the centres and the other items belonging to their respective clusters. Constraint (i) takes care of the upper bound on the number of centres. Constraint (ii) ensures that each item is assigned to exactly one center. Constraint (iii) says that if y_i is 0, then all the corresponding x_{ij} equal 0. The program (10) provides optimum number of groups (less than or equal to M) and their corresponding centres.

ILP for UR-RTe: We will modify the above general k-means algorithm (10) to suit our problem statement. We require fixed number of recommendations. Thus we fix the number of centres in constraint (i), as a result of which it becomes an equality constraint in ILP (11). Additional 'equal size clusters' constraint (iv) is added, as we require that the dataset is divided into equal size clusters, to get:

$$\text{minimize} \qquad \sum_{i \in \mathcal{S}} \sum_{j \in \mathcal{S}} x_{ij}(1 - s_{ij})$$

$$\text{subject to (i)} \quad \sum_{j \in \mathcal{S}} y_j = M,$$

$$\text{(ii)} \quad \sum_{j \in \mathcal{S}} x_{ij} = 1, \forall i \in \mathcal{S}$$

$$\text{(iii)} \quad x_{ij} \le y_j, \forall i \in \mathcal{S}, j \in \mathcal{S}$$

$$\text{(iv)} \quad \sum_{i \in \mathcal{S}} x_{ij} \le \frac{|\mathcal{S}| + M - 1}{M}, \forall j \in \mathcal{S}, \text{ constraint for 'equal size clusters'}$$

$$\text{(v)} \quad x_{ij} \in \{0, 1\}, i, j \in \mathcal{S}$$

$$\text{(vi)} \quad y_i \in \{0, 1\}, i \in \mathcal{S}.$$

$$\tag{11}$$

The objective function minimizes the total inter distances (or equivalently one minus similarity measures, $\{1 - s_{ij}\}$).

For **UR-RTu** the same ILP can be used after discarding the 'equal size clusters' constraint (iv).

We invoke ILP (11) recursively to generate entire tree. At each call to the program we have to update the set S with the output clusters generated by the previous call. Let $\{a_i^k\}_{i,k}$ represent the centres of the nested clusters, with a_i^k denoting the index of the i-th center belonging to k-th level. While deriving nested clusters using ILP (11), say at level k, we exclude the balls $\{\mathcal{B}(a_i^k, \underline{r})\}_i$ around the previous centres $\{a_i^k\}_i$, before considering the clustering for the next level $k + 1$.

The program is written in AMPL and the script solving the program at every node is also written in AMPL and we are using the GUROBI solver for solving the ILP. The script in AMPL generating the tree can easily be extended for any number of items in the dataset. Once the tree is generated we used R Programming Language to read the output and used the package 'data.tree' to store in a proper format. We will be recommending according to the tree but the user will select the item that is closer to V_{ref} in terms of similarity measure. It may happen that we may not reach the V_{ref} in the tree, which we will count as a miss. We compare the expected time to reach V_{ref} with CF and UR-LA.

Recommendation Tree Experiments

From Table 1, the average time $E[\tau]$ to reach V_{ref} is 13.5 and 16 using UR-LA and CF algorithms, respectively. We test the RT based recommendation algorithms for the same test case and the results are tabulated in Table 5. We notice that $E[\tau]$ for UR-RTe algorithm is 11.76 steps, which is a good improvement. And we have even better result with UR-RTu, $E[\tau] = 7.64$. Solving ILP (11) is an NP-Hard problem but there has been a lot of research in the field of k-means clustering algorithms. One can generate the clusters using heuristics that converge in polynomial time. The previous algorithms are computationally intensive and it was not easy to implement them for $M > 4$. *While in clustering based algorithms, one needs to derive and store the optimal nested clusters (offline) once and then actual recommendation algorithm is very simple.* We experimented with more number of recommendations, while testing RT based algorithms and the results are tabulated in Tables 5 and 6.

Table 5. $E[\tau]$ (in steps) for different algorithms, for different number of recommendations

Music	CF	UR-LA	UR-RTe	UR-RTu
2-Reco	16	13.5	11.76	7.64
3-Reco	13.04	11.31	10.02	5.607
4-Reco	11.53	10.55	8.42	4.88

From Corollary 1, if one has

$$\gamma_M^t := \frac{M^{t+1} - M}{M - 1}$$

disjoint balls and if one can partition efficiently (i.e., if one can realize the nested partition as in Fig. 1), the partition and its centres can provide optimal policy. If dataset $\mathcal{A}_0 = \mathcal{S}$ is exact union of the γ_M^t balls, then $E^*[T - \tau] = T - t$ for any $T \geq t$. If the data set $\mathcal{S}$ is a subset of union of γ_M^t such disjoint balls, like in Theorem 1(iii), one can prove that $E^*[T - \tau] \leq T - t$. That is, if the dataset is small and can be enclosed in γ_M^t appropriate balls, then $E[T - \tau] \leq T - t$ and one can use this to determine if a given policy is 'near' optimal policy. Define,

$$\tau_M^* = \inf \left\{ t : \gamma_M^t |\mathcal{B}| \geq |\mathcal{S}| \right\}.$$

It is clear that τ_M^* is an upper bound (in integers) over the optimal time $E^*[\tau]$ (provided the balls enclose the data set). We compare the numerical results with τ_M^* to judge the quality of the proposed algorithms.

We can see that there is a significant improvement from UR-RTe to UR-RTu though UR-RTu is not the optimal policy. This is because of the 'equal size clusters' constraint. This constraint leads to inefficient clustering, as discussed before and can lead to misses. Here some items do not follow the desired path of

Table 6. Number of misses and $E[\tau]$ (in steps) for $T = 20$ and with music dataset of size 285

Misses	UR-RTe	UR-RTu
2-Reco	96	1
3-Reco	86	0
4-Reco	67	1
5-Reco	76	0
6-Reco	60	0
7-Reco	72	0

$E[\tau]$	UR-RTe	UR-RTu	τ_M^*
2-Reco	11.76	7.64	9
3-Reco	10.02	5.607	6
4-Reco	8.42	4.88	5
5-Reco	8.71	4.41	5
6-Reco	7.5	4.12	4
7-Reco	8.1	3.87	4

discovery, if the item is closer to the center of a cluster, but belongs to a different cluster. These cases are almost completely excluded in UR-RTu algorithm leading to few diversions. Thus the actual V_{ref} is hit with a high probability. Below in Table 6 we tabulated the number of misses out of 285 times and the mean time to reach V_{ref} for the case with $T = 20$.

From Table 6, we also notice that $E[\tau]$ of UR-RTu is less than τ_M^* (provided in the last column), and hence is achieving near optimal performance for all most all M.

8 Conclusion

We presented and demonstrated novel recommendation policies, that are based on user-generated responses. Unlike the traditional recommendation schemes, our recommendations not only depend upon the history, but they also exploit the responses of the same user in the same session. We proposed a new 'notion of local angle' in the context of discrete data base, using which we translated continuous space policies to discrete space. The main difference in the new approach is that 'the inter distances between items of the same recommendation list is maximum possible' and 'the distance from the previous recommendation is initially large and decreases geometrically'. These observations readily give good policies, as via user's choices to previous recommendations (of the same session) the user has given a *good hint about not only the items closer to its interest, but also about the items which are not exactly its choice.*

We developed UR-LA (user response and local angle) and hybrid algorithms and tested their performance on two real datasets. We compared them with baseline CF based recommendation algorithm. Our algorithms reduce the search time significantly (up to 40%) in most of the cases.

We developed another set of policies, using clustering approach. These again recommend 'faraway' items, based on the user responses. These algorithms illustrate much better performance than all the algorithms considered in this paper. We showed that they perform close to theoretical limits, based on some numerical results on the data sets. Further the new clustering algorithms require computation (and storage of centres) of 'nested clusters' at one time (offline), while the online part of the algorithm is significantly simplified.

A Appendix: Proofs

Lemma 2. *The new belief B_1 is uniformly distributed over area $\mathcal{A}_1$ which has two choices:*

$$B_1 \sim \mathcal{U}(\mathcal{A}_1) \text{ where } \mathcal{A}_1 = \mathcal{A}_{11}1_{\{X_1=a_{11}\}} + \mathcal{A}_{12}1_{\{X_1=a_{12}\}},$$

where $\mathcal{A}_{11}$, $\mathcal{A}_{12}$ are given by Eq. (3).

Proof of Lemma 2: By definition belief B_1 is the conditional distribution of V_{ref} given history H_1 which includes current observation X_1, the user choice. That is, $B_1 \sim V_{ref}|H_1$. For any subset Λ (Borel if continuous case)[3] from Eq. (3):

$$
\begin{aligned}
rClP(B_1 \in \Lambda) &= P\big(V_{ref} \in \Lambda | B_0, \mathbf{a_1}, X_1\big) \\
&= P\big(V_{ref} \in \Lambda | V_{ref} \in \mathcal{A}_0, \mathbf{a_1} = (a_{11}, a_{12}), X_1\big) \\
&= P\big(V_{ref} \in \Lambda | V_{ref} \in \mathcal{A}_0, V_{ref} \in \mathcal{A}_{11}\big) 1_{\{X_1 = a_{11}\}} \\
&\quad + P\big(V_{ref} \in \Lambda | V_{ref} \in \mathcal{A}_0, V_{ref} \in \mathcal{A}_{12}\big) 1_{\{X_1 = a_{12}\}} \\
&= \frac{\mu(\Lambda \cap \mathcal{A}_{11})}{\mu(\mathcal{A}_{11})} 1_{\{X_1 = a_{11}\}} + \frac{\mu(\Lambda \cap \mathcal{A}_{12})}{\mu(\mathcal{A}_{12})} 1_{\{X_1 = a_{12}\}}.
\end{aligned}
\tag{12}
$$

Thus clearly belief B_1 is a uniform random variable either over $\mathcal{A}_{11}$ or $\mathcal{A}_{12}$, as μ is uniform. $\qquad\square$

Lemma 3. *The new belief B_2 is uniformly distributed, i.e., $B_2 \sim \mathcal{U}(\mathcal{A}_2)$, where the area $\mathcal{A}_2$ has two choices for any given X_1:*

$$
\mathcal{A}_2(X_1) = \mathcal{A}_{21} 1_{\{X_2 = a_{21}\}} + \mathcal{A}_{22} 1_{\{X_2 = a_{22}\}},
$$

with $\mathcal{A}_{21}, \mathcal{A}_{22}$ defined in (4). These two choices depend further upon X_1, and hence in total $\mathcal{A}_2$ can be one among four choices.

Proof: The belief B_2 is again conditional distribution of V_{ref} given the entire history $B_0, B_1, \mathbf{a_1}, \mathbf{a_2}$ and current observation X_2. The proof goes through in exactly the same manner as in Lemma 2, except that $\mathbf{A}_2$ can now have four choices based on X_1, X_2. $\qquad\square$

Lemma 4. *The belief B_k at time step k $(k > 1)$ is uniformly distributed, i.e., $B_k \sim \mathcal{U}(\mathcal{A}_k)$, where the area $\mathcal{A}_k$ has two choices for any given X_{k-1}:*

$$
\mathcal{A}_k(X_{k-1}) = \mathcal{A}_{k1} 1_{\{X_k = a_{k1}\}} + \mathcal{A}_{k2} 1_{\{X_k = a_{k2}\}},
$$

where $\mathcal{A}_{k1}, \mathcal{A}_{k2}$ are partitions of $\mathcal{A}_{k-1}$ as in definitions (3) and (4). These two choices depend further upon $X_1, \cdots, X_{k-1}$, and hence in total $\mathcal{A}_2$ can be one among 2^k choices.

Proof: The proof goes through in exactly the same manner as in Lemmas 2 and 3. $\qquad\square$

B   Appendix: L^1 Metric with $(2^{T+1} - 2) > \overline{R}^2 / \underline{r}^2$

Basic idea is to obtain the optimal policy using Corollary 1 till k^* where

$$
k^* = \arg\max_k \left\{ (2^{k+1} - 2) \le \frac{\overline{R}^2}{\underline{r}^2} \right\}
$$

---

[3] This is basically belief propagation. The state $S = (X, V_{ref})$ observation $O = X$, the choice of user and then belief of the unobserved state needs to be computed.

and then using Corollary 2 for the time steps from $k^* + 1$ till T. Basically this policy achieves the upper bound of Théorem 1(iii), where the minimum on the right hand side is achieved using k^*.

The exact details are as below for the case when $\overline{R}/\underline{r}$ is an appropriate power of 2 such that $2^{k^*+1} - 2 = \overline{R}^2/\underline{r}^2$. One can give similar construction even otherwise. But some minor details need to be considered.

Note that we exactly have $(2^{k^*+1} - 2)$ disjoint balls and hence one can upper bound all the terms till k^* by $|\mathcal{B}|$ as in Corollary 1. Let $a_{k,i}^*$ be as defined in Eq. (7) for all i and for all $k < k^*$. At k^* all the remaining areas $\{\mathcal{A}_i^{k^*}\}_{i \leq 2^{k^*}}$ are already of size $\underline{r}$. As in Corollary 2, define for any $k > k^*$ and i

$$a_{k,i}^* = X_{k-1} = X_{k^*}.$$

One can easily verify that $E[\tau]$ is strictly less than k^*, thus the user satisfied in an average time, less than k^*.

$$E[\tau] = k^* - \frac{(2^{k^*+1} - 2k^* - 2)|\mathcal{B}|}{\mu(\mathcal{A}_0)}.$$

C   Appendix: Optimal Policies in Discrete Space

We consider binary database with F features, similarity based distance and cardinality based measure. A ball $\mathcal{B}(v, r)$ here includes all those items which match in more than $F(1 - r)$ features with v, e.g., $\mathcal{B}((10), 0.5) = \{(10)\}$, $\mathcal{B}((10), 1) = \mathcal{S}$.

We again use Corollary 1 to obtain optimal policies in some example scenarios. One can easily verify the following.

Case I: $F = 7$, $T = 2$ **and** $\underline{r} = 2/7$: Optimal $\mathcal{Q}_{\pi^*}$ is

$$\begin{aligned} a_1^1 &= 1111111, \ a_2^1 = 0000000, && a_1^2 = 0011111, \\ a_2^2 &= 1111100, \ a_3^2 = 1100000 && \text{and} \ a_4^2 = 0000011. \end{aligned}$$

Case II: $F = 7$, $T = 2$ **and** $\underline{r} = 3/7$: Optimal $\mathcal{Q}_{\pi^*}$ is

$$\begin{aligned} a_1^1 &= 1111111, \ a_2^1 = 0000000, && a_1^2 = 0001111, \\ a_2^2 &= 111100, \quad a_3^2 = 1110000 && \text{and} \ a_4^2 = 0000111. \end{aligned}$$

Case III: $F = 9$, $T = 2$ **and** $\underline{r} = 4/9$: Optimal $\mathcal{Q}_{\pi^*}$ is

$$\begin{aligned} a_1^1 &= 111111000, \ a_2^1 = 000000111, && a_1^2 = 001111001, \\ a_2^2 &= 110001110, \ a_3^2 = 110000110 && \text{and} \ a_4^2 = 001110001. \end{aligned}$$

References

1. Hill, W., Stead, L., Rosenstein, M., Furnas, G.: Recommending and evaluating choices in a virtual community of use. In: Proceedings of the SIGCHI Conference on Human Factors in Computing Systems, Denver (1995)
2. Grossman, L.: How Computers Know What We Want Before We Do. http://content.time.com/time/magazine/article/0,9171,1992403,00.html
3. Kavitha, V., Memon, S., Hanawal, M.K., Altman, E., Devanand, R.: User response based recommendations: a local angle approach. In: 10th International Conference on Communication Systems & Networks (COMSNETS) (2018)
4. Adomavicius, G., Tuzhilin, A.: Toward the next generation of recommender systems: a survey of the state of the art and possible extensions. IEEE Trans. Knowl. Data Eng. **17**(6) (2005)
5. Gaillard, J., El Beze, M., Altman, E., Ethis, E.: Flash reactivity: adaptive models in recommender systems. In: International Conference on Data Mining (DMIN), WORLDCOMP (2013)
6. Sarwar, B., Karypis, G., Konstan, J., Riedl, J.: Item-based collaborative filtering recommendation algorithms. In: Proceedings of the 10th International Conference on World Wide Web. ACM (2001)
7. Rashid, A.M., et al.: Getting to know you: learning new user preferences in recommender systems. In: Proceedings of the International Conference on Intelligent User Interfaces, San Francisco (2002)
8. Rashid, A.M., Karypis, G., Riedl, J.: Learning preferences of new users in recommender systems: an information theoretic approach. ACM SIGKDD Explor. Newsl. **10**(2), 90–100 (2008)
9. Lika, B., Kolomvatsos, K., Hadjiefthymiades, S.: Facing the cold start problem in recommender systems. Expert Syst. Appl. **41**, 2065–2073 (2014)
10. Stritt, M., Tso, K.H.L., Schmidt-Thieme, L.: Attribute aware anonymous recommender systems. In: Decker, R., Lenz, H.-J. (eds.) Advances in Data Analysis, pp. 497–504. Springer, Heidelberg (2007). https://doi.org/10.1007/978-3-540-70981-7_57
11. MovieLens Dataset. https://grouplens.org/datasets/movielens/
12. Music Dataset. https://labrosa.ee.columbia.edu/millionsong/lastfm

Correction to: Implementation of Energy Efficient WBAN Using IEEE 802.15.6 Scheduled Access MAC with Fast DWT Based Backhaul Data Compression for e-Healthcare

Tanumay Manna and Iti Saha Misra

Correction to:

Chapter "Implementation of Energy Efficient WBAN Using IEEE 802.15.6 Scheduled Access MAC with Fast DWT Based Backhaul Data Compression for e-Healthcare" in:
S. Biswas et al. (Eds.): *Communication Systems and Networks*, LNCS 11227, https://doi.org/10.1007/978-3-030-10659-1_2

The original version of this chapter was revised. Reference no. 23 ("References" section) was updated because the chapter which was under review has now been published.

The updated version of this chapter can be found at
https://doi.org/10.1007/978-3-030-10659-1_2

Author Index

Printed in the United States
By Bookmasters